# Management Accounting Techniques

GW00587183

C I *m* A

Published in association with
the Chartered Institute of
Management Accountants

**Other titles in the CIMA series**

*Stage 1*
*Economics for Accountants*
Keith West

*Quantitative Methods*
Kevin Pardoe

*Stage 2*
*Accounting Information Systems and Data Processing*
Krish Bhaskar and Richard Housden

*Cost Accounting*
Mark Lee Inman

*Financial Accounting*
Peter Taylor and Brian Underdown

*Management*
Cliff Bowman

*Stage 3*
*Advanced Financial Accounting*
Peter Taylor and Brian Underdown

*Control and Audit in Management Accounting*
Jeff Coates, Colin Rickwood and Ray Stacey

*Management Accounting Techniques*
David Benjamin and Colin Biggs

*Stage 4*
*Financial and Treasury Management*
Paul Collier, Terry Cooke and John Glynn

*Management Accounting: Strategic Planning and Marketing*
Patrick McNamee

*Revision Guides*
*Quantitative Methods Revision Guide*
Paul Goodwin

*Cost Accounting Revision Guide*
Colin Drury

*Company Accounting Revision Guide*
Peter Taylor and Brian Underdown

*Economics Revision Guide*
Rob Dixon and Keith West

*Business Law Revision Guide*
Stan Marsh

*Advanced Accounting Techniques Groups and Special Transactions Revision Guide*
Peter Taylor and Brian Underdown

# Management Accounting Techniques

## An Integrated Approach

### Stage 3

Colin Biggs MBA, BSc,
ITP(Harvard)
David Benjamin FCCA

Heinemann Professional Publishing

*We would like to dedicate the book to our parents:*

*Hetty and Simon Benjamin*
*Irene and Henry Biggs*

Heinemann Professional Publishing Ltd
Halley Court, Jordan Hill, Oxford OX2 8EJ

OXFORD  LONDON  MELBOURNE  AUCKLAND  SINGAPORE
IBADAN  NAIROBI  GABORONE  KINGSTON

First published 1989

**British Library Cataloguing in Publication Data**
Biggs, Colin
   Management accounting techniques.
   1. Management accounting
   I. Title   II. Benjamin, David
   658.1′511

ISBN 0 434 90151 2

Printed in Great Britain by
Redwood Burn Limited, Trowbridge, Wiltshire

# Contents

*Preface*                                                                    vii

*List of mathematical content*                                               viii

1   The classification of costs                                              1

2   Linear cost estimation                                                   21

3   Cost estimation – learning curve                                         54

4   Marginal costing – an introduction                                       73

5   Marginal costing – cost–volume–profit analysis                          90

6   Marginal costing – pricing and common costs                            114

7   Budgeting and forecasting methods                                       139

8   Behavioural aspects of budgeting                                        174

9   Capital budgeting                                                       190

10  Further aspects of capital budgeting                                    222

11  Cost, profit and investment centres                                     257

12  Standard costing and variance analysis                                 277

13  Further aspects of variance analysis                                   321

14 Computerized accounting information systems (CAIS) and the cost and management accountant     362

*Appendix*    *Mathematical tables*     390

*Index*     410

# Preface

The aim of this book is to be the main textbook for the Chartered Institute of Management Accountants' Stage 3 syllabus Management Accounting Techniques. The topics covered should also be useful for students studying management accounting as a part of a professional studies course or on an undergraduate degree course.

The title of the book – *Management Accounting Techniques: an integrated approach* – clearly states our philosophy. Today's management accountant must be familiar with, and be able to apply, quantitative models to management accounting. The emphasis must be on the application and not purely on the knowledge. We have attempted to follow the stages:

1 Identify the problem.
2 Explain the quantitative model.
3 Applied the model to the situation.
4 Interpret the results.

It is not necessary for students to have a detailed mathematical understanding of a topic in the way that a mathematician needs, but they must understand the general principles and particularly the requirements of a model. There is a danger that without this knowledge they will apply quantitative models in inappropriate situations. In Chapter 14 we have dealt with the modelling approach. This is the methodology which should be used when analysing a problem situation.

This is essentially a book on management accounting which applies quantitative techniques to management accounting problems. However the complexity of the analysis or the amount of the data to be processed often requires the use of a computer. Therefore wherever possible we have made use of widely available software packages to analyse the problem.

At the end of each chapter we have included some past examination questions along with model answers. This is so that readers can see how the techniques covered in the chapter (sometimes including techniques from previous chapters) can be applied in the problem situation. Using past examination questions also makes sure that readers are familiar with the types of question they are going to meet in the examination.

The content of the book covers not only the Management Accounting Technique syllabus but also some topics from Cost Accounting in Stage 2, as well as a few topics from the Quantitative Methods syllabus in Stage 1. This is because of the considerable amount of overlap between the syllabuses (a deliberate policy of CIMA) and an attempt by us to ease the student's transition from the earlier levels. This has meant, for example, starting with a chapter on cost classification which is really more of a Stage 2 topic than a Stage 3.

We would like to thank Daphne Biggs who managed to turn our scribbled jottings into neat typescript only to be given a revised version five minutes after she had completed our first draft.

*Colin Biggs and David Benjamin*

# List of mathematical content

Our philosophy is for the mathematical techniques to be integrated with the management accounting. However there are occasions when it will be necessary to go directly to a specific mathematical technique.

The following list gives the chapters in which the techniques are explained or used.

List of mathematical topics:

| Subject | 1 | 2 | 3 | 4 | 5 | 6 | 7 | 8 | 9 | 10 | 11 | 12 | 13 | 14 |
|---|---|---|---|---|---|---|---|---|---|---|---|---|---|---|
| Analysis of variance | | 2 | | | | | | | | | | | | |
| Calculus | | | | | | 6 | | | | | | | | |
| Chi-squared | | | | | | | | | | | | | | 14 |
| Confidence interval | | 2 | | | | 6 | | | | | | | | |
| Correlation | | 2 | | | | | | | | | | | | |
| Critical path method | | | | | | | | | | | | 12 | | |
| Decision analysis | | | | 4 | | 6 | | | | 10 | | | | |
| Economic order quantity | | | | | | 6 | | | | | | | | 14 |
| Exponential smoothing | | | | | | | 7 | | | | | | | |
| F distribution | | 2 | | | | | | | | | | | | |
| Forecasting | | | | | | | 7 | | | | | | | |
| Internal rate of return | | | | | | | | | 9 | 10 | | | | 14 |
| Learning curve | | | 3 | | | | | | | | | 12 | | |
| Linear programming | | | | | 5 | | | | | 10 | | | | |
| Moving average method | | | | | | | 7 | | | | | | | |
| Net present value | | | | | | | | | 9 | 10 | | | | 14 |
| Normal distribution | | | | | | 6 | | | | | | 12 | | |
| Pert | | | | | | | | | | | | 12 | | |
| Quality control chart | | | | | | | | | | | | | 13 | |
| Queueing theory | | | | | | | | | | | | | | 14 |
| Regression | | 2 | 3 | | | | 7 | | | | | | | |

ix

| | | | |
|---|---|---|---|
| Sensitivity analysis | | 5 | 10 |
| Simulation | | | 10 | 14 |
| t-distribution | 2 | | |
| Tests of significance | 2 | | | 14 |

# 1 The classification of costs

## Introduction

A cost can be defined as the value attributed to a resource. There are three elements of a cost – material, labour and services (expenses).

It is important to note that costing is the provision of cost information for different purposes and therefore the classification of a cost depends on the purpose for which it is required.

The main areas in which costs can be classified are decision making, planning, control and stock valuation. In this chapter costs are classified into the above categories in order to meet the requirements of the various users of accounting information.

## Classification of costs for stock valuation

### Product and period costs

Product costs are those costs which are identified as part of stock, and only become expenses in the form of cost of goods sold when the stock is sold.

Period costs are those costs which are not identified with stock and are deducted as expenses during the period in which they are incurred. They are not carried forward in stock to the next accounting period.

In a manufacturing enterprise all manufacturing (production) costs are considered as product costs. Non-manufacturing costs, such as administration, distribution and selling expenses are treated as period costs, because:

1  they are not expected to generate future revenue as they do not represent any value added to units of output;
2  some non-manufacturing costs e.g. delivery costs are not incurred

when output is stored, and should not therefore be included in the stock valuation.

### Direct and indirect costs

Direct costs are those costs which are identifiable with the end product and include the following: raw material used in manufacturing the product (direct material); machine operators who make the product (direct labour); royalties paid or special plant hired (direct expenses). The total of these direct costs is called the prime cost.

Indirect costs are costs which cannot be identified with, or traced to the end product and include the following: lubricants and scrap material (indirect material); the salaries of factory supervisors (indirect labour); rent, rates and depreciation (indirect expenses). Indirect costs are often called overheads.

It is important to know the reason why a cost is being identified. If identification is with a sales area, then a salesman's salary is a direct cost to that area but indirect to the end product.

### Analysis of indirect costs (overheads)

Overheads can be categorized broadly into three functions – manufacturing, administration, selling and distribution functions.

Manufacturing (production) overheads are those costs incurred within the factory e.g. rent, rates depreciation, and supervisors' salaries. Administration overheads include the rent, rates, power and salaries incurred within the office. Selling and distribution overheads include such costs as advertising, salesmen's salaries, transportation, insurance and depreciation on salesmen's vehicles.

Let us consider an example, which illustrates the classification of costs for stock valuation and profit determination purposes.

*Example*
A company produces 10,000 units of a product during its accounting period. The costs for the period are as follows:

| | |
|---|---|
| Direct material | £30,000 |
| Direct labour | £40,000 |
| Direct expenses | £10,000 |
| Manufacturing overheads | £50,000 |
| Administration overheads | £30,000 |
| Selling overheads | £20,000 |

During the period 5000 units were sold for £150,000 and the remaining 5000 units were unsold. There was no opening stock at the beginning of the period.

*Solution*
Profit and loss account for the period (£)

| | | |
|---|---:|---:|
| Sales (5000 units) | | 150,000 |
| Direct material | 30,000 | |
| Direct labour | 40,000 | |
| Direct expenses | 10,000 | |
| Prime cost | 80,000 | |
| Manufacturing overheads | 50,000 | |
| (Product costs) manufacturing (factory) cost | 130,000 | |
| Less closing stock (5000 units) | (65,000)* | |
| Cost of goods sold | | (65,000) |
| Gross profit | | 85,000 |
| Less non-manufacturing (period costs) | | |
| Administration overheads | 30,000 | |
| Selling overheads | 20,000 | |
| | | (50,000) |
| | Net Profit | 35,000 |

* Cost determined on a pro-rata basis.

## Classification of costs for decision making

### Cost behaviour

Cost behaviour indicates the way in which costs react to changes in activity levels. Activity or volume may be expressed in terms of units of output, sales, hours worked etc.

*Fixed costs*
These are costs which are unaffected by changes in the level of activity e.g. salaries, rent, rates and depreciation (see Figure 1.1).

Although the total fixed costs are constant, the fixed costs per unit will decrease as output increases (fixed costs are spread over a greater number of units).

However, total fixed costs are subject to managerial decisions and will not therefore remain constant. In the long run as activity increases and more plant and staff are required, fixed costs will increase in a step-like fashion (see Figure 1.2).

*Variable costs*
These are costs which vary in direct proportion to changes in the level of activity, i.e. if the activity level is trebled total variable costs will treble. Total variable costs are therefore linear (see Figure 1.3).

Examples of variable costs are direct material, direct labour and direct expenses.

Although total variable costs increase as activity increases, the variable cost per unit is constant.

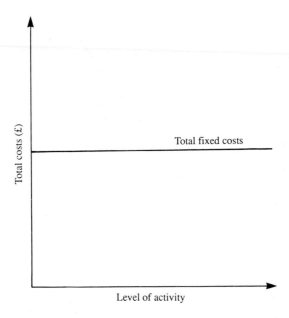

Figure 1.1

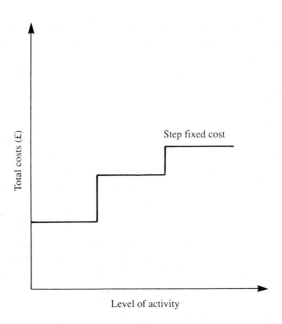

Figure 1.2

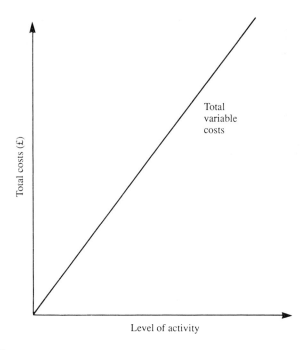

Figure 1.3

*Semi-variable (mixed) costs*
These costs are comprised of both fixed and variable elements, e.g. a telephone cost which consists of a fixed rental charge, and variable costs associated with the calls made.

The total costs of an organization are the sum of its fixed and variable costs and therefore have the same cost behaviour pattern as semi-variable costs (see Figure 1.4).

*Semi-fixed costs*
These are costs which are fixed for a certain level of activity but eventually increase by a constant amount at some particular point, e.g. supervisors' salaries – can cope with up to 1000 hours of activity per week, beyond which the costs will increase by say 20 per cent of the existing cost, for each increase in 1000 hours of activity (see Figure 1.5).

If the above steps are close together the semi-fixed costs may be represented by a variable cost (an approximation) (see Figure 1.6).

The above accounting models assume that over relevant ranges of activity levels, price levels (wage rates and material prices) and efficiency levels are constant and that fixed costs will remain unchanged.

However, the economic model shown in Figure 1.7 assumes that over wide ranges of output, price and efficiency levels will change first because of economies and then diseconomies (law of diminishing returns) arising as output increases.

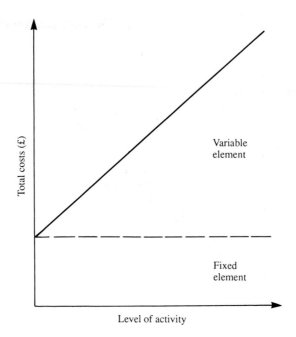

Figure 1.4

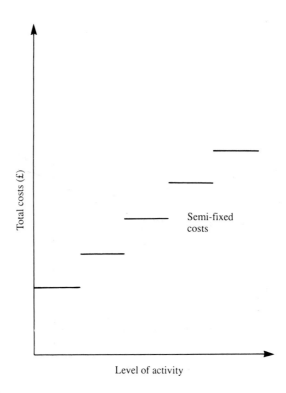

Figure 1.5

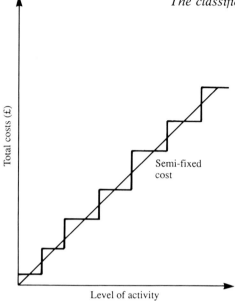

Figure 1.6

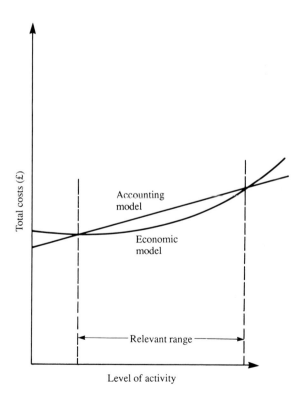

Figure 1.7

It can be seen that over the relevant range both models provide similar cost estimates.

### Relevant costs

For decision making purposes it is not only important to classify costs according to the way in which they behave, but also as to whether or not they are relevant to a particular decision.

A relevant cost is a future cost which differs between alternatives. It can also be defined as any cost which is affected by the decision at hand.

The main features of a relevant cost are:

1  It must be a future cost, i.e. one which is expected to be incurred and not a historic (sunk) cost, which has already been incurred and cannot therefore be affected by a decision.
2  It must be an incremental (additional) or avoidable cost, i.e. fixed overheads which are allocated by head office are not relevant, but incremental or avoidable fixed overheads are relevant.

*Example*

A company purchased a machine for £10,000. It has a book value of £3000, but has become obsolete, and cannot be sold in its present condition. However, if the firm is willing to modify the machine at a cost of £2000 it can be sold for £6000. Advise.

*Solution*

The £10,000 has been incurred and is therefore a sunk cost and irrelevant to this decision. Similarly the book value of £3000, which will have to be written off, no matter what possible alternative future action is taken, is also irrelevant as it cannot be changed by any future decision.

However, both the £2000 modification cost and £6000 sale value are relevant as they represent future, incremental costs and revenues.

It can therefore be seen that the firm would be advised to modify and sell, thus showing an incremental benefit of:

£6000 − £2000 = £4000

### Opportunity costs

An opportunity cost is an imputed cost which represents the greatest benefit foregone or sacrifice made as a result of using a particular resource or choosing an alternative course of action. If, for example, a choice lies between alternatives A, B and C, then the opportunity cost of choosing alternative A is the more profitable of alternatives B and C which has been foregone.

Although opportunity costs are not collected within the accounting system as they are not based on past payments or future commitments, they can be affected by decisions and are therefore relevant.

*Example*

A company has decided to use material A in a particular contract, and therefore needs to value 500 kg of this material in order to set a price for the contract.

Material A is in stock, and has a book cost of £2 per kg. Its scrap value is £1 per kg. Also material A can be used as a substitute for material X, which currently costs £3 per kg and is out of stock. Value material A.

*Solution*

The book cost of £2 per kg is a historic, sunk cost and therefore irrelevant to the valuation.

However, there are two opportunities for this material:

1  to realize the material A and obtain future revenue of £1 per kg;
2  to use the material A as a substitute for material X, and thus save a cost of £3 per kg. A possible saving in cost is the same as a benefit receivable.

The opportunity cost of using material A in the contract is the greater of the two opportunities foregone, i.e. £3 per kg. The relevant valuation of material A is therefore:

500 kg at £3 = £1500

## Classification of costs for planning and control

### Historic and standard costs

Historic costs are costs which have already been incurred and, as explained earlier, are irrelevant for decision making purposes. However, these past costs can be used to estimate future costs, and to provide a basis for comparison with budgeted information in order to highlight areas where control action may be necessary.

Standard costs are predetermined (planned) cost estimates for a unit of output in order to provide a basis for comparison with actual costs. Standards are the building blocks which are used to compile budgets. The term 'budgeted costs' is a total concept, i.e. the budgeted cost of material is £5000 if 5000 units are to be produced and the standard cost of material is £1 per unit.

Product costs do not pinpoint costs to areas of responsibility. To overcome this problem, a system of responsibility accounting is necessary which recognizes individual areas of responsibility in a firm's organizational structure.

There are three types of areas of responsibility:

1  Cost centres, where managers are responsible for costs under their control.
2  Profit centres, where managers are responsible for costs and revenues.

3  Investment centres, where managers are responsible for costs, revenues and capital investment decisions.

### Controllable and uncontrollable costs

When distinguishing between controllable and uncontrollable costs it is necessary to consider both the time scale of the cost and the level of authority involved.

Some fixed costs called discretionary costs, e.g. advertising, accounting and research and development expenditure, can be controlled in the short run. Other fixed costs called committed costs, e.g. rent, rates, depreciation and insurance, cannot be reduced without injuring the firm's ability to meet long range goals and are therefore uncontrollable.

Also a manager should have the level of authority to influence a cost before he is made responsible for it. Hence production salaries may be noncontrollable costs on a manager's performance report, but controllable costs on his superior's report.

A responsibility centre performance report can take the following format:

Department P

|  | Budget (£) | Actual (£) | Variance (£) |
| --- | --- | --- | --- |
| Controllable costs | | | |
| Direct labour | XX | XX | XX |
| Direct material | XX | XX | XX |
| Power | XX | XX | XX |
| Idle time | XX | XX | XX |
| Stationery | XX | XX | XX |
| Noncontrollable costs | | | |
| Salaries | XX | XX | XX |
| Insurance | XX | XX | XX |
| Depreciation | XX | XX | XX |

It is the difference between the actual and budget, i.e. the variances, which may prompt managerial control action.

Students should note that the classification of costs by their behaviour to changes in activity levels is also very important for control purposes.

*Example*
Budgeted performance – £50,000 of costs. 10,000 units to be produced.
Actual performance – £45,000 of costs. 8000 units produced.

The actual and budgeted costs cannot be compared as they are based on different levels of activity. It is therefore necessary to flex the budget to the actual level of 8000 units in order that a comparison can be made. However, some of the budgeted £50,000 costs are fixed costs and unaffected by changes in activity levels. It is therefore necessary to classify costs into their fixed, variable and other elements so that the budgeted costs can be adjusted to the level of activity under which the manager operated.

Flexible budgeting forms the basis of standard costing and variance analysis.

In this chapter costs have been classified in three different ways. However, students should note that this categorization is not exhaustive. Furthermore from a financial point of view costs can be of a revenue nature, i.e. associated with the running of a business and charged to the profit and loss account. Also they can be of a capital nature, i.e. associated with the acquisition of long-term assets, which are not purchased for resale purposes. This expenditure is shown in the balance sheet.

Finally, it is the context in which a cost is used which determines its classification.

## Examination questions

### Questions 1 (ACA)

*Cost classification*
The diagrams in Figure 1.8 represents nine cost-volume relationships. They have been drawn on the following bases and assumptions:

1  The independent variable is productive activity
2  The dependent variable is total cost
3  The graphs are not necessarily drawn to scale
4  The zero point is at the intersection of the axes
5  The period being considered is a year
6  Each relationship which is represented should be interpreted as being independent of those shown on other diagrams.

### Required

(a)  A brief statement of which relationship each diagram could represent, together with an example, taken either from your reading or your own experiences, of a cost that could follow the pattern illustrated. In your answer, clearly indicate which diagram you are discussing.
(b)  A brief discussion on how a knowledge of the major cost–volume relationships can be helpful to the management accountant.

### Answer 1

(a)  Diagram (a) illustrates a variable cost, i.e. one which varies with the level of activity. The variability here is directly proportional as

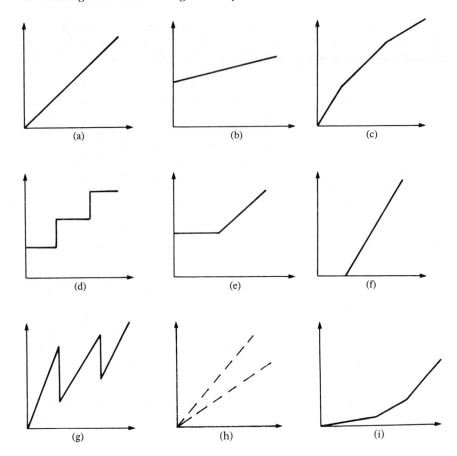

Figure 1.8

shown by the linear relationship. Examples of variable costs include direct material, direct labour and direct expenses.

Diagram (b) could represent a firm's total costs, being the sum of its fixed and variable costs, or an individual cost which has a fixed and variable element. The latter is called a semi-variable or mixed cost. Examples include maintenance costs and telephone costs consisting of a fixed rental and variable costs relating to the number of calls made.

Diagram (c) shows a decreasing variable cost. The straight lines could be smoothed out to produce a curvilinear relationship. An example is the purchase of raw materials where discounts are obtained on quantities in excess of certain level of purchase, e.g. £10 per kilo for the first 2000 kilos, £8 per kilo for the next 2000 kilos and £7 per kilo for any further supplies.

Diagram (d) illustrates a step-cost or semi-fixed cost. It is a cost which is fixed over a certain level of activity, but increases by a fixed amount when activity rises above this level. Examples include most fixed costs, i.e. salaries, rent and depreciation. Some variable costs, such as raw materials ordered in economic batch quantities, also fall into this category. However, the steps are too small to be significant.

Diagram (e) shows a cost which is initially fixed, and then behaves in a variable fashion. An example could be the hiring of a machine where a certain number of units can be made at no charge, i.e. only the fixed charge is incurred. However, after this number has been exceeded, charges are incurred for additional units on a reducing scale.

Diagram (f) illustrates a variable cost which is incurred after a certain level of activity is achieved. Examples include overtime premiums or bonuses.

Diagram (g) shows a variable cost, whose straight lines could be smoothed out to produce a curvilinear function. This diagram is similar to that of (c), except that in (g) discounts received in bulk purchases of raw materials are on every unit bought, including those in lower levels of units supplied.

Diagram (h) represents variable costs which are difficult to forecast, and therefore two cost functions have been drawn to show possible behaviour patterns.

Diagram (i) is and increasing variable cost, whose straight lines could be curvilinear. An example is where the purchase cost of a resource changes, as increases in activity, and therefore demand, for a limited supply increases the cost of the resource. Petrol requirements during an oil crisis would be characteristic of such a cost.

(b)   A knowledge of major cost–volume relationships enables the management accountant to estimate budgeted costs of cost centres and thereby prepare budgets.

Budgetary control and variance analysis are also facilitated, as by knowing cost behaviour the cost that should have been incurred for a given actual level of activity can be estimated. The diagrams in part 1 of the question provide the following assistance:

Diagram (h) is useful in a break-even analysis situation, where uncertainty exists, and sensitivity analysis can be used to appraise the situation in the event of the higher and lower cost existing.

Diagram (d) helps a firm to decide whether or not it should increase its activity level and therefore incur the costs associated with such an increase.

Diagram (i) might cause the firm to make economies with respect to scarce resources, or search for substitutable resources.

Diagrams (c) and (g) show that buying more of a resource may be cheaper than buying less, even if it means wasting the surplus; e.g. 100 units at £10 would cost £1000 whereas 101 units at £8 (discount received) only cost £808. As movement is made from one price level to another, the average unit cost falls.

The above presentation of cost information in diagram form is an excellent way of communication particularly for non-accountants.

It can be seen that an understanding of cost behaviour is invaluable to the management accountant for decision-making, planning and control purposes.

### Question 2 (ACCA)

Slick Sales Ltd have a sales force structure based upon a national sales manager situated in Birmingham, and 15 representatives who cover the United Kingdom. The sales force, including the sales manager, are all provided with the same sort of car. This costs £3200 when new and there is a replacement programme when it is traded in after two years for a guaranteed £1200. The salesman covering the lowest mileage, which is 18,000 miles annually, operated in the London area. The one with the highest mileage travels 40,000 miles throughout the Scottish Highlands. The sales manager has averaged an annual 25,100 miles over the last three years. The annual average mileage of the complete sales team works out at 30,000 miles per vehicle.

Members of the sales force are allowed to use their cars for local private journeys at no cost to them. However, if they wish to use their company car for a long holiday journey, they are expected to make a contribution towards the annual running costs of the vehicle, based upon the mileage that they cover whilst on holiday.

The average annual cost of operating a salesman's vehicle is:

|  | £ |
|---|---|
| Petrol and oil | 1200 |
| Road tax | 40 |
| Insurance | 160 |
| Repairs (see note (i)) | 240 |
| Miscellaneous (see note (ii)) | 100 |
| Total | £1740 |

*Notes*

(i)  Annual repairs include £80 for regular maintenance. Tyre life is around 30,000 miles and replacement sets cost £120. No additional repair costs incurred during the first year of vehicle life because a special warranty agreement exists with the supplying garage to cover these. However, on average £200 is paid for repairs in the second year. Repair costs are averaged over the two years with regular maintenance and repairs being variable to mileage rather than time.

(ii) This includes such things as subscriptions to motoring organizations, cleaning vehicles, parking fees, allowances for garaging etc.

*Required*

It is important that you clearly state any assumptions that you make when answering the various parts of this question.

(a) Computations showing the cost of operating the organization's highest and lowest mileage vehicles each year.
(b) The salesman based in London wishes to take his car on a holiday tour of Wales and the Lake District. He expects to cover 1800 miles. Suggest ways in which the contribution that he should pay to Slick Sales Ltd for use of the car during this tour should be calculated.
(c) The sales manager has to make a special journey to Ireland to carry out negotiations with a potential large new customer. If he takes his car he will have to cover an additional mileage to that normally incurred in a year. This will be 151 miles to the ferry, where he will have to pay £35 for the return ferry for himself and his car, and then travel for another 100 miles on the other side to his ultimate destination. He could fly directly to the potential customer's offices for £60 return. Which method of transportation would you advise him to use?

Note that the cost of capital, taxation considerations and inflation can all be ignored in answers to this question.

## Answer 2

(a)

| Annual costs for | London (lowest mileage 18,000 miles) (£) | Highlands (highest mileage 40,000 miles) (£) |
|---|---|---|
| Fixed costs | | |
| Road tax | 40 | 40 |
| Insurance (note i) | 160 | 160 |
| Miscellaneous (note ii) | 100 | 100 |
| Depreciation (note iii) | 1000 | 1000 |
| | 1300 | 1300 |
| Variable costs | | |
| Repairs at 0.6p per mile (note iv) | 108 | 240 |
| Petrol and oil at 4p per mile (note v) | 720 | 1600 |
| Semi-variable costs | | |
| Tyre replacement (note vi) | 60 | 120 |
| Total annual cost | 2188 | 3260 |

In the above table costs have been classified into fixed, variable and semi-variable. The following notes state the assumptions made in this classification.

*Notes*

(i) The insurance costs are the same for each area. In reality this is unlikely because of different risk factors. (There is more traffic in

London than in the Highlands and therefore there is a greater risk of an accident occurring in London. Insurance premiums should be higher.)

(ii)   Because of lack of information in the question, miscellaneous costs are assumed to be fixed. This is a valid assumption for motoring subscriptions and garaging allowances, but not necessarily correct for the other items. Parking fees should vary with number of calls made rather than mileage. More parking will occur in London where there is less distance between cells. Cleaning will be a function of both time and mileage.

(iii)   Annual depreciation charge $= \dfrac{£3200 - £1200}{2 \text{ years}} = £1000$

The trade-in value appears to be based on time and unaffected by mileage, which is rather unrealistic.

|  | (£) |
|---|---|
| (iv)   Annual repairs | 80 |
| Average annual additional repairs | 100   i.e. (200/2) |
|  | 80 |

Therefore average cost per mile $= £180$ per 30,000 miles
$= 0.6\text{p per mile}$

Repairs are a function of use, and therefore treated as a variable cost.

(v)   Petrol and oil are also based on usage and treated as a variable cost; 30,000 miles divided into £1200 $= 4\text{p per mile}$. This ignores driving conditions, length of journeys, and the way an individual drives, all of which affect fuel consumption. It is assumed that the cost of petrol does not vary in different parts of the country.

(vi)   It is assumed that in the case of the lowest mileage only one replacement set of tyres will be required during the two-year cycle as a new set of tyres can be avoided at the end of the second year when the vehicle is traded in.

$$\frac{£120}{2 \text{ yrs}} = £60$$

Tyres will move in a step function and are therefore classified as semi-variable cost. (The way a person drives and road conditions have been ignored.)

(b)   One possible way would be to charge a proportion of the total cost which reflects the mileage expected to be covered.

$$£2188 \times \frac{1800 \text{ miles}}{18,000 \text{ miles}} = £218.80$$

A more likely way is to ignore fixed costs and consider only the variable costs. Tyre costs for this purpose would be treated as variable costs.

$$\text{Tyre costs} \quad = \frac{£120}{30,000 \text{ miles}} = 0.4\text{p per mile}$$

$$\text{Repair costs} = \frac{£180}{30,000} = 0.6\text{p per mile}$$

$$\text{Petrol costs} \quad = \frac{4\text{p per mile}}{5\text{p} \times 1800 \text{ miles}} = £90$$

Perhaps a charge between £90 and £218.80 would be made depending whether the firm wishes to use the availability of a car as a perk in order to motivate the salesman.

(c)  If the car is used for the journey to Ireland, the relevant costs are the variable costs, petrol and oil 4p per mile and repairs 0.6p per mile, i.e. 4.6p per mile. The fixed costs and tyre replacement costs* are irrelevant as they will be unaffected by the 502 mile (return trip), and are therefore not incremental (additional) costs.

502 miles at 4.6p per mile = £23
Ferry charge                 = £35
                              ‾‾‾‾‾
                               £58

This is cheaper than the £60 air fare. However, qualitative benefits of air transport should be considered, and these include speed, convenience and the prestige of flying.

Perhaps these benefits outweigh the small savings in travelling costs of £2 (£60 − £58).

## Question 3 (CIMA)

An electrical goods manufacturing company made a ten per cent profit on sales of £1 million in its last trading year. The composition of its costs was direct labour 25 per cent, direct materials 60 per cent and fixed overhead 15 per cent.

The general manager has drawn your attention to the fact that, although sales were just below forecast, the profit was very much lower than he had expected.

Your initial investigation shows that the significant difference appears to be caused by the direct labour costs. The company uses the marginal cost accounting principle to price its products. In all price quotations the direct labour was treated as a variable cost directly related to volume output. However the review indicates that the direct

---

* The additional 502 miles would not cause a second replacement set in the two year period.

labour cost showed little change when output decreased for any reason.
  You are required to:

(a)  State whether you agree that direct labour costs should be treated
     as wholly variable with output.
(b)  Calculate using the last year's results, the sales value at break-even
     point and the margin of safety when the direct labour costs are
     treated as:

     (i)  wholly variable;
     (ii) fixed.

(c)  Comment on the results obtained in part 2 above.


### Answer 3

(a)  Whether or not direct labour costs should be treated as wholly
variable with output is largely a question of fact. In practice, the only
time that this treatment reflects reality is when direct labour payments
are made strictly on piecework. To treat direct labour as a variable cost
implies the following:

• Working at 100 per cent of standard levels (on which direct labour
  costs are based).
• No downtime or excess over standard. This means no gap in work
  due to failure of organization or nonavailability of materials, no
  machine breakdown and no absence for which payments are made.
• No situation where a standard total labour force, and thus the cost,
  is at a given level to cover a range of activity, e.g. a vat that requires
  three men to operate it, whether a small or a large amount of liquid
  is being processed in any given period.
• No overtime, unless it is being treated as overheads.

  Clearly, the above constraints mean that direct labour is very rarely
strictly variable with output. A review of the industrial scene today
reinforces this fact. There is relatively stable employment with negoti-
ated manning levels, guaranteed working weeks and minimum payments. Direct labour has almost become a fixed cost, eliminatable only
after long trade union negotiation and often with redundancy payments. Additionally, changing technology, whereby operatives become
machine-minders rather than product-makers, means that the relationship between output and production costs is no longer a simple linear
one.

  It may well be, however, that in the long run there will be a tendency
for direct labour to approximate to a variable cost. Thus, if the
company quoted in the question were to find its sales dropping to
£500,000, for example, it is quite likely that its direct labour force
would drop fairly closely into line. Conversely, if its sales were to
double, its labour force might increase substantially, though it would
not necessarily double. Thus, over a wide range of output, something

approximating to direct variability might be achieved. It must be recognized, however, that in the short run, such direct variability of direct labour is much less likely.

The situation is somewhat improved by the treatment in the costing system given to the sort of differences indicated above. For example, if excess labour costs arising from machine breakdowns or nonavailability of materials are treated as overheads, the remaining direct labour cost might remain fairly closely variable with output. For this rather technical approach to be valid from the standpoint of being able to forecast costs, the total overhead increments from such causes would need to be able to be budgeted with considerable accuracy.

(b)   Break-even points and margins of safety

|  | (£000) | (£000) |
|---|---|---|
| Sales |  | 1000 |
| Direct materials | 540 |  |
| Direct labour | 225 | } 85% |
| Fixed overhead | 135 |  |
|  | 900 |  |
|  | 100 |  |

(i)   Direct labour costs as wholly variable:
Fixed overhead + sales quantity × variable cost
= sales value at break-even point (S)

$$£135 + 0.90 \times 0.85S = S$$
$$£135 + 0.765S = S$$
$$£135 = 0.235 \, S$$

Sales value at break-even point = £574,468
Margin of safety
£1,000,000 − £574,468 = £425,532

(ii)   Direct labour costs as fixed

$$£360 + 0.54 \times S = S$$
$$£360 = 0.46S$$

Sales value at break-even point = £782,609
Margin of safety
£1,000,000 − £782,609 = £217,391

(c)   The break-even point when direct labour is treated as wholly fixed is 36 per cent higher than when direct labour is treated as wholly variable. Conversely, the margin of safety is about one half.

When direct labour is treated as wholly variable, there is a substantial margin of safety.

The two treatments above are, of course, the extremes, but the importance of correct treatment is thus strongly highlighted.

## Further reading

Mepham, M.J., *Accounting Models*, Polytech., 1980.
Solomon, D., *Studies in Cost Analysis*, 2nd edn, Sweet and Maxwell, 1968.
Wells, M.C., *Accounting for Common Costs*, Centre for International Education and research in accounting, University of Illinois, 1978.
*Management Accounting: Official Terminology*, CIMA, 1982.

# 2 Linear cost estimation

## Introduction

This chapter deals with the methods used to develop estimates of costs for planning and controlling operations. Earlier in Chapter 1 it was shown that a cost item may be classified by behaviour, i.e. as variable, fixed, semi-fixed or semi-variable when related with some activity measure X. If we ignore semi-fixed costs and assume linear cost functions then a cost item can be defined by the equation

TC (total cost) = a + bX

where X may take the form of units of output, material weight, direct labour hours, or machine hours, a represents fixed costs and b is the variable cost per unit.

Two methods are used to obtain cost estimates

1  the engineering method which relies on the physical relationship between the inputs to a productive process and the observed output from the process;
2  the analysis of past cost data and the relationship between different cost and activity levels.

Although most of this chapter is focused on the various methods of using historical data, the engineering method, which does not require historic data, is discussed first.

## The engineering method

Every productive process involves employing a particular mix of materials, labour, and capital equipment in order to yield physical output. When the relationship between the input and output is established by the engineer or technical expert, e.g. 2 kilos of material + 3 hours of labour = 1 unit of output, the material and labour costs can be estimated by imputting material prices and wage rates to the physical input needs. It is important to note that these costs are estimates because of possible uncertainty with regards to wastage in material usage and changes in labour efficiency, in the production process.

The engineering method is particularly useful when applied to material and labour costs which represent a large proportion of the total output cost. If the relationships between material and labour inputs and outputs remain static over time, then these cost estimates can be used in the future without significant adjustment. When costing new products the engineering method is the only approach that can be used due to the lack of historic data.

However there are three main disadvantages of the engineering method:

1   it is expensive as work measurement involves detailed analysis of the physical movements required in each task, in order to produce one unit of output;
2   there are other costs incurred in the production process, e.g. machine maintenance and supervision which cannot be associated with specific units of output, but may be direct costs of the department. The engineering method cannot be applied to these costs, whose equations will have to be derived from an analysis of past data or from subjective evaluation.
3   different mixes of materials and skills may be used to produce the same unit of output, leading to several conflicting cost estimates.

Although the engineering method is usually associated with production, work study techniques are applied to other areas, such as selling and administrative functions of the organization.

## The analysis of historical data

The analysis of past cost data to estimate future costs is based on the cost and activity relationships of previous periods. These past relationships will only provide a reliable means of estimating the future, if there has not been any significant change in the firm's underlying cost structure, otherwise historical cost data will have to be adjusted.

Before we study the different methods of cost estimation from past data, it is necessary to analyse the historical cost data in order to ensure that it is suitable information.

The following stages are useful in increasing the reliability of results.

## Examination of information

1   To ensure that cost and activity data are of the same period, otherwise the costs of period 1 may be matched against the output of

period 2. This misallocation would have a serious effect on the estimation of variable cost.

2  Cost classifications by costing units must be correct and consistent over past periods.

3  Time periods under consideration should be of suitable length, i.e. long enough to enable the collection of meaningful data, yet short enough to reflect different activity rates, e.g. if cost data were collected hourly, then the hourly observations would include the effect of time of day on cost. However, if monthly observations were used an artificial smoothing of production and costs may occur, concealing the exact relationships between costs and activities at high and low readings.

4  It is important to ensure that the allocation of fixed costs does not make such costs appear as variable costs of different departments, otherwise the variable cost coefficient in the cost equation will be overstated.

## Selection of activity rate

An activity variable should be chosen which has the greatest effect on the level of cost observed (i.e. strong causality) and which is convenient to use. Direct labour hours, machine hours and number of units produced are widely used.

## Observation for homogeneity

Data collected should reflect only changes in the activity variable, and not changes in labour skills, technology or price levels of inputs from one period to another.

## Plotting

It is important to plot cost observations against activity levels as valuable information, not previously detected, may become available. For example, any extreme observations (or outliers) may be observed and then should be investigated to see if they are due to measurement error or are events of extreme behaviour which are likely to be nonrecurring. If an outlier (see Figure 2.1) is assumed to be an unusual occurrence, unlikely to occur again, it can be dropped from the analysis as it is not representative of a future occurrence. If however it is a value that could easily occur, then it should be included in the analysis to show the variability in the cost behaviour.

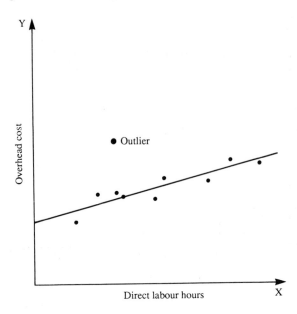

Figure 2.1

## Methods applied to past data

There are four methods of estimating costs described in this chapter, the first three of which provide rough estimates of cost–volume behaviour: visual curve-fitting, account classification, and the high–low methods.

There is a need to obtain accurate cost estimates and measures of the reliability of such estimates for flexible budgeting. The complexity of cost behaviour means that the cost accountant must use more sophisticated techniques such as the fourth method of statistical regression to analyse complex cost relationships.

### Visual curve-fitting

Where more than two cost and activity observations exist, a total cost line can be visually drawn to best fit these plotted observations as long as the points lie within reasonable proximity to the line. For example assume the Barsands company has determined the following overhead costs and direct labour hours (activity) for the production of an item over the last twelve months:

| Month | Overhead cost (£1000) | Direct labour hours |
|---|---|---|
| Jan | 22.8 | 624 |
| Feb | 19.3 | 587 |
| Mar | 22.3 | 686 |

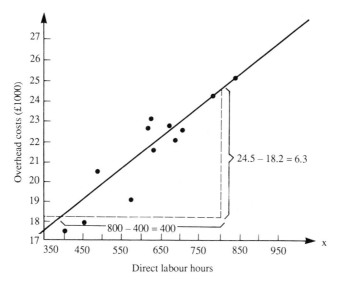

Figure 2.2

| Apr | 20.6 | 481 |
| May | 21.7 | 642 |
| Jun | 24.2 | 766 |
| Jul | 22.7 | 673 |
| Aug | 22.9 | 636 |
| Sep | 17.5 | 394 |
| Oct | 18.0 | 450 |
| Nov | 25.1 | 835 |
| Dec | 22.7 | 698 |

Plotting the overhead costs on the y-axis (the dependent variable) and the direct labour hours (the independent variable) on the x-axis gives the graph shown in Figure 2.2.

Note, the overhead costs (the variable we want to estimate) is assumed to depend upon the direct labour hours; i.e. if the demand in a given month increases then the direct labour hours required will increase resulting, we assume, in an increase in overhead costs.

It can be seen from the above graph that the points are clustered about a straight line, drawn by eye on the graph. Where the straight line crosses the y-axis, the y intercept at 17.5 provides an estimate of the fixed cost of £17,500. The slope of the line (from the graph 6.3/400 or 0.01575) gives an estimate of the variable cost per unit of £15.75. If the points were more widely scattered, or were scattered about a curve or formed a step pattern then fitting a straight line would be wrong. However, valuable information about the cost relationship would have been obtained.

The problem with this method is that each accountant using the same cost data to estimate the cost equation may draw different total costs lines by eye, to describe the relationship between cost and activity.

### Account classification

This method is a fast and inexpensive way of estimating costs as it simply involves examining each account and subjectively classifying the account's total cost into either fixed or variable elements.

*Example*

Total cost for department XXX with a value of 7,000 units

| Account | Amount (£) | Variable (£) | Fixed (£) |
|---|---|---|---|
| Direct labour | 150,000 | 150,000 | |
| Raw material | 125,000 | 125,000 | |
| Repairs and maintenance | 5,000 | 5,000 | |
| Depreciation | 15,000 | | 15,000 |
| Administrative overheads | 1,000 | | 1,000 |
| Indirect labour | 4,000 | | 4,000 |
| | 300,000 | 280,000 | 20,000 |

Total cost = Fixed costs + Variable cost per unit × (no. of units)

TC = 20,000 + 40* (no. of units)

* 280,000/7,000 = £40

However, this technique has the following limitations:

1  It depends heavily on the initial decision to classify an account as fixed or variable.
2  It fails to recognize that semi-variable costs exist.
3  It relies on a single observation of the account to determine the cost equation rather than using an average based on several observations of each account.
4  It assumes that transactions have been correctly charged to one account or another.

The account classification method should be used only when a crude approximation of cost behaviour is sufficient for making decisions.

### The high–low method

This approach uses two observations, the highest and the lowest activity levels, to reflect the change in cost that results from changes in activity.

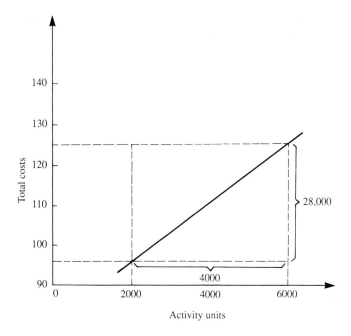

Figure 2.3

*Example*

|  | Total costs (£) | Activity units |
|---|---|---|
| Highest | 123,000 | 6,000 |
| Lowest | 95,000 | 2,000 |

The slope of the line (shown in Figure 2.3) can be derived by dividing the change in the total costs (123,000 − 95,000) by the change in the activity levels (6,000 − 2,000).

£28,000 per 4,000 units = £7 per unit (the variable cost per unit).

The fixed costs can be found in the following way:

|  | Highest level (£) | Lowest level (£) |
|---|---|---|
| Total costs | 123,000 | 95,000 |
| Less variable costs | 42,000 (£7 × 6,000 units) | 14,000 (7 × 2,000) |
| Fixed costs | 81,000 | 81,000 |

Hence variable cost is £7 per unit and fixed cost is £81,000. The total cost can therefore be expressed as a linear equation:

TC = 81,000 + 7X

where X is the number of units produced.

Although the high–low method provides a quick means of estimating costs, it relies on two extreme values to calculate the slope and intercept of the cost functions, and does not take into consideration the occurrence of any unusual situations. Two extreme values may not be truly representative of the observations.

A further example will illustrate the difference between the high–low and the account classification methods.

| Output levels (units) | | Classification of accounts | | |
|---|---|---|---|---|
| Units level | 40,000 | 60,000 | 80,000 | At 80,000 |
| Costs (£) | | | | |
| Material | 80,000 | 120,000 | 160,000 | variable |
| Labour | 120,000 | 180,000 | 240,000 | variable |
| Overheads: | | | | |
| Indirect supplies | 40,000 | 60,000 | 80,000 | variable |
| Indirect labour | 72,000 | 88,000 | 104,000 | variable |
| Supervision | 40,000 | 40,000 | 40,000 | fixed |
| Depreciation | 48,000 | 48,000 | 48,000 | fixed |
| Others | 24,000 | 30,000 | 36,000 | fixed |
| | 424,000 | 566,000 | 708,000 | |

*Using the accounts classification method* (at 80,000 level)

When the output level is 80,000 the total of the variable cost is £584,000 and the total of the fixed cost is £124,000. The variable cost per unit £584,000/80,000 or £7.30.

i.e.   TC (total cost) = 124,000 + 7.30X

*Using the high-low method*

$$\text{The variable cost per unit} = \frac{£708,000 - £424,000}{80,000 \text{ units} - 40,000 \text{ units}} = £7.1 \text{ per unit}$$

Fixed costs at high level = £708,000 − £7.1 × 80,000 = £140,000

Fixed costs at low level = £424,000 − £7.1 × 40,000 = £140,000

TC = 140,000 + 7.1X

For material, labour and indirect supplies the intercept is zero so that TC/X = a constant over all output observations.

However this does not apply to indirect labour. Also 'Others' has been wrongly classified as fixed. Both the indirect labour and 'others' can be considered as semi-variable costs.

Indirect labour

Variable cost per unit $b = \dfrac{£104,000 - £72,000}{80,000 - 40,000 \text{ units}} = £0.80$ per unit

Therefore fixed cost $\quad a = £40,000$

'Others'

$b = \dfrac{£36,000 - 24,000}{80,000 - 40,000 \text{ units}} = £0.30$ per unit

Therefore fixed costs a $= £12,000$

### Reconciliation of the two methods

Variable cost per unit of £1.30 (104,000/80,000). Therefore £1.30 − £0.80 = £0.50 excess.

Fixed costs were understated by £40,000.

*Others*
Variable cost per unit of zero. Therefore £0.30 − 0 = £0.30 deficiency.

Fixed costs were overstated by £36,000 − £12,000 = £24,000. The two variable costs per unit net out to £0.50 − £0.30 = £0.20.

The two fixed costs net out to £40,000 − £24,000 = £16,000. Hence:

$$
\begin{array}{r}
£124,000 + £7.3X \\
+ \underline{£\ \ 16,000 - £0.2X} \\
£140,000 + \ \ 7.1X
\end{array}
$$

The differences between the accounts classification and the high–low methods arise because they are based on different simplifying assumptions. Both methods should only be used when a rough approximation is required or no previous data is available. The more sophisticated linear regression method should be used if an accurate estimate is required.

### Simple regression and correlation

Simple linear regression analysis is a statistical technique for fitting a set of data to a straight line. It is used by the cost and management accountant to forecast the cost (dependent variable) from an activity (independent variable).

Like the visual curve-fitting method, regression analysis fits a linear cost function to all the past data. The approach used is called the method of least squares as it finds the line $Y = a + bX$, mathematically, which minimizes the sum of the squares of the vertical distances from the points to the line (see Figure 2.4).

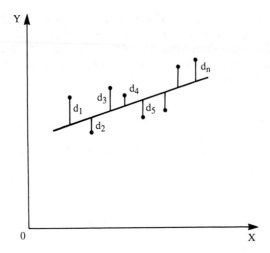

Figure 2.4

$$S = d_1^2 + d_2^2 + \ldots + d_n^2$$

The regression line $Y = a + bX$ is that line that gives the minimum value of $S$, and hence gives the line that best fits the data.

It can be proved using the differential calculus that:

$$b = \frac{n\Sigma xy - \Sigma x\Sigma y}{n\Sigma x^2 - (\Sigma x)^2} \quad \text{and} \quad a = \bar{y} - b\,\bar{x}$$

Where n equals the sample size. (See mathematical tables for students published by CIMA.)

Let us reconsider the Barsands problem which we looked at in the visual curve-fitting section.

Barsands plc need to estimate how overhead costs vary with direct labour hours (activity). They have collected 12 months' data as follows:

| Month | Overhead cost (£1000) | Direct labour hours |
|-------|------------------------|----------------------|
| Jan | 22.8 | 624 |
| Feb | 19.3 | 587 |
| Mar | 22.3 | 686 |
| Apr | 20.6 | 481 |
| May | 21.7 | 642 |
| Jun | 24.2 | 766 |
| Jul | 22.7 | 673 |
| Aug | 22.9 | 636 |
| Sep | 17.5 | 394 |
| Oct | 18.0 | 450 |
| Nov | 25.1 | 835 |
| Dec | 22.7 | 698 |

A visual curve-fitting of overhead costs against the direct labour hours shows a good fit as shown in the graph (Figure 2.2). Using overhead cost as the dependent variable (Y) and the direct labour hours as the independent variable (X) we can formulate a simple linear regression model of the form:

$$Y = \alpha + \beta X + e$$

where $\alpha$ = constant or intercept term, $\beta$ = slope of the regression line, e = error term or residual.

Our best estimates of $\alpha$ and $\beta$ are respectively the sample values a and b.

In the example

$$n = 12 \ \Sigma x = 7472. \ \Sigma y = 259.8$$

$$\Sigma x^2 = 4834412 \ \Sigma y^2 = 5685.76 \ \Sigma xy = 164870.9$$

$$b = \frac{12 \times 164870.9 - 7472 \times 259.8}{12 \times 4834412 - (7472)^2}$$

$$b = 0.01706$$

$$a = \frac{259.8}{12} - 0.01706 \times \frac{7472}{12}$$

$$a = 11.03$$

Least squares regression line is

$$Y = 11.03 + 0.017X$$

Remember the overhead costs Y is measured in £1000s hence the equation may be written as:

$$Y = 11030 + 17.1X$$

measuring Y in pounds.

This means for direct labour hours in the range 394 to 835 we obtain a fixed overhead cost estimate of £11,030 and a variable overhead cost estimate of £17.1 per direct labour hour.

The cost and management accountant can use this cost equation to determine a flexible budget, e.g. if a budget is required when direct labour hours is 600 hours.

Then substituting X = 600 in our regression line gives;

$$\hat{Y} = 11030 + 17.1(600)$$

$$\hat{Y} = 21,290$$

Giving a budget estimate of £21,290.

Note, the estimate of the unit variable cost of £17.1 obtained by regression is a more accurate estimate than the estimate of £15.75 found by a visual curve-fit.

It is assumed for this analysis that the total overhead cost depends upon the activity (labour hours). However there are several activities that could have been used such as machine hours or units of production. One of the advantages of a more sophisticated mathematical approach is that various tests of the reliability of the cost function can be determined. We can evaluate how accurate each of these activities are in forecasting the costs.

One of these measures of reliability is the correlation coefficient (r) where

$$r = \frac{n\Sigma xy - \Sigma x \Sigma y}{\sqrt{(n\Sigma x^2 - (\Sigma x)^2)(n\Sigma y^2 - (\Sigma y)^2)}}$$

Giving $r = \dfrac{12 \times 164870.9 - 7472 \times 259.8}{\sqrt{(12 \times 4834412 - (7472)^2)(12 \times 5685.76 - (259.8)^2)}}$

$r = 0.931$

As r is positive and numerically close to one there is a high positive correlation, i.e. the cost function of costs depending on direct labour hours is a reliable cost function.

Hence the least squares regression line of total overhead cost on direct labour hours can be used for estimating total overheads from a knowledge of direct labour hours.

If the correlation coefficient had been close to zero say in the range −0.3 to +0.3 then the correlation would be zero meaning that the activity selected should not be used for cost estimation.

## Coefficient of determination

A further insight into the problem is obtained by examining a sketch of the least squares line (see Figure 2.5). Consider the June figures: When direct labour hours (x) = 766 and overhead cost (y) = 24.2, the estimate Y given by the regression line for X = 766 is:

$\hat{Y} = 11.03 + 0.0171 (766)$

$\hat{Y} = 24.10$

Note, ˆ means estimated as distinct from knowing the value. The average overhead cost over the year is 21.65 hence $\bar{y} = 21.65$.

If there was no regression, i.e. r = 0 and b = 0 the best estimate of the total overhead costs (Y) would be the sample mean $\bar{y} = 21.65$. This is the base figure for comparison purposes. The estimate for Y using the regression line (with r = 0.931, b = 0.0171) is 24.1 compared with an observed figure in June of 24.2. The total difference (or variation) between the observed value of 24.2 and the base figure of 21.65 is 2.55, while the difference between $\hat{Y}$ estimate of 24.1 and the base figure of 21.65 is 2.45. This difference of 2.45 can be explained by the regression, i.e. the increase of 2.45 above the average of 21.65 is due to the fact that

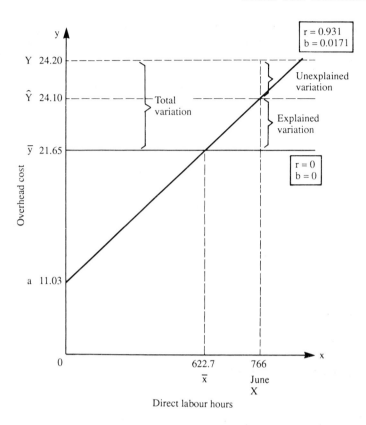

Figure 2.5

as x increases y increases. The remainder of 0.10 is unexplained by the regression line (see Figure 2.5).

In practice the total variation is defined as the sum of the square of all the observed values from the mean value called the total sum of squares (TSS), i.e. total variation $= \Sigma(y - \bar{y})^2$.

The explained variation is defined as the sum of the squares of the difference between the forecasted values (calculated from the observed x values) and the mean value called the regression sum of squares (RSS), i.e. explained variation $= \Sigma(\hat{y} - \bar{y})^2$.

It therefore follows that the error sum of squares (ESS) or unexplained variation $= \Sigma(y - \hat{y})^2$ as TSS = RSS + ESS.

It can be shown that the ratio explained variation/total variation or RSS/TSS $= r^2$. This is called the coefficient of determination. In the example $r = 0.931$ $r^2 = 0.866$. This means that 86.6 per cent of the variation is explained by the regression line leaving 13.4 per cent unexplained.

The coefficient of determination is a more useful statistic for comparing the fit of a regression line than the correlation coefficient. In multiple regression cases we will be more concerned with the increase in $r^2$ (or explained variation) rather than in the absolute value of r or $r^2$.

## Computer output

To do a complete statistical analysis of the fit of the data to the line it is convenient to use a statistical package like STATPACK, MINITAB or SPSS. These are commercial software packages available on most mainframe computers. There are equivalent packages available on both mini- and micro-computers.

The computer output shown in Figure 2.6 was generated by MINITAB (on an IBM mainframe computer) on the overhead cost and direct labour hour data of Barsands. The computer printout confirms our calculations. The coefficient of determination is 0.8662 and hence the correlation coefficient is 0.9307 and in the parameter estimates section, the parameter estimate column gives the coefficient of direct labour hours (DLH) as 0.017059, i.e. b=0.017059 and the constant term a=11.028 giving the regression line as Y = 11.028 + 0.017059X.

## Significance test − t test

A more powerful test for reliability of the cost function is to carry out a test of significance on the slope of the regression line b. For cost estimation, we will need to know if the b value is significantly different from zero, i.e. is there a variable cost element?

In the computer printout the standard error of b is 0.002120, usually written as SE(b)=0.002120 which will enable a test on the slope of the regression line to be carried out. Initially assume that there is no regression of OHCOS (Y) on DLH (X) i.e. r = 0. This means that as X changes Y remains constant, therefore, the slope of the line (b) must be zero. There would be no variable cost element.

When carrying out a test of significance the scientific method is followed. Start with an hypothesis and then using sample results as evidence attempt to refute the hypothesis.

In statistics the first hypothesis is called the 'null hypothesis', in the example that is b=0. This is written $H_0$:b=0.

Also formulate an 'alternative hypothesis' to accept if the null hypothesis is rejected. This is $H_1$:b≠0.

Note, assume the null hypothesis is true. The alternative hypothesis is to be used only if the null hypothesis is rejected.

We will test if our sample b value of 0.017059 is significantly different from zero. Sampling theory says that the 'sampling distribution' of all possible b values, follows a t-distribution. The students' t-distribution is a bell-shaped probability distribution (see Figure 2.7). If the sample

```
MTB >
REGRESS C1 ON 1 PREDICTORS C2

The regression equation is
C1 = 11.0 + 0.0171 C2

Predictor                  Coef           Stdev          t-ratio
Constant                 11.028          1.345            8.20
C2                      0.017059        0.002120           8.05

s = 0.9040    R - sq = 86.6%    R - sq(adj) = 85.3%

Analysis of Variance

SOURCE                     DF              SS              MS
Regression                  1           52.918          52.918
Error                      10            8.172           0.817
Total                      11           61.090

Continue?

                                                    VM Read IBMA

Unsual Observations
Obs.      C2            C1        Fit      Stdev. Fit  Residual  St. Resid
 2       587        19.300     21.042       0.272      -1.742    -2.02A

A denotes an obs. with a large st. resid.
MTB >
```

Figure 2.6

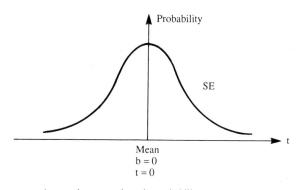

Area under curve gives the probability

Figure 2.7

size was above 30 we would carry out a similar test using a normal distribution.

The t-test statistic can be calculated by

$$t = \frac{\text{sample b} - \text{b (under H}_0)}{\text{SE}}$$

Where SE is the standard error of b.

$$\text{i.e.} \quad t = \frac{0.017059 - 0}{0.002120}$$

$$t = 8.047$$

Note, this approach is common to a number of significance tests which have the form:

$$\text{test statistic} = \frac{\text{sample result} - \text{result under H}_0}{\text{SE of statistic being tested}}$$

The value of t calculated from the sample b value needs to be compared with the table value (see t table in the appendix).

The concept of degrees of freedom must be introduced in order to use the t table. The concept has confused many people partly because the formal definition is heavily mathematical and partly because there exists several equivalent definitions.

For our purpose it should be sufficient to define the degrees of freedom (V) for regression to be equal to $n-k$, where n = sample size and k = number of variables used (including the dependent variable).

Therefore in our example $V = 12 - 2 = 10$. The level of significance to be tested needs to be decided. Common levels used are 5 per cent or 1 per cent. Let us use a 5 per cent level. This means that there is a probability of 0.05 that we will reject $H_0$ when $H_0$ is true. Of course there is the possibility that we will accept $H_0$ when $H_0$ is false.

From the t tables $t_{0.05}$ (V=10), a two tailed test, is 2.228. The use of a two tailed test is consistent with the alternative hypotheses $H_1:b\neq0$. That is, we will reject $H_0$ if our sample t value is significantly less than zero or significantly greater than zero (see Figure 2.8).

The t value, just like the z value of the normal distribution, is measured from the mean of the distribution. Hence the test t values are $+2.228$ and $-2.228$ giving a total rejection area of 5 per cent (the level of significance).

The sample t value of 8.047 lies in the shaded rejection region. Hence reject $H_0:b=0$, concluding that b is significantly different from zero. Therefore there must be a regression situation and the best estimate of b is the sample b of 0.017059. It follows mathematically that r is also significantly different from zero.

This means that our cost function $Y = 11.028 + 0.017059X$ has passed the reliability test and may be used by the cost accountant for cost estimation.

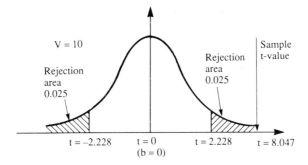

Figure 2.8 *Sampling distribution of b*

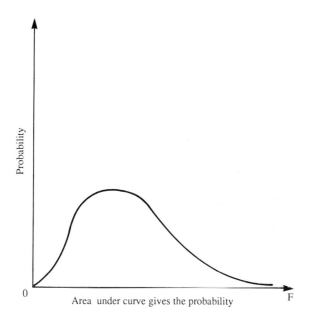

Figure 2.9 *The F distribution*

## Significance test F test

An alternative test of reliability can be carried out using the F distribution. The F distribution is a probability distribution, like the t or normal distribution. However it is positively skewed (see Figure 2.9).

The F test considers the problem from a related but different point of view. The null hypothesis is still $H_0:b=0$ and the alternative hypothesis is $H_1:B \neq 0$. However the F test is concerned with the spread of the observations and is a ratio of variances (i.e. standard deviations squared).

The numerator measures how much the estimates are spread about the assumed mean under $H_0$. The denominator measures how much the observations are spread about the regression line.

If $H_0$ is true than the variances should be approximately equal, only differing due to sample errors, and hence F should be close to one. If F is significantly greater than one then the null hypothesis is rejected.

To apply the F test the degrees of freedom of the numerator and of the denominator need to be calculated. The degrees of freedom for the numerator is one, and for the denominator is $n-k$ where k is the number of variables in the regression. Hence DF = (1,10). From the F table using a 5 per cent test of significance test $F(1,10)$ 5 per cent = 4.96 (see Figure 2.10). As the F sample value lies in the rejection region, reject $H_0$, accept $H_1$.

Note, the F distribution is a skewed distribution and is used with one rejection area as if it was a one tailed test. As the variances are concerned with spread it is in reality a two tailed test and consequently $H_1:b\neq0$.

## Analysis of variance for overall regression

When analysing a cost relationship we can carry out a t test examining individual parts of the regression equation, i.e. testing 'a', the fixed cost estimate, and 'b', the variable cost estimate, separately. Alternatively the total fit of the observations to the line can be determined by considering the correlation coefficient r or the coefficient of determination $r^2$. Similarly the F test can be applied to the individual values of 'a' and 'b' or we can consider the total fit by carrying out an analysis of variance test for the overall regression.

The analysis of variance table takes the following form:

| Source of variation | Degrees of freedom | Sum of squares | Mean square | F value |
|---|---|---|---|---|
| Regression | k − 1 (a) | $\varepsilon(\hat{y} - \bar{y})^2$ (c) | (a)/(c) = (f) | (f)/(g) |
| Residuals | n − k (b) | $\varepsilon(y - \hat{y})^2$ (d) | (a)/(d) = (g) | |
| Total | n − 1 | $\varepsilon(y - \bar{y})^2$ (e) | | |

Where y is the value of Y for an observed value of X, (c) is the explained variation (RSS), (d) is the unexplained variation (ESS), and (e) is the variation (TSS).

The mean squares (or variance estimates) are obtained by dividing the third column results by the second column. Finally the F value (the variance ratio) is calculated by dividing the variances (or mean squares).

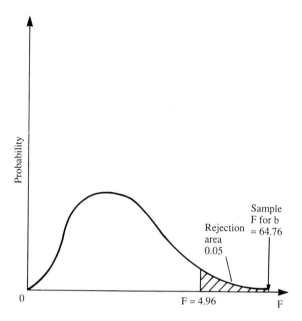

Figure 2.10   *The F distribution*

In the computer run F = 52.9/0.817 = 64.77 (the same as for the F value for b in the linear regression case) is significantly larger than the test value of F, F(1,10) 0.05 = 4.96. Hence there is a significant linear regression, i.e. the cost relationship Y = 11.028 + 0.017059X has passed the test of reliability and may be used for cost forecasting.

Note, the degree of freedom for the numerator is k−1 and for the denominator n−k as given in the table above.

Steps in an analysis of variance table for simple linear regression using a calculator with statistical functions are as follows:

1   Calculate degrees of freedom 1,10,11.
2   Calculate standard deviation of the y values ($\sigma_n$ on calculator) $\sigma_y$ = 2.256.
3   Calculate total sum of squares as $n\sigma_y^2$ TSS = 61.09, (4) in table.
4   Calculate regression sum of squares as $r^2$TSS; RSS = 52.92.
5   Calculate ESS from TSS–RSS; ESS = 8.17.
6   Then proceed to calculate the mean square and F as explained earlier.

## Summary of simple linear regression analysis

The relationship between the overhead costs and the direct labour hour has now been fully analysed providing the following regression line.

Y = 11.028 + 0.01706X

The correlation coefficient is 0.9307, a high positive value of correlation indicating a good fit. The coefficient of determination is 0.8662 showing that 86.62 per cent of the variation is explained by the regression line leaving 13.38 per cent of the variation unexplained. This is due to sampling errors or to factors not taken into account in the analysis.

The analysis of variance gives a significant F value of 64.76 showing that r is significantly different from zero and hence a linear regression relationship exists.

At the micro level, testing each coefficient in turn, the t, F values of 8.047 and 64.77 respectively for b are significant showing that b=0.01706 is significantly different from zero. Similarly the t and F values for 'a' being respectively 8.196 and 67.1788 are significant, showing that 'a' is significantly different from zero.

Hence the regression line passes all the tests and therefore may be used for prediction purposes when constructing flexible budgets.

## Limitations and interpretation of the statistical analysis

When cost relationships are determined by statistical analysis of historic cost data the relationships represents the behaviour experienced in the past. They do not necessarily represent the current or future cost relationships. These relationship can be used as a standard to compare the future performance to the past performance.

Some indication of the past efficiency of the cost centre can be determined from the statistical analysis. If the standard error of the estimate of the regression line is large, leading to a wide confidence interval, it would indicate a lack of control in the cost centre. If the correlation coefficient r or the coefficient of determination r is low, close to zero, then there are large unexplained fluctuations in the cost centre. If any of the statistical tests using t or F distributions fail (i.e. we accept $H_0$) then the cost relationship is a poor fit to the data and indicates that the cost centre is not operating in a state of statistical control. Costs are changing due to factors outside of the analysis. This would indicate that the operating procedures should be investigated in an attempt to identify the source of variation in the cost behaviour.

It might be that using a simple linear regression model for the cost relationship is too simplistic a model. The cost behaviour may not just depend upon one activity such as labour hours but may depend also upon the level of machine hours or level of output. To analyse these situations a similar approach is adopted called multiple regression.

## Multiple regression

Multiple regression is used for forecasting cost relationships where the cost depends, in a linear way, on two or more activities.

Having achieved some success at forecasting overhead costs using direct labour hours (DLH) in the Barsands example, let us now include as an extra independent variable direct machine hours (DMH) to see if the percentage explained variation is increased.

For this we need to obtain the direct machine hours for the twelve month period and using all three variables run the multiple regression package with two independent variables DLH and DMH.

The data are as follows:

| Month | Overhead cost (£1000) | Direct labour hours | Direct machine hours |
|-------|------------------------|----------------------|------------------------|
| Jan | 22.8 | 624 | 1389 |
| Feb | 19.3 | 587 | 949 |
| Mar | 22.3 | 686 | 1120 |
| Apr | 20.6 | 481 | 1169 |
| May | 21.7 | 642 | 1437 |
| Jun | 24.2 | 766 | 1425 |
| Jul | 22.7 | 673 | 1267 |
| Aug | 22.9 | 636 | 1474 |
| Sep | 17.5 | 394 | 962 |
| Oct | 18.0 | 450 | 925 |
| Nov | 25.1 | 835 | 1584 |
| Dec | 22.7 | 698 | 1303 |

The output from the multiple regression run is given in Figure 2.11.

The multiple regression line reading from the computer printout is:

$$Y = 9.09 + 0.0108DLH + 0.00467DMH$$

The multiple correlation coefficient is 0.9731 (square root of 0.947) compared with 0.9307 in our simple linear regression model. However, using the same set of data points (n=12) the value of r is mathematically bound to increase. The question is whether the increase is significant. The coefficient of determination is 0.947, an increase of 8 per cent (94.7–86.7) in explained variation. A common rule of thumb in practice is to take the increase as significant if the $r^2$ has increased by at least 5 per cent. Hence this result would be taken as increasing the explained variation significantly.

The analysis of variance table gives an F value of 28.922/0.361=80.12 compared with the table value of F(2,9) 0.05=5.12. The sample F value of 80.12 is greater than the test value of 5.12. Therefore the correlation coefficient is significantly different from zero. This is not surprising, because a good fit exists using DLH as an independent variable. The introduction of any extra variable, however irrelevant, will not reduce the fit, or value of $r^2$.

Tests of significance must be performed on the individual coefficients and constant term.

```
MTB >
REGRESS C1 ON 2 PREDICTORS C2 C3

The regression equation is
C1 = 9.09 + 0.0108 C2 + 0.00467 C3

Predictor               Coef        Stdev        t-ratio
Constant                9.085       1.037         8.76
C2                      0.010807    0.002201      4.91
C3                      0.004688    0.001263      3.70

s = 0.6006    R-sq = 94.7%    R-sq(adj) = 93.5%

Analysis of Variance

SOURCE                  DF          SS            MS
Regression              2           57.844        28.922
Error                   9           3.246         0.361
Total                   11          61.090

                                           MORE... 18MA

Continue?
Y
SOURCE                  DF          SEQ SS
C2                      1           52.918
C3                      1           4.926

MTB >
```

Figure 2.11   *Multiple linear regression*

$$t (DLH) = (0.0108 - 0)/0.002201 = 4.91$$
$$t (DMH) = (0.00467 - 0)/0.001263 = 3.70$$
$$t (constant) = (9.0851 - 0)/1.0371 = 8.76$$

Test t (v=9) 2.5 per cent = 2.262 (using two tailed test).

The sample t values exceed the test t value of 2.262 therefore all the coefficients and the constant term are significantly different from zero. The overhead costs depend upon both DLH and DMH.

A similar result comes from the F test where the test F (1,9) 5 per cent = 5.12 and all the individual F values exceed the test value.

The conclusion is therefore that our multiple linear regression line

$$Y = 9.085 + 0.108DLH + 0.00467DMH$$

provides a better fit than the simple linear regression line. Therefore for cost estimation the cost and management accountant should use the cost relationship determined from the multiple regression analysis.

The approach to multiple linear regression and simple linear regression is similar because the statistics have the same interpretation at each level.

## Forecasting using regression analysis

Earlier in this chapter, in the section on simple regression and correlation, we used the simple linear regression line

$$Y = 11030 + 17.1X$$

to forecast the overhead cost for the activity level of 600 direct labour hours. The estimate was

$$Y = 11030 + 17.1(600)$$

$$Y = £21,290$$

This figure is only an estimate obtained from the regression line. In addition we know that unless the correlation coefficient is one the points will lie about the regression line and not on the line. Regression theory states that the points will be distributed about the regression line following a normal distribution. The theory will allow us to calculate a range of values around the point estimate of £21,290, in which the true cost is likely to fall. This range is called a confidence interval.

As the sample size is less than 30 the sampling distribution of the estimate is a t distribution with an estimated mean of £21,290. The standard error of the estimate is given by the formula:

$$SE \text{ (estimate)} = \sqrt{\frac{\Sigma y^2 - a\Sigma y - b\Sigma xy}{n-2}}$$

Previously the following calculations were made: $n=12$, $\Sigma y=259.8$, $\Sigma y^2=5685.76$, $\Sigma xy=164870.9$, $a=11.027$, and $b=0.01706$

$$SE \text{ (estimate)} = \sqrt{\frac{5685.76 - 11.027 \times 259.8 - 0.01706 \times 164870.9}{12-2}}$$

$$= 0.908$$

Note, this could have been determined from the computer printout. The standard error of the estimate is the square root of the mean square of the residuals (or error term).

Hence SE (estimate) $= \sqrt{0.817}$

$$= 0.904$$

(the difference is purely due to rounding errors).

Now we can determine a 95 per cent confidence interval for the true cost.

### *Sampling distribution of the estimate*

From the t tables (see appendix)

$t_{0.025}$ ($v=10$) is 2.228

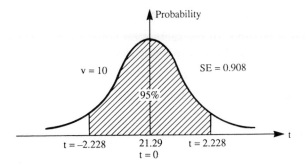

Figure 2.12   *Sampling distribution of the estimate*

95 per cent confidence interval is:

$$= \mu \pm t \times SE$$
$$= 21.29 \pm 2.228 \times 0.908$$
$$= 21.29 \pm 2.02$$
$$= 19.27 \text{ to } 23.31$$
$$= £19,270 \text{ to } £23,310$$

There is a 95 per cent probability that the true cost is between £19,270 and £23,310. We have a cost estimate accurate to within £2000.

The probability of obtaining a value outside the range is 0.05 (5 per cent). Hence if an observed cost is outside the range there is a high probability that costs are out of control.

Other percentage confidence limits may be calculated depending upon the level the company finds it most economical to operate.

This analysis can be used to calculate flexible budgets for different levels of direct labour hours, e.g. 500, 600 and 700 hours, to provide the following flexible budgets obtained from confidence intervals.

Flexible budgets

| Activity level (DLH) | Lower limit (£) | Average (£) | Upper limit (£) |
|---|---|---|---|
| 500 | 17,560 | 19,580 | 21,600 |
| 600 | 19,270 | 21,290 | 23,310 |
| 700 | 20,980 | 23,000 | 25,020 |

A similar approach can be adopted using the multiple regression line:

$$Y = 9.085 + 0.0108(DLH) + 0.00468(DMH)$$

The standard error of the estimate is the square root of the error mean square given in the computer printout 2.2 (see Figure 2.13).

$$SE = \sqrt{0.361} = 0.601$$

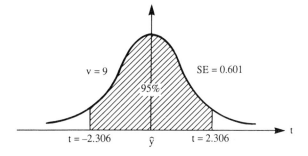

Figure 2.13 *Sampling distribution of the estimate*

From tables $t_{0.25}$ (v=9) = 2.306.

Using these results we can obtain the following flexible budgets for various levels of direct labour hours and direct machine hours.

Flexible budgets

| Activity 1 DLH | Activity 2 DMH | Lower limit (£) | Average (£) | Upper limit (£) |
|---|---|---|---|---|
| 500 | 1000 | 17,779 | 19,165 | 20,551 |
| 500 | 1100 | 18,247 | 19,633 | 21,019 |
| 600 | 1000 | 18,859 | 20,245 | 21,631 |
| 600 | 1100 | 19,327 | 20,713 | 22,099 |

We have discussed linear multiple regression, its assumptions and tests. The topics have been covered in depth so that you are aware of the problems and the power of the technique. The emphasis should be on the interpretation of the results of computer runs as micro-computers with multiple regression software areas are widely available today.

## Examination questions

### Question 1 (CIMA)

A management accountant is analysing data relating to retail sales on behalf of marketing colleagues. The marketing staff believe that the most important influence upon sales is local advertising undertaken by the retail store. The company also advertises by using regional television areas. The company owns more than 100 retail outlets, and the data below relate to a sample of ten representative outlets.

| Outlet | Monthly sales (£000) $y$ | Local advertising by the retail store (£000 per month) $x_1$ | Regional advertising by the company (£000 per month) $x_2$ |
|---|---|---|---|
| 1 | 220 | 6 | 4 |
| 2 | 230 | 8 | 6 |
| 3 | 240 | 12 | 10 |
| 4 | 340 | 12 | 16 |
| 5 | 420 | 2 | 18 |
| 6 | 460 | 8 | 20 |
| 7 | 520 | 16 | 18 |
| 8 | 600 | 15 | 30 |
| 9 | 720 | 14 | 36 |
| 10 | 800 | 20 | 46 |

The data have been partly analysed and the immediate results are available below

$\Sigma y = 4550$ $\quad\quad$ $\Sigma y^2 = 2451300$ $\quad\quad$ $\Sigma x_1 y = 58040$

$\Sigma x_1 = 113$ $\quad\quad$ $\Sigma x_1^2 = 1533$ $\quad\quad$ $\Sigma x_2 y = 121100$

$\Sigma x_2 = 212$ $\quad\quad$ $\Sigma x_2^2 = 6120$ $\quad\quad$ $\Sigma x_1 X_2 = 2780$

(a)  You are required to examine closely, using coefficients of determination, the assertion that the level of sales varies more with movements in the level of local advertising than with changes in the level of regional company advertising.

(b)  Further analysis of the raw data reveals a coefficient of multiple correlation of 0.99 and hence a coefficient of multiple determination of 0.98. Using the least squares multiple regression equation, a sales forecast for an outlet in the same area as outlet 8 in the original data has been prepared for a planned level of £12,000 of local advertising. This produces a sales forecast of £597,333 for the next month.

Your are required to interpret the above information for the marketing manager and to explain the value and limitations of regression analysis in sales forecasting. What other factors should be taken into account when preparing a sales forecast?

Note that the coefficient of determination for $y$ and $x_1$ may be calculated from

$$r^2 = \frac{(n\Sigma x_1 y - \Sigma x_1 \Sigma y)^2}{(n\Sigma x_1^2 - (\Sigma(x_1)^2)(n\Sigma y_1^2 - (\Sigma y_1)^2)}$$

### Answer 1

(a)  Coefficient of determination

$$r^2 = \frac{(n\Sigma xy - \Sigma x \Sigma y)^2}{(n\Sigma x^2 - (\Sigma x)^2)(n\Sigma y^2 - (\Sigma y)^2)}$$

Apply to $x_1$

$$r^2 = \frac{((10 \times 58040) - (113 \times 4550))^2}{(10 \times 1533 - 12769)(10 \times 2451300 - 20702500)}$$

$$= \frac{66250^2}{2561 \times 3810500}$$

$$= 0.4498$$

Apply to $x_2$

$$r^2 = \frac{((10 \times 121100) - (212 \times 4550))^2}{(10 \times 6120 - 44944)(10 \times 2451300 - 20702500)}$$

$$= \frac{246400^2}{16250 \times 3810500}$$

$$= 0.9801$$

*Conclusion*
Based on the validity of the proposition that there is a causal link between the level of advertising and the level of sales, it appears that the level of sales varies more with the level of regional advertising than with local advertising: the regional $r^2$ of 0.9801 is far higher than the local $r^2$ of 0.4498.

(b)  $y = 158.25 - 4.81x_1 + 16.56x_2$

Therefore $a = 158.25$; $b_1 = -4.81$; $b_2 = 16.56$

$$r^2 = \frac{a\Sigma y + b_1\Sigma x_1 y + b_2\Sigma x_2 y - (\Sigma y)^2/n}{\Sigma y^2 - (\Sigma y)^2/n}$$

$$= \frac{(158.25 \times 4550) + (-4.81 \times 58040) + (16.56 \times 121100) - 2070250}{2451300 - 2070250}$$

$$= 0.9868$$

$r^2$ has increased over either of the individual $r^2$ figures calculated in part (a), thus the use of the multiple regression model appears to improve very slightly the managers' understanding of the situation. However, it should be noted that $r^2$ always increases when more independent variables are added. In order to avoid including insignificant variables an adjusted coefficient of determination, $r^2$, may be calculated.

Regression analysis can be useful in forecasting in that it can help managers to predict the outcome of specified actions. It has measures of probable error and can be used when there are several independent variables. However, it should not be applied in a mechanical manner. A good knowledge of underlying business operations is essential.

Regression analysis must be used properly – the assumptions of regression must be applicable to the data. A fundamental assumption is that past relationships will continue – it is therefore particularly useful when applied to repetitive operations, but sales forecasting cannot necessarily assume that past relationships will continue. Regression analysis may be used to provide base information, but this should be carefully examined in the light of changing conditions.

Note

$$\hat{y} = 158.25 - 4.81x_1 + 15.56x_2$$

Therefore $\hat{y} = 158.25 - (4.81 \times 12) + (16.56 \times 30)$

$$\hat{y} = 597.33$$

Other factors in sales forecasting:

1   Number of sales staff employed.
2   Floor shop area.
3   Local economic conditions, plus changes thereof.
4   Local tastes/demand patterns, plus changes thereof.
5   Changes in general economic conditions and demand patterns.
6   Market research may be undertaken.

## Question 2 (ACA)

Abourne Ltd manufactures a micro-computer for the home use market. The management accountant is considering using regression analysis in the annual estimate of total costs. The following information has been produced for the twelve months ended 31 December 1988.

| Month | Total cost<br>Y<br>(£) | Output<br>$X_1$<br>(Numbers) | Number of employees<br>$X_2$<br>(Numbers) | Direct labour<br>hours worked<br>$X_3$<br>(Hours) |
|---|---|---|---|---|
| 1 | 38,200 | 300 | 28 | 4,480 |
| 2 | 40,480 | 320 | 30 | 4,700 |
| 3 | 41,380 | 350 | 30 | 4,800 |
| 4 | 51,000 | 500 | 32 | 5,120 |
| 5 | 52,980 | 530 | 32 | 5,120 |
| 6 | 60,380 | 640 | 35 | 5,700 |
| 7 | 70,440 | 790 | 41 | 3,200 |
| 9 | 75,800 | 250 | 41 | 7,300 |
| 10 | 71,920 | 780 | 39 | 7,200 |
| 11 | 68,380 | 750 | 38 | 6,400 |
| 12 | 33,500 | 270 | 33 | 3,960 |

$\Sigma Y = 637,200 \qquad \Sigma X_1 = 6,300 \qquad \Sigma X_2 = 420 \qquad \Sigma X_3 = 65,220$

Additionally

$$\Sigma Y^2 = 36,614.05 \times 10^6 \qquad \Sigma X_1^2 = 3.8582 \times 10^6$$

$$\Sigma X_2^2 = 14954 \qquad \Sigma X_3^2 = 374{,}423 \times 10^6$$
$$\Sigma X_1 Y = 373.5374 \times 10^6 \qquad \Sigma X_2 Y = 22.81284 \times 10^6$$
$$\Sigma X_3 Y = 3692.2774 \times 10^6$$

The management accountant wants to select the best independent variable ($X_1$, $X_2$, or $X_3$) to help in future forecasts of total production costs using an ordinary least squares regression equation. He is also considering the alternatives of using the high–low and multiple regression equations as the basis for future forecasts.

You are required to:

(a) Identify which of the three independent variables ($X_1$, $X_2$, $X_3$) given above is likely to be the least good estimator of total cost (Y). Give your reasons, but do not submit any calculations.

(b) Compute separately, for the remaining two independent variables, the values of the two parameters and for each regression line. Calculate the coefficient of determination ($r^2$) for each relationship.

(c) State, with reasons, which one of these independent variables should be used to estimate total costs in the future given the results of (b) above.

(d) Devise the two equations which should be used, using the high–low technique, instead of the two regression lines computed in (b) above and comment on the differences found between the two sets of equations.

(e) Comment critically on the use of high–low and ordinary least squares regression as forecasting and estimating aids using the above results as a basis for discussion. In addition, comment on the advantages and problems using multiple regression for forecasting and estimating; and state whether, in your opinion, the management accountant should consider using it in the present circumstances.

## Answer 2

(a) *Identification of the least good estimator of total costs*
'Number of employees ($X_2$)' is likely to be the independent variable which is the least good estimator of total production costs.

The reason for this is not based on any calculations nor on any theoretical ideas of cost volume relationships but by scanning the columns of figures shown. It can be seen that in month 8, total costs fall dramatically as do the figures for output and direct labour hours worked whereas number of employees remains constant for months 7, 8 and 9.

Theoretical arguments could be advanced for or against each independent variable, Suggesting that number of employees is the 'odd man out' assumes that the work force are paid not a fixed monthly wage but rather by the hour, according to production or a combination of an hourly rate and piece work rate. It might also be said to assume that 'materials' rather than labour still represents a significant element of the production cost of micro-computers.

Reasons why number of employees is most likely to be the least good estimator of total production cost might include:

(i)  number of employees could include production and non-production workers;
(ii)  holiday periods, idle time, sickness payments etc. have to be paid for,

though these again make assumptions about the accounting or costing system that Abourne use.

(b)  *Regression coefficients and coefficient of determination*
Having decided that $X_2$ is the least good estimator of total costs, regression coefficients and coefficients of determination are found for $X_1$ and $X_3$. Corresponding figures for $X_2$ are shown at the end of the section.

(i)  $X_1$ and Y

$$b = \frac{3735374 \times 10^6 - 6300 \times 637200/12}{3.8582 \times 10^6 - 6300^2/12}$$

$$= 70.83$$

$$a = \frac{637200}{12} - 70.83 \times \frac{6300}{12}$$

$$= 15912.99$$

$$r^2 = \frac{15912.99 \times 637200 + 70.83 \times 373.5374 \times 10^6 - 637200^2/12}{36614.05 \times 10^6 - 637200^2/12}$$

$$= 0.9943$$

(ii)  $X_3$ and Y

$$b = \frac{3692.277 \times 10^6 - 65220 \times 637200/12}{374423 \times 10^6 - 65220^2/12}$$

$$= 11.48$$

$$a = \frac{637200}{12} - 11.48 \times \frac{65220}{12}$$

$$= -9305.51$$

$$r^2 = \frac{-9305.51 \times 637200 + 11.48 \times 3692.277 \times 10^6 - 637200^2/12}{36614.05 \times 10^6 - 637200^2/12}$$

$$= 0.9467$$

Summary

| | | | |
|---|---|---|---|
| $X_1$ | 15,912.99 | 70.83 | 0.9943 |
| $X_2$ | −17,291.34 | 2,011.18 | 0.3697 |
| $X_3$ | − 9,305.51 | 11.48 | 0.9467 |

(c) *Comments on the most useful estimator of total costs*
By comparing the three coefficients of determinations, based as it is on the same number of data points in each case, $X_1$ (output), should be used to estimate total production costs in the future.

A coefficient of determination of 0.9943 implies that 99.43 per cent of the variation in the dependent variable, total cost, is explained by variation in the independent variable, output.

Another factor in favour of using $X_1$ rather than $X_3$ is the difficulty in interpreting the value of b for $X_3$ which suggests that any number of employees might pay for the privilege of sitting in Abourne's premises and doing nothing. Really, negative fixed costs have no practical significance; in this case they may indicate that employees are regularly working overtime.

(d) *Devising equations using the high–low technique*
Concentrating now on $X_1$ and $X_3$:

(i)  Output ($X_1$) as the independent variable

$$\text{Unit variable cost} = \frac{£75{,}800 - £32{,}720}{820 - 250} = £75.58$$

Monthly fixed costs = £32,720 − 250 × £75.58 = £13,825

The equation that should be used is:

$Y = 13825 + 75.58X_1$

(as compared with $Y = 15912.99 + 70.83X_1$ from (b)). Where $X_1$ is in units and Y in £s.

(ii)  Direct labour worked ($X_3$) as the independent variable

$$\text{Hourly variable cost} = \frac{£75{,}800 - £32{,}720}{7300 - 3200} = £10.51$$

Monthly fixed costs = £32,720 − 3200 × £10.51 = −£903

The equation that could be used is:

$Y = -903 + 10.51X_3$

(as compared with $Y = -9305.51 + 11.48X_3$ from (b)). Where $X_3$ is in hours and Y is in £s.

(iii)  Comments
The differences stem from the fact that part (b) makes use of all the data, whereas (d) uses only some of the data – the extreme values.

It is likely that these extreme values are not typical and any reasons for non-linearity are more likely to affect these extreme values. Such reasons might be economies or perhaps diseconomies of scale. The most likely factor here is probably the need for overtime payments as hours worked per employee increases and possibly certain stepped fixed costs that result from the need to employ more supervisors or checkers as the number of employees increase.

(e)   *Comments on the use of various estimation and forecasting methods*
(i)   High–low methods
A comparison of the two methods has been made in (d) above, the high–low method being less reliable, having no statistical basis which means that further analysis is impossible and having simplicity as its only redeeming feature. Even ordinary least square regression has its limitations when used as a forecasting and estimation aid, these include:

- Linearity over the range of the data – it is possible to use regression to find a line of best fit through a snow storm. This does not give any indication that there is a linear relationship between the two variables. In this case sufficient coefficients of determination suggest a reasonable relationship for $X_1$ and $X_3$ but not for $X_2$.
- Linearity beyond the range of the data – having found the equation relating, say, cost and output over a limited range, it is dangerous to use that equation for levels of activity outside that range where factors may well change the relationship between the variables.
- Sample size – here a full year's results have been used and a reasonably large sample should have led to a reliable set of values for the regression coefficients. In addition the effects of seasonal variations should have been ironed out (if this is required).
- Cause and effect – some time was spent in (a) considering which was the major factor influencing costs. None of the identified variables may be suitable, time may be the most suitable as costs rise with inflation and output with consumer tastes. If however both output and total costs remain constant functions of time, output could be used to make forecasts of total costs under such circumstances. Also several variables may influence total costs as indicated below.

(ii)   Use of multiple regression
If it were felt that cost was a function of several independent variables then multiple regression would be more appropriate than simple linear regression. An example of two such variables might be output and time. (Though total cost is undoubtedly a function of materials used and labour hours, one would assume that they were both functions of output.) However there are now even greater problems in deciding which of several variables are appropriate and, in the case of the two mentioned, there might be simpler methods of coping with the problem; for example adjusting all prices by the relevant rates of inflation. What's more, it might be better to modify the analysis to use polynomial regression if non-linear functions are expected.

The use of multiple regression has been successful in one particular area of forecasting, despite limited historic data being available, and that is in the field of forecasting potential collapses of companies.

# Further reading

Benston, G., *Contemporary Issues in Cost Accounting and Control*, Dickenson, 1977.

Levin, R.I., *Statistics for Management*, 3rd edn, Prentice Hall, 1984.

Simmonds, K., Strategic Management Accounting, *Management Accounting*, April 1981.

# 3 Cost estimation – learning curve

In our analysis of cost functions we have assumed that the cost was a linear function of output. This is not always true as economies of scale accrue resulting in curvilinear cost functions. It is beyond the scope of this book to apply regression analysis in general to curvilinear functions. However one important curvilinear function which needs to be examined occurs when learning takes place. This is because firms have become large and complex, thus resulting in increased output, which causes lower production costs. Selling prices can therefore be reduced and a larger share of the market is captured.

Learning curve theory was first studied in the USA in the 1920s in the aircraft industry, where it was discovered that the material and unit labour costs decreased as the number of aircraft produced increased.

At the beginning of the learning stage initial progress was substantial. However, as individuals became more experienced with their tasks the rate of learning decelerated.

Since these early days the learning concept has been studied in various business environments. Hirschmann (1964) showed how the learning curve phenomenon affected costs and competitiveness. He illustrated that a linear relationship exists between costs and cumulative units produced when plotted on a double logarithmic scale. On a uniform scale with linear coordinates the relationship is curvilinear. Hirschman showed the slope of the curve could be expressed as an exponential function of activity, and for each doubling of accumulated output, the unit cost would fall to around 80 per cent of the previous level.

Recent research has shown that there are three levels of learning – operator, managerial and technological. The operator or shop-floor level ranges from 80–90 per cent. At managerial level, relating to planning and control, the rate is 70 per cent and for technological developments 60 per cent can be achieved.

## Necessary conditions for the learning curve theory

The learning curve theory is more applicable in a labour intensive industry where repetition of operations or processes enables learning to take place.

Ideally breaks between production runs should be short, or learning is forgotten, and it assumes that the labour mix is stable with a negligible labour turnover.

Finally it is implicit in the theory that all employees are motivated in order to learn. This important topic of motivation is featured in Chapter 8.

## Learning curve problem

Barsands plc have been asked to give a quote for the production of 50 units of a new product. Estimates for the assembly of the first unit are:

|  | (£) |
| --- | --- |
| Direct materials | 100 |
| Direct labour | 50 |
| Variable overhead | 30 |

Notes:
1   Labour costs are £5 an hour.
2   Variable overhead is based on labour hours (activity based) at a rate of £3 per labour hour.
3   The company quotes prices on a 20 per cent mark up on the estimated costs to cover fixed overheads and profits.
4   The company operates an 80 per cent learning curve.

The company wishes to estimate the marginal cost of making the 50 units and hence calculate the quoted price per unit.

As the direct labour for the first unit is £50 at a £5 an hour rate the number of hours required to produce the first unit is 10. Hence using the learning curve rule we can generate the following table.

| Number of units<br>$X$ | Average time/unit<br>over life of product<br>$Y$ | Cumulative time used<br>$T$ |
| --- | --- | --- |
| 1 | 10 | 10 |
| 2 | 8 | 16 |
| 4 | 6.4 | 25.6 |
| 8 | 5.12 | 40.96 |
| 16 | 4.096 | 65.54 |
| 32 | 3.277 | 104.86 |
| 64 | 2.2621 | 167.74 |

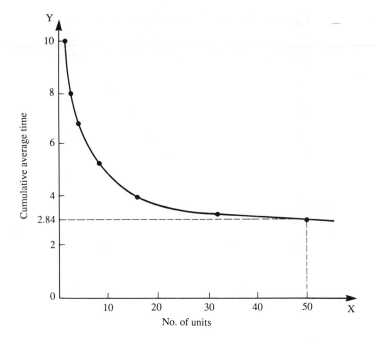

Figure 3.1   *80 per cent learning curve*

Plotting the average time/unit against the number of units gives the 80 per cent learning curve (see Figure 3.1). When X = 50, Y = 2.84 (from graph). Therefore T = 50 × 2.84 = 142 hours.

Alternatively plot the cumulative time against the number of units (Figure 3.2). From the graph when X = 50, T = 142. Therefore the estimated marginal costs (50 units):

|                    | (£)  |                     |
|--------------------|------|---------------------|
| Direct materials   | 5000 | (50 × 100)          |
| Direct labour      | 710  | (142 × £5)          |
| Variable overheads | 426  | (142 hours × £3)    |
| Total              | 6136 |                     |

Hence marginal cost of making 50 units is £6136.
Therefore quoted price for 50 units = £6136 × 1.20 (20 per cent mark-up) = £7363.20

Therefore quoted price per item = £7363.20/50 = £147.26

Barsands plc should therefore quote a price of £147.26 per item for the batch of 50 items.

If Barsands plc did not appreciate that a learning curve effect was present then the estimated price based on the first unit costs would be:

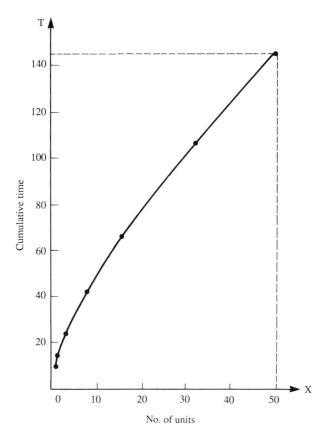

Figure 3.2  *Cumulative time–learning curve*

|  | Costs based on<br>1st unit costs<br>(£) | Costs based on<br>learning curve<br>(£) |
| --- | --- | --- |
| Direct materials | 100.00 | 100.00 |
| Direct labour | 50.00 | 14.20 |
| Variable overhead | 30.00 | 8.52 |
| Total | 180.00 | 122.72 |
| 20 per cent mark-up | × 1.20 | × 1.20 |
| Price | 216.00 | 147.26 |

Hence ignoring the learning curve effect would lead to substantial overpricing to the competitors' advantage.

## Equation of the learning curve

The problem with the graphical approach is that to obtain either the average or total cost it is necessary to interpolate between two values on a curve. This makes the cost estimate depend upon a visual judgement which is subject to errors. A more suitable approach is to use the equation of the learning curve.

$$Y = a\, X^{-b}$$

where a = the time to produce the first unit and b = $-\log L/\log 2$. Where L is the learning curve rate expressed as a decimal and X = number of units.

In our example a = 10 hours

$$b = \frac{-\log(0.80)}{\log 2} = \frac{-(-0.09691)}{0.3010}$$

b = 0.3219

Therefore the learning curve is:

$$Y = 10\,(X)^{-0.3219}$$

when X = 50, Y = $10\,(50)^{-0.3219}$

$$Y = 2.84$$

Therefore T = XY = 50 × 2.84 = 142 hours.
    The same total hours as determined graphically, leading to a quoted price of £147.26.

## Learning curve tables

An alternative approach to the graphical or equation method is to use learning curve tables. Consider the following problem.
    Jennings plc, a large garage, has been asked to quote for a contract to service fleets of lorries. The customer requires separate price quotations for each of the following possible orders:

| Order | Lorries |
|-------|---------|
| First | 100 |
| Second | 60 |
| Third | 40 |

The company's standard costs per unit for the first order are:

| | |
|---|---|
| Direct material | £30 |
| Direct labour | |
| Dept A (highly automated) | 2 hours at £5 per hour |
| Dept B (skilled labour) | 4 hours at £8 per hour |
| Variable overheads | 20 per cent of direct labour |

Fixed overheads absorbed

| | |
|---|---|
| Dept A | £4 per hour |
| Dept B | £2 per hour |

Determine a price per unit for each of the three orders, assuming that Jennings plc uses a mark up of 25 per cent on total costs, and allows for an 80 per cent learning curve.

Extract from learning curve table:

### 80 per cent LEARNING CURVE TABLE

| X | Y (%) |
|---|---|
| 1.0 | 100.0 |
| 1.1 | 96.9 |
| 1.2 | 93.3 |
| 1.3 | 91.7 |
| 1.4 | 89.5 |
| 1.5 | 87.6 |
| 1.6 | 86.1 |
| 1.7 | 84.4 |
| 1.8 | 83.0 |
| 1.9 | 81.5 |
| 2.0 | 80.0 |

X represents the cumulative total volume produced to date expressed as a multiple of the initial order. Y is the learning curve factor, for a given X value, expressed as a percentage of the cost of the initial order.

*Solution*
First order – 100 lorries

| | £ | £ |
|---|---|---|
| Direct material | | 30.0 |
| Direct labour | | |
| Dept A (2 hours at £5 per hr) | 10.0 | |
| Dept B (4 hours at £8 per hr) | 32.0 | 42.0 |
| Variable overheads (20% of £42) | | 8.4 |
| Fixed overheads | | |
| Dept A (2 hours at £4 per hr) | 8.0 | |
| Dept B (4 hours at £2 per hr) | 8.0 | 16.0 |
| Total cost | | 96.4 |
| Profit (25% of 96.4) | | 24.1 |
| Selling price per unit (lorry) | | 120.5 |

Second order – 60 lorries

Cumulative total – 160 lorries
The cumulative total is now 160 lorries, which is denoted by the

multiple of 160/100 i.e. 1.6. From the 80 per cent learning curve table the relevant percentage factor is 86.1 per cent of the labour cost

|  | £ | £ |
|---|---|---|
| Direct material |  | 30.0 |
| Direct labour |  |  |
| Dept A (2 hours at £5 per hr) | 10.0 |  |
| Dept B (4 hours × 86.1% × £8 per hr) | 27.5 | 37.5 |
| Variable overheads (20% of £37.5) |  | 7.5 |
| Fixed overheads |  |  |
| Dept A (2 hours at £4/hr) | 8.0 |  |
| Dept B (4 hours × 86.1% × £2/hr) | 6.9 | 14.9 |
| Total cost |  | 89.9 |
| Profit (25% of £89.9) |  | 22.5 |
|  |  | 112.4 |

|  | £ |
|---|---|
| Cumulative order 160 at £112.4 | 17,984 |
| Previous orders 100 at £120.5 | 12,050 |
| Increment order 60 | 5,934 |
| Therefore charge price per unit | 5,934/60 |
|  | =£98.9 |

Third order – 40 lorries
Cumulative total – 200 lorries
   The cumulative total is now 200 lorries with a X multiple of 2.0 giving, from the learning curve, a relevant factor of 80 per cent of the labour cost.

|  | £ | £ |
|---|---|---|
| Direct material |  | 30.0 |
| Direct labour |  |  |
| Dept A (2 hours at £5 per hr) | 10.0 |  |
| Dept B (4 hours × 80% × £8 per hr) | 25.6 | 35.6 |
| Variable overheads (20% of £35.6) |  | 7.1 |
| Fixed overheads |  |  |
| Dept A (2 hours at £4 per hr) | 8.0 |  |
| Dept B (4 hours × 80% × £2 per hr). | 6.4 | 14.4 |
| Total cost |  | 87.1 |
| Profit (25% of £87.1) |  | 21.8 |
|  |  | 108.9 |

|  | £ |
|---|---|
| Cumulative orders 200 at £108.9 | 21,780 |
| Previous orders 160 at £112.4 | 17,984.0 |
| Incremental order 40 | 3,796.0 |
| Therefore charge per unit (lorry)          = | £94.9 |

Before submitting these quotes Jennings plc would take into consideration the following factors:

- Possible union non-cooperation in time reduction.
- Motivation or apathy in the workforce.
- Is the 80 per cent learning curve applicable in department B?
- Has the rate been correctly estimated?
- Has previous experience (i.e. some learning) reduced the learning effect?
- If the learning curve is no longer applicable the costs of the 2nd and 3rd orders will have been underestimated resulting in orders being underpriced.

## Regression and the learning curve

A completely new product, that is subject to the learning curve effect, requires the determination of the learning curve rate. Regression analysis can be used to determine the learning curve rates as follows:

The learning curve is expressed by

$$y = a\, x^{-b}$$

Take logs of both sides

$$\log y = \log a - b \log x$$

Let

$$Y = \log y, \quad A = \log a, \quad B = -b, \quad X = \log x$$

Then the equation becomes

$$Y = A + BX$$

The simple linear regression model.

This log transformation results in simple linear regression determining the learning rate. The correlation coefficient measures the fit of the learning curve to the cost data.

*Example*
Given the following cumulative average costs determine the learning curve and hence the appropriate learning rate.

| Number of units (x) | 1 | 2 | 3 | 4 | 5 | 6 | 7 | 8 |
|---|---|---|---|---|---|---|---|---|
| Cumulative average cost (y) | 49 | 33 | 29 | 25 | 20 | 18 | 17 | 17 |

First calculate the log of x and y

| | 1 | 2 | 3 | 4 | 5 | 6 | 7 | 8 |
|---|---|---|---|---|---|---|---|---|
| log x: | 0 | 0.3010 | 0.4771 | 0.6021 | 0.6990 | 0.7782 | 0.8451 | 0.9031 |
| log y: | 1.690 | 1.5190 | 1.4620 | 1.3980 | 1.3010 | 1.2550 | 1.2300 | 1.2300 |

Now $\Sigma X = 4.6056, \quad \Sigma Y = 11.086, \quad \Sigma XY = 6.0337$

$\quad \Sigma X^2 = 3.3046, \quad \Sigma Y^2 = 15.549$

Using our linear regression formula;

$A = 1.693$, $B = -0.5335$, $r = -0.992$ and $r^2 = 0.985$

hence the learning curve explains 98.5 per cent of the variation.

Now log a = 1.693

Therefore a = £49.32

Cost of first unit = £49.32

As $B = -0.5335$

Therefore b = 0.5335

Now $b = -\log L/\log 2$ can be rearranged to give
$$L = 2^{-b}$$
$$L = 2^{-0.5335}$$
$$L = 0.6908$$

Therefore learning curve rates is 69.1%.

## Applications of the learning curve

### The setting of standard costs

If the learning phase is not recognized, an incorrect standard may be established. When cumulative output is low the standard cost is high, resulting in favourable variances. The converse of this applies when cumulative output is high.

Some companies try to overcome this problem by setting 'normal' standard costs, but introduce a supplementary budget for new products or processes.

### Work scheduling and overtime decisions

Output per employee increases as the learning effect is realized. Production schedules, machine capability, and materials availability must be carefully controlled to avoid potential stockouts and bottlenecks. In the early stages of learning overtime may be required to compensate for poor efficiency.

### The setting of wage incentive schemes

These schemes must recognize the learning curve effects, i.e. that employees will need to be compensated during the early stages of learning for the lower than normal level of performance. This is due to lack of familiarity in the early stages of production rather than any lack of motivation or ability.

### Budgeting cash flows

Because of the learning curve phenomenon, an increase in output will not attract a proportionate increase in variable costs. Direct labour, material, activity related overheads will reduce owing to greater efficiency. A new level of finance for this output must be planned.

### Pricing

This is a very important application of learning curve theory. When a company submits a tender for a contract there is the possibility of follow-up orders. The firm will move along its learning curve with these orders, recognizing the reduction in labour, material and activity related overheads when pricing.

It is necessary to fix prices which are low enough to be competitive yet high enough to reap satisfactory profits when attempting to secure contracts.

Firms must also take into consideration the probability of lower bids being proposed and being accepted. They may therefore have to move further down the learning curve in order to compete. The danger of this approach is that if further orders do not materialize, then costs will have been underestimated, which may lead to losses being incurred.

## Examination questions

### Question 1 (CIMA)

You have been asked about the application of the learning curve as a management accounting technique. You are required to:
(a) Define the learning curve.
(b) Explain the theory of learning curves.
(c) Indicate the areas where learning curves may assist in management accounting.
(d) Illustrate the use of learning curves for calculating the expected average unit cost of making (i) 4 machines; and (ii) 8 machines using the data given below.

*Data:*
Direct labour needed to make the first machine – 1000 hours
Learning curve 80 per cent.
Direct labour cost – £3 per hour.
Direct materials cost – £1800 per machine.
Fixed cost for either size order – £8000.

### Answer 1

(a) *Definition of learning curve*
The learning curve, also known as a cost experience curve, is defined in

the Institute's Terminology as 'the relationship plotted between cost per unit expressed in constant money terms, and cumulative units produced per unit – usually plotted on a double logarithmic scale'. In other words, it is a graphical representation of the way in which cumulative average costs per unit decrease as the cumulative volume of output increases over a period of time.

The extent to which the learning curve operates is denoted by the level of cumulative average costs at each successive doubling of output when compared with those costs at the previous output level. For example, if the initial output level of a product is x and the cumulative average costs for the quantity are £y then if at output 2x the cumulative average costs for the total quantity are £0.8y and at output 4x those costs are £0.64y, the costs are deemed to be subject to an 80 per cent learning curve.

### (b)   *Explanation of the theory*

As an organization repeats the manufacture of a particular product or the provision of a particular service, it becomes more adept at the manufacture or provision as a result of:

1   Familiarity with the detailed activities in its manufacture or provision.
2   Exposure to, and awareness of, the problems that can arise, and consequently more experience in how to deal with those problems.
3   Confidence in its ability to deal with the activity in the most advantageous ways.

The increased adeptness should lead to greater speed in carrying out the task with consequent reduction in the time taken and the costs incurred, particularly in so far as they relate to man-controlled activities.

Improvements in productivity can be expected with each successive batch of output and the effect of the cumulative average cost at each doubled level of output can be expected to be a constant when expressed in percentage terms. On a log log scale, this would appear as a straight line. In absolute terms, of course, the drop in costs from one doubled level to the next will be progressively smaller. The more complex the activity, the greater the general possibility of improvement over time and thus the steeper the slope is likely to be. The rates at which costs fall tend to be between 75 and 90 per cent.

### (c)   *Areas of assistance in costing*

As indicated, the learning curve operates mostly where activities are person-controlled. Thus it is of great relevance in assessing or predicting future levels of direct labour time and cost. It is thus useful in:

- setting labour standard times;
- pricing for successive batches/contracts;
- calculation of incentive rates in wage bargaining;
- evaluating likely wage movements in project evaluation.

The learning curve also influences the absorption of overhead costs when direct labour hour rates are used.

It is not so relevant for processes that are largely governed by machine speeds – such as where the rhythm or speed of a production line (or other machinery) governs the speed of operations.

It should be noted that the concept has been extended to relate to the whole activity of a factory or an industry. Here it is known as the 'cost experience curve' and includes such features as long-term improvements in inventiveness, product development, and manufacturing equipment development (e.g. of specialized equipment for the industry). The developments in the speed/cost of producing pocket calculators over the past, say 5–10 years, is an evident example of the operation of this curve.

(d)

| Cumulative order size | Cumulative average hours | Cumulative average costs (£) | Materials (£) | Overhead costs (£) | Total (£) |
|---|---|---|---|---|---|
| 1 | 1000 | 3000 | — | — | — |
| 2 | 800 | 2400 | — | — | — |
| 4 | 640 | 1920 | 1800 | 2000 | 5720 |
| 8 | 512 | 1536 | 1800 | 1000 | 4336 |

## Question 2 (CIMA)

A company is asked to quote for a contract taking account of an 80 per cent learning curve which is normal for its industry. There are three variations to the contract.

Variation 1: A single order for 200 units.
Variation 2: An initial order for 200 units following by a succession of orders totalling 600 units altogether (including the initial order).
Variation 3: A first order for 200 units;
a possible second order for 100 units;
a possible third order for 100 units;
a possible fourth order for 80 units.
There is no obligation on the customer to place the second, third or fourth orders but he requires a separate price quotation for each of them now.

Based on standard for comparable work the company's cost estimates per unit for variation 1 of the contracts are:

Direct materials: 15 metres at £8 per metre

Direct labour
   Dept AR      8 hours at £3 per hour
   Dept AS   100 hours at £3.60 per hour
   Dept AT    30 hours at £2.40 per hour
Variable overhead: 25% of direct labour

Fixed overhead absorption
   Dept AR   £5 per direct labour hour
   Dept AS   £3 per direct labour hour
   Dept AT   £2 per direct labour hour

The three departments differ in their work composition. Department AR is highly automated and its output, predominantly machine-controlled, is little influenced by operator efficiency. By contrast, output in departments AS and AT is almost exclusively influenced by operator skills.
   You are required to:

(a)   Calculate prices per unit for each of the three variations to the contract, allowing a profit margin of 3 per cent on direct materials cost and 10 per cent on conversion cost. Note, variation 3 calls for four separate prices.
(b)   List three major factors that would influence you *against* taking account of the learning curve when setting labour standards in a standard costing system. Note, an 80 per cent learning curve on ordinary graph paper would show the following relationship between the x axis (volume) and y axis (cumulative average price of elements subject to the learning curve).

| X | Y (%) | X | Y (%) |
|---|---|---|---|
| 1.0 | 100 | 2.1 | 78.9 |
| 1.1 | 96.9 | 2.2 | 77.8 |
| 1.2 | 93.3 | 2.3 | 76.8 |
| 1.3 | 91.7 | 2.4 | 76.0 |
| 1.4 | 89.5 | 2.5 | 74.9 |
| 1.5 | 87.6 | 2.6 | 74.0 |
| 1.6 | 86.1 | 2.7 | 73.2 |
| 1.7 | 84.4 | 2.8 | 72.3 |
| 1.8 | 83.0 | 2.9 | 71.5 |
| 1.9 | 81.5 | 3.0 | 70.7 |
| 2.0 | 80.0 | 3.1 | 70.0 |

**Answer 2**

(a)   *Variation 1*
Selling price per unit

|  | £ | £ | £ |
|---|---|---|---|
| Direct material cost |  |  | 120.00 |
| Direct labour |  |  |  |
| AR   8 hours at £3.00 per hour | 24 |  |  |
| AS 100 hours at £3.60 per hour | 360 |  |  |
| AT   30 hours at £2.40 per hour | 72 |  |  |
|  |  | 456 |  |
| Variable overhead 25% of 456 |  | 114 |  |
| Fixed overhead |  |  |  |
| AR   8 hours at £5 per hour | 40 |  |  |
| AS 100 hours at £3 per hour | 300 |  |  |
| AT   30 hours at £2 per hour | 60 |  |  |
|  |  | 400 |  |
|  |  |  | 970.00 |
|  |  |  | 1090.00 |
| Profit  3% on direct materials of £120 |  |  | 3.60 |
| Profit 10% on conversion cost of £970 |  |  | 97.00 |
| Selling price per unit |  |  | £1190.60 |

*Variation 2*
Total order is for 600 units, that is three times variation 1. The 3x curve with a 70.7 per cent cumulative average price will apply to departments AS and AT where output is influenced by operator skills.

Selling price per unit for a total order for 600 units using the learning curve of 3x or 70.7 per cent

|  | £ | £ | £ |
|---|---|---|---|
| Direct material cost |  |  | 120.00 |
| Direct labour |  |  |  |
| AR   8 hours at £3.00 per hour | 24 |  |  |
| AS 100 hours at 70.7% = |  |  |  |
|       70.7 at £3.60 per hour | 254.52 |  |  |
| AT   30 hours at 70.7% = | 50.90 |  |  |
|       21.21 at £2.40 per hour |  |  |  |
|  |  | 329.42 |  |
| Variable overhead 25% of 39.424 |  | 82.36 |  |
| Fixed overhead |  |  |  |
| AR  8   hours at £5 per hour | 40 |  |  |
| AS 70.7 hours at £3 per hour | 212.10 |  |  |
| AT 21.21 hours at £2 per hour | 42.42 |  |  |
|  |  | 294.52 |  |
|  |  |  | 706.30 |
|  |  |  | 826.30 |
| Profit    3% on direct materials of £120 |  |  | 3.60 |
|          10% on conversion cost of £706.30 |  |  | 70.63 |
| Selling price per unit |  |  | £900.53 |

*Variation 3*
Selling price per unit for four possible orders of 200, 100, 100 and 80 units respectively giving cumulative production of 300, 400 and 480 units and a learning curve benefit of 1.5×(87.6%), 2.0×(80.0%) and 2.4×(76.0%) to departments AS and AT direct labour costs.

| | | | | | |
|---|---|---|---|---|---|
| Order No. 1 | as variation 1 | | £1190.6 per unit | | |
| Order No. 2 | | | Order No. 3 | Order No. 4 | |
| Cumulative 300 units | | | Cumulative 400 | Cumulative 480 | |
| Conversion costs | | | | | |
| Direct labour AR at £3 | 24.00 | | | 24.00 | | 24.00 |

| | | | | | |
|---|---|---|---|---|---|
| Conversion costs | | | | | |
| Direct labour AR at £3 | 24.00 | | 24.00 | | 24.00 |
| (87.6hr) AS at £3.60 | 315.36 | (80hr) | 288.00 | (76hr) | 273.60 |
| (26.28hr) AT at £2.4 | 63.07 | (24hr) | 57.60 | (22.8hr) | 54.72 |
| | 402.43 | | 369.60 | | 352.32 |
| Variable overhead 25% | | | | | |
| of (£402.43) | 100.61 | | | | |
| of (£369.60) | | | 92.40 | | |
| of (£352.32) | | | | | 88.08 |
| Fixed overhead | | | | | |
| AR at £5 | 40.00 | | 40.00 | | 40.00 |
| AS at £3 | 262.80 | | 240.00 | | 228.00 |
| AT at £2 | 52.56 | | 48.00 | | 45.60 |
| | 858.40 | | 790.00 | | 754.00 |
| Direct materials cost | 120.00 | | 120.00 | | 120.00 |
| Profit 3% on £120 | 3.60 | | 3.60 | | 3.60 |
| 10% on £858.40 | 85.84 | | | | |
| on £790 | | | 79.00 | | |
| on £754 | | | | | 75.40 |
| | 1067.84 | | 992.60 | | 953.00 |

| | | |
|---|---|---|
| Order No. 2 | | £ |
| Cumulative orders | 300 at £1067.84 | 320,352 |
| Previous orders | 200 at £1190.60 | 238,120 |
| Incremental order | 100 at a cost of | 82,232 |

Unit selling price £822.32

| | | |
|---|---|---|
| Order No. 3 | | £ |
| Cumulative orders | 400 at £992.60 | 397,040 |
| Previous orders | 300 at £1067.84 | 320,352 |
| Incremental order | 100 at a cost of | 76,688 |

Unit selling price £766.88

| | | |
|---|---|---|
| Order No. 3 | | £ |
| Cumulative orders | 480 at £953.00 | 457,440 |
| Previous orders | 400 at £992.60 | 397,040 |
| Incremental order | 80 at a cost of | 60,400 |

Unit selling price £755.00

(b)   Some of the factors that would influence against taking account of the learning curve when setting labour standards in a standard costing system are given below.

- Previous experience in similar work had shown the learning curve to be inappropriate.
- Pre-knowledge of union non-cooperation in time reduction would make it easier to set an initial lower time.
- Workers' inherent skill in the same type of work would enable them to assimilate new tasks very quickly.
- Keenness and interest of workers to do a good job from the start would give above average initial results.
- New jobs themselves as a series are subject to learning curves – the greater the number of new jobs tackled the less formidable a new job becomes.
- The rate at which the learning curve volume becomes operative – if too quickly there is no learning curve; if too slowly the work force may change and benefits do not materialize.
- If standards are linked to a productivity-type bonus then operators may not understand the basis of repeated changes, particularly when these are downwards and they appear to be penalized for their growing efficiency.
- If the production techniques used for the product are liable to considerable change.

### Question 3 (CIMA)

A company is considering investing in a project with the following characteristics.

Equipment is to be purchased costing £70,000 payable at once and having a life span of five years with no residual value. The equipment is used to produce one type of product whose sales are budgeted as follows:

| Year to 30th June | Number of units |
|---|---|
| 1983 | 20 |
| 1984 | 40 |
| 1985 | 50 |
| 1986 | 30 |
| 1987 | 10 |
| Total | 150 |

The selling price of the unit is to be £4000 each.
Costs of units are:

| | |
|---|---|
| Direct materials | £1200 each |
| Variable production overhead | 50% of direct wages |
| Variable selling and administration overhead | 10% of selling price |

Direct wages are paid at £3 per hour. The first unit to be produced is budgeted to take 1505.3 man-hours of work and an 80 per cent learning curve applies to direct wages.

Fixed overhead relating to this project is £12,000 per annum.

The company requires a 12 per cent DCF return on its investments.

You are required to:

(a) Calculate whether or not the project meets the company's investment criterion, based on:

  (i)  the average direct wages rate for the whole quantity of units budgeted to be sold;
  (ii) the direct labour times expected to be required in each individual year.

(b) Comment briefly on the relative merits of bases (a)(i) and (a)(ii) above. Ignore the effects of tax and inflation.

Note, an 80 per cent learning curve on ordinary graph paper would show the following relationship between x axis (volume) and y axis (cumulative average cost of elements subject to the learning curve):

| x | Y% | x | y% |
|---|---|---|---|
| 1 | 100.00 | 70 | 25.48 |
| 2 | 80.00 | 80 | 24.40 |
| 10 | 47.65 | 90 | 23.50 |
| 20 | 38.13 | 100 | 22.71 |
| 30 | 33.46 | 110 | 22.03 |
| 40 | 30.50 | 120 | 20.86 |
| 50 | 28.39 | 140 | 20.38 |
| 60 | 26.77 | 150 | 19.93 |

## Answer 3

*Workings*

Cash flows exclusive of items relating to the learning curve:

|  | £ |
|---|---|
| Selling price | 4000 |
| Direct material | 1200 |
| Variable selling and administration | 400 |
|  | 1600 |
| Margin | 2400 |

| Year | 1 | 2 | 3 | 4 | 5 |
|---|---|---|---|---|---|
| Units | 20 | 40 | 50 | 30 | 10 |
|  | £ | £ | £ | £ | £ |
| Margin | 48,000 | 96,000 | 120,000 | 72,000 | 24,000 |
| Fixed | 12,000 | 12,000 | 12,000 | 12,000 | 12,000 |
|  | 36,000 | 84,000 | 108,000 | 60,000 | 12,000 |

Learning curve impact:

1st unit 1505.3 hours

Therefore entire 150, the average hours per unit will be:

19.93% of 1505.3 = 300.0062 hr (say 300)

Therefore unit direct wages and variable production overhead:

300 hr (£3.00 + £1.50) = £1350

(a)(i)

| Year | 1 | 2 | 3 | 4 | 5 |
|---|---|---|---|---|---|
| Margin from workings (£) | 36,000 | 84,000 | 108,000 | 60,000 | 12,000 |
| Direct labour etc at £1,350 unit (£) | 27,000 | 54,000 | 67,500 | 40,500 | 13,500 |
| | 9,000 | 30,000 | 40,500 | 19,500 | (1,500) |
| 12% Discount factors | 0.89 | 0.80 | 0.71 | 0.64 | 0.57 |
| Discounted cash flow | 8,010 | 24,000 | 28,755 | 12,480 | (855) |

| | |
|---|---|
| Present value | £72,390 |
| Equipment | 70,000 |
| Net present value | 2,390 |

The project meets the company's investment criterion

(a)(ii)  Workings for learning curve impact:

| Year | Units | Cum. units | Cum.hrs at 1505.3 | % factor | Hours | Incremental hours | at £4.50 (£) |
|---|---|---|---|---|---|---|---|
| 1 | 20 | 20 | 30,106 | 38.13 | 11,479 | 11,479 | 51,655 |
| 2 | 40 | 60 | 90,318 | 26.77 | 24,178 | 12,699 | 57,145 |
| 3 | 50 | 110 | 165,583 | 22.03 | 36,478 | 12,300 | 55,350 |
| 4 | 30 | 140 | 210,742 | 20.38 | 42,949 | 6,471 | 29,120 |
| 5 | 10 | 150 | 225,795 | 19.93 | 45,000 | 2,051 | 9,230 |
| | | | | | | 45,000 | 202,500 |

| Year | 1 | 2 | 3 | 4 | 5 |
|---|---|---|---|---|---|
| Margin from workings for (a)(i) | 36,000 | 84,000 | 108,000 | 60,000 | 12,000 |

| Direct labour and variable production overhead | 51,655 | 57,145 | 55,350 | 29,120 | 9,230 |
|---|---|---|---|---|---|
| | (15,655) | 26,855 | 52,650 | 30,880 | 2,770 |
| Discount factor (12%) | 0.89 | 0.80 | 0.71 | 0.64 | 0.57 |
| Present value | (13,933) | 21,484 | 37,382 | 19,763 | 1,579 |

| Net present value | £66,275 |
|---|---|
| Less equipment | 70,000 |
| | (3,725) |

The project does not meet the company's investment criterion.

(b) (a)(i)  This approach reflects the experience effect on labour costs over the five year period to establish average hours per unit.

(a)(ii)  This approach recognizes that whilst 300 hours per unit is the average time per unit over the whole five year period, hours per unit will exceed this figure in the early years. In cash flow terms therefore (a)(ii) is correct and (a)(i) is incorrect and the correct conclusion is that the company's investment criterion is not met.

## Further reading

Hirschmann, W.B., 'Profit from Learning Curve', *Harvard Business Review*, Jan.–Feb. 1964.

Liao, W.M., Simulating learning curve parameters for managerial planning and control, *Accounting and Business Research*, 12, Spring 1982.

Yelle, L.E., The learning curve: historical review and comprehensive survey, *Decision Sciences*, X2, April 1979.

# 4 Marginal costing – an introduction

## Introduction

Marginal costing (period costing) is a costing techniques whereby each unit of output is charged with variable production costs. Fixed production costs are not considered to be real costs of production, but rather costs which provide the facilities for an accounting period thus enabling production to take place. They are therefore treated as costs of the period and charged to the period in which they are incurred. Stock is valued on a variable production cost basis and excludes fixed production costs.

Marginal costing should be contrasted with absorption costing, which is another costing technique whereby each unit of output is charged with both fixed and variable production costs. The fixed production costs are treated as part of the actual production costs. Stock is therefore valued on a full production cost basis. When the stock is sold in the next accounting period these costs are released and matched with the revenue of that period.

Both techniques can be used for reporting profits as shown by the following example.

## Comparative income statements

*Example*
A firm budgets to produce 22,000 units, but actually produces 24,400 units. Its sales were 20,400 units at a price of £200 per unit.
Budgeted costs were as follows:

| | |
|---|---|
| Direct material | £72 per unit |
| Direct labour | £16 per unit |
| Variable production costs | £12 per unit |

Fixed costs
Production costs                         £396,000
Administration costs                     £104,000
Selling costs                            £ 56,000

A sales commission is to be paid at 10 per cent of sales revenue. There is no opening stock and budgeted costs were the same as actual costs.

(a)   Prepare income statements for the period using marginal and absorption costing techniques.
(b)   Reconcile any differences in the resulting profits/losses.
(c)   Show the fixed production overhead account.

(a)   *Comparative income statements*

| Marginal costing | (£) | (£) |
|---|---|---|
| Revenue | | 4,080,000 |
| Variable production costs | | |
| (24,400 units × £100*) | 2,440,000 | |
| Plus opening stock | — | |
| Less closing stock | | |
| (4000 units × £100) | (400,000) | |
| Cost of sales | | (2,040,000) |
| Gross contribution | | 2,040,000 |
| Less sales commission | | (408,000) |
| Net contribution | | 1,632,000 |
| Less fixed costs | | |
| Production | 396,000 | |
| Administration | 104,000 | |
| Selling | 56,000 | |
| | | (556,000) |
| Net profit | | 1,076,000 |

| Absorption costing | | |
|---|---|---|
| Revenue | | 4,080,000 |
| Full production costs | | |
| (24,400 units × £118*) | 2,879,200 | |
| Plus opening stock | — | |
| Less closing stock | | |
| (4000 units × £118) | (472,000) | |
| Cost of sales | | (2,407,200) |
| | | 1,672,800 |
| Gross profit | | |
| Less other expenses | | |
| Sales commission | 408,000 | |
| Administration | 104,000 | |
| Selling | 56,000 | |

|                                        |           | (568,000) |
| -------------------------------------- | --------- | --------- |
| Plus over-absorbed fixed               |           | 1,104,800 |
| production overheads                   |           | 43,200[†] |
| Net profit                             |           | 1,148,000 |

\* Workings
Production costs per unit

|                              | (£) |               |
| ---------------------------- | --- | ------------- |
| Direct material              | 72  |               |
| Direct labour                | 16  |               |
| Variable production overhead | 12  |               |
| Variable production cost     | 100 |               |
| Fixed production overhead    | 18  | (see note, below) |
| Full production cost         | 118 |               |

Note, $\dfrac{\text{Budgeted fixed production cost}}{\text{Budgeted level of activity}} = \dfrac{£396,000}{22,000} = £18$ per unit

[†] Over-absorbed fixed production overheads
(Actual production − Budget production) × Fixed production overhead rate per unit
(24,400 units − 22,000 units) × £18 per unit = £43,200

(b) *Reconciliation of difference between profits*
The absorption costing profit is higher than that under the marginal approach because under the former technique stock is valued at full production costs, the fixed production costs being carried forward in the stock to the next period instead of being charged to the current period as in marginal costing.

*Stock valuation/unit*
Closing stock × (Absorption − Marginal) = Profit difference
4000 units × (£118 − £100) = £72,000

(c) *Fixed production overhead account*

|                              | £       |                              | £       |
| ---------------------------- | ------- | ---------------------------- | ------- |
| Overheads incurred           |         | Work in progress             |         |
| (Bank)                       | 396,000 | (24,400 units × £18)          | 439,200 |
|                              |         | Overheads absorbed           |         |
| Over-absorbed                |         |                              |         |
| overheads P and L            | 43,200  |                              |         |
|                              | 439,200 |                              | 439,200 |

Under/over-absorbed overheads represent the difference between overheads incurred and overheads absorbed. Over-absorbed overheads are credited to the profit and loss account, as in the above example, and under-absorbed overheads are debited to the profit and loss account.

In this example the over-absorption was caused by the actual production level deviating from the budgeting level of production. However, it is important to note that deviations (variances) can arise due to differences between actual and budgeted volumes, and/or actual and budgeted expenditure.

Before the advantages of both techniques are considered it is important for students to understand that the difference between them is one of timing; the actual amount of expenses does not differ, only the periods in which it is charged against profits.

   (i)   When stock levels are constant or nil there is no difference in profits.

  (ii)   When stock levels are increasing, i.e. closing stock exceeds opening stock, higher profits are reported under absorption costing, as some fixed costs are carried forward in the stock valuation.

 (iii)   When stock levels are decreasing, the converse applies and higher profits are reported under marginal costing.

### Advantages of absorption costing

1   Absorption costing conforms with the accrual concept of SSAP2 by matching costs with revenue for a particular accounting period, as in the full costing of stocks.

2   Stock valuation complies with SSAP9, as an element of fixed production costs is absorbed into stocks.

3   It avoids the separation of costs into fixed and variable elements, which is not easily and accurately achieved.

4   The analysis of under/over-absorbed overheads reveals any inefficient utilization of production resources.

5   The apportionment and allocation of fixed production overheads to cost centres (e.g. departments), makes managers more aware of the costs and services provided.

6   Cost plus (full cost) pricing ensures that all costs are covered, as is true of absorption costing. Pricing at the margin may, in the long run, result in contribution failing to cover the fixed costs. It is important in absorption costing that sales are equal to or exceed the budgeted level of activity otherwise fixed costs will be under-absorbed.

### Advantages of marginal costing

1   It avoids the arbitrary apportionment of fixed overheads as mentioned in 5 above.

2   Most fixed production overheads, e.g. factory rent, rates, salaries, and depreciation are periodic, i.e. relate to time and therefore should be charged to the period in which they are incurred.

3   It avoids the problem of determining a suitable basis (i.e. units, labour hours, machine hours, etc.) which is needed for a predetermined overhead absorption rate.

4   Fixed production costs may not be controllable at departmental level and therefore should not be included in production costs at cost centre level, as it is important to match control with responsibility.

5 In absorption costing, profits vary with both production and sales, so that if sales are depressed profits can be artificially increased by merely increasing production and thereby increasing stocks. However, profits cannot be manipulated in this way in marginal costing because stocks exclude fixed costs and profits therefore vary directly with sales.

6 The contribution approach enables the firm to determine break-even points and plan profits.

7 Marginal costing facilitates control in the following ways:

(a) Costs are more easily controlled, when pooled into separate fixed and variable totals.

(b) Flexible budgets can be prepared which provide a comparison for actual levels of activity (see flexible budgeting).

8 The exclusion of fixed overheads from production costs enables an organization to price its goods on a marginal basis and be more competitive.

9 Stock is valued on a variable production cost basis, which conforms with the view that the additional cost of stock is limited to its variable costs.

10 Marginal costing is prudent in that fixed production costs are charged to the period in which they are incurred, and are not carried forward in stock which may be unsaleable, resulting in earlier profits being overstated.

11 Marginal costing is a powerful decision making tool as it focuses attention on these costs which are affected by the decision at hand. The following example illustrates this point:

*Example Company XYZ*
Departments

|  | A (£) | B (£) | C (£) |
|---|---|---|---|
| Sales | 60,000 | 80,000 | 40,000 |
| Variable costs | 40,000 | 60,000 | 34,000 |
| Fixed costs (allocated) | 6,000 | 10,000 | 8,000 |

It has been suggested that department C should be closed as it appears to be making a loss. Advise the company.

*Solution*
Using an absorption basis

|  | A (£) | B (£) | C (£) | Total (£) |
|---|---|---|---|---|
| Sales | 60,000 | 80,000 | 40,000 | 180,000 |
| Total costs | 46,000 | 70,000 | 42,000 | 158,000 |
| Profit (Loss) | 14,000 | 10,000 | (2,000) | 22,000 |

C is loss making and therefore should be closed.

Using a marginal basis

| | A (£) | B (£) | C (£) | Total (£) |
|---|---|---|---|---|
| Sales | 60,000 | 80,000 | 40,000 | 180,000 |
| Variable costs | 40,000 | 60,000 | 34,000 | 134,000 |
| Contribution | 20,000 | 20,000 | 6,000 | 46,000 |
| Less fixed costs | | | | 24,000 |
| Profit | | | | 22,000 |

Profits are the same under both approaches as there are no stocks involved. However if C is closed the effect under the marginal basis is as follows:

| | A (£) | B (£) | C (£) | Total (£) |
|---|---|---|---|---|
| Sales | 60,000 | 80,000 | — | 140,000 |
| Variable costs | 40,000 | 60,000 | — | 100,000 |
| Contribution | 20,000 | 20,000 | — | 40,000 |
| Less fixed costs | | | | 24,000 |
| Profit | | | | 16,000 |

Students can see that the closure of department C results in a reduction in profits of £22,000 − £16,000 = £6000, caused by the £6000 lost contribution of department C.

This simple illustration shows that department C should be kept open because it yields a contribution towards covering the fixed costs.

The marginal approach focuses attention on the variable costs, which are affected by the decision and segregates them from the fixed costs which are unaffected by, and therefore irrelevant to the decision. The allocated fixed costs are irrelevant because the closure of department C will not result in any saving of its fixed costs, for such costs would be shared between the other departments.

If in this example the fixed costs were directly attributable to each department, instead of being allocated, then the closure of C would result in a saving of £8000 of fixed costs. Our advice would then have been to close C as this saving of £8000 exceeds the department's contribution of £6000.

One of the advantages of marginal costing, mentioned earlier, was that it enables a firm to determine break-even points and plan profits. Let us now consider break-even analysis.

## Break-even analysis

The break-even point is that point where total costs equal revenue, and there is no profit or loss. The break-even chart shown in Figure 4.1 illustrates the break-even point.

Contribution = Profit + Fixed costs

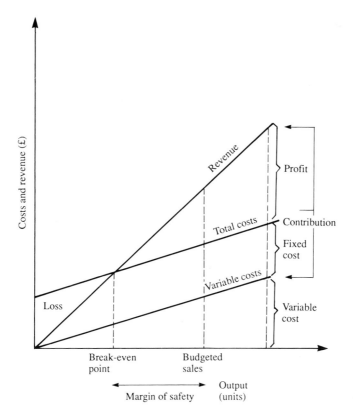

Figure 4.1  *Break-even analysis*

At the break-even point (BE)

Contribution = Fixed costs

This total contribution is comprised of the contribution per unit times the number of units at the break-even point.

Number of units at BE × contribution/unit = fixed costs

$$\text{Number of units at BE} = \frac{\text{fixed costs}}{\text{contribution per unit}}$$

$$\text{BE in sales value £} = \frac{\text{fixed costs}}{\text{contribution/unit}} \times \text{selling price}$$

Also it can be seen from the break-even chart that after the break-even point has been reached any further contribution is equal to profit.

*Example*

A firm PX Ltd manufactures calculators, which have a variable cost of £20 per unit and a selling price of £30 per unit. Fixed costs are budgeted at £80,000

(a)   How many calculators must be sold in order to break even.
(b)   What is the break-even point in sales value.
(c)   How many calculators are required to be sold, to generate a profit of £30,000.

*Solution*

(a)   BE in units $= \dfrac{\text{Fixed costs}}{\text{Contribution per unit}} = \dfrac{£80,000}{£30 - 20} = 8000$ units

(b)   BE in sales value = 8000 units × £30 = £240,000

(c)   After the break-even point contribution and profit are the same.

$\dfrac{£30,000 \text{ (Profit or contribution)}}{£10 \text{ (Contribution per unit)}} = 3000$ (Additional units)

Number of units required to          $\underline{\phantom{xx}8,000}$ (at BE)
make £30,000 profit                              11,000 units

Alternatively students may just use the formula:

$\dfrac{\text{Number of units to make}}{£30,000 \text{ profit}} = \dfrac{\text{Fixed cost + Required profit}}{\text{Contribution per unit}}$

$= \dfrac{£80,000 + £30,000}{£10}$

$= 11,000$ units

## Contribution/sales ratio (C/S ratio)

This ratio, which is sometimes referred to as the P/V (profit/volume) ratio, shows the amount of contribution generated per pound of sales.

If both the variable cost per unit and selling price per unit remain unaltered then the C/S ratio will be equal to a constant.

*Example*

|  | 1 unit | 20 units | 50 units |
|---|---|---|---|
| Sales (£) | 5 | 100 | 250 |
| Variable costs (£) | 3 | 60 | 150 |
| Contribution (£) | 2 | 40 | 100 |
| C/S | 40% | 40% | 40%   (a constant) |

The C/S ratio, as seen above, is equal to a constant on a unit or total basis. It has the following important uses:

1   It acts as a means of evaluating performance.
2   It can determine the break-even point in sales value

$$\text{i.e. BE in sales value} = \frac{\text{Fixed costs}}{\text{Contribution per unit}} \times \text{Selling price}$$

$$\text{BE in sales value} = \text{fixed costs} \times \frac{1}{\text{C/S}} = \frac{\text{fixed costs}}{\text{C/S ratio}}$$

3   If the contribution and constant are known then the sales value can be found for a particular level of profit.

*Example*
In PX Ltd (see example 1) if only 10,000 calculators can be sold at £30 each, and thereafter any additional units will be sold at £24 each, what is the sales value needed to make the same profit as before. Assume the cost structure remains unchanged.

*Solution*
   Contribution = Profit + Fixed costs

   110,000      = £30,000 + £80,000

£110,000 of contribution must be generated in order to make the same profit as before.

| C/S ratio | £ Contribution | £ Sales |
|---|---|---|
| 10/30 | 100,000* | 300,000 (10,000 units of £30) |
| 4/24 | 10,000 | 60,000† |
| | 110,000 | 360,000 |

£360,000 of sales will produce £110,000 of contribution and thereby generate the same £30,000 profit as before.

$$^*\frac{\text{Contribution}}{\text{£ Sales}} = \frac{10}{30} \qquad \text{Contribution} = \frac{10}{30} \times 300,000$$

$$= 100,000$$

$$^\dagger\frac{\text{Contribution}}{\text{£ Sales}} = \frac{4}{24} \qquad \text{Sales} = 10,000 \times \frac{24}{4}$$

$$= 60,000$$

## Profit/volume graph (P/V graph)

This graph is an aid to profit planning as it shows not only the break-even point, but also profits or losses at different levels of activity.

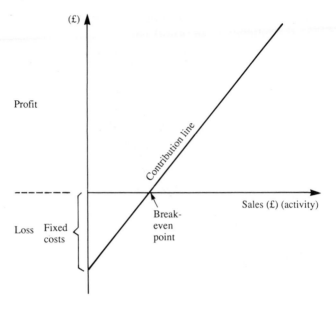

Figure 4.2   *Profit/volume graph (P/V graph)*

In the chart shown in Figure 4.2 a loss equal to the fixed costs will exist when activity is zero. As activity increases contribution is generated which covers the fixed costs until the break-even point is reached. After this point any additional contribution is the same as profit, and the profits for different activity levels can be planned.

*Example*
Company Z spells three products D, E and F. The following information is provided.

|  | D (£) | E (£) | F (£) |
|---|---|---|---|
| Variable cost per unit | 4 | 7 | 3 |
| Selling price per unit | 6 | 8 | 7 |
| Sales volume | 6000 units | 6000 units | 7600 units |

Fixed costs are £20,000

Construct a multi-product P/V chart.

*Solution*

|  | D (£) | E (£) | F (£) | Total (£) |
|---|---|---|---|---|
| Contribution | 12,000 | 6,000 | 30,400 | 48,400 |
| Less fixed costs |  |  |  | 20,000 |
| Profit |  |  |  | 28,400 |

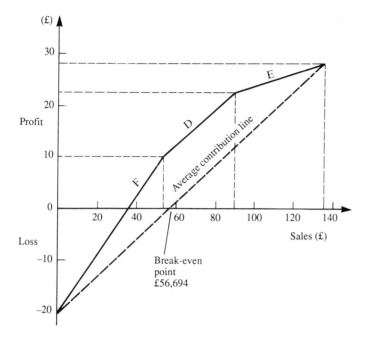

Figure 4.3  *Multi-product P/V chart*

| Sales revenue | 36,000 | 48,000 | 53,200 | 137,200 |
|---|---|---|---|---|
| C/S Ratio | 33.3% | 12.5% | 57.1% | |

A multi-product P/V chart can be drawn, plotting the products in order of the highest ranking C/S ratios.

$$\text{The break-even point in sales value} = \frac{\text{Fixed costs}}{\text{C/S ratio}}$$

$$= £20,000 \times \frac{137,200}{48,400}$$

$$= £56,694$$

The multi-product P/V chart is shown in Figure 4.3.

## Examination questions

### Question 1 (CIMA)

As the first management accountant employed by a manufacturer of power tools you have been asked to supply financial results by product line to help in marketing decision making.

The following account was produced for the year ended 30th September 1988.

|  | (£000) | (£000) |
|---|---|---|
| Sales |  | 1200 |
| Cost of goods sold |  |  |
| Materials | 500 |  |
| Wages | 300 |  |
| Production expenses | 150 |  |
| Marketing costs | 100 |  |
|  |  | 1050 |
| Net profit |  | 150 |

A statistical analysis of the figures shows the following variable element in the costs.

|  | (%) |
|---|---|
| Materials | 90 |
| Wages | 80 |
| Production expenses | 60 |
| Marketing costs | 70 |

Below is given, as a percentage, the apportionment of the sales and variable elements of the costs among the five products manufactured.

|  | Product | | | | | |
|---|---|---|---|---|---|---|
|  | A | B | C | D | E | Total |
| Sales | 30 | 15 | 7 | 28 | 20 | 100 |
| Materials | 40 | 20 | 10 | 20 | 10 | 100 |
| Wages | 15 | 25 | 10 | 25 | 25 | 100 |
| Production expenses | 30 | 10 | 10 | 30 | 20 | 100 |
| Marketing costs | 10 | 30 | 20 | 30 | 10 | 100 |

From the information given you are required to:

(a) (i) prepare a statement for the year showing contribution by products,

   (ii) comment on these contributions.

(b) Calculate the following:

   (i) the break-even sales level;

   (ii) the order of sales preference for additional orders to maximize contribution as a percentage of sales;

   (iii) a revised mix of the £1,200,000 sales to maximize contribution assuming that existing sales by products can only be varied 10 per cent either up or down;

   (iv) a product mix to maximize contribution if manpower availability were reduced by 10 per cent but the product mix could be varied by up to 20 per cent;

   (v) the percentage commission which could be offered to an overseas agent on an order of £30,000 of each product A, C and E to obtain a 20 per cent contribution on the total sales value.

## Answer 1

(a)(i)   *Analysis of overall performance*

|  | (£000) | (£000) |
|---|---|---|
| Sales | | 1200 |
| Variable costs of goods sold | | |
| Materials | 450 | |
| Wages | 240 | |
| Production expenses | 90 | |
| Marketing costs | 70 | |
| | | 850 |
| Contribution | | 350 |
| Fixed costs | | 200 |
| Net profit | | 150 |

*Product line analysis*

|  | A | B | C | D | E | Total |
|---|---|---|---|---|---|---|
| Sales | 360 | 180 | 84 | 336 | 240 | 1200 |
| Material | 180 | 90 | 45 | 90 | 45 | 450 |
| Wages | 36 | 60 | 24 | 60 | 60 | 240 |
| Production expenses | 27 | 9 | 9 | 27 | 18 | 90 |
| Marketing costs | 7 | 21 | 14 | 21 | 7 | 70 |
| | 250 | 180 | 92 | 198 | 130 | 850 |
| Contribution | 110 | — | (8) | 138 | 110 | 350 |

(a)(ii)   Three of the product lines make a contribution to fixed costs and to profit. The other two do not although individual products within a product line may do so. Product lines B and C should not therefore be discontinued, particularly since it is likely that some inter-relationship of sales exists between the product lines. It is also possible that B and C are recently introduced product lines.

For those product lines making contribution, contribution/sales percentages are:

A   30.56%
D   41.07%
E   45.83%

(b)(i)   Assuming a constant mix of sales, average contribution/sales percentage is 350/1200 = 29.16 per cent. Break-even sales is therefore:

$$\frac{200}{29.16\%} = £685,714$$

(ii)   Preference order is E, D, A, B, C

(iii)   Assumption: As in (iv), variation is up to ± 10 per cent. Therefore:

|   | Min Sales (£) | Distribution of balance (£) | Total (£) |
|---|---|---|---|
| A | 324 | 4.8 | 328.8 |
| B | 162 | — | 162 |
| C | 75.6 | — | 75.6 |
| D | 302.4 | 67.2 | 369.6 (max) |
| E | 216 | 48 | 264 (max) |
|   | 1080 | 120 | 1200 |

(iv)   Contribution/wages

|   | A | D | E |
|---|---|---|---|
|   | $\dfrac{110}{36}$ | $\dfrac{138}{60}$ | $\dfrac{110}{60}$ |
|   | 306% | 230% | 183% |
| Ranking | 1 | 2 | 3 |

|   | Min sales (£) | Wages used (£) | Distribution of balance (£) | Total wages (£) | Sales (£) |
|---|---|---|---|---|---|
| A | 288 | 28.8 | 14.4 | 43.2 | 432 (max) |
| B | 144 | 48 |   | 48 | 144 |
| C | 67.2 | 19.2 |   | 19.2 | 67.2 |
| D | 268.8 | 48 | 9.6 | 57.6 | 322.56 |
| E | 192 | 48 |   | 48 | 192 |
|   | 960 | 192 | 24 | 216 | 1157.76 |

90% of 240 = 216.

(v)

|   | A | C | E |   |
|---|---|---|---|---|
| Sales | 30 | 30 | 30 | 90 |
| C/Sales | 30.56% | (9.52%) | 45.83% |   |
| = | 9.17 | (2.86) | 13.75 | 20.06 |
|   |   | 20% of 90 = |   | 18.00 |
| Available for commission |   |   |   | 2.06 |

Percentage commission $\dfrac{2.06}{90}$ = 2.29%

### Question 2 (CIMA)

E Ltd manufactures a hedge-trimming device which has been sold at £16 per unit for a number of years. The selling price is to be reviewed and the following information is available on costs and likely demand.
   The standard variable cost of manufacture is £10 per unit and an

analysis of the cost variances for the past 20 months show the follow-ing pattern which the production manager expects to continue in the future.

Adverse variances of +10 per cent of standard variable cost occurred in ten of the months
Nil variances occurred in six of the months.
Favourable variances of −5 per cent of standard variable cost occured in four of the months.

*Monthly data*
Fixed costs have been £4 per unit on an average sales level of 20,000 units but these costs are expected to rise in the future and the following estimates have been made for the total fixed costs.

|  | (£) |
|---|---|
| Optimistic estimate (probability 0.3) | 82,000 |
| Most likely estimate (probability 0.5) | 85,000 |
| Pessimistic estimate (probability 0.2) | 90,000 |

The demand estimates at the two new selling prices being considered are as follows:

| If the selling price per unit is | £17 | £18 |
|---|---|---|
| Demand would be: | (Units) | (Units) |
| Optimistic estimate (probability 0.2) | 21,000 | 19,000 |
| Most likely estimate (probability 0.5) | 19,000 | 17,500 |
| Pessimistic estimate (probability 0.3) | 16,500 | 15,500 |

It can be assumed that all estimates and probabilities are independent. You are required to:

(a) Advise management, based only on the information given above, whether they should alter the selling price and, if so, the price you would recommend.
(b) Calculate the expected profit at the price you recommend and the resulting margin of safety, expressed as a percentage of expected sales.
(c) Criticize the method of analysis you have used to deal with the probabilities given in the question.
(d) Describe briefly how computer assistance might improve the analysis.

## Answer 2

*Workings*
Average variable cost

| Standard variance | | Weighting | | (£) |
|---|---|---|---|---|
| £10 + 10% | = | £11 | × 10m = | 110 |
| £10 | = | £10 | × 6m = | 60 |
| £10 − 5% | = | £ 9.5 × | 4m = | 38 |
| | | | 20 | 208 |

Variable cost per unit = £10.40

Fixed cost per month (£000)

82 × 0.3 = 24.6
85 × 0.5 = 42.5
90 × 0.2 = 18.0
        85.1

Total fixed cost   £85,100

Demand

| Selling price | £17 | | £18 |
|---|---|---|---|

| (000 units) | | (000 units) | |
|---|---|---|---|
| 21.0 × 0.2 = | 4.20 | 19.0 × 0.2 = | 3.80 |
| 19.0 × 0.5 = | 9.50 | 17.5 × 0.5 = | 8.75 |
| 16.5 × 0.3 = | 4.95 | 15.5 × 0.3 = | 4.65 |
| | 18.65 | | 17.20 |

(a)

| | | | |
|---|---|---|---|
| Unit selling price | £16.00 | £17.00 | £18.00 |
| Unit variable cost | £10.40 | £10.40 | £10.40 |
| Unit contribution | £5.60 | £6.60 | £7.60 |
| Total demand (units) | 20,000 | 18,650 | 17,200 |
| Contribution | £112,000 | £123,090 | £130,720 |

(b)  *Profit statement*

| | (£) |
|---|---|
| Contribution | 130,720 |
| Fixed cost | 85,100 |
| Profit | 45,620 |

Margin of safety = Actual sales − Sales at break-even point.

$$\text{Break-even point (BE)} = \text{Fixed cost (FC)} \times \frac{\text{Sales}}{\text{Contribution}}$$

$$= £85,100 \times \frac{£18.00}{£7.60} = £201,553$$

| | |
|---|---|
| Actual sales = 17,200 units × £18 | £309,600 |
| Margin of safety | £108,047 |
| | 34.9% of sales |

(c)   The method of analysis used assumes that the assigned probabilities can be weighted and the resultant single figure used. Although this is simple to understand and calculate it ignores other characteristics of distribution, e.g. range and skewness.

The method could be amended to produce combined figures showing throughout the use of:

1  optimistic estimates;

2   most likely estimates;
3   pessimistic estimates;

and thus a range of possible outcomes.

(d) Computer assistance would enable more complex and sophisticated analysis to take place. Different scenarios could be constructed based on different assumptions and combinations of assumptions of variable cost, fixed cost, selling price and sales demand.

## Further reading

Ghosh, B.C., Fixed costs in break-even analysis, *Management Accounting*, May 1980.

Kaplan, R.S., *Advanced Management Accounting*, Prentice Hall, 1982.

Middleton, K., A critical look at break-even analysis, *Australian Accountant*, May 1980.

Richardson, A.W., Some extensions with the application of cost–volume–profit analysis, *Cost and Management*, September 1978.

# 5 Marginal costing – cost–volume–profit analysis (C–V–P)

Cost–volume–profit analysis studies the effects of changes in costs, volume and selling price on profits. Break-even analysis is only one particular aspect of C–V–P, which can be useful for profit planning, sales mix decisions, production capacity decisions and pricing decisions.

*Example*
A company sells 30,000 units of a product at £8 each and incurs variable costs of £3.30 per unit, and fixed costs of £64,000. What are the consequences of a price increase or decrease of 10 per cent?

*Solution*
The existing profit = Contribution − Fixed costs
$$= (30,000) \times £4.70 − £64,000$$
$$= £77,000$$

|  | Price increase (+10%) unit (£) | Price reduction (−10%) unit (£) |
|---|---|---|
| Price | 8.80 | 7.20 |
| Variable cost | 3.30 | 3.30 |
| Contribution | 5.50 | 3.90 |

Number of units needed to be sold to maintain the existing profit of £77,000:

$$= \frac{\text{Fixed costs} + \text{Required profit}}{\text{Contribution per unit}}$$

$$= \frac{£64,000 + £77,000}{£5.50} \quad \frac{£64,000 + £77,000}{£3.90}$$

$$= \quad 25,636 \text{ units} \quad\quad 36,153 \text{ units}$$

90

Therefore if prices are raised by 10 per cent sales volume must not fall by more than

$$\frac{(30{,}000 - 25{,}636)}{30{,}000} \times 100 = 14.5\%$$

If prices are reduced by 10 per cent sales volume must increase by at least

$$\frac{(36{,}154 - 30{,}000)}{30{,}000} \times 100 = 20.5\%$$

The above example assumes that a new pricing policy will not be accepted if it provides a smaller profit than the existing one.

## Multiple product C–V–P analysis with production constraints

One benefit of cost–volume–profit analysis in the multi-product case is to focus attention on products with high contribution margins. Management can decide on the output of the high contribution products and therefore maximize the contribution to cover fixed costs and generate profits. However, there is not usually an unlimited supply of production resources and hence there may be constraints due to limits on materials, labour hours and machine hours or demand for the products.

*One constraint problem*
Consider for example a situation with just one binding constraint. There may well be other constraints (e.g. availability of materials) but only one constraint is binding.

Exeter PLC produces two products on one machine. A unit of product A requires five hours of machine time while a unit of product B required eight hours. There are only 2000 hours of machine time available.

The unit selling prices are £120 for product A and £180 for product B with unit variable costs of £40 for product A and £60 for product B. Budgeted fixed costs are £10,000.

*Solution*
This problem may be formulated as a linear programming model to maximize contribution to overheads and profit.

Let $X_1$ be the number of items of product A to be produced.
Let $X_2$ be the number of items of product B to be produced.

The contribution per item are:

    A   $120 - 40 = £80$
    B   $180 - 60 = £120$

Hence the contribution for producing $X_1$ items of A is $80X_1$, and the centribution for producing $X_2$ items of product B is $120X_2$.

Therefore total contribution is:

$$80X_1 + 120X_2$$

This is called the objective function and is written as:

$$Z \text{ (max)} = 80X_1 + 120X_2$$

Z is the contribution which needs to be maximized.

The machine hour constraint can also be expressed algebraically by using a similar approach.

If one item of product A is produced then five machine hours will be used. If however $X_1$ items of product A were produced then $5X_1$ machine hours would be used. Similarly it can be shown that to produce $X_2$ items of product B would use $8X_2$ hours of machine time. Hence total machine time used is $5X_1 + 8X_2$.

Now

Total machine hours used ≤ Total machine hours available
$$5X_1 + 8X_2 \leq 2000$$

$X_1$ and $X_2$ also need to be restricted to positive or zero values

$$X_1, X_2 \geq 0$$

These are called non-negativity constraints.

The machine hour constraints can be plotted on a graph with the $X_1$ variable on the horizontal axis and the $X_2$ variable on the vertical axis as shown in Figure 5.1. The axes represent the non-negativity constraints, and the area below the machine hour constraint represents the feasibility region, i.e. that area that contains all the possible solutions.

The objective function cannot be plotted directly as it contains three unknowns rather than two. If Z is set to a value, say 30,000 then the objective function becomes a straight line. If Z is varied than all the objective function lines lie parallel to one another (see the graph for Z = 30,000).

It can be seen from the graph, or by considering the two extreme cases, that the highest contribution occurs when 400 units of A and none of B is produced giving a maximum contribution of 80(400) + 120(0) = £32,000 and a maximum profit of 32,000 − 10,000 = £22,000.

Note that the product B with the highest unit contribution does not give the maximum contribution. If product B is produced, a product mix of 250 Bs and no As will result in a total contribution of £30,000.

It is the contribution per unit of the scarce resource which is important, i.e. 80/5 = £16 for A and 120/8 = £15 for B.

Hence producing product A gives more contribution for each unit of scarce resource than product B.

Ranking by contribution per unit of resource will only work when there is just one scarce resource. If there is more than one constraint, linear programming is required.

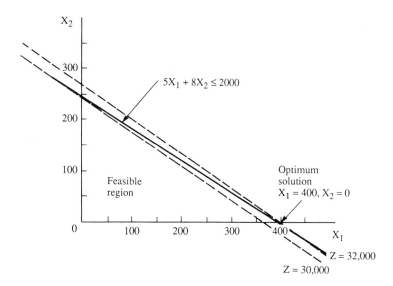

Figure 5.1

*Problem 2*
Assume that product A and B also have to be processed on a second machine, with each unit of A requiring five hours and each unit of B requiring three hours. There being only 1500 hours. The prices and costs remain unchanged.

*Solution*
The linear programming model is:

$$5X_1 + 8X_2 \leqslant 2000$$
$$5X_1 + 3X_2 \leqslant 1500$$
$$80X_1 + 120X_2 = Z \text{ (max)}$$
$$X_1, \qquad X_2 \geqslant 0$$

The previous maximum contribution line Z = 32,000 does not now cross the feasible region which is bounded by the points OLMN. Clearly the new maximum contribution must be less than £32,000 as an additional constraint has been added. As the right-hand side value of £32,000 is reduced the objective function line (broken line on the graph shown in Figure 5.2) moves down the diagram parallel to the original line of $80X_1 + 120X_2 = 32,000$.

It first touches the feasible region at M. Hence M, where $X_1 = 240$ and $X_2 = 100$ (read from the graph), is the new optimum point. The optimal contribution is given by Z (max) = 80(240) + 120(100) = £31,200 giving a maximum profit of £31,200 − 10,000 = £21,200.

The important point to realize from this example is that the optimal solution to a linear programming problem must occur at one of the

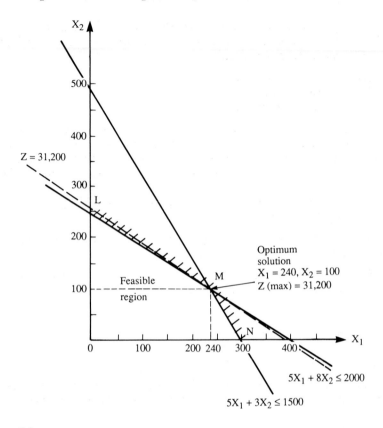

Figure 5.2

vertices of the feasible region (0, L, M, or N). An alternative method of determining the optimal point in small graphical problems is to evaluate the objective function for each vertex of the feasible region, e.g.:

L   (0,250)     $Z = 80 (0)+120(250)$     $= 30,000$
M   (240,100)   $Z = 80 (240)+120(100) = 31,200$
N   (330,0)     $Z = 80 (300)+120(0)$    $= 24,000$

showing the optimum point is at M.

## Simplex method

If more than two products are produced a graphical approach which only uses two variables cannot be applied. A more general algebraic approach called the simplex method is used. Because the simplex method is designed for solving linear programming problems using a computer it is rather tedious for manual use. It is a powerful technique that provides more information than the graphical method.

To illustrate the simplex method consider the two product LP problem that was solved graphically:

$$5X_1 + 8X_2 \leqslant 2000$$
$$5X_1 + 3X_2 \leqslant 1500$$
$$80X_1 + 120X_2 = Z \text{ (max)}$$

The simplex method starts at the origin 0 and moves around the points of the feasible region until the optimal solution is reached. At each vertex of the feasible region the simplex method tests to see if the point is optimal and if not, it will check to see to which point it should move.

The first step is to remove the inequalities by adding to each constraint a slack variable.

Let $S_1$, be the slack variable for the first constraint. Hence $S_1$ = the unused capacity on the first machine

Let $S_2$ be the slack variable for the second constraint. Hence $S_2$ = the unused capacity on the second machine.

Giving:

$$5X_1 + 8X_2 + S_1 = 2000$$
$$5X_1 + 3X_2 + S_2 = 1500$$
$$80X_1 + 120X_2 = Z \text{ (max)}$$

Nowadays it is usual to express these equations in tableau (or matrix) form as they would be held in the computer as a tableau of coefficients.

### First tableau

| $X_1$ | $X_2$ | $S_1$ | $S_2$ | Value | |
|---|---|---|---|---|---|
| 5 | 8* | 1 | 0 | 2000 | Pivot row |
| 5 | 3 | 0 | 1 | 1500 | |
| 80 | 120 | 0 | 0 | 0 | |
| | Pivot column | | | | |

* Pivot element.

Each tableau represents a point on the vertex of the feasible region. The first tableau represents the point 0 (the origin). At this point Z is zero and occurs in the bottom right hand corner of the simplex tableau.

To determine the coordinates of the point of any tableau first look for the unit matrix columns ($S_1$ and $S_2$) (this is the 2×2 unit matrix).

Only the variables in the unit matrix column will have positive values. All the other variables ($X_1$ and $X_2$) will be zero.

In the $S_1$ column we have a 1 in the first row (indicated by a box round the number) and in the first row of the value column we have 2000 (also in a box). This means that for this tableau $S_1$ = 2000. Similarly the 1 in the $S_2$ column occurs in the second row and hence is equal to the second row entry in the value column, i.e. $S_2$ = 1500. There are no other non-zero entries. Therefore, all other variables ($X_1$ and $X_2$) must be zero. Hence the first solution is $X_1$ = 0, $X_2$ = 0, $S_1$ = 2000, $S_2$ = 1500 and Z = 0. This is the trivial solution at the origin.

Produce none of the products A or B and there will be 2000 unused hours on machine 1 and 1500 unused hours on machine 2 with a contribution of zero.

This solution is not optimal. The rule to apply: the solution is not optimal (maximum) if the objective function contains any positive coefficients. If there is a positive coefficient, then increasing the associated variable above zero will increase the contribution above the existing level.

Looking at the first tableau, $X_2$ has the greatest coefficient (contribution) in the objective function hence $X_2$ should be increased. However, if $X_2$ is increased the other variables will change. (Geometrically we are moving away from the origins 0 along the $X_2$ axis towards point L.)

$X_2$ cannot be increased indefinitely as these are limited resources. The next step is to determine by how much we can increase $X_2$. Remember, for each unit of $X_2$ produced the contribution will rise by £120.

Consider in tableau 1 the $X_2$ and value columns only. For each extra $X_2$ produced, eight hours of machine 1 are used. There are only 2000 hours available, hence the limit on $X_2$ from this constraint is 2000/8 = 250 units.

Similarly the limit on $X_2$ from the second constraint is 1500/3 = 500.

The limit of 250 on $X_2$ is the binding constraint (i.e. it occurs before 500).

This means that $X_2$ will rise from zero to 250 using all the available hours on machine 1 causing $S_1$ to go from 2000 to zero. Consequently that part of the unit matrix which appeared in the $S_1$ column will now move to the $X_2$ column. There will be other consequential changes to the rest of the tableau.

The procedure is, as stated earlier, rather tedious and is best summarized by a set of rules.

First summarize the steps already covered:

1  Add in slack variables.
2  Write out first tableau setting Z equal to zero.
3  Identify greatest positive coefficient in objective function row. This is the pivot column ($X_2$).
4  To find which variable becomes zero, calculate the test ratios for each pivot column element:

$$\text{Test ratio} = \frac{\text{Value}}{\text{Pivot column element}}$$

Select lowest positive test ratio to determine pivot row (row 1).

5 The pivot element (8) is the element at the intersection of the pivot row (row 1) and the pivot column ($X_2$).

The remaining steps are known as pivoting. This determines the next point and next tableau.

6 Divide pivot row by pivot element (divide by 8)

| $X_1$ | $X_2$ | $S_1$ | $S_2$ | Value |
|---|---|---|---|---|
| 0.625 | 1 | 0.125 | 0 | 250 |
| | 0 | | 1 | |
| 0 | | | 0 | |

and replace rest of pivot column by zero to give a part of the unit matrix in the old pivot column.

If any element in the pivot row is zero ($S_2$ column) enter the old elements in the column which contains that zero element.

The same rule applies for any zero elements in the old pivot column (there are not any in this example), where the old row would be repeated.

The tableau is as above with six elements still to be filled in.

7 To determine the remaining elements, use the following formula.

$$\frac{\text{New}}{\text{element}} = \frac{\text{Old}}{\text{element}} - \frac{\substack{\text{Element in} \\ \text{pivot row and} \\ \text{old element} \\ \text{column}} \times \substack{\text{Element in} \\ \text{pivot column} \\ \text{and old element} \\ \text{row}}}{\text{Pivot element}}$$

It may help to realize that the four terms involved in each calculation form a rectangle.

Applying the formula to the element in the

2nd row 1st column

$$5 - \frac{5 \times 3}{8} = 3.125$$

2nd row 3rd column

$$0 - \frac{1 \times 3}{8} = 0.375$$

2nd row 5th column

$$1500 - \frac{2000 \times 3}{8} = 750$$

3rd row 1st column

$$80 - \frac{5 \times 120}{8} = 5$$

3rd row 3rd column

$$0 - \frac{1 \times 120}{8} = -15$$

3rd row 5th column

$$0 - \frac{2000 \times 120}{8} = -30,000$$

giving the second tableau.

**Second tableau**

| $X_1$ | $X_2$ | $S_1$ | $S_2$ | Value | Test ratio |
|-------|-------|-------|-------|-------|------------|
| 0.625 | 1 | 0.125 | 0 | 250 | 400 |
| 3.125 | 0 | -0.375 | 1 | 750 | 240 |
| 5 | 0 | -15 | 0 | -30,000 | |

This is not optimal as there is still a positive coefficient in the objective function row. The whole process continues until the optimum solution is found.

**Third tableau**

| $X_1$ | $X_2$ | $S_1$ | $S_2$ | Value |
|-------|-------|-------|-------|-------|
| 0 | 1 | 0.20 | -0.20 | 100 |
| 1 | 0 | -0.12 | 0.32 | 240 |
| 0 | 0 | -14.40 | -1.60 | -31,200 |

This is the final tableau as there are no positive coefficients in the objective function row.

From the tableau $X_2 = 240$, $X_2 = 100$, $S_1 = 0$, $S_2 = 0$, $Z = 31,200$.

Note, ignore the minus sign of the objective function value, as the bottom line in equation form is:

$$-14.40S_1 - -1.60 \ S_2 = Z \ (max) - 31,200$$

which when rearranged is:

$$Z(max) = 31,200 - 14,40 \ S_1 - 1.60 \ S_2$$

As $S_1 = S_2 = 0$ then $Z(max) = 31,200$

This was the same solution as obtained by the graphical method.

Produce 240 units of product A and 100 units of product B giving a maximum contribution of £31,200.

The slack variables $S_1$ and $S_2$ are both zero showing that there are no unused machine hours.

## Shadow prices and sensitivity analysis

Sensitivity analysis is a technique whereby the effects of changes in the coefficients and constraint values on the final solution are gauged.

The coefficient of the slack variables ($S_1$ and $S_2$) in the objective function are known as the shadow prices (or dual prices), i.e. the shadow prices are 14.40 for $S_1$ and 1.60 for $S_2$ (ignore the signs).

If the first constraint is relaxed by one hour, i.e. 2000 hours is increased by one hour to 2001 hours the increase in contribution (above £31,200) is £14.40.

Similarly for the second constraint an extra hour added to the second machine would increase the contribution by £1.60 (shadow price of $S_2$ = £1.60).

This can be shown by considering that if one extra hour is to be used on machine 1 over what is currently available then $S_1$ goes from zero to minus 1.

But $\quad$ $Z \text{ (max)} = 31{,}200 - 14.40\,S_1 - 1.60\,S_2$
$$\text{and then } S_1 = -1 \text{ and } S_2 = 0$$
$$Z \text{ (max)} = 31{,}200 - 14.40(-1) - 1.60(0)$$
$$= 31{,}200 + 14.40$$

An increase in contribution of £14.40.

If, however, an hour was lost on machine 1 then the contribution would be reduced by £14.40 for each hour lost. The shadow prices can be regarded as opportunity costs and hence provide useful information to the management accountant.

These shadow prices, or opportunity costs, are only valid over a range of values. To determine these values it is useful to arrange the cost tableau in vector equation form.

$$\begin{pmatrix} X_2 \\ X_1 \\ 0 \end{pmatrix} + S_1 \begin{pmatrix} 0.20 \\ -0.12 \\ -14.40 \end{pmatrix} + S_2 \begin{pmatrix} -0.20 \\ 0.32 \\ -16.60 \end{pmatrix} = \begin{pmatrix} 100 \\ 240 \\ Z - 13{,}200 \end{pmatrix}$$

rearranging

$$\begin{pmatrix} X_2 \\ X_1 \\ -Z \end{pmatrix} = \begin{pmatrix} 100 \\ -240 \\ -13{,}200 \end{pmatrix} - S_1 \begin{pmatrix} 0.20 \\ -0.12 \\ -14.40 \end{pmatrix} - S_2 \begin{pmatrix} -0.20 \\ 0.32 \\ -1.60 \end{pmatrix}$$

Consider ranging on $S_1$ leaving $S_2 = 0$
We can ignore the last vector as $S_2 = 0$
Therefore:

$$\begin{pmatrix} X_2 \\ X_1 \\ -Z \end{pmatrix} = \begin{pmatrix} 100 \\ 240 \\ -13{,}200 \end{pmatrix} - S_1 \begin{pmatrix} 0.20 \\ -0.12 \\ -14.40 \end{pmatrix}$$

$X_2$ must not become negative as a negative number of items cannot be produced.

Now $X_2 = 100 - 0.20\ S_1 \geqslant 0$
Therefore $S_1 \leqslant 100/0.20 \leqslant 500$
Similarly for $X_1$

$$X_1 = 240 - S_1\ (-0.12) \geqslant 0$$
$$S_1 \geqslant -\ 2000$$

(This method of analysis is known as ranging and most linear programming computer packages will print out the permitted ranges for each constraint.)

The shadow prices for $S_1$ of 14.40 will be valid up to a loss of 500 hours ($S_1 = 500$) and up to a gain of 2000 hours ($S_1 = -2000$) on machine 1. The maximum the company should pay for extra hours on machine 1, in excess of the current cost, is £14.40 and should not take on more than 2000 extra hours on top of the existing 2000 hours.

This may be summed up by:

$$\text{Relevant cost of a resource} = \text{Resource cost} + \begin{array}{c}\text{Shadow price of}\\ \text{resource (opportunity}\\ \text{cost)}\end{array}$$

This analysis may be used to price an additional product using the same resources.

*Example*
Product C is being considered using the same two machines, but with no further machine hours available. Each item of product C requires four hours on machine 1 and three hours on machine 2. The variable costs are £80 per item.

What is the minimum price that should be charged for product C?

*Solution*
Relevant costs (including opportunity costs)

|  |  | (£) |
|---|---|---|
| Machine 1: 4 hr at £14.40 (Shadow price of m/c 1) | = | 57.60 |
| Machine 2: 3 hr at £1.60 (Shadow price of m/c 2) | = | 4.80 |
| Variable cost per item | = | 80.00 |
| Total relevant cost |  | 142.40 |

Therefore minimum price for product C is £142.40. If the price is less than this then the existing product mix is better.

**Sensitivity analysis on the unit contribution**

It is important to know how sensitive the optimum solution is to change in the unit contributions.

The solution to the LP problem $X_1 = 240$, $X_2 = 100$ is based on unit contributions of 80 and 120 respectively.

How much can the contribution of product A differ from 80 before the values of $X_1$ and $X_2$ will change?

Consider the graph of the problem (shown in Figure 5.3). As long as

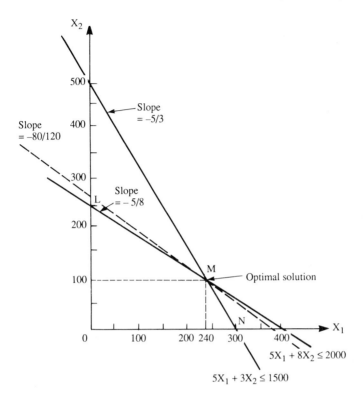

Figure 5.3

the slope of the objection function line $-80/120$ is between the slopes of the two constraints $-5/8$ and $-5/3$ the solution will not change.

Let the contribution for $X_1$ be C1 instead of 80.

Then $-5/8 \geqslant \dfrac{-C1}{120}$ and $\dfrac{-C1}{120} \geqslant -5/3$

Therefore $C1 \geqslant 75$    $C1 \leqslant 200$

The contribution may vary from 80 down to 75 or up to 200.

A similar analysis for the contribution 120 for B shows that it may vary from 120 down to 48 or up to 128 before the solution changes. Although the product mix does not change the contribution does and will have to be recalculated. These results can be obtained from the final simplex tableau.

| $X_1$ | $X_2$ | $S_1$ | $S_2$ | Value |
|---|---|---|---|---|
| 0 | 1 | 0.20 | −0.20 | 100 |
| 1 | 0 | −0.12 | 0.32 | 240 |
| 0 | 0 | −14.40 | −1.60 | −31,200 |

Test Ratio

1st constraint:    −72    8
2nd constraint:    120   −5

Divide the non-zero coefficients in the objective function by the coefficients in each constraint to calculate the test ratio for the objective ranging.

e.g. −14.4/0.2 = −72 and −14.4/−0.12 = 120 etc.

The first row of the tableau gives the solution to $X_2$. Therefore the first set of test ratios give the maximum possible changes from the contribution of $X_2$ before the product mix changes.

i.e. 120 − 72 to 120 + 80 = 48 to 120

The second row and hence the second set of test ratios are concerned with $X_1$. Therefore contributions range for $X_1$ is:

80 − 5 to 80 + 120 = 75 to 200

The same results as determined graphically.

### Problems of using LP

1   The linear programming model assumes that the objective function and the constraints are linear. This implies that the contribution per unit of product and hence the price and variable cost per unit are constant. It does not allow for curvilinear cost functions such as learning curve situations or the economics of scale. It also assumes that fixed costs are constant over the range of output considered.

   The non-linearity can be overcome if curvilinear cost functions are approximated by a set of straight lines.

2   It assumes that the coefficients are known with certainty and are constant. In practice the coefficients are usually estimated by some averaging method. Sensitivity analysis helps to solve this problem as described early. However this technique only considers one variable changing at a time and not the interaction of changes in all the variables simultaneously.

3   The variables are assumed to be continuous while in reality they are more likely to be discrete, i.e. only a whole number. You cannot make 16.7 fridges, you either make 16 or 17.

   Integer programming packages can be used where necessary to overcome this problem.

4   There is only one objective function. However it might be necessary for management to meet several objectives or goals at the same time. There is an extension to LP called goal programming which has had some limited success in coping with this problem.

   Most of these objections to LP can also be aimed at most management accounting techniques. It is important to be aware of the limitations of any technique. The final solution should be tested against the practical situation to see if any obvious errors exist.

## Examination questions

### Question 1 (CIMA)

A company makes two products X and Y. Product X has a contribution of £124 per unit and product Y £80 per unit. Both products pass through two departments for processing and the times in minutes per unit are:

|              | Product X | Product Y |
|--------------|-----------|-----------|
| Department 1 | 150       | 90        |
| Department 2 | 100       | 120       |

Currently there is a maximum of 225 hours per week available in department 1 and 200 hours in dependent 2. The company can sell all it can produce of X but EEC quotas restrict the sale of Y to a maximum of 75 units per week.

The company which wishes to maximize contribution, currently makes and sells 30 units of X and 75 units of Y per week.

The company is considering several possibilities including

1 altering the production plan if it could be proved that there is a better plan than the current one;
2 increasing the availability of either department 1 or department 2 hours. The extra costs involved in increasing capacity are £0.5 per hour for each department;
3 transfering some of their allowed sales quota for product Y to another company. Because of commitments the company would always retain a minimum sales level of 30 units.

You are required to:

(a) calculate the optimum production plan using the existing capacities and state the extra contribution that would be achieved compared with the existing plan;
(b) advise management whether they should increase the capacity of either department 1 or department 2 and, if so, by how many hours and what the resulting increase in contribution would be over that calculated in the improved production plan;
(c) calculate the minimum price per unit for which they could sell the rights of their quota, down to the minimum level given the plan in (a) as a starting point.

### Answer 1

(a)  Maximize $C = 124x + 80y$ subject to:

Department 1 $150x + 90y \leqslant 13{,}500$
Department 2 $100x + 120y \leqslant 12{,}000$
Demand $\qquad\qquad\quad y \leqslant \quad 75$
$\qquad\qquad x, \quad y \geqslant \quad 0$

From the graph shown in Figure 5.4 $x = 60$, $y = 50$.

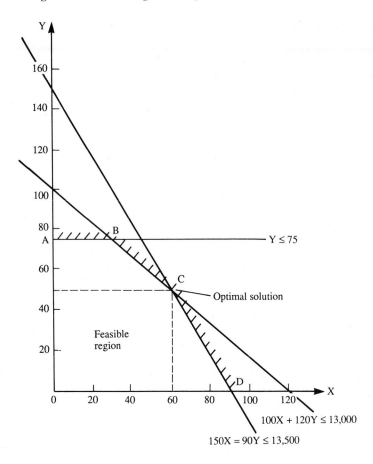

Figure 5.4

Revised contribution = (60 × 124) + (50 × 80) = £11,440
Current contribution = (30 × 124) + (75 × 80) = £  9,720
                                    Increase      = £  1,720

(b)  Maximize production of product X as it has the highest contribution per unit.
From the graph, maximum output of X = 120 units

|  | Hours required | Hours available | Additional hours |
|---|---|---|---|
| Department 1 | $\dfrac{120 \times 150}{60}$ = 300 | 225 | 75 |
| Department 2 | $\dfrac{120 \times 100}{60}$ = 200 | 200 | — |

Contribution        = 120 × £124 = £14,880.00
Less additional cost =   75 × £0.5  = £     37.50

                            14,842.50
Less contribution per (a) above    11,440.00
Increased contribution           3,402.50

Advise: Increase Department 1 by 75 hours; and hence increase contribution by £3,402.50

| (c) | Department 1 | | Department 2 |
|---|---|---|---|
| Total hours | 225 | | 200 |
| Hours required for | | | |
| 30 units of Y   (×1.5) | 45 | (×2) | 60 |
| Hours available for X | 180 | | 140 |
| Hours per unit of X | 2.5 | | 1.67 |
| Production of X | 72 units | | 84 units |

Therefore maximum production of X = 72 units.

Revised contribution = £124 × 72 + £80 × 30 = £11,328
Contribution in (a)                       = £11,440
           Decrease in contribution = £    112

Note: Y – sales quota       = 75
        Production plan (a)   = 50
             Unsold quota    = 25

Thus, under the production plan per (a) above, 25 units of the quota remain unsold. Since the company currently derives no benefit from this element of the quota the rights to it could be sold at the minimum price of zero.

The rights to the remaining 20 units of the quota (50 − 30) should be sold to negate the decrease in contribution of £112.

$$\text{Minimum price} = \frac{£112}{20} = £5.60 \text{ per unit.}$$

### Question 2 (ACA)

The Milton Carpet Company has been manufacturing two ranges of carpet for many years, one for commercial use, the other for private use. The main difference between the two ranges is in the mix of wool and nylon; with the commercial range having 80 per cent wool and 20 per cent nylon and the private range 20 per cent wool and 80 per cent nylon. The designs of each range are the same and each range can be made in five different colours. There are variations in the cost of the dyes used for the different colours in the range, but they are all within five per cent of each other so the accountant takes an average cost of dyeing in her costing.

The Board has just decided to use up its remaining stocks of wool and nylon and transfer its production over to making acrylic carpets in three months' time. The company's objective is to maximize the contribution from the running down of the stocks of wool and nylon over the period subject to any operating constraints. Data concerning its present carpet range is given below. It is assumed that sufficient demand exists to ensure all production can be sold at the stated price.

|  | Per roll | |
|---|---|---|
|  | Private use | Commercial use |
|  | (£) | (£) |
| Selling price | 2400 | 3200 |
| Manufacturing costs |  |  |
| Material – wool | 140 | 700 |
| – nylon | 320 | 100 |
| Direct labour | 90 | 108 |
| Variable production costs | 250 | 312 |
| Fixed production overheads |  |  |
| based on 200 per cent direct labour | 180 | 216 |
| Standard full cost | 980 | 1436 |
| Production requirements |  |  |
| Wool (lbs) | 40 | 200 |
| Nylon (lbs) | 160 | 50 |
| Direct machine time (hours) | 30 | 36 |

There are 24,000 lbs of wool and 25,000 lbs of nylon in the stores to be used up. At the end of the quarter, when it changes to production of the new carpet, any wool or nylon can be sold for £1 per lb. The production manager forecasts that the machines can operate for a total of 6600 hours during the next quarter.

You are required to:

(a) Formulate the above problem in a linear programming format. Solve the problem and provide the production manager with the required output mix of rolls of private and commercial carpets. State whether any of the raw material has to be sold off as scrap at the end and thus what the total contribution for the quarter's production should be.

(b) Show whether or not it will be necessary to recompute the optimum solution if due to economic difficulties, the cost of the dyes of the carpets are to be increased by £110 and £40 per roll of private and commercial carpet respectively.

(c) Describe what would happen in physical and financial terms if the availability of one of the fully utilized resources were to be increased by a small amount.

(d) Comment on the advisability of introducing the concept of opportunity costs into the budgetary control framework, by using the output from the linear programming solution to the optimum production mix.

**Answer 2**

(a) *Linear programming formulation and solution*
Working
The material costs are sunk costs and should not therefore be used in the calculation of the contribution. The realizable value of £1 per lb should be used to value the materials.

Calculation of contribution:

|  | Private (£) | Commercial (£) |
|---|---|---|
| Selling price | 2400 | 3200 |
| Full cost | (980) | (1436) |
| Profit | 1420 | 1764 |
| Fixed overheads | 180 | 216 |
| Contribution before | 1600 | 1980 |
| Material cost (sunk cost) | 460 | 800 |
| Sales cost | (200) | (250) |
|  | 1860 | 2530 |

(i) Let $x$ = number of rolls for private use; and
$y$ = number of rolls for commercial use made in the period.

The aim is to maximize contribution,

$$Z(\text{max}) = 1860x + 2530y$$

Subject to:
Wool:      $40x + 200y \leqslant 24{,}000$   (1)
Nylon:     $160x + 50y \leqslant 25{,}000$   (2)
Capacity   $30x + 36y \leqslant 6{,}600$   (3)
$x, \quad y \geqslant 0$

The feasibility region (shown in Figure 5.5) is ABCDO.
Draw the iso-profit line $Z = 303{,}600$ (the value of the contribution at D). From the graph, using the iso-profit line it can be seen that the optimal solution occurs at C where $x = 100$ and $y = 100$.
The optimum mix requires producing 100 rolls for private use and 100 rolls for commercial use.

(ii) This requires 24,000 lb of wool to be used but only 21,000 lb of nylon. Therefore 4000 lb of nylon are sold off at £1 per lb.

(iii) The historic cost of wool and nylon is irrelevant and therefore the contribution is given by:

$100 \times (£1860 + £200) + 100 \times (£2530 + £250) + 4{,}000 \times £1$
$= £488{,}000$

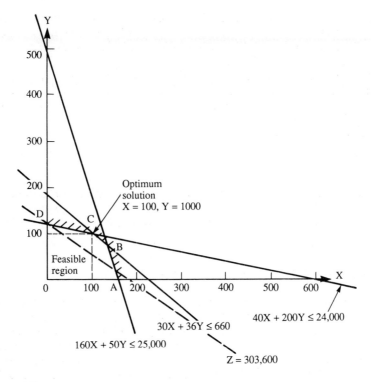

Figure 5.5

**(b)  *Effect of increased cost of dyes***
The objective function changes with contribution figures of:

Private      : 1860 − 110 = £1750
Commercial: 2530 −   40 = £2490

The objective function becomes

Z(max) = 1750x + 2490y

The optimum point does not change although the value of the contribution will decrease.

**(c)  *Effect of marginal increases in availability of constraining resources***
The effect of the availability of a small additional amount of wool or machine capacity can be seen by reference to the graph (Figure 5.5). One or other of the lines of constraint moves further away from the origin expanding the feasible region and allowing a new optimum mix to be produced to generate a greater contribution. It might be worthwhile extending the capacity constraint until it went through point F and the wool constraint until it went through G.

In physical terms the availability of extra machine capacity would result in extra private rolls and fewer commercial rolls being produced. Extra wool available would result in more commercial and fewer private rolls.

The additional contribution gained by relaxing a constraint by one unit (the shadow or dual price) can either be obtained from a computer run of an LP package or by graphical means, e.g. increase the machine capacity by one hour.

Binding constraints are:

$$40x + 200y \leqslant 24{,}000$$
$$30x + 36y \leqslant 6{,}601$$

Solving as equalities gives $x = 100.04$; $y = 99.99$ giving an increase in contribution of £59.39.

A similar calculation for one extra lb of wool gives a shadow price of £1.96.

(d)  *Comment on the introduction of opportunity costs in the budgetary control framework*

The major advantage of the use of opportunity cost in budgetary control has been illustrated here. Opportunity costs represent the true cost of a (limited) resource to a business and are therefore of greater use to management. Here they have been used to provide input to a linear programming problem to help decision making. They could just as easily be derived from a linear programming formulation to provide costs for further decisions or for performance evaluation.

For example, it is often stated of fixed overhead capacity variances that they do not represent the true cost to a firm of under-used resources. This could be overcome if the opportunity costs of such resources are measured. If managers fail to utilize a scarce resource they could be 'charged' with the loss of contribution resulting from their decision or control failure.

The output of a linear programming solution has also been used in the context of budgetary control by Demski and others. He proposed a form of ex-post evaluation of performance which involved the reformulation of a linear programming problem in the light of more up-to-date standards.

On the assumption that differences between ex-ante decision inputs and ex-post decision inputs were uncontrollable, differences between the two optimal results could form the basis of a measure of planning or prediction variances. Similarly differences between actual results and ex-post optimal plans (as could be produced by a linear programming approach) would produce variances showing the opportunity cost of sub-optimal decisions and control failures. This approach therefore improves the traditional analysis by:

1   attempting to identify the value of cost of errors in the original decision inputs;

2  attempting to measure variances in a way which is consistent with objectives.

The disadvantages of the use of such opportunity costs for budgetary control are the limitations placed on such values by the limitations of the linear programming method.

1  Objective function and constraints need to be linear functions of the variables. This does not allow for economies or diseconomies of scale, stepped fixed costs or the need to reduce selling price to increase demand.
2  Estimates of costs and revenues must be known with certainty. The distinction between the fixed and variable elements of costs must be known and the way such costs vary with time established.
3  All constraints must be included.
4  The organization's objective must be quantifiable and not of a qualitative nature.

## Question 3 (CIMA)

A chemical manufacturer is developing three fertilizer compounds for the agricultural industry. The product codes for the three products are X1, X2, and X3 and the relevant information is summarized below:

Chemical constituents: percentage make-up per tonne

|    | Nitrate | Phosphate | Potash | Filler |
|----|---------|-----------|--------|--------|
| X1 | 10      | 10        | 20     | 60     |
| X2 | 10      | 20        | 10     | 60     |
| X3 | 20      | 10        | 10     | 60     |

Input prices per tonne
| Nitrate   | £150 |
| Phosphate | £ 60 |
| Potash    | £120 |
| Filler    | £ 10 |

Maximum available input in tonnes per month
| Nitrate   | 1200     |
| Phosphate | 2000     |
| Potash    | 2200     |
| Filler    | No limit |

The fertilizers will be sold in bulk and managers have proposed the following prices per tonne.

| X1 | £83 |
| X2 | £81 |
| X3 | £81 |

The manufacturing costs of each type of fertilizer, excluding materials, are £11 per tonne.

You are required to:

(a) Formulate the above data into a linear programming model so that the company may maximize contribution.

(b) Construct the initial simplex tableau and state what is meant by 'slack variables' (define X4, X5, X6 as the slack variables for X1, X2 and X3 respectively).

(c) Indicate, with explanations, which will be the 'entering variable' and 'leaving variable' in the first iteration. You are not required to solve the model.

(d) Interpret the final matrix of the simplex solution given below:

| Basic Variable | X1 | X2 | X3 | X4 | X5 | X6 | Solution |
|---|---|---|---|---|---|---|---|
| X1 | 1 | 0 | 3 | 20 | −10 | 0 | 4,000 |
| X2 | 0 | 1 | −1 | −10 | 10 | 0 | 8,000 |
| X6 | 0 | 0 | −0.4 | −3 | 1 | 1 | 600 |
| Z | 0 | 0 | 22 | 170 | 40 | 0 | 284,000 |

(e) use the final matrix to investigate:

(i) the effect of an increase in nitrate of 100 tonnes per month;

(ii) the effect of a minimum contract from an influential customer for 200 tonnes of 3 per month to be supplied.

## Answer 3

(a) To calculate contribution one must first work out the material cost per tonne for each product:

$X1 = £(0.1 \times 150) + (0.1 \times 60) + (0.2 \times 120) + (0.6 \times 10) = £51$
$X2 = £(0.1 \times 150) + (0.2 \times 60) + (0.1 \times 120) + (0.6 \times 10) = £45$
$X3 = £(0.2 \times 150) + (0.1 \times 60) + (0.1 \times 120) + (0.6 \times 10) = £54$

So that Selling Price − Material costs − Manufacturing costs = contribution

| | (£) | (£) | (£) | (£) |
|---|---|---|---|---|
| X1 | 83 | 51 | 11 | 21 |
| X2 | 81 | 45 | 11 | 25 |
| X3 | 81 | 54 | 11 | 16 |

Contribution must then be maximized subject to constraints representing the maximum available input of three of the four materials:

Maximize  $Z = 21X1 + 25X2 + 16X3$
Subject to   $0.1X1 + 0.1X2 + 0.2X3 \leqslant 1200$ Nitrate
$0.1X1 + 0.2X2 + 0.1X3 \leqslant 2000$ Phosphate
$0.2X1 + 0.1X2 + 0.1X3 \leqslant 2200$ Potash

and the non-negativity requirements that X1, X2, X3 are all >=0.

(b)  The slack variables X4, X5, X6 are introduced to represent the amount of each of the scarce resources left unused; the inequality constraints are thus converted into equations, e.g. $0.1X1 + 0.2X2 + 0.2X3 + X4 = 1200$ and the simplex tableau is:

|     | X1    | X2    | X3    | X4 | X5 | X6 | Solution |
|-----|-------|-------|-------|----|----|----|----------|
| X4  | 0.1   | 0.1   | 0.2   | 1  | 0  | 0  | 1200     |
| X5  | 0.1   | 0.2   | 0.1   | 0  | 1  | 0  | 2000     |
| X6  | 0.2   | 0.1   | 0.1   | 0  | 0  | 1  | 2200     |
| Z   | −21   | −25   | −16   | 0  | 0  | 0  | 0        |

(c)   To select the entering variable for the first iteration, look at the Z row: as this is a maximizing problem, choose the variable corresponding to the column with the most negative entry in that row. In this case, it is −25, so the entering variable is X2.

To determine the leaving variable, it is necessary to compare the elements in the entering variable column (X2) with those in the solution column. For each basic variable (row) calculate the ratio. Solution column entry/2nd column entry and choose the smallest non-zero positive one.

In this case the values are:   X4 1200/0.1 = 12,000
X5 2000/0.2 = 10,000
X6 2200/0.1 = 22,000

The smallest non-zero positive is 10,000, so the leaving variable is X5.

(d)   From the tableau, the optimal solution is to produce 4000 tonnes of X1, 8000 tonnes of X2, and no X3 each month. This gives a contribution of £284,000 per month, uses all the nitrate and phosphate, but leaves 600 tonnes of potash unused. The shadow price of X3 is £22 and the marginal values of nitrate and phosphate are £170 per tonne and £40 per tonne.

(e)(i)   The availability of nitrate is constraining the optimal solution at present, so any increase will change the optimal solution. The elements in the X4 column of the final tableau show the changes which will result from each extra tonne of nitrate per month, so that with 100 extra tonnes per month the new values will be:

| X1 | $4,000 + (20 \times 100)$    | = | 6,000   |
|----|------------------------------|---|---------|
| X2 | $8,000 + (-10 \times 100)$   | = | 7,000   |
| X6 | $600 + (-3 \times 100)$      | = | 300     |
| Z  | $284,000 + (170 \times 100)$ | = | 301,000 |

So the new optimal solution is to make 6000 tonnes of X1 and 7000 tonnes of X2 per month for a contribution of £301,000.

(ii)   The optimal policy at present is to produce no X3 at all; this contract will reduce the total contribution, assuming the normal selling price. The changes in the solution for each tonne of X3 sold each month are given by the elements in the X3 column of the final tableau, so the changing results are:

X1    4,000 − (  3  × 200) =    3,400
X2    8,000 − (−1  × 200) =    8,200
X6      600 − (−0.4× 200) =      680
Z   284,000 − (  22 × 200) = 279,600

(Note that the changes are deducted from the original values because each tonne of X3 reduces the overall contribution.) Thus 3400 tonnes of X1, 8200 tonnes of X2 and 200 tonnes of X3 would be produced, for a contribution of £279,600

## Further reading

Baker, K.R. and Taylor, R.E., A linear programming framework for cost allocation and external acquisition when reciprocal services exist, *Accounting Review*, LIV 4, October 1979.

Dev, S., Linear programming dual prices in management accounting and their interpretation, *Accounting and Business Research*, Winter 1978.

Dury, J.C., Linear programming for decision making and control, *Accountancy*, January 1979.

Gee, K.P., *Advanced Management Accounting Problems*, Macmillan, 1986.

# 6 Marginal costing – pricing and common costs

In the previous two chapters, cost–volume–pricing analysis was outlined. However this analysis has the following limitations:

1  It assumes that output is the only factor affecting costs, but there are other variables which can affect costs, e.g. inflation, efficiency and economic and political factors.
2  Not all costs can be easily and accurately separated into fixed and variable elements.
3  Total fixed costs do not remain constant beyond certain ranges of activity levels but increase in a step-like fashion.
4  It assumes that where a firm sells more than one product the sales mix is constant. However, the sales mix will be continually changing owing to changes in demand.
5  There is an assumption that there are either no stocks, or no changes in stock levels. Profit is therefore dependent on the sales volume. However, when changes in stock levels occur and such stocks are valued using absorption costing principles, then profit will vary with both production and sales. If sales are depressed, profit can be raised by increasing production and thereby increasing stock levels. Profit is therefore a function of two independent variables (sales and production). The conventional break-even chart is two dimensional and cannot cope with two independent variables.
   It is important to note that if stocks are valued using marginal costing principles then profit is a function of sales, only, and the conventional C–V–P analysis applies.
6  C–V–P analysis assumes that costs and sales can be predicted with certainty. However, these variables are uncertain and the cost and management accountant must try to incorporate the effects of uncertainty into his information.

*Problem on uncertainty under C–V–P analysis*

Dual plc has to decide between launching one or two similar new products. (It does not have the production capacity to launch both products.)

The fixed costs are £20,000 pa. Product A can be sold for £400 per item and Product B for £350 per item. The variable unit costs are £240 for product A and £200 for product B.

The likely demand for both products are given by the following probability distributions:

| Likely demand | Probability | |
|---|---|---|
| | Product A | Product B |
| 100 | 0.1 | 0.3 |
| 200 | 0.3 | 0.4 |
| 300 | 0.4 | 0.2 |
| 500 | 0.2 | 0.1 |
| | 1.0 | 1.0 |

(a) Calculate the break-even point for each product and estimate the probability of making a loss.
(b) Which product should Dual decide to launch.

*Solution*

(a) Break-even points:

| Product A | Product B |
|---|---|

$$\frac{20,000}{400 - 240} = 125 \qquad \frac{20,000}{350 - 200} = 133$$

Probability of a loss:

A:   0.1
B:   0.3

(b) Expected demand

Product A:

$$100 \times 0.1 + 200 \times 0.3 + 300 \times 0.4 + 500 \times 0.2 = 290$$

Product B:

$$100 \times 0.3 + 200 \times 0.4 + 300 \times 0.2 + 500 \times 0.1 = 220$$

Expected contribution for A $= 290 \times (400 - 240) = £46,400$
Hence expected profit $= 46,400 - 20,000 = £26,400$

Expected contribution for B $= 220 \times (350 - 200) = £33,000$
Hence expected profit $= 33,000 - 20,000 = £13,000$

Product A has a probability of a loss of 0.1 compared with product B's higher probability of 0.3. This therefore makes product B unattractive.

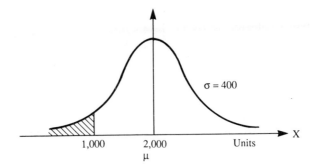

Figure 6.1

Product A has a much higher expected profit than product B and is therefore more attractive from the profitability point of view.

*Problem on uncertainty using a probability distribution*
Annual sales of product Kassel are normally distributed with a mean of 2000 units and a standard deviation of 400 units. Kassel has a selling price of £80 with a variable cost of £50. Budgeted fixed costs are £30,000.

(a) Determine the breakeven quantity and hence the probability of a loss.
(b) What is the expected profit?
(c) Determine the probability of a loss greater than £5000.
(d) Calculate a 95 per cent confidence interval for the expected profit and comment on the viability of this product for the company.

*Solution*
(a)  Break-even quantity (see Figure 6.1)

$$\frac{30000}{80 - 50} = 1000$$

$$Z = \frac{1000 - 2000}{400} = -2.5$$

From tables area = 0.4938
Therefore table area = 0.5 − 0.4938
$$= 0.0062$$
Therefore probability of a loss is 0.0062

(b)  Expected profit = 2000 × (£80 − 50) − 30,000
$$= £30,000$$

(c)  The demand distribution is normal and therefore the profit dis-

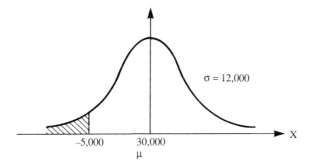

Figure 6.2

tribution is normal. The fixed cost is a constant and cannot affect the variability of the profit distribution. Hence the standard deviation of the profit is the standard deviation of demand multiplied by the contribution per unit, i.e. 400 × (80 − 50) = 12,000 (See Figure 6.2.)

$$Z = \frac{-5000 - 30,000}{12,000} = -2.9$$

From tables area = 0.4981
Therefore tail area = 0.5 − 0.4981 = 0.0019
Hence, probability of a loss greater than £5,000 is 0.0019.

(c)  From tables Z = 1.96
95% confidence interval for the profit is:

  £30,000 ± 1.96 × 12,000
= £30,000 ± 23,520

i.e. £6480 to 53,520.
  The probability of a loss is very small. The expected profit is £30,000 and there is a probability of 95 per cent that it will be in the range £6480 to 53,520. The project would seem to be a profitable one. (See Figure 6.3.)

7  C–V–P analysis assumes linearity of costs and revenue. However in reality both the revenue and total cost functions will be curvilinear for the following reasons:

(a)  It may be necessary to reduce sales prices in order to induce further demand. Total revenue will not increase proportionately with output.

(b)  As output increases efficiencies are gained, and these economies of scale will reduce the marginal costs per unit. Eventually diseconomies of scale (diminishing returns) will cause the marginal costs to rise (see Figure 6.4).

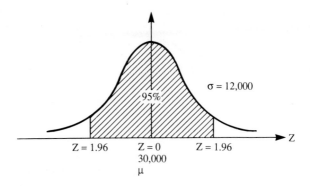

Figure 6.3

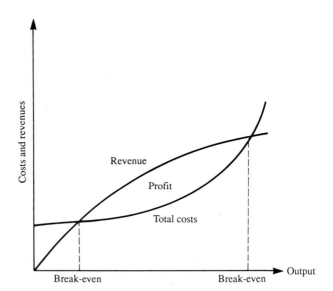

Figure 6.4

Although the economist's chart is theoretically correct, it is time consuming and expensive to plot mathematically complex curvilinear functions. Also over relevant ranges of activity levels the difference between this chart and the accountant's model is small, so the latter is often used.

The profit in Figure 6.4 can be determined using the mathematical technique called calculus.

The method of pricing used earlier, where prices are set in order to maximize contributions towards fixed costs and profit, is called marginal pricing. It is useful for short run pricing decisions as it focuses attention on future costs and revenues, and ignores past, sunk costs, which are irrelevant to these decisions. A typical application of this method of pricing is in seasonal industries where spare capacity often arises and a price is set above the marginal cost, but lower than the normal price, in order to generate contribution towards profits. Absorbed, allocated fixed costs are ignored as they are unaffected by the decision. However, any incremental fixed costs must feature in the decision analysis.

Marginal pricing considers demand and volume and is therefore similar to the classical economic approach towards pricing. Under this approach a price is set at a level of output where the marginal revenue (the additional revenue obtained by selling one extra unit) is equal to the marginal cost (the additional cost of producing one extra unit).

Both of these pricing methods should be contrasted with the cost plus pricing method which is frequently used in practice. Full cost plus pricing is the same as absorption costing, in that conventional cost accounting principles are employed to arrive at a total cost for a product to which is added a mark up, thus providing a selling price.

The following example illustrates the cost plus and economic approaches towards pricing.

*Example*
(a) Nantderyn Products has two main products, Exco and Wyeco, which have unit costs of £12 and £24 respectively. The company uses a mark-up of $33\frac{1}{3}$ per cent in establishing its selling prices and the current prices are thus £16 and £32. With these prices, in the year which is just ending, the company expects to make a profit of £300,000 from having produced and sold 15,000 units of Exco and 30,000 units of Wyeco. This programme will have used all the available processing time in the finishing department. Each unit of Exco requires an hour of processing time in this department and every unit of Wyeco correspondingly requires half an hour.

Fixed overhead was £360,000 for the year and this has been charged to the products on the basis of the total processing hours used. All other costs may be assumed variable in relation to processing hours. In the current year it is estimated that £60,000 of the fixed overhead will be absorbed by Exco and £300,000 by Wyeco. With the existing selling prices it is considered that the potential annual demand for Exco is 20,000 units and that for Wyeco 40,000 units.

You are required to comment critically on the product mix adopted by Nanderyn Products. Calculate what would have been the optimal plan given that there was no intention of changing the selling prices.

(b) For the forthcoming year increased capacity has been installed in the finishing department so that this will no longer be a constraint for any feasible sales programme. Annual fixed overhead will be increased to £400,000 as a consequence of this expansion of facilities, but variable costs per unit are unchanged.

A study commissioned by the Sales Director estimates the effect that alterations to the selling price would have on the sales that could be achieved. The following table has been prepared.

|  | Exco |  | Wyeco |  |
|---|---|---|---|---|
| Price (£) | 13.50 | 18.50 | 29.00 | 35.00 |
| Demand in 000's | 30 | 10 | 60 | 20 |

It is, thought, reasonable to assume that the price/demand relationship is linear. Assuming that the company is now willing to abandon its cost plus pricing practices, if these can be shown to be deficient, you are required to calculate the optimal selling price for each product and the optimal output levels for these prices. State clearly any assumptions that you find it necessary to make.

*Solution*
(a)   Product Exco

The fixed overhead per unit $= \dfrac{£60,000}{15,000 \text{ units}} = £4$ per unit

Therefore variable cost per unit = £12 (total cost) − £4 = £8

Therefore contribution/unit = £16 − £8 = £8

Contribution per hour of finishing time $= \dfrac{£8}{£1 \text{ hr}} = £8$ per hr

Product Wyeco

The fixed overhead per unit $= \dfrac{£300,000}{30,000 \text{ units}} = £10$ per unit

Variable cost per unit = £24 (total cost) − £10 = £14

Contribution per unit = £32 − £14 = £18

Contribution per hour of finishing time $= \dfrac{£18}{0.5 \text{ hr}} = £36$ per hr

Available hours:

   15,000 for making (15,000) Exco
   <u>15,000</u> for making (30,000) Wyeco
   30,000 hours

Recommended mix:

Make maximum of Wyeco − 40,000 units needing 20,000 hrs
                 Exco   − 10,000 units needing <u>10,000</u> hrs
                                     30,000 hrs

(b)   From the graph shown in Figure 6.5, the slope of the demand

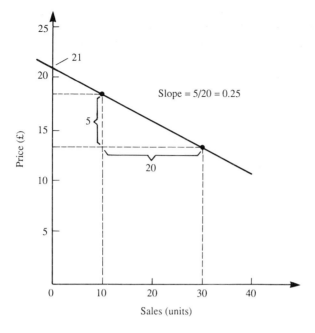

Figure 6.5 *Exco*

function for Exco is 0.25 and the y-intercept is 21, giving a demand function:

P = 21 – 0.25X

where P = unit selling price of Exco, X = demand for Exco.

R = PX   where R = revenue

Therefore R = (21 – 0.25X)X
R = 21X – 0.25X²

Using calculus

MR = 21 – 0.5X, where MR = Marginal revenue.

Now MC = 8,       where MC = Marginal cost.

The optimal level of output is where MC = MR,

8 = 21 – 0.5X

Therefore X = 26 i.e. produce 26,000 of Exco
Optimal price = £21 – 0.25 × 26
= £14.5

A similar approach for Wyeco gives the following results:

P = 38 – 0.15Y
R = 38Y – 0.15Y²

$$MR = 38 - 0.3Y$$
$$MC = 14$$
$$Y = 80$$
$$P = £26$$

Optimal policy is produce 80,000 unit of Wyeco to sell at £26.

This is below the lowest selling price and may be unacceptable.

Cost plus pricing is widely used in practice for the following reasons:

(i)   it is easily understood by management;
(ii)  it standardizes pricing, thereby enabling pricing decisions to be delegated to lower management;
(iii) it is consistent with absorption costing, a technique which is used by most firms;
(iv)  it covers all costs which is important when setting prices for the long run.

However, this method of pricing has a number of limitations which include:

(i)   its failure to consider the price elasticity of demand, i.e. the responsiveness of demand to changes in selling price, which can lead to the under or over pricing of a product.
(ii)  Cost plus systems include past, irrelevant costs and therefore do not have the flexibility to cope with short run pricing decisions.
(iii) cost plus pricing involves the arbitrary allocation and apportionment of fixed costs in determining overhead absorption rates. Different types of overhead recovery rates give different overhead charges and therefore can result in different selling prices.

Students should also be aware of the criticisms which can be levelled at the economic approach towards pricing. Firstly, it assumes perfect knowledge of all information involved. Secondly, the marginal approach assumes that profit maximization is the firm's sole objective. Thirdly, it assumes that demand is only a function of price, whereas demand is dependent on many other variables which include sales promotion, incomes, social and political factors.

*Problem*
Uniform PLC produce a product which in recent years has shown a decline in profits and made its first loss in 1988.

Income statement for year ending 31 December 1988

|  | (£000) |
|---|---|
| Unit sales | 350 |
| Sales | 3500 |
| Less variable costs | 2100 |
| Contribution | 1400 |
| Fixed costs | 1560 |
| Profit (Loss) | (160) |

A determined sales drive has been started in an attempt to improve sales in 1989, and unit sales are expected to increase by ten per cent during 1989. However, the unit variable costs are also likely to increase by ten per cent on the 1988 levels although the fixed costs are estimated to remain at £1,560,000.

The company is considering whether to increase the unit price by five per cent in order to improve profitability. However, the marketing department has forecasted that a price increase of five per cent is likely to have an effect upon the expected increase in demand. Competition will also affect demand.

The marketing department forecasts are:

Increase in demand on 1988

| (%) | Probability |
|---|---|
| +10 | 0.5 |
| + 5 | 0.3 |
| − 2.5 | 0.2 |
| | 1.0 |

(a) Calculate Uniform's expected profit for 1989 if the price increase of five per cent is implemented and the unit sales do increase by five per cent.
(b) Calculate Uniform's expected profit for 1989 using the marketing department's probability distribution.
(c) Assuming that the probability distribution is unlikely to change substantially for price increases up to 20 per cent, what percentage change in price is required for the company to break even?

*Solution*
(a)   Income statement for year ending 31 December 1989

| | (£000) |
|---|---|
| Unit sales | 385 |
| Sales (385 × £10 × 1.05) | 4042.50 |
| Less variable costs | |
| (385 × £6 × 1.10) | 2541.00 |
| Contribution | 1501.50 |
| Fixed costs | 1560.00 |
| Profit (Loss) | (58.50) |

(b)   Expected percentage increase in unit sales volume = 10 × 0.5 + 5 × 0.3 + (−2.5) × 0.2 = 6%

Income statement for year ending 31 December 1989

| | (£000) |
|---|---|
| Unit Sales | 371 |
| Sales (385 × £10 × 1.05) | 3895.50 |
| Less variable costs | |
| (385 × £6 × 1.10) | 2448.60 |
| Contribution | 1446.90 |
| Fixed costs | 1560.00 |
| Profit (Loss) | (113.10) |

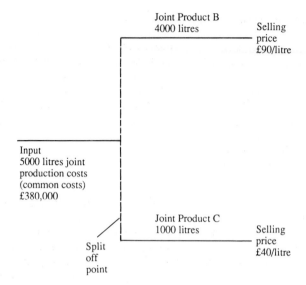

Figure 6.6

(c)   Profit has to increase by £113.10. Hence sales must increase by £113.10 with no increase in units sold. Therefore price must rise by a further £113.10/371 = £0.305, i.e. a further percentage increase of 0.305/10 × 100 = 3.05%.

A total increase in price of 5 + 3 = 8% is necessary for the company to expect to break even.

## Joint product costing

When two or more products are simultaneously produced from a common process these products are called joint products. Any products arising incidentally to, and of relatively lower sales value than, the joint products are by-products. The different products become separately identifiable at the split-off point. Joint and by-products frequently arise in the chemical, food and other industries.

The following example illustrates how common costs (i.e. the joint production costs incurred prior to the split-off point) are apportioned between the joint products in order to value stock and determine income.

*Example*
One method available for the allocation of common costs between the joint products is the physical quantity basis. This method allocates on the basis of each product's relative portion of the total quantity (see Figure 6.6).

## Physical quantity basis

| Joint products | Physical quantity (Litres) | Allocation of common costs (£) | Unit cost (£) | Net income (£) |
|---|---|---|---|---|
| B | 4000 | 304,000* | 76/litre | 56,000 |
| C | 1000 | 76,000[†] | 76/litre | (36,000) |
| Total | 5000 | 380,000 | | 20,000 |

\* 4/5 × 380,000 = 304,000
[†] 1/5 × 380,000 = 76,000

This method of allocation is satisfactory when a close relationship exists between the selling price of individual products and the physical measure, and the joint products are homogeneous.

However, if this close relationship does not exist, then a sales value basis should be used, which allocates common costs on the basis of each product's relative proportion of the total sales value, and will result in an equitable apportionment of profitability between the joint products.

## Sales value basis

| Joint products | Sales value (£) | Allocation of common costs (£) | Unit cost (£) | Net income (£) |
|---|---|---|---|---|
| B | 360,000 | 342,000* | 85.5 | 18,000 |
| C | 40,000 | 38,000[†] | 38.0 | 2,000 |
| Total | 400,000 | 380,000 | | 20,000 |

\* 380,000 × 0.9 = 342,000
[†] 380,000 × 0.1 = 38,000

This method provides a more equitable apportionment of profitability between the joint products (gross profit margins of five per cent each).

Net income is determined by substracting allocated costs from sales revenue:

360,000 − 342,000 = £18,000
40,000 −  38,000 =  £2,000

Assume that in the above example the facts are unchanged except that product C does not have a market, and must be converted into 1000 litres of product D. Product D sells for £160 per litre, after incurring additional processing costs of £40 per litre. The sales value basis needs to be modified. The additional costs are deducted from the sales to arrive at a net realizable value (NRV) at the split-off point. These relative NRVs form the basis of joint cost allocation

Net realizable value (NRV) basis

| Joint products | Sales value (£) | Additional costs (£) | NRV (£) | Allocation of common costs (£) | Unit costs (£) | Net income (£) |
|---|---|---|---|---|---|---|
| B | 360,000 | — | 360,000 | 285,000[†] | 71.25[§] | 75,000 |
| C | 160,000 | 40,000 | 120,000 | 95,000[†] | 95.00[§] | 25,000 |
| Total | | | 380,000 | 380,000 | | 100,000 |

Plus additional cost 40.135 per litre.

[*] Net income is determined by subtracting allocated costs from the NRV
$(36,000 - 285,000 = £75,000$ and $(120,000 - 95,000) = £25,000$.
[†] $380,000 \times 0.75 = 285,000$
$380,000 \times 0.25 = 95,000$
[§] $285,000/4,000 = 71.25$
$95,000/1,000 = 95$

The gross profit margins are 20.8 per cent for B and 15.6 per cent for D.

The above methods for allocating common costs are irrelevant with respect to making decisions about whether or not joint products should be further processed.

Common costs are historic, sunk costs and a marginal cost approach should be used for joint product costing decision making purposes.

Under this approach incremental revenue (i.e. the difference between the revenue obtained after further processing and revenue received if sold at the split-off point) is compared with incremental cost (i.e. the additional processing costs).

*Example*
X Ltd produced two joint products, 400,000 units of A and 200,000 units of B with respective selling prices at the split-off point of £5 per unit and £8 per unit. The joint production costs are £600,000.

A could be processed further to produce 240,000 units of C which would sell for £13 per unit. However, extra fixed costs of £80,000 and variable cost of 60p per unit of A processed would be incurred.

Should X Ltd process further?

*Solution*

| | (£) | (£) |
|---|---|---|
| Revenue after further processing | | |
| (240,000 units × £13 per unit) | 3,120,000 | |
| Revenue at split-off point (A) | | |
| (4,000,000 units × £5 per unit) | 2,000,000 | |
| Therefore incremental revenue | | 1,120,000 |
| Extra fixed costs | 80,000 | |
| Extra variable costs | | |
| (400,000 × 60p) | 240,000 | |
| Therefore incremental costs | | 320,000 |
| Gain by processing further | | 800,000 |

Therefore A should be processed to produce C.

The last three chapters have described the major applications of marginal costing, i.e. cost–volume–pricing analysis, pricing and the treatment of common costs. A major feature, linear programming was introduced to extend the analysis of the marginal costing model. The linear programming technique was explained in detail because its analytical approach is widely used in many areas of management accounting.

## Examination questions

### Question 1 (CIMA)

Z Ltd is considering various product pricing and material purchasing options with regard to a new product it has developed. Estimates of demand and costs are as follows:

| If selling price per unit is | £15 per unit<br>Sales volume<br>(000 units) | £20 per unit<br>Sales volume<br>(000 units) |
|---|---|---|
| Forecasts probability | | |
| Optimistic    0.3 | 36 | 28 |
| Most likely    0.5 | 28 | 23 |
| Pessimistic    0.2 | 18 | 13 |
| Variable manufacturing costs | | |
| (excluding materials) per unit | £3 | £3 |
| Advertising and selling costs | £25,000 | £96,000 |
| General fixed costs | £40,000 | £40,000 |

Each unit requires 3 kg of material and because of storage problems any unused material must be sold at £1 per kg. The sole suppliers of the material offer three purchase options, which must be decided at the outset, as follows:

(i)  any quantity at £3 per kg; or
(ii)  a price of £2.75 per kg for a minimum quantity of 50,000 kg; or
(iii)  a price of £2.50 per kg for a minimum quantity of 70,000 kg.

You are required, assuming the company is risk neutral, to:

(a)  Prepare calculations to show what pricing and purchasing decisions the company should make, clearly indicating the recommended decisions.
(b)  Calculate the maximum price you would pay for perfect information as to whether the demand would be optimistic or most likely or pessimistic.

### Answer 1

(a)  *Purchasing option (i)*

|                                | (£) |    |    |    | (£) |    |
|--------------------------------|----:|----|----|----|----:|----|
| Selling price                  | 15  |    |    |    | 20  |    |
| Variable manufacturing costs   | 3   |    |    |    | 3   |    |
| Gross contribution             | 12  |    |    |    | 17  |    |

|                                | (£000) |    |    |    | (£000) |    |
|--------------------------------|-------:|----|----|----|-------:|----|
| Advertising and selling costs  | 25     |    |    |    | 96     |    |
| General fixed costs            | 40     |    |    |    | 40     |    |
|                                | 65     |    |    |    | 136    |    |

| Sales (000)                          | 36     | 28     | 18     | 28     | 23     | 13     |
|--------------------------------------|-------:|-------:|-------:|-------:|-------:|-------:|
|                                      | (£000) | (£000) | (£000) | (£000) | (£000) | (£000) |
| Gross contribution                   | 432    | 336    | 216    | 476    | 391    | 221    |
| Materials at £3 per kg × 3 kg        | 324    | 252    | 162    | 252    | 207    | 117    |
| Total fixed costs                    | 65     | 65     | 65     | 136    | 136    | 136    |
| Conditional profit (loss)            | 43     | 19     | (11)   | 88     | 48     | (32)   |
| Probability                          | 0.3    | 0.5    | 0.2    | 0.3    | 0.5    | 0.2    |
| Expected profit (loss)               | 12.9   | 9.5    | (2.2)  | 26.4   | 24.0   | (6.4)  |
|                                      |        |        | 20.2   |        |        | 44.0   |

*Purchasing option (ii)*

| Sales (000) × 3 kg                   | 36     | 28     | 18     | 28     | 23     | 13     |
|--------------------------------------|-------:|-------:|-------:|-------:|-------:|-------:|
| Material usage (000 kg)              | 108    | 84     | 54     | 84     | 69     | 39     |
| Minimum purchase (50,000 km)         |        |        |        |        |        | 50     |
| Actual purchase                      | 108    | 84     | 54     | 84     | 69     |        |
| Returns                              |        |        |        |        |        | 11     |
| Purchase × £2.75                     | 297    | 231    | 148.5  | 231    | 189.75 | 137.5  |
| Less: Returns at £1                  |        |        |        |        |        | (11)   |
| Material cost (£000)                 | 297    | 231    | 148.5  | 231    | 189.75 | 126.5  |

|                                      | (£000) | (£000) | (£000) | (£000) | (£000) | (£000) |
|--------------------------------------|-------:|-------:|-------:|-------:|-------:|-------:|
| Gross contribution                   | 432    | 336    | 216    | 476    | 391    | 221    |
| Less material cost                   | 297    | 231    | 148.5  | 231    | 189.75 | 126.5  |
| Total fixed costs                    | 65     | 65     | 65     | 136    | 136    | 136    |
| Conditional profit (loss)            | 70     | 40     | 2.5    | 109    | 62.25  | (41.5) |
| Probability                          | 0.3    | 0.5    | 0.2    | 0.3    | 0.5    | 0.2    |
| Expected profit (loss)               | 21.0   | 20.0   | 0.5    | 32.7   | 32.625 | (8.3)  |
|                                      |        |        | 41.5   |        |        | 57.0   |

*Purchasing option (iii)*

| Sales (000) × 3 kg                   | 36     | 28     | 18     | 28     | 23     | 13     |
|--------------------------------------|-------:|-------:|-------:|-------:|-------:|-------:|
| Material usage (000 kg)              | 108    | 84     | 54     | 84     | 69     | 39     |
| Minimum purchase (50,000 km)         |        |        | 70     |        | 70     | 70     |
| Actual purchase                      | 108    | 84     |        | 84     |        |        |
| Returns                              |        |        | 16     |        | 1      | 31     |
| Purchase × £2.50                     | 270    | 210    | 175    | 210    | 175    | 175    |
| Less: Returns at £1                  |        |        | (16)   |        | (1)    | (31)   |
| Material cost (£000)                 | 270    | 210    | 159    | 210    | 174    | 144    |

|  | (£000) | (£000) | (£000) | (£000) | (£000) | (£000) |
|---|---|---|---|---|---|---|
| Gross contribution | 432 | 336 | 216 | 476 | 391 | 221 |
| Less material cost | 270 | 210 | 159 | 210 | 174 | 144 |
| Total fixed costs | 65 | 65 | 65 | 136 | 136 | 136 |
| Conditional profit (loss) | 97 | 61 | (8) | 130 | 81 | (59) |
| Probability | 0.3 | 0.5 | 0.2 | 0.3 | 0.5 | 0.2 |
| Expected profit (loss) | 29.1 | 30.5 | (1.6) | 39.0 | 40.5 | (11.8) |
|  |  |  | 58.0 |  |  | 67.7 |

The following combination offers the highest expected profit:
Selling price of £20 and purchase option (iii), £2.50 per kg for a minimum quantity of 70,000 kg.

(b) Purchasing option

| | | Conditional profit (£000) | |
|---|---|---|---|
| | Optimistic | Most likely | Pessimistic |
| (i) | 43/88 | 19/48 | (11)/(32) |
| (ii) | 70/109 | 40/65.25 | 2.5/(41.5) |
| (iii) | 97/130 | 61/81 | (8)/(59) |
| Select best result: | | | |
| Conditional profit | 130 | 81 | 2.5 |
| Probability | 0.4 | 0.5 | 0.2 |
| Expected profit | 39.0 | 40.5 | 0.5 |

|  | (£000) |
|---|---|
| Total expected profit with perfect information | 80.0 (39.0 + 40.5 + 0.5) |
| Expected profit per (a) above | 67.7 |
| Maximum price for perfect information | 12.3 |

## Question 2 (CIMA)

A national boutique chain sells a wide range of high quality customized fashion goods. One particular outfit is bought in at £80 and sold at £130. Mean holding costs per season per outfit work out at £5 and it costs £800 to order and receive goods into stock. The manufacturers require orders in advance and once a batch has been made, it is not possible to place a repeat order. Further, it is not possible for delivery to be staggered over the fashion season.

When a customer buys an outfit, she has a fitting, any alterations or adjustments are made, and she collects the outfit a day or so later. Generally, if an outfit is out of stock at one boutique it can be readily obtained from another branch, usually in a matter of hours. However, if the chain as a whole runs out of an item, then not only is the profit not earned, but the £20 or so profit that comes from the extras that customers buy is also lost. Should the chain over buy for a season then it is expected that the chain will be able to dispose of the surplus outfits at £50 each.

The pattern of past sales of a comparable outfit shows the following probability distribution for the chain as a whole.

| Outfits sold | Probability |
|---|---|
| 1100 | 0.30 |
| 1200 | 0.40 |
| 1300 | 0.20 |
| 1400 | 0.10 |

The problem facing the management accountants of the chain is to decide how many outfits to order for the season ahead in order to maximize expected profit, bearing in mind the penalties for over and under ordering.

You are required to:

(a)  Determine the number of outfits to order to maximize expected profits.
(b)  Compare and contrast the model that you have developed with the classical economic order model.

### Answer 2

(a)  Unit contribution £130 − (80 + 5) = £45

Unit loss when surplus sold £85 − 50 = £35

Unit penalty when demand not satisfied £20 per outfit not sold

Probability of sales levels:

| Sales | Probability |
|---|---|
| 1100 | 0.3 |
| 1200 | 0.4 |
| 1300 | 0.2 |
| 1400 | 0.1 |

*Contribution calculations*
(1100 units purchased)

| Demand | Contribution | £ |
|---|---|---|
| 1100 | 1100 × £45 | = 49,500 |
| 1200 | 1100 × £45 − 100 × £20 | = 47,500 |
| 1300 | 1100 × £45 − 200 × £20 | = 45,500 |
| 1400 | 1100 × £45 − 300 × £20 | = 43,500 |

(1200 units purchased)

| Demand | Contribution | £ |
|---|---|---|
| 1100 | 1100 × £45 − 100 × £35 | = 46,000 |
| 1200 | 1200 × £45 | = 54,000 |
| 1300 | 1200 × £45 − 100 × £20 | = 52,000 |
| 1400 | 1200 × £45 − 200 × £20 | = 50,000 |

(1300 units purchased)

| Demand | Contribution | £ |
|---|---|---|
| 1100 | 1100 × £45 − 200 × £35 | = 42,500 |
| 1200 | 1200 × £45 − 100 × £35 | = 50,500 |
| 1300 | 1300 × £45 | = 58,500 |
| 1400 | 1300 × £45 − 100 × £20 | = 56,500 |

(1400 units purchased)

| Demand | Contribution | £ |
|--------|-------------|---|
| 1100 | $1100 \times £45 - 300 \times £35 =$ | 39,000 |
| 1200 | $1200 \times £45 - 200 \times £35 =$ | 47,000 |
| 1300 | $1300 \times £45 - 100 \times £35 =$ | 55,000 |
| 1400 | $1400 \times £45$ $=$ | 63,000 |

*Summary of outcomes*

| Order quantity | 1100 | 1200 | Demand 1300 | 1400 | Expected value |
|----------------|------|------|------|------|----------------|
| 1100 | 49.5 | 47.5 | 45.5 | 43.5 | 47.3 |
| 1200 | 46.0 | 54.0 | 52.0 | 50.0 | 50.8 |
| 1300 | 42.5 | 50.5 | 58.5 | 56.5 | 50.3 |
| 1400 | 39.0 | 47.0 | 55.0 | 63.0 | 46.8 |
| Probability | 0.3 | 0.4 | 0.2 | 0.1 | |

Therefore on the basis of expected contribution, order 1200 outfits. (Note, the order/receipt costs of £800 are constant throughout and therefore have been ignored.)

(b) The above model is perhaps not sophisticated mathematically, but it does enable managers to cope with uncertainty. It clearly differs from the classic economic order quantity model at the most fundamental level in that in the latter model demand is known and certain whereas, in the former, the whole model is concerned with uncertain demand. Further, the basic EOQ model assumes no stock out situation and so does not give managers the tools to handle the case. A further development of the model does allow stock outs. The Marie-Claire model does not allow back ordering because of the fact that no repeat orders are possible. The main point to bear in mind concerning the EOQ model is that it was conceived in a manufacturing environment where the aim of the production manager is a constant usage of stock and where there is a regular replacement of items used up. Finally, in the Marie-Claire context, the £800 ordering cost is really irrelevant to the decision-making process because only one order is possible and so it may as well be merged into general overheads or fixed costs. In any case, it is not a material cost.

### Question 3 (CIMA)

Homeworker Ltd is a small company that manufactures a lathe attachment called the Homelathe for the DIY market. The data for manufacturing the attachment are as follows:

For each batch of 10 Homelathes

| Components | A | B | C | D | E | Total |
|---|---|---|---|---|---|---|
| Machine hours | 10 | 14 | 12 | | | 36 |
| Labour hours | | | | 2 | 1 | 3 |
| | (£) | (£) | (£) | (£) | (£) | (£) |
| Variable cost | 32 | 54 | 58 | 12 | 4 | 160 |
| Fixed cost (apportioned) | 48 | 102 | 116 | 24 | 26 | 316 |
| Total component costs | 80 | 156 | 174 | 36 | 30 | 476 |

Assembly costs (all variable)          £40 per 10

Selling price          £600 per 100

General purpose machinery is used to make components A, B and C and is already working to the maximum capability of 4752 hours and there is no possibility of increasing the machine capacity in the next period. There is labour available for making components D and E and for assembling the product.

The marketing department advises that there will be a 50 per cent increase in demand next period so the company has decided to buy one of the machine-made components from an outside supplier in order to release production capacity and thus help to satisfy demand.

A quotation has been received from General Machines Ltd for the components, but because this company has not made the components before, it has not been able to give single figure prices. Its quotation is as follows:

| Component | Pessimistic price probability (£) | | Most likely price probability (£) | | Optimistic price probability (£) | |
|---|---|---|---|---|---|---|
| A | 96 | 0.25 | 85 | 0.5 | 54 | 0.25 |
| B | 176 | 0.25 | 158 | 0.5 | 148 | 0.25 |
| C | 149 | 0.25 | 127 | 0.5 | 97 | 0.25 |

It has been agreed between the two components that audited figures would be used to determine which one of the three prices would be charged for whatever component is bought out.

As management accountant of Homeworker Ltd it is your responsibility to analyse the financial and production capacity effects of the proposed component purchase and you are required to:

(a) Show in percentage form the maximum increased production availability from the three alternatives, i.e. buying A or B or C.
(b) Analyse the financial implications of the purchase and, assuming a risk neutral attitude, recommend which component to buy out, noting that the production availability will be limited to a 50 per cent increase.
(c) Prepare a profit statement for the period assuming that the component chosen in (b) is bought out and that the extra production is made and sold (show your workings).
(d) State three other factors you would consider if you were advised that management had decided to avoid risk as much as possible

when buying out a component. (Calculations are not required for this section.)

## Answer 3

*Workings*
Present output
General purpose machinery

| | | |
|---|---|---|
| Capacity | | 4752 hours |
| Machine hours per batch of Homelathes | | |
| A | 10 hours | |
| B | 14 hours | |
| C | 12 hours | 36 hours |

| | |
|---|---|
| Present output | 132 batches |
| + 50% increase in demand | 66 batches |
| Projected output | 198 batches |

Present and projected fixed costs

| | | |
|---|---|---|
| TFC per batch | £316 | |
| | × | 132 batches |
| TFC | £41,712 | |

Expected price

| Probability | A | | B | | C | |
|---|---|---|---|---|---|---|
| | (£) | (£) | (£) | (£) | (£) | (£) |
| 0.25 | 96.00 | 24.00 | 176.00 | 44.00 | 149.00 | 37.25 |
| 0.50 | 85.00 | 42.50 | 158.00 | 79.00 | 127.00 | 63.50 |
| 0.25 | 54.00 | 13.50 | 148.00 | 37.00 | 97.00 | 24.50 |
| Expected price | | 80.00 | | 160.00 | | 125.00 |

Present contribution

| | | | |
|---|---|---|---|
| Per batch | | (£) | (£) |
| Selling price | | | 600 |
| Less: | | | |
| Variable production cost | | 160 | |
| Variable assembly costs | | 40 | 200 |
| | | | 400 |
| Present output | | | 132 batches |
| Present contribution | | | £52,800 |

(a)  *Increased production availability*

| | | | |
|---|---|---|---|
| Present capacity | | 4752 hours | 132 batches |
| (1)  Buy  A | — hours | | |
| Make B | 14 hours | | |
| Make C | 12 hours | | |
| | | 26 hours | |
| No of batches 4,752/26 | | | 182.8 |
| Increase = 50.8 batches | | | 38.5% |

(2)  Buy  B  — hours
     Make A  10 hours
     Make C  12 hours

                                22 hours
     No of batches 4,752/22                    216
     Increase = 84 batches                     63.6%

(3)  Buy  C  — hours
     Make A  10 hours
     Make B  14 hours

                                24 hours
     No of batches 4,752/24                    198
     Increase = 66 batches                     50%
Notes: Increase in market demand =  66 batches = 50%
       Market demand         = 198 batches

(b)  *Financial implications*

|  | A (£) | B (£) | C (£) |
|---|---|---|---|
| TVS per batch | 32 | 54 | 58 |
| Expected purchase price | 80 | 160 | 125 |
| Increase in VC per batch | 48 | 106 | 67 |
| Present contribution per batch | 400 | 400 | 400 |
| Revised contribution per batch | 352 | 294 | 333 |
| Revised number of batches | 182.8 | 198* | 198 |
| Revised contribution | £64,346 | £52,212 | £65,934 |

* limited to 50% increase.

Decision – buy out C; this offers the greatest revised contribution.

(c)  *Revised profit statement*

|  |  | Per batch (£) | Total (per 198 batches) (£) |
|---|---|---|---|
| Sales |  | 600 | 118,800 |
| Variable costs | (£) |  |  |
| Production A | 32 |  |  |
| B | 54 |  |  |
| C | 125 |  |  |
| D | 12 |  |  |
| E | 4 |  |  |
|  | 227 |  |  |
| Assembly | 40 | 267 | 52,866 |
| Contribution |  | 333 | 65,934 |
| Fixed cost |  |  | 41,712 |
| Profit |  |  | 24,222 |

(d) *Other factors in risk avoidance*

(i) Component prices and costs
The expected price of component C, £125, is based upon the prob-
abilities given. Even using these probabilities there is a 25 per
cent chance it could be as high as £149 per batch. Does General
Machines Ltd have any incentive to keep costs down if the price of
C is to be based on actual costs?

(ii) General Machines Ltd
Should Homeworker Ltd reply entirely on one supplier?
General Machines Ltd must be responsible for meeting delivery
dates, quality standards etc.

(iii) Matching of supply and demand
The projections show a perfect matching – 50 per cent in each
case, but market demand may possibly exceed 50 per cent. How
would Homeworker cope?

(iv) Would fixed cost actually remain constant given a 50 per cent
increase in output?

(v) How reliable is the marketing department's estimate of 50 per
cent increase in demand? Why has a range of probabilities not
been used?

## Question 4 (ACA)

The Alternative Sustenance Company is considering introducing a new
franchized product Wholefood Waffles.

Existing ovens now used for making some of the present 'Half-Baked'
range of products could be used instead for baking the Wholefood
Waffles. However, new special batch mixing equipment would be
needed. This cannot be purchased, but can be hired from the franchizer
in three alternative specifications, for batch sizes of 200, 300 and 600
units respectively. The annual cost of hiring the mixing equipment
would be £5000, £15,000 and £21,500 respectively.

The 'Half-Baked' product which would be dropped from the range
currently earns a contribution of £90,000 per annum, which it is con-
fidently expected could be continued if the product were retained in the
range.

The company's marketing manager considers that, at the market
price for Wholefood Waffles of 40 pence per unit, it is equally probable
that the demand for this product would be 600,000 or 1,000,000 units
per annum.

The company's production manager has estimated the variable cost
per unit of making Wholefood Waffles, and the probabilities of those
costs being incurred, as follows:

| Batch size | 200 units | 300 units | 600 units | 600 units |
|---|---|---|---|---|
| Cost per unit (pence) | | Probability if annual sales are | | |
| | either | either | | |
| | 600,000 or | 600,000 or | | |
| | 1,000,000 | 1,000,000 | 600,000 | 1,000,000 |
| | units | units | units | units |
| 20 | 0.1 | 0.2 | 0.3 | 0.5 |
| 25 | 0.1 | 0.5 | 0.1 | 0.2 |
| 30 | 0.8 | 0.3 | 0.6 | 0.3 |

You are required to:

(a)　(i)　draw a decision tree setting out the problem faced by the company; and

　　(ii)　show in each of the following three independent situations which size of mixing machine, if any the company should hire:

　　　1　to satisfy a 'maximin' criterion
　　　2　to maximize the expected value of contribution per annum
　　　3　to minimize the probability of earning annual contribution of less than £100,000.

(b)　Outline briefly the strengths and limitations of the methods of analysis which you have used in part (a) above.

### Answer 4

(a)(i)　See decision tree (Figure 6.7).

(ii)　The approach of the maximin criteria is rather negative, in that it attempts to avoid the worst outcomes. The decision maker selects the values of the worst possible outcome for each decision alternative. Then from this set of worst outcomes he selects the alternative with the largest payoff. From the decision tree the worst pay-offs are:

| | Payoff (£000) |
|---|---|
| Hire equipment 200 | 55.00 |
| Hire equipment 300 | 45.0 |
| Hire equipment 600 | 38.5 |
| Do not franchize | 90.0 |

The maximin decision is not to franchize.

2　The expected values for each decision alternative, see decision tree, are:

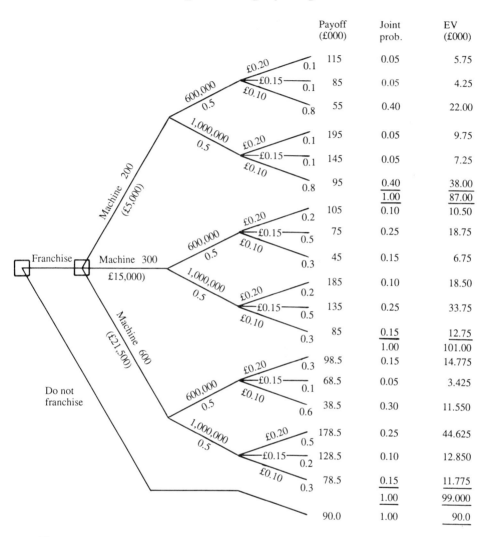

Figure 6.7

|  | Payoff (£000) |
|---|---|
| Hire equipment 200 | 87.0 |
| Hire equipment 300 | 101.0 |
| Hire equipment 600 | 99.0 |
| Do not franchize | 90.0 |

The expected value decision is to hire equipment 300 giving a maximum expected value of £101,000.

3   The probability of a contribution of less than £100,000 can be found for each decision alternative, by adding the joint probabilities for each payoff of less than £100,000.

|                       | Probability of less than £100,000 |
|-----------------------|:---------------------------------:|
| Hire equipment 200    | 0.85 |
| Hire equipment 300    | 0.55 |
| Hire equipment 600    | 0.65 |
| Do not franchize      | 1.00 |

The minimum probability solution is to hire equipment 300.

(b)   The approaches in part (a) enable uncertainty to be incorporated into the analysis and for decisions to be based on a range of outcomes rather than a single outcome. This result should produce better results in the long run. The main problem with this approach is that only a few selected outcomes with related probabilities are chosen as being representative of the entire distribution of possible outcomes. There is also a problem in determining the correct probabilities.

*Maximin*   A method that minimizes risk. This risk averse method does not lead to maximum long term profits. It may be seen as being too conservative, and can lead to inconsistency in decision making.

*Expected value*   Leads to maximum long term profits hence is appropriate in repetitive situations where the risk level is not high. It ignores risk (but in conjunction with the standard deviation this weakness may be overcome).

*Probability of less than £100,000*   This approach allows the decision maker to reduce the likelihood of an unsatisfactory outcome occurring.


## Further reading

Amey, L.R., Joint product decisions: The fixed proportion case, *Journal of Business Finance and Accounting*, **XI3**, 1984.

Driscoll, D.A., Lin, W.T. and Watkins, P.R., Cost–volume–profit analysis under uncertainty: a synthesis and framework for evaluation, *Journal of Accounting Literature*, **III**, Spring 1984.

Humphreys, R.G., *Analysis Uncertainty: An Introductory Workbook for Decision-making*, CIMA, 1978.

Scapens, R.W., Gameil, M.Y. and Cooper, J., Accounting information for pricing decisions, In Cooper, D. et al. (eds), *Management Accounting Research and Practice*, CIMA, 1983.

# 7 Budgeting and forecasting methods

## Introduction

A budget is a financial and/or quantitative plan for a defined period of time. It is usually prepared for one year, although it can be prepared for shorter periods in order to facilitate control.

Budgetary control is a control technique whereby actual and budgeted information are compared, and any differences, i.e. variances, are made the responsibility of certain managers who can either take the necessary control action or revise the original budgets.

Budgeting is therefore concerned with the planning and control functions of management accounting, which ensure that corporate goals are attained. The planning process involves cost estimation and allocating resources in order to achieve corporate objectives. Budgeting determines in detail how the resources are to be used.

## Advantages of budgeting

1   Budgetary control establishes a basis for internal audit by regularly evaluating departmental results.
2   Only reporting information which has not gone according to plan, it economizes on managerial time and maximizes efficiency. This is called management by exception reporting.
3   Scarce resources should be allocated in an optimal way, thus controlling expenditure.
4   It forces management to plan ahead so that long term goals are achieved.
5   Communication is increased throughout the firm and coordination should be improved. For example the purchasing department will base its budget on production requirements. This will reduce or prevent sub-optimality.

6   An effective budgetary control system will allow people to partici-pate in the setting of budgets, and thereby have a motivational impact on the workforce. Individual and corporate goals are aligned.

7   Areas of efficiency and inefficiency are identified. Variance analysis will prompt remedial action where necessary.

8   The budget provides a yardstick against which the performance of the firm can be evaluated. It is better to compare actual with budget rather than with the past, since the latter may no longer be suitable for current and expected conditions.

9   People are made responsible for items of cost and revenue, i.e. areas of responsibility are clearly delineated.

## Problems in budgeting

1   Budgets are perceived by the workforce as pressure devices imposed by top management. This can have an adverse effect on labour rela-tions.

2   It can be difficult to motivate an apathetic workforce.

3   The pressure in the budgeting system may result in inaccurate re-cord keeping.

4   Managers may overestimate costs in order that they will not be held responsible in the future should they overspend. The difference between the minimum necessary costs and the costs built into the budget is called slack.

5   Departmental conflict arises because of competition for resource allocation. Departments blame each other if targets are not achieved.

6   Uncertainties can occur in the system, e.g. uncertainty over demand, inflation, technological change, competition, the weather, etc.

7   It may be difficult to align individual and corporate goals. Indi-vidual goals often change and may be much lower than the firm's goals.

8   It is important to match responsibility with control, otherwise a manager will be demotivated. Costs can only be controlled by a mana-ger if they occur within a certain time span and can be influenced by that manager. A problem arises when a cost can be influenced by more than one person.

9   Managers are often accused of wasting expenditure when they either:

(a)   demand a greater budget allowance than is really needed, or
(b)   unnecessary spend in order to fully utilize their allowance through fear of future cut-backs.

Zero base budgeting can overcome this problem.

10   Sub-optimal decisions may arise when a manager tries to enhance his short run performance in a way which is detrimental to the orga-nization as a whole, e.g. delaying expenditure on urgently needed re-pairs.

## Budget organization and administration

An effective system of budgetary control should contain the following:

1 *Budget officer*, his task will be to control the budget administration. His duties include ensuring that deadlines are met, teaching people about budgetary control procedures, liaising between the budget committee and managers responsible for budgets are dealing with budgetary control problems.

2 *Budget committee*, this consists of senior managers and provides support to the budgetary control system. Other functions include establishing long term goals, authorizing the master budget, reviewing budgets and reviewing of actual results compared with budgets.

3 *Budget centres*, these are clearly defined parts of the firm where responsibility lies for the preparation of budgets.

4 *Budget manual*, this is a clearly defined rule book which provides details of budgetary control procedures. It delineates areas of responsibility and contains timetable, account codes and standardized forms to be used.

## Budgets for planning and budgets for control purposes

Planning budgets reflect management's real beliefs. However control budgets are based, for motivational reasons, on standards which are unlikely to reflect actual levels of achievement, e.g. if management believes that a strike is likely to happen, the potential effects of the strike will not be shown in the departmental budgets. In practice it can be confusing to have two types of budgets and a single compromise budget is usually employed.

The similarities and differences between planning and control budgets are as follows:

1 Both types of budgets must be flexible – planning budgets to change in circumstances, and control budgets to changes in activity levels.

2 They both need feedback in order to evaluate performance and ensure that standards are up to date.

3 Control budgets analyse costs and revenues on a departmental basis, whereas planning budgets analyse costs and revenues on a product line basis.

4 Planning budgets are prepared for the whole firm whereas control budgets can be sectionalized.

5 Participation is encouraged in control budgets but not in planning budgets.

6 In planning budgets the standards reflect what management believe will happen. However, in control budgets the standards are set to influence behaviour in a way which is beneficial to the organization.

## Budget preparation

Since the output of most firms is determined by demand, the limiting budget factor is sales, and is usually the first budget to be prepared.

1  *Sales budget* is based on a realistic sales forecast and expressed in financial and quantitative terms. Sales forecasting methods include market research, expert opinions and statistical techniques such as moving averages and exponential smoothing. When forecasting demand it is important to consider economic and political conditions, competition, the availability of substitute products, consumers' tastes and incomes, sales promotion techniques and the company's pricing policy.

2  *Production budget* is geared to the sales budget and expressed in quantitative terms (i.e. units). The production manager will have to consider capacity requirements to satisfy demand, i.e. should he subcontract, introduce overtime or shiftwork, hire or buy additional plant.

3  *Raw materials and purchasing budget*, the materials usage budget is expressed in quantitative terms, i.e. units of raw material, whereas the purchases budget is quantitative and financial.

These budgets are geared to production requirements and will recognize planned stock levels, storage space, normal loss and material price inflation.

*Labour budget* is geared to the production budget and expressed in quantitative (standard hours) and financial terms. It is influenced by the grades of labour required, man hours available, wage rates, wage inflation, union agreements and the need for bonus schemes.

*Cash budget* is a cash plan for a defined period of time. It is comprised of monthly cash receipts and payments, resulting in monthly surpluses and/or deficits.

Its main uses are:

(a)   to enable a firm to take precautionary measures and arrange for investment and loan facilities when budgeted surplus and deficits are anticipated;
(b)   to show how feasible management's plans are in terms of cash resources;
(c)   to exercise control over a firm's cash requirements and thereby maintain the correct level of liquidity;
(d)   to illustrate the financial impact of some major changes in corporate policy, e.g. a change in the firm's credit control policy.

The master budget encompasses all of the above budgets plus other budgets for research and development, advertising, administration, selling and distribution expenses, working capital and capital expenditure.

In the example that follows try and prepare the required budgets before looking at the solution. The solution illustrates a mechanical step-by-step approach to formulating a master budget.

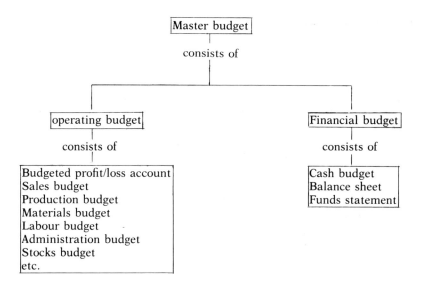

## Example 1

B Ltd manufactures three types of product for the building industry. Budgeted sales of the products A, B and C are as follows:

| Product | Quantity | Price (£) |
|---------|----------|-----------|
| A | 3000 | 60 |
| B | 7000 | 70 |
| C | 5000 | 80 |

Materials used in manufacture of the company's products are:

| Components | X1 | X2 | X3 | X4 |
|------------|----|----|----|----|
| Component unit cost | £2 | £3 | £4 | £5 |
| Quantities used; | | | | |
| A | 5 | 3 | 1 | 2 |
| B | 4 | 4 | 2 | 3 |
| C | 3 | 2 | 1 | 5 |

Two types of labour are used, fitters and machinists, the standard unit times for each product being:

| | Fitters (Hourly rate £0.50) (hours) | Machinists (Hourly rate £0.60) (hours) |
|---|---|---|
| A | 3 | 1.5 |
| B | 4 | 2 |
| C | 5 | 2.5 |

Production overheads which are absorbed into product costs on a direct basis are budgeted as follows:

|  | (£) |
|---|---|
| Building occupancy | 30,050 |
| Equipment utilization | 16,100 |
| Personal services | 12,150 |
| Materials handling | 9,310 |
| Production planning and control | 9,790 |

Selling and distribution costs budgeted are:

|  | (£) |
|---|---|
| Representation | 101,300 |
| Sales office | 30,100 |
| Advertising and publicity | 29,100 |

and are charged to products in proportion to the sales income of the period.

Stocks at the beginning of the budget period are expected to be:

| Finished goods | Quantity | £ unit cost |
|---|---|---|
| A | 1000 | 39 |
| B | 3000 | 51 |
| C | 2000 | 51 |

| Components | Quantity | £ unit cost |
|---|---|---|
| X1 | 40,000 | 2 |
| X2 | 20,000 | 3 |
| X3 | 10,000 | 4 |
| X4 | 30,000 | 5 |

The company plans an increase of 10 per cent in quantities of finished stocks held at the end of the budget period, and a reduction of 20 per cent in the quantities of component stocks.

(a) Prepare budgets for:

   (i) sales;
   (ii) production;
   (iii) material usage;
   (iv) material purchases;
   (v) direct labour.

(b) Prepare a statement showing the valuation of finished stocks at the end of the budget period.

(c) Prepare a budget profit statement for the period, showing the amount of profit contributed by each product.

*Solution*

(a)(i) *Sales budget*

| Product | Quantity | Selling price (£) | Sales volume (£) |
|---|---|---|---|
| A | 3000 | 60 | 180,000 |
| B | 7000 | 70 | 490,000 |
| C | 5000 | 80 | 400,000 |
| | | | £1,070,000 |

(ii) *Production budget*

| Product | Sales budget | Stock increases | Products |
|---|---|---|---|
| A | 3000 | 100 | 3100 |
| B | 7000 | 300 | 7300 |
| C | 5000 | 200 | 5200 |

(iii) *Materials usage budget*

| Product | X1 | Components X2 | X3 | X4 |
|---|---|---|---|---|
| A | 15,500 | 9,300 | 3,100 | 6,200 |
| B | 29,200 | 29,200 | 14,600 | 21,900 |
| C | 15,600 | 10,400 | 5,200 | 26,000 |
| | 60,300 | 48,900 | 22,900 | 54,100 |

(iv) *Materials purchases budget*

| Total | X1 | Components X2 | X3 | X4 | |
|---|---|---|---|---|---|
| Budgeted usage | 60,300 | 48,900 | 22,900 | 54,100 | |
| Stock decrease | 8,000 | 4,000 | 2,000 | 6,000 | |
| Purchase quantities | 52,300 | 44,900 | 20,900 | 48,100 | |
| | (£) | (£) | (£) | (£) | (£) |
| Cost prices | 2 | 3 | 4 | 5 | |
| Purchase values | 104,600 | 134,700 | 83,600 | 240,500 | 563,400 |

(v) *Direct labour utilization and cost budget*

| Product | Production budget | Fitters | Machinist | Total |
|---|---|---|---|---|
| A | 3,100 | 9,300 | 4,650 | |
| B | 7,300 | 29,200 | 14,600 | |
| C | 5,200 | 26,000 | 13,000 | |
| Total direct labour hours | | 64,500 | 32,250 | |
| | | Fitters | Machinists | |
| Budgeted labour rates | | £0.50 | £0.60 | |
| Total direct labour costs | | £32,250 | £19,350 | £51,600 |

(b)   *Finished stock valuation*

| Product | Quantity | Unit cost £ | Stock value £ |
|---|---|---|---|
| A | 1,100 | 39 | 42,900 |
| B | 3,300 | 51 | 168,300 |
| C | 2,200 | 51 | 112,200 |
| | | | £323,400 |

(c)   *Budgeted profit statement*

| | A | | B | | C | | Total |
|---|---|---|---|---|---|---|---|
| Sales units | 3000 | per unit | 7000 | per unit | 5000 | per unit | 15,000 |
| | (£) | (£) | (£) | (£) | (£) | (£) | (£) |
| Sales revenue | 180,000 | 60 | 490,000 | 70.00 | 400,000 | 80 | 1,070,000 |
| Production cost | 117,000 | 39 | 357,000 | 51.00 | 255,000 | 51 | 729,000 |
| Selling and distribution costs | 27,000 | 9 | 73,500 | 10.50 | 60,000 | 12 | 160,500 |
| Profit | £36,000 | 12 | 59,500 | 8.5 | 85,000 | 17 | 180,500 |

*Workings*
Calculation of unit product costs

(i)   Components (usage and costs per materials budget)

| | | A | (£) | B | (£) | B | (£) |
|---|---|---|---|---|---|---|---|
| | X1 | 10 | | 8 | | 6 | |
| | X2 | 9 | | 12 | | 6 | |
| | X3 | 4 | | 8 | | 4 | |
| | X4 | 10 | | 15 | | 25 | |
| | | 33 | | 43 | | 41 | |

(ii)   Direct labour hours (hours and rates per direct labour budgets)

| | A | B | B |
|---|---|---|---|
| Fitter | 1.5 | 2.0 | 2.5 |
| Machinist | 0.9 | 1.2 | 1.5 |
| | 2.4 | 3.2 | 4.0 |

(iii)   Production overheads:
Total overheads:

£(30,050 + 16,100 + 12,150 + 9,310 + 9,790) = £77,400

Total direct labour

(64,500 + 32,250) = 96,750

Therefore rate per hour (77,400 divided by 96,750) = £0.80

| | A | | B | | C | |
|---|---|---|---|---|---|---|
| | Hr | £ | Hr | £ | Hr | £ |
| | 4.5 | 3.60 | 6.0 | 4.80 | 7.5 | 6.0 |

(iv) Unit cost of production

| | A (£) | B (£) | C (£) |
|---|---|---|---|
| Components | 33.00 | 43.00 | 41.00 |
| Labour | 2.40 | 3.20 | 4.00 |
| Overheads | 3.60 | 4.80 | 6.00 |
| | £39.00 | £51.00 | £51.00 |

(v) Apportionment of selling and distribution costs:

$$\frac{\text{Total costs}}{\text{Sales value}} = \frac{£160,500}{£1,070,000} = 15\%$$

| | A (£) | B (£) | C (£) |
|---|---|---|---|
| Selling price | 60 | 70 | 80 |
| Selling and distribution | 9 | 10.5 | 12 |

*Example 2*

Textiles Ltd operates a subsidiary, the Sunny Textile Company Ltd, which manufactures ladies swimwear. Following the success of this subsidiary it has been decided to expand it by diversifying into the production of swimwear for all the family. An extension to the Sunny Textile Company Ltd's factory is now being built for this purpose. The contract for this extension is for £100,000. Ten per cent of the contract price had to be paid on signing the contract in December 19X5. Another £50,000 has to be paid on the 30 March 19X6 with the balance due no later than 30 May 19X6 on completion.

The financial year of the Sunny Textile Company Ltd runs from April and budgeted figures for the 19X6 calendar year have been produced as follows:

| Month | Sales (before discounts allowed) (£) | Purchase of raw materials (before discounts received) (£) | Wages (£) | Fixed overheads including depreciation of £1,000 per month (£) |
|---|---|---|---|---|
| Jan | 6,000 | 10,000 | 5,000 | 2,000 |
| Feb | 6,000 | 10,000 | 5,000 | 2,000 |
| Mar | 24,000 | 10,000 | 5,000 | 2,000 |
| Apr | 48,000 | 10,000 | 5,000 | 2,000 |
| May | 48,000 | 10,000 | 5,000 | 2,000 |
| Jun | 48,000 | 10,000 | 5,000 | 7,000 |
| Jul | 24,000 | 10,000 | 5,000 | 2,000 |
| Aug | 12,000 | — | 4,000 | 2,000 |
| Sep | 2,000 | 10,000 | 5,000 | 2,000 |
| Oct | 4,000 | 10,000 | 5,000 | 2,000 |
| Nov | 4,000 | 10,000 | 5,000 | 2,000 |
| Dec | 2,000 | 10,000 | 6,000 | 7,000 |
| Total | £228,000 | £110,000 | £60,000 | £34,000 |

In budgeting cash at bank on 1 April 10X6 at £50,000 the company has overlooked the contract payment for the factory extension due on 30 March 19X6.

Although the Sunny Textile Company Ltd requires payment for its sales in the month following that in which the sale is made, and offers a settlement discount of five per cent for accounts settled within this period, experience has taught it to expect only half the payments when due. One-quarter of the payments following during the second month after sale and the balance comes in the third month. Bad debts average 2.5 per cent of sales.

It is the company's policy to pay for supplies during the month in which they are delivered in order to take advantage of the ten per cent prompt settlement discount offered by all its suppliers.

The level of stocks at the end of December 19X6 are expected to remain unchanged from those prevailing in January. These are valued on a variable cost basis. The architect issued a final certificate for the factory extension on 19 April.

You are required to prepare for the Sunny Textile Company Ltd

(i)   a budgeted profit and loss account;
(ii)  a cash budget for a monthly basis;

both for the six months commencing 1 April 19X6, stating clearly any assumptions that you need to make.

*Solution*
(i)  Budgeted profit and loss account for the six months commencing 1 April 19X6

|  | (£) | (£) | (£) |
|---|---|---|---|
| Sales |  | 182,000 |  |
| Less discounts (5% of £91,000) | 4,550 |  |  |
| Bad debts (2.5% of £182,000) | 4,550 |  |  |
|  |  | 9,100 |  |
|  |  |  | 172,900 |
|  |  |  |  |
| Less: expenses and costs: |  |  |  |
| Discounts received (10% of £50,000) |  | (5,000) |  |
| *Material costs of sales (48.25% of revenue) |  | 87,800 |  |
| *Wages (26.3% of revenue) |  | 47,900 |  |
| Fixed overheads |  | 11,000 |  |
| Depreciation |  | 6,000 |  |
|  |  |  | 147,000 |
| Budget net profit |  |  | £25,200 |

*Workings*
To ascertain the material and labour cost of sales for the six month period a decrease in the volume of stocks over the period must be recognized. A percentage cost of materials and labour to sales for the

| Month | Apr | May | Jun | Jul | Aug | Sep | Total |
|---|---|---|---|---|---|---|---|
| Balance of cash | 0 | (750) | (25,600) | (5,400) | 25,200 | 54,400 | 0 |
| Cash from sales | | | | | | | |
| Jan | 1,350 | | | | | | 1,350 |
| Feb | 1,500 | 1,350 | | | | | 2,850 |
| Mar | 11,400 | 6,000 | 5,400 | | | | 22,800 |
| Apr | | 22,800 | 12,000 | 10,800 | | | 45,600 |
| May | | | 22,800 | 12,000 | 10,800 | | 45,600 |
| Jun | | | | 22,800 | 12,000 | 10,800 | 45,600 |
| Jul | | | | | 11,400 | 6,000 | 17,400 |
| Aug | | | | | | 5,700 | 5,700 |
| Cash received from debtors | 14,250 | 30,150 | 40,200 | 45,600 | 34,200 | 22,500 | 186,900 |
| Payment | | | | | | | |
| Suppliers | 9,0000 | 9,000 | 9,000 | 9,000 | 0 | 9,000 | 45,000 |
| Wages | 5,000 | 5,000 | 5,000 | 5,000 | 4,000 | 5,000 | 29,000 |
| Fixed overheads | 1,000 | 1,000 | 6,000 | 1,000 | 1,000 | 1,000 | 11,000 |
| Building | | 40,000 | | | | | 40,000 |
| Total | 15,000 | 55,000 | 20,000 | 15,000 | 5,000 | 15,000 | 125,000 |
| Balance | (750) | (25,600) | (5,400) | 25,200 | 54,400 | 61,900 | 61,900 |

Figure 7.1 *Cash budget for the six months commencing 1 April 19X6 in £s*

year is taken as applicable to the six month period, as a basis for cost of sales (and conversely stock valuation).

$$* \text{Materials} = \frac{£110,000}{£228,000} \times 100 = 48.25\%$$

$$* \text{Labour} = \frac{£60,000}{£228,000} \times 100 = 26.3\%$$

Fixed overheads are treated as period expenses, and therefore problems of stock valuation do not arise.

Discounts received have been treated as financial items in the period in which the discount is taken (see Figure 7.1).

## Flexible budgets

All budgets discussed so far have been fixed (inflexible), i.e. tailored to a single level of activity. In contracts, flexible budgets are prepared for a range of activity levels in order to provide a basis for comparison with actual.

*Example*
The planned level of activity for a machining department is 10,000 finished units for next month, with the following budgeted variable overhead:

|                 | (£)  |
|-----------------|------|
| Indirect labour | 4200 |
| Material        | 1000 |
| Maintenance     | 800  |
|                 | 6000 |

Actual output was only 9400 units and the actual variable overhead was:

|                 | (£)  |
|-----------------|------|
| Indirect labour | 4160 |
| Material        | 960  |
| Maintenance     | 800  |
|                 | 5920 |

*Performance report: variable overhead*

|                 | Actual | Budget | Variance       |
|-----------------|--------|--------|----------------|
| Units           | 9400   | 10,000 | 600 Adverse    |
|                 | (£)    | (£)    | (£)            |
| Indirect labour | 4160   | 4200   | 40 Favourable  |
| Material        | 960    | 1000   | 40 Favourable  |
| Maintenance     | 800    | 800    | —              |
|                 | 5920   | 6000   | 80 Favourable  |

The above report illustrates that comparing performance at one activity level with a plan developed at some other activity level is wrong from the viewpoint of judging how efficiently a manager has produced a given output.

*The flexible budget: variable overhead*

| Units produced  | per unit | 9200 | 9400 | 9600 | 10,000 | 10,400 |
|-----------------|----------|------|------|------|--------|--------|
|                 | (£)      |      |      |      |        |        |
| Indirect labour | 0.42     | 3864 | 3948 | 4032 | 4200   | 4368   |
| Materials       | 0.10     | 920  | 940  | 960  | 1,000  | 1,040  |
| Maintenance     | 0.08     | 736  | 752  | 768  | 800    | 832    |
|                 | £0.60    | 5520 | 5640 | 5760 | 6000   | 6240   |

The actual output was 9400 units, and a better indication of true performance would be as follows:

|                 | Actual | Budget | Variance    |
|-----------------|--------|--------|-------------|
| Units           | 9400   | 9400   | —           |
|                 | (£)    | (£)    | (£)         |
| Indirect labour | 4160   | 3948   | 212 Adverse |
| Materials       | 960    | 940    | 20 Adverse  |
| Maintenance     | 800    | 752    | 48 Adverse  |
|                 | 5920   | 5640   | 280 Adverse |

The flexible budget presents a more meaningful comparison of the manager's day-to-day overhead cost control because the level of activity underlying the comparison is the same.

The problem of measuring and reporting the resulting variances is dealt with in the chapters on standard costing and variance analysis.

The flexible budget approach is based on an adequate knowledge of cost behaviour patterns. Cost behaviour and methods of cost classification have been discussed in Chapter 1.

*Example 4*

Thomas Ltd is a small firm which manufactures cleaning fluid. Its management realize that, as a small company it must constantly strive to control and reduce costs in order to be competitive. The accounting department provided the following information to aid the planning process:

Plant capacity 2,250,000 gallons of cleaning fluid per year. Selling price will average an expected 52 p per gallon next year.

| | Worst | | | Best | Actual |
|---|---|---|---|---|---|
| Gallons of product sold in (000s) | 1,200 | 1,400 | 1,750 | 2,000 | 1,800 |
| | (£) | (£) | (£) | (£) | (£) |
| Revenue from sales | 600,000 | 650,000 | 750,000 | 900,000 | 850,000 |
| Cost of goods sold: | | | | | |
| Materials | 300,000 | 340,000 | 375,000 | 500,000 | 495,000 |
| Labour | 120,000 | 154,000 | 200,000 | 250,000 | 240,000 |
| Factory overhead | 17,000 | 19,000 | 22,500 | 25,000 | 23,000 |
| Total | 437,000 | 513,000 | 597,500 | 775,000 | 758,000 |
| Gross profit | £163,000 | 137,000 | 152,500 | 125,000 | 92,000 |
| Marketing expenses | 16,000 | 16,000 | 18,000 | 20,000 | 20,000 |
| Administration expenses | 30,000 | 30,000 | 30,000 | 30,000 | 30,000 |
| Total | 46,000 | 46,000 | 48,000 | 50,000 | 50,000 |
| Net profit before tax | £117,000 | 91,000 | 104,500 | 75,000 | 42,000 |

Prior to his resignation, the former chief accountant had devised a standard labour cost for 19X6 at 10.909p per gallon for the entire process. An examination of the figures indicates that they are quite adequate except for an expected rise of ten per cent in wage rates since 19X6 prices. The average cost of the mix of materials was 26p per gallon of fluid. Materials usage seldom varies. Overhead expenses are anticipated to remain at 19X6 price levels.

Prepare a flexible budget in profit statement form for the year 19X7, to cover a range from 1,250,000 to 2,250,000 gallons, with increments of 250,000 gallons. Use the high and low method in segregating the fixed and variable elements of any semi-variable expenses. You may assume that only administrative expenses are fixed costs.

*Solution*

Profit statement for the year 19X7

| | | | | | |
|---|---|---|---|---|---|
| Sales (gallons) | 1,250,000 | 1,500,000 | 1,750,000 | 2,000,000 | 2,250,000 |
| Revenue (£) | | | | | |
| 52p/gall | 650,000 | 780,000 | 910,000 | 1,040,000 | 1,170,000 |
| Cost of goods sold | | | | | |
| Materials (26p/gall) | 325,000 | 390,000 | 455,000 | 520,000 | 585,000 |
| Labour (12p/gall) | 150,000 | 180,000 | 210,000 | 240,000 | 270,000 |
| Factory overhead | | | | | |
| Fixed | 5,000 | 5,000 | 5,000 | 5,000 | 5,000 |
| Variable | 12,500 | 15,000 | 17,500 | 20,000 | 22,500 |
| Total | £492,500 | 590,000 | 687,500 | 785,000 | 882,500 |
| Gross profit | £157,500 | 190,000 | 222,500 | 255,000 | 287,500 |
| Marketing expenses | | | | | |
| Fixed | 10,000 | 10,000 | 10,000 | 10,000 | 10,000 |
| Variable | 6,250 | 7,500 | 8,750 | 10,000 | 11,250 |
| Admin. expenses | 30,000 | 30,000 | 30,000 | 30,000 | 30,000 |
| Total | £46,250 | 47,500 | 48,750 | 50,000 | 51,250 |
| Net profit | £111,250 | 142,500 | 173,750 | 205,000 | 236,250 |

Workings*

Factory overheads

| | Gallons (000s) | Total cost (£) |
|---|---|---|
| High | 2000 | 25,000 |
| Low | 1200 | 17,000 |
| Difference | 800 | 8,000 |

$$\frac{8000}{800 \text{ galls}} = £10 - \text{Variable cost per gallon}$$

$2000 \times £10 =$ £20,000 Variable factory overhead
£25,000 Total factory costs
£5,000 Fixed factory overhead

Marketing expenses are segregated into fixed and variable elements in the same way.

# Zero based budgeting (ZBB)

Zero based budgeting is a method of budgeting whereby all activities are re-evaluated each time a budget is formulated. It involves starting from zero, i.e. justifying every item of expenditure in the budget.

### Application of ZBB

1   Each manager's area of control is analysed into separate activities. The documents which identify and describe these specific activities are called decision packages.

2   Each decision package must be justified, i.e. does it promote the firm's goals?
3   If justified, then the minimum effort required to sustain each package is costed.
4   Are there any cheaper alternatives for each package?
5   Incremental decision packages are similarly justified and costed. These packages describe the costs and benefits of additional work that could be done above that required by the base package for the minimum amount of work needed to carry out the activity.
6   Decision packages are ranked in order of priority for resource allocation.
7   Resources are allocated to the packages.

### Advantages of ZBB

1   It should improve the allocation of resources.
2   Communication within the firm is increased.
3   Increased participation in the ZBB process should have a motivational impact.
4   It should ensure that the best methods of performing jobs are used, and that new ideas emerge.
5   Wastage and obsolete operations should be clearly identified and eliminated.
6   Decision packages improve coordination within the firm.
7   ZBB is particularly useful for service departments where it can be difficult to identify output. Last year's budgets tend to be subjectively increased to allow for next year's budgeted expenditure, thus resulting in inefficiency and wastage. ZBB should overcome this problem.
8   Managers are made more aware of the value of inputs, which helps them to identify priorities.

### Disadvantages of ZBB

1   Bad managers feel threatened by ZBB and may resist new ideas and changes.
2   It is expensive to justify and requires a vast number of decision packages in a large firm. This involves a large amount of extra paperwork.
4   ZBB may emphasize short-term benefits at the expense of long-term benefits.
5   Some activities have qualitative rather than quantitative benefits, e.g. money spent on working conditions.
6   The ranking of decision packages and the allocation of resources is subjective, which can result in departmental conflict.

## Uncertainty in budgeting

It was mentioned earlier in this chapter (see page 140) that uncertainty is a major problem in budgeting. There are many ways of dealing with uncertainty some of which are described elsewhere in this book, e.g. the use of probabilities to ascertain expected values, simulation and sensitivity analysis. Other methods include market research, shorter budget periods, Government indices to allow for inflation, rolling budgets and certain forecasting techniques. These last two methods are now described in more detail.

## Rolling budgets

This involves continuous budgeting, i.e. extending the current budget by an extra period (month or quarter) as the current period ends. The budget is therefore continuously updated so that it reflects current conditions.

The advantages of rolling budgets include the following: they reduce uncertainty in budgeting, make performance evaluation more meaningful, force managers to regularly reconsider the budget, the use of up-to-date information in them has a motivational impact on the work force.

Their disadvantages include the following:

(a)   The extra clerical work involved is time consuming and costly.
(b)   The problem of persuading managers that the benefits of this continuous updating process are worthwhile.
(c)   The problem of deciding whether the budgets should be updated on a monthly or quarterly basis.
(d)   If stock valuations and wage incentive schemes are based on standard costs then the budget revision will require stocks to be revalued and wage incentive schemes to be reset.

## Cost reduction techniques

Budgetary control is a cost control technique whereby costs are contained within some predetermined target. Budgetary control should be distinguished from cost reduction, which results in costs being reduced from some predetermined norm, while maintaining the functional value of the product or service.

Unnecessary costs arise because of inefficiency, lack of information, and absence of new ideas and a resistance to change. It is therefore useful to apply cost reduction programmes to certain areas such as material, financial and labour costs.

(a)   *Work study*
Work study investigates every aspect of existing or proposed work in order to find the best way of performing tasks. It involves setting standards and solving problems which include bottlenecks, low morale, large amounts of defective work and low productivity. Work study is comprised of method study and work measurement.

*Method study* is usually undertaken in the following stages.

1 The area of study is defined. This will be determined by cost/benefit considerations.
2 Information is gathered by observing and interviewing employees. Flow charts and management reports are analysed.
3 Alternative methods of performing work are considered. This process involves analysing current methods used and the following questions are asked:

Is the job and all aspects of it necessary?
Is the best equipment used?
Are controls adequate?
Do bottlenecks and idle time occur?
Is the standard set for the job acceptable?
4 The best alternative is developed and installed.
5 Feedback is obtained and progress is monitored.

*Work measurement* determines the time it should take an average worker to perform a particular job at an acceptable standard of performance. Statistical sampling techniques can be applied to mass labour in order to measure the time taken by employees to perform their tasks. Method study is carried out before work measurement.

(b) *Value analysis*
Value analysis examines all aspects of an existing or proposed product or component, in order to reduce costs, whilst maintaining or improving quality. It is particularly useful in areas of design, planning, buying and manufacturing.

The stages involved in a value analysis programme are the same as those for method study, except that in the third stage the following questions are asked:

Is the product and all its features necessary?
Is there a better alternative product or component?
Can it be standarized?
Can a cheaper material be used in its manfucture?
Are components and products stored in the optimal way?

It is important to note that standardization will result in longer production runs, and therefore lower unit costs. However, a reduction in the variety of product may have an adverse effect on customer goodwill.

## Limitations of cost reduction schemes

1 These schemes are undertaken by experts whose services are expensive.
2 Some employees may feel threatened and pressurized by these schemes, and will therefore resist change.

3   They are usually carried out on an ad hoc basis but should be reformed on a continual process, embracing all activities, where cost effective.
4   They are often applied hurriedly to achieve short-run benefits, resulting in harmful long-term effects.

Cost reduction schemes, which are designed to reduce expenditure, should be long-term, cost effective programes. They will cover all important areas of activity in a firm, including expenditure on energy.

## Forecasting

A budget is a plan, whereas a forecast is a prediction of future events and conditions. Forecasts are needed in order to prepare budgets. The sales manager will prepare sales forecasts and the production manager will forecast production resource requirements.

In forecasting events that will occur in the future, a forecaster must rely on information concerning events that have occurred in the past. That is, in order to prepare a forecast, the forecaster must analyse past data and must base the forecast on the results of the analysis. Forecasters use past data in the following way:

1   The forecaster analyses the data in order to identify a pattern that can be used to describe it.
2   The pattern is extrapolated, or extended, into the future in order to prepare a forecast.

This basic strategy is employed in most forecasting techniques and rests on the assumption that the pattern that has been identified will continue in the future. A forecasting technique cannot be expected to give good predictions unless this assumption is valid. If the data pattern that has been identified does not persist in the future, the forecasting technique being used will likely produce inaccurate predictions. A forecaster should not be surprised by such a situation, but rather must try to anticipate when such a change in pattern will take place so that appropriate changes in the forecasting system can be made before the predictions become too inaccurate.

There is no one single best forecasting model available. In fact, there are many forecasting methods that can be used to predict future events. The problem is finding a forecasting model that matches the pattern of historical data that is available.

## Forecasting methods

Forecasting methods can be classified initially into two types; qualitative methods and quantitative methods.

## Qualitative forecasting methods

Qualitative forecasting methods generally use the opinions of experts to subjectively predict future events. Such methods are often required when historical data either is not available at all or scarce, e.g. if a new product is being introduced, no past sales data for that product will exist. In order to forecast sales for the new product, a company must rely on expert opinion, which can be supplied by members of its sales force and market research team. Historical data will also not exist if a company is trying to predict when new technology will emerge. This might be critical to a company if the emergence of a new technology means that an existing product might become obsolete.

There are several qualitative forecasting methods of which the following three methods are the most widely used.

### Subjective curve fitting

Consider the case of a company introducing a new product and wishing to forecast sales of the product over the next three years. When predicting sales of a new product, it might be appropriate to consider the 'product life cycle'. The product life cycle model splits the life of the product into three stages, growth, maturity and decline. During the growth stage the sales of the product start slowly, then increase rapidly, and then continue to increase at a slower rate. During the maturity stage, sales of the product stabilize, increase slowly, reach a plateau and then decrease slowly. During the decline stage, sales of the product decline at an increasing rate (see Figure 7.2).

When forecasting sales of the product during the growth stage, the company might use the expert opinion of its sales and marketing personnel to subjectively construct an S-curve (see the shape of the curve in the growth stage in Figure 7.2). The S-curve could then be used to forecast sales during this stage. The company must use its experience with other products, and knowledge concerning the new product, in constructing the S-curve. It will need to determine how long it will take for the rapid increase in sales to begin, how long this rapid growth will continue, and when sales of the product will begin to stabilize. Estimating such a curve is an example of subjective curve fitting. In general the difficulty is in deciding on the form of the curve to be used. In a product life cycle situation the use of an S-curve may be appropriate. But many other functional forms can be used. For example, an exponential curve or a logarithmic curve might be appropriate. Thus, the forecaster must first subjectively determine the form of the curve to be used. The subjective construction of such curves is very difficult and requires a great deal of expertise and judgement.

### Delphi method

This technique involves using a panel of experts to produce predictions concerning a specific question, such as when a new development would

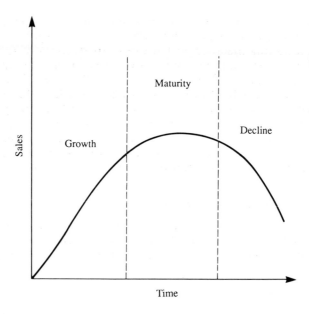

Figure 7.2    *Product life style*

occur. The use of the Delphi method assumes that the panel members are recognized experts, and it also assumes that the combined knowledge of the panel members will produce predictions at least as good as those that would be produced by one member. The Delphi method keeps the panel members physically separated. Each participant is asked to respond to a series of questionnaires and to return the completed questionnaires to a panel chairman. When the first questionnaire is complete subsequent questionnaires are accompanied by information concerning the opinions of the group as a whole. Thus, the participants can review their predictions relative to the group response. It is hoped that after several rounds of questionnaires the group response will converge on a consensus that can be used as a forecast. However, the Delphi method does not require that consensus be reached. Instead, the method allows for justified differences of opinion rather attempting to produce unanimity.

### Independent technological comparisons

This method is often used to produce technological change. The method involves predicting changes in one area by monitoring changes that take place in another area. That is, the forecaster tries to determine a pattern of change in one area, called a primary trend, which he believes will result in new developments being made in some other area. A forecast of developments in the second area can then be made by monitoring developments in the first area. Forecasting when a new metal alloy of a very high tensile strength will be used commercially, might be related to metallurgical advances in the space programme. Then, by following metallurgical advances made in the space programme, the forecaster can predict when similar advances will take place in industry. Thus the development of high tensile strength alloys in the space programme will allow the forecasters to predict when such alloys will be available for commercial use. This type of forecasting poses two basic problems. Firstly, the forecaster must identify a primary trend that will reliably predict events in the area of interest. Secondly, the forecaster must use his expertise to determine the precise relationship between the primary trend and the events to be forecast.

### Quantitative forecasting methods

These techniques involve the analysis of historical data in an attempt to predict future values of a variable of interest. Quantitative forecasting models can be classified as univariate models or causal models.

### Univariate models

Univariate models predict future values of a time series solely on the basis of the past values of the time series. When a univariate model is used, historical data is analysed in an attempt to identify a data pattern. Then, assuming that the same pattern will continue in the future, the pattern is extrapolated in order to produce forecasts. Univariate forecasting models are, therefore, most useful when conditions are expected to remain the same. They are not very useful in forecasting the impact of changes in management policies. For example a univariate model can be used to predict sales if a firm expects to continue using its present marketing strategy. However such a model would not be useful in predicting the changes in sales that might result from a price increase, increased advertising expenditure, or a new advertising campaign.

## Exponential smoothing

Exponential smoothing is a forecasting technique that attempts to 'track' changes in time series by using newly observed time series values to 'update' the estimates of the parameters describing the time series.

The model used is:

$$\text{Forecast for period } T+1 = \text{Forecast for period } T + \text{Alpha} \times \left\{ \text{Actual for period } T - \text{Forecast for period } T \right\}$$

The terms in the brackets are regarded as the error term, as it is the difference between the actual result and its forecast. The forecast for the next period is the previous forecast plus a proportion of the error term.

The proportion alpha lies between 0 and 1 and is known as the smoothing constant.

Each new forecast depends upon the previous result and its forecast, but this old forecast depends upon the previous result and so on. Hence each new forecast can be shown to be a weighted average of all previous results, the weights being made up of increasing powers of the alpha value. This means in general that the most recent results are given higher weights than earlier results. The closer the value of alpha is to one the more weight is being given to the most recent results and little weight to older results. If the alpha value is low more weight is given to the most recent results. The effects of earlier results will still be significant.

*Example*

| Month | Jan | Feb | Mar | Apr | May | Jun |
|-------|-----|-----|-----|-----|-----|-----|
| Sales (£000) | 17.5 | 18.3 | 19.0 | 18.6 | 19.2 | 18.4 |

The forecast for January was £16,800. Let alpha be 0.80. The forecast can be obtained by use of the following table

| *Month* | *Actual* | *Forecast (T)* | *Error*<br>*A − F* | *Alpha × Error*<br>*0.8 × (A − F)* | *Forecast (T + 1)*<br>*F + 0.8 (A − F)* |
|---------|----------|----------------|----------|----------------|-----------------|
| Jan | 17.5 | 16.80 | 0.70 | 0.56 | 17.36 Feb |
| Feb | 18.3 | 17.36 | 0.94 | 0.75 | 18.11 Mar |
| Mar | 19.0 | 18.11 | 0.89 | 0.71 | 18.82 Apr |
| Apr | 18.6 | 18.82 | −0.22 | −0.18 | 18.64 May |
| May | 19.2 | 18.64 | 0.56 | 0.45 | 19.09 Jun |
| Jun | 18.4 | 19.09 | −0.69 | −0.55 | 18.54 Jul |
| Jul | | 18.54 | | | |

The February forecast of 17.36 is obtained by using the exponential model on the January data. The February forecast is recorded in the F column in the February row, ready to be used to forecast March sales. This process is repeated every month.

When the smoothing constant is high, lag problems may occur if either the time series is steadily rising or falling, i.e. the forecasts consistently lag behind the trend in the actual sales. In the majority of situations in which exponential smoothing is applied, the smoothing constant lies between 0.01 and 0.30.

## Method of moving average

If the sales appear to vary according to some seasonal pattern (which may be weekly, quarterly or some other fixed period) and the data does not indicate a high positive or negative trend, then the method of moving averages may be used to deal with the seasonal effects.

The model used is:

$$\text{Actual sales} = \text{Trend} + \text{Seasonal factor} + \text{Residual}$$
$$A = T + S + R$$

*Example*
Using the method of moving averages forecast sales by quarter for 1989 from the following data:

|  | Quarter | | | |
|---|---|---|---|---|
|  | 1 | 2 | 3 | 4 |
| **Year** |  |  |  |  |
| 1986 | 966 | 1042 | 1051 | 1041 |
| 1987 | 1040 | 1128 | 1134 | 1122 |
| 1988 | 1118 | 1207 | 1228 | 1208 |

*Solution*

| Year Deviation | Quarter | Actual Moving Sales A | Total | Moving Total | Centred Moving Average (trend) T | From trend A–T |
|---|---|---|---|---|---|---|
| 1986 | 1 | 966 | — | — | — | — |
|  | 2 | 1042 | — | — | — | — |
|  |  |  | 4100 |  |  |  |
|  | 3 | 1051 |  | 8274 | 1034.250 | 16.750 |
|  |  |  | 4174 |  |  |  |
|  | 4 | 1041 |  | 8434 | 1054.250 | — |
| −13.250 |  |  | 4260 |  |  |  |
| 1987 −35.375 | 1 | 1040 |  | 8603 | 1075.375 | — |
|  |  |  | 4343 |  |  |  |
|  | 2 | 1128 |  | 8767 | 1095.875 |  |
| 32.125 |  |  | 4424 |  |  |  |
|  | 3 | 1134 |  | 8926 | 1115.750 |  |
| 18.250 |  |  | 4502 |  |  |  |
|  | 4 | 1122  4502 |  | 9083 | 1135.375 | — |
| −13.375 |  |  | 273 |  |  |  |
|  |  |  | 4581 |  |  |  |
| 1988 −39.000 | 1 | 1118 |  | 9256 | 1157.000 | — |
|  |  |  | 4675 |  |  |  |
|  | 2 | 1207 |  | 9436 | 1179.500 |  |
| 27.500 |  |  | 4761 |  |  |  |
|  | 3 | 1228 |  | — | — | — |
|  | 4 | 1208 |  | — | — | — |

Deviation from trend table

| Year | Quarter | | | | | |
|------|---------|---|---|---|---|---|
| | 1 | 2 | 3 | 4 | | |
| 1986 | — | — | 16.750 | −13.250 | | |
| 1987 | −35.375 | 32.125 | 18.250 | −13.375 | | |
| 1988 | −39.000 | 27.500 | — | — | | Total |
| Average | −37.188 | 29.812 | 17.500 | −13.312 | = | −3.188 |
| Correction | 0.797 | 0.797 | 0.797 | 0.797 | = | 3.188 |
| | −36.391 | 30.609 | 18.297 | −12.515 | = | 0 |
| | $S_1$ | $S_2$ | $S_3$ | $S_4$ | | |

To forecast quarterly sales figures for 1989, first estimate the quarterly trend figures for 1989:

Increase in trend from 1986 quarter 3 to 1988 quarter 2
= 1179.5 − 1034.25 = 145.25

Therefore the average increase in trend $= \dfrac{145.25}{7} = 20.75$

(Note, divide by 7 as the time period between the end of 1986 quarter 3 to the end of 1988 quarter 2 is 7 quarters not eight quarters.)
    The last trend figure determined is 1179.5 for 1988 quarter 2, hence assuming a linear trend the forecasted trend figures for 1989 are:

Quarter 1   1179.50 + 3 × 20.75 = 1241.75
Quarter 2   1241.75 +      20.75 = 1262.50
Quarter 3   1262.50 +      20.75 = 1283.25
Quarter 4   1283.25 +      20.75 = 1304.00

Adjusting for seasonal variations the forecasted sales are:

Quarter 1   1241.75 + (−36.391) = 1205
Quarter 2   1262.50 +    30.609  = 1293
Quarter 3   1283.25 +    18.297  = 1302
Quarter 4   1304.00 + (−12.515) = 1291

(Rounding to the nearest whole number.)

### Causal models

The use of causal forecasting models involves the identification of other variables that are related to the variable to be predicted. Once these related variables have been identified, a statistical model which describes the relationship between these variables and the variable to be forecasted is developed. The statistical relationship derived is then used to forecast the variable of interest. The sales of a product might be related to the price of the product, advertising expenditure to promote the product, and competitors' prices charged for similar products. In such a case, sales would be the dependent variable, while the other variables would be the independent variables. The forecaster's job is to statistically estimate the functional relationship between sales and the independent variables. The forecaster can then predict future values of sales using future values of the independent variables.

Causal models are advantageous because they allow the management accountant to evaluate the impact of various different policies, e.g. different price levels. However causal models have several disadvantages. They are quite difficult to develop. They require historical data on all the variables included in the model. The forecaster also needs to predict the future values of the independent variables so as to forecast the dependent variable. This approach can only be realistically used when the problem of forecasting the independent variables is simpler than forecasting the dependent variables.

### Causal model using linear regression

*Example*
The sales of a product in industry A are believed to be related to the movement in the industry A index. The monthly index and monthly sales have been recorded for the last ten months.

| Month no. | Industry A index | Sales (£000) |
|---|---|---|
| 1 | 110 | 20.4 |
| 2 | 115 | 21.3 |
| 3 | 121 | 23.2 |
| 4 | 116 | 22.8 |
| 5 | 114 | 22.4 |
| 6 | 120 | 23.4 |
| 7 | 125 | 24.1 |
| 8 | 128 | 25.3 |
| 9 | 131 | 25.9 |
| 10 | 133 | 26.7 |

Fit a regression line to the data and comment on the fit of the model to the data.

*Solution*
The Minitab statistical computer package was used with the following results (see Figure 7.3):

The regression line is:

Sales = −6.960 − 0.25153 (index)

The R-sq value is 95.4 showing that 95.4 per cent of the variation is explained by the regression line. The correlation coefficient is the

```
MTB > REGRESS C2 ON 1 PREDICTOR C1

The regression equation is
C2 = −6.96 + 0.252 C1

Predictor            Coef         Stdev        t-ratio          P
Constant           −6.960         2.378         −2.93        0.019
C1                 0.25153       0.01957        −12.85        0.000

s=0.4548      R−sq=95.4%      R−sq(adj)=94.8%

Analysis of Variance

SOURCE              DF           SS           MS            F          P
Regression           1        34.170       34.170       165.17      0.000
Error                8         1.655        0.207
Total                9        35.825
```

Figure 7.3

square root of R-sq and is therefore equal to 0.977. Hence the regression line is a good fit to the data. Note, the F value = 34.170/0.207 = 165.17, showing a significant result, confirming the good fit of the regression line to the data.

There appears to be a relationship between the sales and the industrial index. Hence the regression line can be used for forecasting sales providing good forecasts of the industrial index can be obtained.

### Choosing a forecasting technique

In choosing a forecasting technique the forecaster must consider the following factors.

1   *The forecast form desired*
The forecast form can vary between obtaining a point estimate or a prediction interval. The form of the forecast can influence the choice of forecasting method used.

2   *The time pattern*
The time frame or time horizon is the total period over which forecasts are required. Is it a week, a year or perhaps ten years? The longer the time period the more difficult the forecasting becomes, and the more useful qualitative methods become.

3   *The pattern of data*
The important aspect about the pattern of data is whether a time series or some cyclical pattern exists within the data. This will dictate the forecasting technique to be used.

### 4   *The cost of forecasting*

The cost of forecasting may vary significantly depending on the cost of collecting and storing the data. The costs of forecasting should be compared with the value of having good accurate forecasts.

### 5   *The accuracy required*

Perhaps crude forecasts are sufficient in a particular situation. In a different problem a very accurate forecast is required.

### 6   *The availability of data*

The choice between quantitative and qualitative approaches will depend upon whether suitable data is available or can be collected.

### 7   *The ease of operation and understanding*

The management accountant must be able to understand and explain the forecast methodology used. If he does not understand the methodology he will not have confidence in the results. There is also a danger that he will not foresee when the parameter of the model needs to be changed because of underlying changes in the data.

Choosing the forecasting method to be used in a particular situation involves finding a technique that balances all the factors 1 to 7. The best technique is usually the technique that meets the needs of the situation at the least cost and inconvenience.

A general guide to the choice of technique is as follows. Quantitative forecasting methods are used when historical data is available. Univariate models are used to predict future values when it is believed that the historical pattern will continue; causal models are used when the historical pattern is likely to change due to changes in some other uncontrollable but predictable variable or variables. Qualitative forecasting techniques are employed when historical data is scarce or not available at all.

In practice most forecasting systems involve both quantitative and qualitative methods. Quantitative methods are used when the existing data pattern is expected to persist, while qualitative methods are used to predict when the existing data patterns might change. Thus forecasts generated by quantitative methods are almost always subjectively evaluated by management. This evaluation may result in a modification of the forecast based on the management accountant's expert opinion.

## Examination questions

### *Question 1 (CIMA)*

Branch Ltd is to be established as a subsidiary of Tree Ltd and is to be given the task of producing and selling a new gardening product called the Acorn. As part of the initial planning, an analysis of working capital requirements is to be undertaken and the following information has been obtained:

*Acorn*

| | |
|---|---|
| Cost of revenue | £7.50 per unit |
| Direct labour | £2.50 per unit |
| Overhead | £36,000 per week |
| Selling price | £18.00 per unit |

*Expected demand*

Demand is subject to considerable uncertainty. The most optimistic estimate is 15,000 units per week but this could be as few as 10,000 units per week for the most pessimistic.

*Production*

The length of the production cycle is three weeks and the production level can be set to suit the expected weekly level of demand.

*Stocks*

Raw material stocks of £150,000 will be held if production is at the lowest level and £225,000 if set at the highest level. Six weeks' supply of finished goods will be kept.

*Credit terms*

Typically, six weeks' credit is given to customers but experience shows that when there is a general credit squeeze the average payment period extends to eight weeks. Creditors for overhead and materials are normally paid four weeks after supply but if there is a credit squeeze, payments may be delayed for another four weeks.

*Profit options*

Two possibilities are being considered by Tree Ltd for any profits which may arise from the sale of Acorns:

1   that any profits made by Branch Ltd be remitted to Tree Ltd at the time the sale is made;
2   alternatively, that Branch Ltd retains any profit made.

You are required to

(a)   Prepare a working capital budget for Branch Ltd showing the least and greatest amounts of working capital required for both the optimistic and pessimistic demand levels, assuming that the 'profit transferred' basis is adopted.
(b)   Show the effects on the working capital budget prepared in (a) if the 'retained profit' basis is adopted.
(c)   State what assistance could be provided by a computer to aid management in the production and analysis of working capital and other types of budget.

**Answer 1**

The weekly operating statements would be:

|  | Pessimistic | Optimistic |
|---|---|---|
| Number of units | 10,000 | 15,000 |
|  | (£) | (£) |
| Sales | 180,000 | 270,000 |
| Materials | 75,000 | 112,500 |
| Labour | 25,000 | 37,500 |
| Overheads | 36,000 | 36,000 |
| Profit | £44,000 | £84,000 |

(a) *Budget of working capital required if profits are remitted*

|  |  | (£) |  | (£) |
|---|---|---|---|---|
| Debtors (at cost) |  |  |  |  |
| 6 weeks | at £136,000 | 816,000 | at £186,000 | 1,116,000 |
| Finished stocks |  |  |  |  |
| (at cost) 6 weeks | at £136,000 | 816,000 | at £186,000 | 1,116,000 |
| Work-in-progress |  |  |  |  |
| (at cost) 3 weeks | at £136,000 | 408,000 | at £186,000 | 558,000 |
| RM Stock |  | 150,000 |  | 225,000 |
|  |  | 2,190,000 |  | 3,015,000 |
| Less creditors |  |  |  |  |
| 8 weeks | at £111,000 | 888,000 | at £148,500 | 1,188,000 |
|  |  | 1,302,000 |  | 1,827,000 |
| Plus profit paid |  |  |  |  |
| over 6 weeks | at £ 44,000 | 264,000 | at £84,000 | 504,000 |
| Therefore least budget |  | 1,566,000 |  | 2,331,000 |
| Plus 2 weeks |  |  |  |  |
| extra Debtors | at £136,000 | 272,000 | at £186,000 | 372,000 |
| Plus 4 weeks |  |  |  |  |
| extra creditors | at £111,000 | 444,000 | at £148,000 | 594,000 |
| Therefore greatest budget |  | 2,282,000 |  | 3,297,000 |

(b) *Budget assuming that profits are retained*

|  | (£) | (£) |
|---|---|---|
|  | 1,566,000 | 2,331,000 |
| Less profit | 264,000 | 504,000 |
| Therefore least budget | 1,302,000 | 1,827,000 |
|  | 2,282,000 | 3,297,000 |
| Less profit | 264,000 | 504,000 |
| Therefore greatest budget | 2,018,000 | 2,793,000 |

(c) The conclusions arrived at above could have emerged from a manual spreadsheet. Computer-based packages are ideally suited to a detailed preparation of working capital budgets. The values entered in columns, rows and cells are either derived from external information or current or logged internal information appearing elsewhere on the spreadsheet, which is held in the computer's memory. The spreadsheet can be much larger than can be handled manually, though only a portion of it can be seen at one time on a VDU. There is an automatic ability to recalculate when input values are changed so that 'what if' questions can be addressed to it. Thus, different options and assumptions can be tested and evaluated.

## Question 2 (CIMA)

For a company making one product you are required to produce:

(a)   The budgeted production requirement (in units) for each of the months of March, April and May.
(b)   The budgeted purchase requirements of raw material (in units) for each of the months of March and April.
(c)   The budgeted profit and loss statement for April.
(d)   The cash forecast for April.

The following data are available as at 1st March:

1   Budgeted Sales

|  | Units |
|---|---|
| March | 180,000 |
| April | 240,000 |
| May | 250,000 |
| June | 230,000 |

The selling price is £2 per unit.

Sales are invoiced twice per month, in the middle of the month and on the last day of the month. Terms are 2 per cent for 10 days and net for 30 days. Sales are made evenly through the month and 50 per cent of sales are paid within the discount period. The remaining amounts are paid within the 30 day period except for bad debts which average 0.5 per cent of gross sales. Estimated cash discounts and bad debts are treated as deductions from sales in the company's profit and loss statements.

2   Stocks of finished goods were 36,000 units on 1 March. The company's rule is that stocks of finished goods at the end of each month should represent 20 per cent of their budgeted sales for the following month. No work-in-progress is held.

3   Stocks of raw materials were 45,600 kilogrammes on 1 March. The company's rule is that at the end of each month, a minimum of 40 per cent of the following month's production requirement of raw materials should be in stock. Payments for raw materials are to be made in the month following purchase, and materials can only be bought in lots of 40,000 kilogrammes or multiples thereof.

4 The standard production cost of the product, based on a normal monthly production of 230,000 units is:

|  | Cost per unit (£) |
|---|---|
| Direct materials (1/2 kilogramme per unit) | 0.50 |
| Direct wages | 0.40 |
| Variable overhead | 0.20 |
| Fixed overhead | 0.10 |
| Total | £1.20 |

Fixed overhead includes £8000 per month depreciation on production plant and machinery. Any volume variance is included in cost of sales.
5  Production salaries and wages are paid during the month in which they are incurred.
6  Selling expenses are estimated at 10 per cent of gross sales. Administration expenses are £60,000 per month of which £800 per month relates to depreciation of office equipment. Selling and administration expenses and all production overhead are paid in the month following that in which they are incurred.
7  The cash balance is expected to be £12,000 on 1 April.

*Answer 2*

(a)

|  | March 000 units | April 000 units | May 000 units |
|---|---|---|---|
| Budgeted sales | 180 | 240 | 250 |
| Closing stock | 48 | 50 | 46 |
|  | 228 | 290 | 296 |
| Opening stock | 36 | 48 | 50 |
| Budgeted production | 192 | 242 | 246 |

(b)

|  | (000 kg) | (000 kg) |
|---|---|---|
| Material requirements at 0.5 kg per unit produced | 96 | 121 |
| Minimum month end stock | 48.4 | 49.2 |
|  | 144.4 | 170.2 |
| Opening stock | 45.6 | 69.6* |
|  | 98.8 | 100.6 |
| 3 purchase batches will be needed therefore | 120.0 | 120.0 |
| Additional stock c/f | 21.2 | 19.4 |

* 21.2 + 48.4

Budgeted purchase requirements for each month are therefore 120,000 kg (3 batches).

(c)

| | | (£) |
|---|---|---|
| Sales 240,000 units at £2 | | 480,000 |
| Standard production cost at £1.20 | | 288,000 |
| | | 192,000 |

Budgeted volume variance on fixed overhead:

| | | |
|---|---|---|
| Budgeted production | 242,000 units | |
| Normal production | 230,000 units | |
| | 12,000 at £0.10 | 1,200F |
| | | 193,200 |

| | | |
|---|---|---|
| Administrative expenses | 60,000 | |
| Selling expenses | 48,000 | |
| | | 108,000 |
| | | 85,200 |

| | | |
|---|---|---|
| Bad debts 0.5% provision* | 2,400 | |
| Discounts 2% provision on 50% of sales* | 4,800 | |
| | | 7,200 |
| | | 78,000 |

* These items could alternatively be entered as items arising in the month of April, e.g. discounts given on April settlements in respect of earlier sales.

(d)

| | | | (£) |
|---|---|---|---|
| Cash receipts in April | | | 384,000 |
| Cash payments in April: | | | |
| Payment for March raw material purchases | | | 120,000 |
| Wages 242,000 units × £0.40 | | | 96,800 |
| Variable overhead 192,000 units × £0.20 | | | 38,400 |
| Fixed overhead: | | | |
| | | (£) | (£) |
| Budget 230,000 × £0.10 | | 23,000 | |
| Less depreciation content | | 8,000 | |
| | | | 15,000 |
| Administrative overhead | | 60,000 | |
| Less depreciation content | | 800 | |
| | | | 59,200 |
| Selling expenses 10% of March sales | | | 36,000 |
| | | | 365,400 |
| Cash surplus on month | | | 18,600 |
| Opening balance | | | 12,000 |
| | | | 30,600 |

### Question 3 (CIMA)

Prepare brief notes about zero-base budgeting covering the following topics:

(a) What zero-base budgeting means.
(b) How zero-base budgeting would operate.
(c) What problems might be met in introducing zero-base budgeting.
(d) What special advantages could be expected from zero-base budgeting, as compared with more traditional budgeting methods, for an organization operating in an economic recession.

### Answer 3

(a) Zero-base budgeting is an approach to resource allocation. There is an assumption of zero spending. This represents a departure from the status quo concept, in which the existence of current spending is taken as justifying the activity which is in receipt of allocated resources.

(b) The technique would need to be carefully introduced to managers in the organization so that they appreciate both the concept and the manner in which it would be applied. Decision units should be designated. These may be departments, sections or functions – or perhaps a specific development or capital project. Decision units must be independent of each other. Responsibility for identifying the definition, concept and targets of the unit should be identified. The manager concerned should describe the nature, purpose and goals of his unit in such a way that outside observers would understand the importance of the unit to the company.

Alternative ways of making the necessary unit provision should be considered – perhaps brainstorming sessions may be of value in this direction. Variation in activity level should be considered. For example, a lower level of service could be considered, or a lower quality of service, or perhaps what kind of service could be provided with a lower level of resource allocation. Priorities will need to be identified as between a number of approved decision packages for (say) a department.

A final selection of packages will be made with a view to necessary goal achievements and to the resources available for allocation.

(c) There is likely to be a communication problem. Zero-base budgeting may be seen as another variation in already troublesome budgetary procedures. The traditional budgeting process in which the actual costs of the current year provide a basis for next year's resource allocation, protects the empire that a manager has built. The zero-base budgeting approach challenges this in requiring justification from zero level.

It is doubtful if zero-base budgeting could be successfully applied throughout the company. It is more likely to be successfully applied in service areas – administration, marketing, research and development etc. – rather than to direct production operations. There is a need to combat the natural feeling that current operations are efficient.

(d) A time of recession presents particular difficulty in terms of profitability and available resources. Zero-based budgeting therefore has

the advantage that it generates a different approach to resource allocation just when most needed.

Some elements in the zero-base budgeting process are useful in causing managers to rationalize the value of the services provided. There is
a lower degree of preoccupation with historical cost and performance.

### Question 4 (CIMA)

The managing director of your company believes that the existing
annual budget system is costly to operate and produces unsatisfactory
results due to:

- long preparation period;
- business decisions being made throughout the year;
- unpredictable changes in the rate of general inflation;
- sudden changes in the availability and price of raw materials.

He has read about rolling budgets and wonders whether these might
be more useful for his decision making.

You are required, as the management accountant, to prepare a paper
for him covering the following areas:

(a)  A brief explanation of rolling budgets.
(b)  How a rolling budget system would operate.
(c)  Three significant advantages of a rolling budget system.
(d)  Three problems likely to be encountered in using a rolling budget
     system.

### Answer 4

(a)  The ICMA 'terminology' defines a rolling budget as 'the continuous
updating of a short-term budget by adding, say, a further month or
quarter and deducting the earliest month or quarter so that budget can
reflect current conditions.'

(b)  *How it operates*
Every quarter (or month, if that period is chosen) all normal budgeting
activities are repeated in respect of the next quarter, for which a budget
has not yet been prepared, e.g. on 31 March 1984, the budget for the
quarter ending 31 March 1985 is prepared. A comparison is then made
between the quarter just completed and the new quarter just budgeted.

The master budget for the year, and for the intervening quarters,
ending 30 June, 30 September, and 31 December 1984 are then adjusted
to reflect the difference disclosed by the comparison. Actual results for
subsequent quarters can then be compared with the updated budgets.

(c)  *Three advantages*
1  Management is able to concentrate on a suitable managerial time-
span which it can visualize and for which it can more fairly be accountable.

2 Management is forced to think in the light of the implications of practical changes/developments rather than in theoretical or generally optimistic terms. The budgets may thus have more motivational impact.

3 This approach minimizes the historical elements in budgeting (i.e. what people planned for up to 11 months ago). It eliminates the artificial separation of one financial year from another, as regards operational activities, and allows a more evolutionary type of development.

(d) *Problems*

1 Can one motivate managers to accept the value (and the work) associated with the greater frequency of budget preparation – even if the time span covered is short?

2 Can one get executives to take this new routine seriously to devote their time to it, and not to belittle it?

3 Will one be able to have accounting staff available to handle the new data in sufficiently short time periods, and can one afford any extra costs?

4 If the budget is built up from basic standard costs there may be four changes each year in standard product costs. As a result, revaluation of period-end stocks, pricing of material issues etc., will become more complex.

5 One will still need longer-term forecasts and plans. Thus some of the old 'log-jam' in budget preparation will remain.

6 How does one decide on the period to be covered, i.e. a quarter or a month? Will the shorter period justify the extra work?

# Further reading

Amey, L.R., *Budget Planning and Control Systems*, Pitman, 1979.

Bowerman, O'Connell, R.T., *Time Series Forecasting*, 2nd edn, Buxbury, 1987.

Makridakis, S., Wheelwright, S.C., McGee, V.E., *Forecasting: Methods and Applications*, Wiley, 1983.

Parker, L.D., Communication in the corporate budgetary system, *Accounting and Business Research*, (Summer 1978).

# 8 Behavioural aspects of budgeting

One of the main objectives of management accounting is to influence the behaviour of the workforce in order that efficiency is maximized and corporate goals are attained. It is important that the organizational goals are congruent with the aspiration levels of individual managers. This, in part, can be achieved by responsibility accounting.

Responsibility accounting is a system of accounting whereby managers are made responsible for items of costs and revenues so that their performance can be assessed. Responsibility must be matched with control otherwise managers will be demotivated. Control is determined by a manager's level of authority, i.e. his power to influence the cost. A junior manager may be unable to hire and fire staff, whereas a senior manager can and should be held responsible for the wage cost in his department.

Pay is often claimed to be a useful motivator when there is a direct link between pay and results. In a wage incentive scheme the following requirements are necessary:

1  The scheme should be easy to understand and acceptable to the workforce.
2  It should be fair, i.e. based solely on merit.
3  There should be no fear of cancellation of the scheme once the new targets are achieved.
4  The time-scale between effort and reward should be short.
5  Any team bonus must be shared fairly between members of the team.

Feedback can be an important motivator. Information supplied to the workforce must be concise, accurate and timely, and should operate by the management exception principle. Management reports will be clear and commensurate with the recipient's level of understanding.

174

## Ways in which motivation can be improved

1 The management accountant should have regular meetings with operational managers in order to discuss control reports.
2 A participative approach in the setting of budgets should be encouraged.
3 Success, i.e. the achievement of targets, should be rewarded. Rewards may take the form of pay (as mentioned earlier), promotion, extra responsibility and job variety.
4 There must be regular training in budgetary control procedures.
5 Performance reports should distinguish between controllable and uncontrollable costs.
6 Standards must be fair and regularly updated so that control information is realistic.
7 Accounting reports must not emphasize short-run effects at the expense of long run considerations. This may prevent managers from making dysfunctional decisions. A dysfunctional decision arises when a manager makes a decision which is beneficial to his department but is not in the best interests of the organization as a whole.
8 The budgeting system should be flexible as opposed to being rigid so that it meets the requirements of the users of the system.
9 Budgets must be flexed to actual activity levels before performance can be appraised.

## Case study

The following case study is characteristic of some of the problems that can arise in a practical situation concerning the motivational aspects of budgeting.

A new private hospital of 100 beds was opened to receive patients on 2 January 1988 though many senior staff members including the supervisor of the laundry department had been in situ for some time previously. The first three months were expected to be a settling-in period, the hospital facilities being used to full capacity only in the second and subsequent quarters.

On 1 May 1988 the supervisor of the laundry department received her first quarterly performance report from the hospital administrator, together with an explanatory memorandum. Copies of both documents are set out below.

The supervisor had never seen the original budget, nor had she been informed that there would be a quarterly performance report. She knew she was responsible for her department and had made every endeavour to run it as efficiently as possible. It had been made clear to her that there would be a slow build-up in the number of patients accepted by the hospital so she would need only three members of staff, but she had had to take on a fourth during the quarter due to the extra work. This extra hiring had been anticipated for May, not late February.

Rockingham Private Patients Hospital Ltd

Memorandum                                    30 April 1988
To: All Department Heads/Supervisors
From: Hospital Administrator

Attached is the Quarterly Performance Report for your department. The hospital has adopted a responsibility accounting system so you will be receiving one of these reports quarterly. Responsibility accounting means that you are accountable for ensuring that the expenses of running your department are kept in line with budget. Each report compares the actual expenses of running your department for the quarter with our budget for the same period. The difference between the actual and forecast will be highlighted so that you can identify the important variations from budget and take corrective action to get back on budget. Any variation in excess of five per cent from budget should be investigated and an explanatory memo sent to me giving reasons for the variations and the proposed corrective actions.

Performance Report – Laundry Department

3 Months to 31 March 1988

|  | Actual | Budget | Variation (over)/under | % Variation |
|---|---|---|---|---|
| Patient days | 8,000 | 6,500 | (1,500) | (23) |
| Weight of laundry processed (lbs) | 101,170 | 81,250 | (19,920) | (24.5) |
|  | (£) | (£) | (£) |  |
| Department expenses |  |  |  |  |
| Wages | 4,125 | 3,450 | (675) | (19.5) |
| Supervisor's salary | 1,490 | 1,495 | 5 | — |
| Washing materials | 920 | 770 | (150) | (19.5) |
| Heating and power | 560 | 510 | (50) | (10) |
| Equipment depreciation | 250 | 250 | — | — |
| Allocated administration costs | 2,460 | 2,000 | (460) | (23) |
| Equipment maintenance | 10 | 45 | (35) | 78 |
|  | 9,815 | 8,520 | (1,295) | (15) |

Comments: We need to have a discussion about the over-expenditure of the department.

You are required to:

(a) Discuss in detail the various possible effects on the behaviour of the laundry supervisor of the way her budget was prepared and the form and content of the performance report, having in mind the published research findings in this area.

(b) Re-draft, giving explanations, the performance report and supporting memorandum in a way which, in your opinion, would make
them more effective management tools.

*Solution*
(a) *Discussions of the behavioural effects of the performance report*
The features of the way in which the budget was prepared and the form
and content of the performance report that might give rise to an
adverse response from the laundry supervisor.

1 Lack of participation – the supervisor was not even consulted over
the preparation of the budget and didn't even know one was being
prepared.
2 Unflexed budget – no attempt has been made to adjust budgeted
costs in the light of the increase in volume presumably because the
fixed and variable elements of costs have not been established.
3 Uncontrollable costs included – the memorandum's reference to
'responsibility accounts' and 'expenses of running your department'
has been ignored when producing the report which includes 'allocated administration costs' and 'equipment depreciation'.
4 Fixed percentage for investigation – this may not be an ideal system
for deciding which variances should be investigated and which
should not. It seems an arbitrary figure and one which is dubiously
being applied to all costs.
5 Aggressive style – the memorandum has been presented in a somewhat authoritarian style based solely on accounting information.

The effects that this might have on the behaviour of the supervisor
include:

1 Creating a negative attitude – a phrase which encompasses a whole
range of behavioural problems such as a dampened initiative (possibly leading to wrong decisions such as not recruiting staff when
needed); reducing cooperation and communication between departments and particularly with the hospital administrator; reducing
morale within the department and giving rise to lack of commitment to the hospital.
2 Reduced performance – with the lack of cooperation mentioned it
is less likely that the supervisor will try to control or reduce costs.
More effort will be put into finding excuses for poor cost control or
even attempting to falsify data where possible.
3 Budget pressure – management could be said to be adopting a
'budget constrained' style of management and the obsession with
the quarterly targets could lead to impaired performance. Steps
might be taken to ensure not that costs do not exceed a budget, but
rather to ensure that they do not fall below the budget – lest the
budget be pruned in the next quarter.
4 Wrong decisions – the possibility of wrong decisions being made
through 'dampened initiative' has already been mentioned; but the

use of a fixed percentage rule for investigating variances could also lead to wasted time looking at variances. Such variances might be small in absolute terms, caused by a poor budget, poor recording of costs or due to random fluctuations and such variances would not be worth investigating.

Research into these various behavioural effects and their possible causes has grown over the years following earlier papers based more on surmise and opinion. Such researchers include:

1  Coch and French, who, following research in an American pyjama manufacturing company, suggested that performance improved as a result of participation by the workforce.
2  Lorsch found the average quality of decisions made by groups to be greater than those made by individuals.
3  Stedry noted that targets set by employees themselves were often tougher than expected imposed standards and performance improved with these tougher standards. Performance, when standards were imposed on employees, was seen to improve then fall off as the required level was increased. Performance was better with informed or accepted budgets rather than imposed budgets.
4  Hofstede found that for budgets to be motivationally positive, they had to be 'internalized' by the budgetee. Also, cultural, organizational and personality factors all had to be taken into account before it is possible to anticipate reactions to budgets and targets. He also found that indiscriminate use of budgets in performance appraisal might lead to negative attitudes.
5  Hopwood in a study of a manufacturing organization in the USA showed some of the undesirable consequences of evaluating performance solely on the basis of short-run budgets. He found extensive manipulation of accounting data, high job-related tension and poor relations with superiors and colleagues. Many of the problems were caused by badly designed accounting systems. These results tended to indicate the necessity for more flexibility, wider information sources and a more supportive attitude as part of performance evaluation. Interestingly, a later UK study by Otley showed that managers might be more likely to make budget in a 'budget-constrained' environment.

It has been a feature of much of the empirical work into the relationship between accounting and the behaviour, that the results have produced conflicting conclusions on matters such as management style, budgetary pressure, design of accounting measures and participation. This has led to the development of a contingency approach. This broader framework considers the impact of accounting information and procedures on individuals in the context of a number of variables including both exogenous and endogenous factors.

Using a contingency approach, the situation of the laundry would therefore need to be reviewed in the light of matters such as:

1 The likely bureaucratic structure of hospital management.
2 The highly regulated throughput of the department with a stable operating environment
3 The well specified task within the department, probably governed by standard procedures.
4 The clearly defined lines of communication.

Overall, the system is not of an 'organic' type and the kind of budgetary control system selected should reflect the fact.

### Redrafted report and memorandum

Rockingham Private Patients Hospital Ltd

Memorandum                                        30 July 1988
To: Mrs A Brown, Laundry Supervisor
From: B C Smith, Hospital Administrator

As you know the hospital has adopted a responsibility accounting system in order to ensure that each department runs as efficiently as possible. To help the operation of such a system it will be useful for you to receive some form of performance report each quarter and I have attached my version of such a report for the first quarter.

This first report is something of a trial run since the first quarter was expected to be a settling-in period and as such not typical and this report having been produced without consultation with department heads or supervisors may need modification. It will, when fully operational, act as a useful aid to cost control and I am very keen that we should meet as soon as possible to discuss the form and content of future reports.

This report shows the actual costs of running the department together with a budget based on the weight of laundry processed. Variations from budget have been calculated and some marked as requiring your attention. Such variations will be those which are large in terms of the total cost of the department and of the actual cost incurred bearing in mind expected variations in certain costs.

I will expect a quick response to such reports by way of an explanatory memo but any queries over either this or subsequent reports could be most easily sorted out by coming to my office.

Performance Report – Laundry Department

3 Months to 31 March 1988

|  | Actual | Flexed budget | Variation (over)/under | Action needed |
|---|---|---|---|---|
| Patient days | 8,000 | | | |
| Weight of laundry processed (lbs) | 101,170 | | | |

|  | (£) | (£) | (£) |  |
| --- | --- | --- | --- | --- |
| Wages (W1) | 4,125 | 4,313 | 188 | None |
| Supervisor's salary | 1,490 | 1,495 | 5 | None |
| Washing materials (W2) | 920 | 959 | 39 | None |
| Heating and power (W3) | 560 | 572 | 12 | None |
| Equipment maintenance | 10 | 45 | 35 | None |
|  | 7,105 | 7,384 | 279 |  |

The memorandum has been toned down a little, made more personal and an attempt made to justify the purpose of the report and encourage cooperation in establishing a system of cost control.

The report itself has been modified by eliminating uncontrollable elements (budgeted activity levels and certain costs). The budget has been flexed by assuming that:

1  wages are variable subject to staff being employed for whole weeks;
2  materials are variable; and
3  heating and power are 50 per cent fixed and 50 per cent variable. (These arbitrarily proposed figures would need to be established properly.)

The report could have been less formally drawn up with the original budgets shown together with calculations to show how it was flexed to take into account the actual weight of laundry processed and variations laid out. In either case the hospital administrator should highlight which variations are to be investigated and, with the flexed budget, no such investigation is needed for the first quarter.

The performance report could also show various figures to assess efficiency such as total labour hours and number of washing loads. With additional information price and usage variances could be found for washing materials. Details of the use of laundry capacity could be established by noting how much laundry was presented and how much processed as opposed to be being sent outside.

*Workings*

1  Wages £3450 × 1.25 = £4313

2  Materials £770 × $\dfrac{101,170}{81,250}$ = £959

3  Heating and power  £255 + 255 × $\dfrac{101,170}{81,250}$
　　　　　　　(fixed)　　　　　(variable)
　　　　= £255 + £317
　　　　= £572

## Writings on motivational theory

The following writers have identified problems which can be encountered in budgeting. They have suggested ways in which these problems can be alleviated and how motivation can be enhanced:

### Hopwood

Hopwood observed some major budget problems.

1 Budgets are too profit orientated and do not always reflect other goals.
2 Management's expectations may not be congruent with the aspirations level of their subordinates.
3 Although the budgeting process appears to be technical and formal it really is an informal bargaining process, whereby managers compete for organizational resources. This can lead to a dilution of original goals, as managers vie for power and recognition.
4 Real participation in the setting of budgets may not always be desirable and will depend on the nature of the work involved. If the work is highly predictable and routine (e.g. in a production department) then there is less scope for participation. Whereas in a research and development department where the type of work performed is innovative and unpredictable, participation can be encouraged.

Hopwood described three distinct styles of using budget and actual cost information to evaluate performance.

1 *Budget – constrained style*   This method of evaluation is based on the cost centre's ability to achieve the budget on a short term basis. The emphasis is on costs and other considerations are ignored. This results in job-related tension, manipulation of accounting information and poor relations with supervisors and colleagues.
2 *Profit – conscious style*   The performance of the cost centre is evaluated on the basis of its ability to increase the effectiveness of its operations in relation to the organization's long-term goals. The emphasis is still on costs. There is some job-related tension, but there is little manipulation of accounting information. Relations with superiors and colleagues are good.
3 *Non-accounting style*   Accounting data plays a relatively unimportant role in the evaluation of the cost centre's performance. There is little involvement with costs, and hardly any manipulation of accounting information. Although some job-related tension exists relations with supervisors and colleagues are good.

### Chris Argyris

Chris Argyris identified four major problems with budgeting.

1   The budget is often perceived by the workforce as a pressure device imposed by management to force lazy employees to work harder. This leads to resentment and distrust thereby having an adverse effect on labour relations.
2   A feeling of 'them and us' exists between the budget staff, i.e. accounts department ('them'), and the other departments ('us'). This is because the budget staff's success is the other's failure, e.g. the accountant's success in finding an adverse variance identifies another employee's failure to achieve his budget.
3   Departmental conflict can arise as a result of:

   (a)   departments competing for scares resources, and
   (b)   departments blaming each other when they fail to achieve their targets.

4   Managers often use the budget as a vehicle for expressing their leadership style. If subordinates resent a particular style of leadership the budget is blamed rather than the leader.

Argyris suggested two approaches towards these problems.

1   Real participation in the setting of budgets by employees should be encouraged. This gives people more responsibility, boosts their morale and should have a motivational impact.
   It is important to note that Argyris distinguished between real participation which involves people in the decision making process and pseudo-participation which pressurizes people into budget acceptance.
2   There should be training in human relations and improvements in communication systems.

### Hofstede

His research indicated that tight standards (i.e. those which assume perfect conditions) are the most difficult standards to achieve and are perceived as being unrealistic by individuals. The end result is a poorer performance than could have been achieved had less demanding goals been set.

However, if very loose standards are set then although they will be achieved, individuals will not be motivated to achieve their full potential.

The best type of standard is a currently attainable standard. This is one that is tight enough to motivate, yet still realistic.

### Becker and Green

These writers suggested that budget changes should be linked to aspiration levels rather than to the calendar.

If actual performance meets or exceeds expectations then aspiration levels will rise and the budgets should be revised upwards accordingly.

If actual performance is slightly below expectations the budget should remain unadjusted. However, if performance is considerably below expectations, aspiration levels will fall and the budget should be revised downwards accordingly.

There are two major problems with this idea,

1 Aspiration levels may continually change.
2 Aspiration levels may not be congruent with corporate goals.

### McGregor – theory X and theory Y

Leadership style has an important role in the behavioural aspects of budgeting as it is important to have the right type of leader for a particular job. In a production department it is necessary to have a theory X type of manager, i.e. one who tends to be authoritarian and does not encourage a high degree of participation.

However, in the research and development department the theory Y type of manager who is democratic and encourages participation is more suitable.

The above writers represent a selection of different opinions on the behavioural aspects of budgeting. The debate is still very active and research on this theme is continuing. The emphasis is moving away from a search for a unique management accounting system towards designing a system for an organization that takes into account all aspects of the organizational control package.

The development of contingency theories of organization structure in the sixties was followed by its application to management accounting in the seventies. The major theme of contingency theory is that there is no universally appropriate accounting system applicable to all organizations in all circumstances. It attempts to identify the features of the accounting system that can be matched with certain defined circumstances. According to Emmanuel and Otley (1985) three major classes of contingent factor have been identified; the environment, organizational structure and technology. The environment includes such factors as its predictability, the competition in the market, and the number of product lines. Organizational structure includes size, interdependence, decentralization and resources available. Technology concerns the nature of the production process, its degree of routineness, the amount of task variability.

At this stage there is still hard evidence that these factors have a major effect upon management accounting systems. However the contingency framework provides guidance for considering conceptual issues in accounting systems design.

## Examination questions

### Question 1 (CIMA)

You are required to discuss separately each of the following statements.

(a)  Most budgeting systems are bureaucratic and reinforce organizational inertia whereas what is required is continuous adaptation to deal with a volatile environment.

(b)  The typical flexible budget is virtually useless as a control device because for convenience it is common practice for all the variable elements in the budget to be flexed according to the same activity indicator whereas in reality the elements vary according to different activity indicators.

(c)  Participation by managers in setting budget levels is a laudable philosophy but it is naïve to think that participative approaches are always more effective than authoritarian styles.

### Answer 1

(a)  Budgeting systems reflect managerial attitudes. In some instances this can mean reinforcement of organizational inertia. However, in the current economic climate inert organizations have a limited future. Given the volatile environment in which many business organizations exist, continuous adaptation is important, but adaptation in itself may not be sufficient.

Successful managers invariably attempt to shape events rather than merely adapt to them. Such managers can use their budgeting systems to develop the necessary mix of adaptive and dynamic behaviour.

(b)  A flexible budget allowance is calculated on the basis of a single output-based activity indicator, e.g. budgeted fixed overhead costs + (budgeted variable overhead cost per unit × the actual number of units produced). These variable costs tend to vary with input rather than output and variable overhead absorption rates based on input of machine/direct labour hours are used to estimate the flexible budget allowance.

However, for control purposes the budget is flexed on the basis of an output rather than input indicator to ensure that input inefficiencies are not covered up. In this manner, the typical flexible budget can be of some value as a control device.

(c)  Much of the conventional wisdom of management accounting is based on the precept that managerial participation in the budgeting process has a positive effect on motivation and thus leads to enhanced managerial performance. This precept is in fact still open to question. What is beyond doubt is that budgeting is not simply a technical accounting system – it interacts with complex human, social and organizational processes. Budgeting depends for its effectiveness on the people who operate the system and authoritarian styles can be as effective as other styles. However, the style adopted does need to be suitable for superior and subordinate and thus relevant to the type of organization within which it is employed.

## Question 2 (CIMA)

The effective use of the control information provided by an organization's accounting department might be reduced by the behaviour of its operating managers.

(a) Explain briefly six motivators or attitudes that would result in less effective use of the control information.
(b) Indicate very briefly what actions the accounting department might take to improve the situation.

## Answer 2

(a)

1  An operating manager may consider that cost control may be first on his list of priorities and that he is more likely to be pressured with regard to delivery delays, machine breakdown, industrial relations problems, etc. He therefore acts according to his perceived priorities.
2  The attitude displayed may simply be disinterest rather than any outright hostility to the information provided. This may be rooted in a lack of understanding of report content or in a belief that costs and their control is within the remit of the accounting function.
3  The attitude may be one of resentment to the control information and its implications with regard to managerial performance, particularly in a system of imposed budgets and standards.
4  Ineffective use of such statements may develop in a state of managerial inertia, e.g. in a large, decentralized organization in which the feelings of urgency, relevance, commercial danger, etc., can easily be lost.
5  The manager may see such reporting as creating situations potentially dangerous to his self-image, and which he will therefore not willingly enter. This is particularly so if senior operating managers use such reports as pressure devices.
6  An operating manager may take the attitude that such statements neither tell him what in fact went wrong nor what action is required, and therefore do little to help him in the control process.

(b)  The accounting department should:

1  Generate a sympathetic relationship with operations management.
2  Try to communicate in understandable rather than jargon terms.
3  Develop a participative process for setting budgets and standards.

4 Concentrate control information on key areas of the manager's tasks.
5 Make it quite clear to operations management that control in its area is its responsibility.
6 Recognize that the value of control information decays rapidly, and produce information whilst it is still 'fresh' enough to be useful.

### Question 3 (CIMA)

One purpose of management accounting is to influence managers' behaviour so that their resulting actions will yield a maximum benefit to the employing organization.
   In the context of this objective, you are required to discuss:

(a)   how budgets can cause behavioural conflict;
(b)   how this behavioural conflict may be overcome;
(c)   the importance of the feedback of information; and
(d)   the purpose of goal congruence.

### Answer 3

(a)   Although it must be accepted that management accounting seeks to influence managerial behaviour, it is also true that budgeting systems do not always influence such behaviour in the most desirable way.
   It is presumed that organizational conflict will produce inefficiencies of performance, with undesirable symptoms in behavioural attitudes.
   It must be recognized that not only do business goals exist, but also that there are financial goals, group goals (e.g. shop stewards' group), departmental goals, individual goals, etc. and it is clearly difficult to produce a congruence of goals (see (d) below) and a unified approach to their achievement.
   The budgetary process may be thought of as providing a format whereby organizational conflicts can be reconciled in the pursuit of organizational goals. This is somewhat idealistic, however, and the way in which the budgetary process is operated will influence the success in dealing with conflict. For example, budgets inevitably reflect top management style and exercise of authority. An imposed autocratic budget system will produce conflict where such imposition is resented. As a continuation of this, conflict will arise as a result of the way in which budgets are used for control. A belief that budgets will be used in a punitive manner will induce defensive reactions such as budget padding. Finally, it is worth noting that major conflicts in business relate to resource allocations. In this sense budgets, when approved, provide a prima facie recognition of resource commitment. The achievement of budget approval is therefore seen as a resolution of the conflict with other department managers for a share of limited resources.

(b)   Overcoming conflict depends first of all upon recognizing and identifying the nature of organizational conflict, and particularly that induced by the manner in which budgetary systems are operated. This might appear obvious, but top management often appear surprised by the reaction of middle and supervisory management to careless, incompetent or even improper application of budgetary procedures.

Some suggestions would include therefore:

- Clear explanations to budget centre managers as to the intentions and operation of budgetary procedures.
- Formalization of procedures in a budget manual.
- Application of a participative system.
- A sound and fair feedback system (see (c) below).
- A determination to modify procedure etc. to deal with new conflict areas and maintain the momentum of managerial involvement.

(c)   Control theory argues that feedback is an important element in a control process, culminating in corrective action to bring activity performance within acceptable limits. It must be emphasized that cost control is a managerial responsibility, and that feedback is necessary to provoke corrective managerial action. However, variations may be random fluctuations, may be self-correcting, or may already have been the subject of managerial action, and these points should be considered in deciding the nature, frequency, detail, etc. of feedback information. Finally, it is worth noting that there is evidence that some managers require the assurance of feedback to confirm that their 'process' is in control.

(d)   The purpose of goal congruence is to provide a unity of goals and of the means and manner of their achievement.

It is of course a rather idealistic concept. It would be nice to think that each of three divisions can produce a budget in its own interests, but which, when combined into a company budget, produces an acceptable company plan. Where goal congruence is not immediately in evidence, intervention may be necessary by a higher level of management to resolve the conflict.

### Question 4 (CIMA)

You are the budget controller of a large organization and are primarily concerned with the budgetary control of large scale administrative expenses.

(a)   Indicate broadly what sort of data you would require to be included in an annual budget proposal from an administrative department.
(b)   In the context of management motivation and involvement explain what is meant by lack of goal congruence, giving two examples of this.
(c)   Explain what other problems you might expect to meet in administrative expense budgets that would not normally be present if you were controlling operating expense budgets.

### Answer 4

(a)   Any answer to this question requires assumptions to be made about the roles of the budget controller and the manager of the administrative department respectively. It is assumed that the budget controller essentially has a critical and/or coordinating role, but that the administrative department manager is responsible for deciding the form and level of activities in his department, and for the cost of providing them.
Data expected would therefore include:

1   A statement of the philosophy underlying the existence of the administrative department.
2   A statement of responsibilities covered and services provided by the department.
3   A statement of costs expected to be incurred in the department for the budgetary period.
4   Explanation of change proposed in comparison to the activities of the current year.
5   An indication of how cost levels will be expected to respond to the change in the nature or level of the service required or provided.

(b)   Lack of goal congruence occurs when the likelihood of achieving corporate objectives is reduced by the way in which functional budgets are prepared. For example, if the relationship between department A and department B is not 'balanced', the resulting conflict is not conducive to the achievement of corporate objectives.
Examples would be (presumably continuing to relate comment to the administrative department).

1   The establishment of levels of cost (staffing, etc.) in the administrative department capable of providing service levels over and above those required or called for departments served. Such lack of goal congruence may be associated with 'budget padding' and the prestige identified with size of budget in £ terms.
2   It may be that the manager of the administrative department plans the development of the department for the future in isolation from plans for the development of the whole organization. It is important that the development of the administrative department should be seen as serving a changing firm in which structural change will also be required.

(c)

1   Difficulty would be experienced in identifying a measurable output from the department.
2   There would be problems in trying to relate cost inputs to service benefits provided.
3   An obvious basis or bases of flexing does not exist and therefore the judgement of changes in cost level is extremely difficult.

4 Cost efficiency as one means of appraising manager performance becomes questionable.

## Further reading

Argyris, C., *Integrating the Individual and the Organization*, Wiley, 1964.

Emmanuel, X. and Oltey, D.T. *Accounting for Management Control*, Macmillan, 1985.

Hopwood, A.G., Accounting and organizational behaviour, in Carsberg, B., and Hope, A. (eds.) *Current Issues in Accounting*, 2nd edn, Philip Allan, 1984.

Lowe, E.A., and Machin, J.L.F. *New Perspectives in Management Control*, Macmillan, 1983.

Otley, D.T., Management accounting and organization theory: a review of their inter-relationship, in Scapens, R.W., Otley, D.T. and Lister, R., *Management Accounting, Organizational Theory and Capital Budgeting: Three Surveys*, Macmillan, 1984.

# 9 Capital budgeting

## Introduction

Capital budgeting has a vital role to play in the broader processes of strategic planning and budgetary control. Investment proposals must be studied within the context of the firm's goals and policies.

Capital budgets may reveal the spending requirements of an organization over a period of several years, and can therefore be easily distinguished from the relatively short-term decisions, involving a time scale of up to one year.

In the private sector, longer term capital investment decisions include investments in plant and machinery, and research and development, whereas in the public sector such decisions include new hospitals, schools, roads, houses and transportation.

Capital budgeting systems should strive to create an atmosphere which encourages the generation of new investment proposals and evaluates them as accurately as possible. However, loss-making proposals must be identified at the earliest possible moment. This may be achieved by ensuring that lower-level managers are made to study, thoroughly, every aspect of a proposal before seeking higher-level approval. Finally, it must be remembered that the investment decision process will provide good control information and feedback on project progress.

## The capital investment process

The following diagram illustrates the framework of the investment process and is discussed below.

Objectives and strategy
Search for opportunities
Screening of opportunities

Analysis of feasible alternatives
Evaluation of alternatives
Authorization
Implementation and control

## Objectives and strategy

### The search

This involves a continuous search for investment opportunities which are compatible with the firm's objectives. Although businesses may pursue many goals, survival and profitability are two of the most important objectives.

### Screening

Each proposal is then subjected to a preliminary screening process in order to assess whether it is technically feasible; resources required are available; and the expected returns are adequate to compensate for the risks involved.

### Analysis of feasible alternatives

If a proposal satisfies the screening process it is then analysed in more detail by gathering technical, economic and other data. Projects are also classified into new products, expansions or improvements, and ranked within each classification with respect to profitability, risk and degree of urgency.

### Evaluation of alternatives

This stage will involve the determination of an investment's inflows and outflows and the application of a special decision criteria in order to evaluate the proposal. Investment appraisal techniques are fully described later in this chapter (see page 192), and range from the simple payback method and accounting rate of return to the more sophisticated discounted cash flow techniques. The technique selected should be the one which enables a manager to make the best decisions in the light of prevailing circumstances.

### Authorization

Once evaluated a proposal will be forwarded to a higher-level of management appraisal.

### Implementation and control

If approved a project will be implemented and progress is monitored with the aid of feedback reports. These reports will include critical path analysis, capital expenditure progress reports, performance reports (comparing actual performance against plan), and post completion audits.

## Qualitative considerations

It is important for students to appreciate that the various investment appraisal techniques, described below, are based on quantitative information. However, information which cannot be easily quantified, i.e. qualitative factors, must be considered by management. These factors are subjective by nature and may be very difficult to evaluate. For example how does one value the quality, reliability, and promptness of supply in a make or buy type of decision, or customer appeal of a particular salesperson.

In the public sector a cost benefit analysis (CBA) is widely used which enables a comparison to be made between the estimated cost of a project and the estimated value and benefits which may arise from the project. However, it differs from financial analysis by being much broader in its application, e.g. when building a plant CBA would recognize the social costs of possible pollution on the health of the population.

## Investment appraisal techniques

### (a)  The payback method

This method calculates the payback period, which is the number of years necessary to recover the capital investment. Under this criterion a business should invest its money in the project with the shortest payback period. The initial investment and yearly returns are expressed in terms of cashflows.

*Example 1*

|  | Project X (£) | | Project Y (£) | |
| --- | --- | --- | --- | --- |
| Initial investment | (100,000) | | (100,000) | |
| Year | Cash inflows | Total cash inflows to date | Cash inflows | Total cash inflows to date |
| 1 | 20,000 | 20,000 | 25,000 | 25,000 |
| 2 | 20,000 | 40,000 | 25,000 | 50,000 |
| 3 | 30,000 | 70,000 | 50,000 | 100,000 |
| 4 | 30,000 | 100,000 | 20,000 | 120,000 |
| 5 | 50,000 | 150,000 | 10,000 | 130,000 |

In this example project Y would be selected as its payback period of three years is shorter than the four year payback period of project X.

*Advantages*

1 It is simple to apply, easy to understand, and of particular import-ance to businesses which lack the appropriate skills necessary for more sophisticated techniques.
2 The payback method is of some value in risk assessment, as cash-flows arising in earlier years are more certain than those of sub-sequent years (i.e. risk and time are related). Investments with shorter payback periods will generally be less risky.
3 It does not involve assumptions about future interest rates.
4 Ranking projects according to their ability to repay quickly may be useful to firms when experiencing liquidity constraints. They will need to exercise careful control over cash requirements.

*Disadvantages*

1 The payback method does not indicate whether an investment should be accepted or rejected, unless the payback period is com-pared with an arbitrary managerial target.
2 Cash flows arising after the payback period are ignored. In the above example project X, year 5, £50,000 and project Y, years 4 and 5, £20,000 and £10,000 were excluded by the decision criterion. Pro-fitability is therefore neglected.
3 It fails to consider the timing of cash flows, e.g. £10,000 received in year 2 is more valuable than £10,000 received in year 3 because the former can be reinvested in the interim year. In order to compare future cash inflows with the initial investment, the cash receipts must be discounted to their present values (see DCF page 195). This disadvantage can be overcome to a certain extent by the discounted payback method. Under this method cash flows are first discounted to their present values and then used to determine the payback period.
4 The traditional payback approach does not consider the salvage value of an investment. It fails to determine the payback period required in order to recover the initial outlay if things go wrong. The bailout payback method concentrates on this abandonment alterna-tive.

*Example 2*
Project A costs £200,000 and project B costs £300,000. Both have a ten year life. Uniform cash receipts expected are A £40,000 and B £80,000. Salvage values expected are A £140,000 declining at an annual rate of £20,000 and B £160,000 declining at an annual rate of £40,000.

Under traditional payback:

$$\text{Project A} = \frac{£200,000}{£40,000} = 5 \text{ years}$$

$$\text{Project B} = \frac{£300,000}{£80,000} = 3.75 \text{ years}$$

Therefore project B is selected as it has the shorter payback period.

Under bailout payback, the bailout payback time is reached when the cumulative cash receipts plus the salvage value at the end of a particular year equal the initial investment.

| Project A | Cumulative Cash receipts | Salvage Value |
|---|---|---|
| End of year 1 | £40,000 + £140,000 = £180,000 | |
| End of year 2 | £80,000 + £120,000 = £200,000 | |

Therefore bailout payback period is 2 years.

| Project B | Cumulative cash receipts | Salvage value |
|---|---|---|
| End of year 1 | £ 80,000 + £160,000 = £240,000 | |
| End of year 2 | £160,000 + £120,000 = £280,000 | |
| End of year 3 | £240,000 + £ 80,000 = £320,000 | |

Bailout period is between 2 and 3 years.

If the major objective is to avoid loss due to the firm's current financial situation, then the bailout approach is preferable and project A is chosen.


### (b)   The accounting rate of return

This method involves *accounting profits*, not cash flows, and is similar to the performance measure of return on capital employed.

$$\text{The accounting rate of return} = \frac{\text{Average annual profit}}{\text{Average (or initial) investment}} \times 100$$

*Example 3*
An investment with expenditure of £500,000 is expected to produce the following profits (after deducting depreciation).

Year 1   £40,000
Year 2   £80,000
Year 3   £90,000
Year 4   £30,000

$$\text{Average annual profits} = \frac{£40,000 + £80,000 + £90,000 + £30,000}{4}$$

$$= £60,000$$

Average investment assuming nil scrap value is the average of the investment at the beginning and the investment at the end.

i.e. $\dfrac{£500.00 + 0}{2} = £250,000$

Note, if the residual value is not zero but say £60,000, then the average investment would be:

$\dfrac{£500,000 + £60,000}{2} = £280,000$

The accounting rate of return $= \dfrac{£60,000}{£250,000} \times £100 = 24\%$

This percentage is compared with those of other projects in order that the investment yielding the highest rate of return can be selected.

## Advantages

1 The computation is simple and easy to comprehend.
2 It is not concerned with cash flows but rather based upon profits which are reported in annual accounts and sent to shareholders.
3 Unlike the payback method, the accounting rate of return does take into consideration all the years involved in the life of a project.

## Disadvantages

1 This method, like the payback method, fails to consider the timing of the cash flows.
2 It ignores the liquidity aspects, i.e. control over cash requirement of investments, as annual returns are expressed in terms of profits, not cash flows.
3 The accounting rate of return does not indicate whether an investment should be accepted or rejected, unless the rate of return is compared with the arbitrary managerial target. It measures the returns in relation to the outlay and does not evaluate the absolute worth of the returns.
4 It is based upon profits not cash flows. However, it is the latter which determines shareholders' wealth and not non-cash items such as accruals and depreciation etc.
5 Problems can arise in defining yearly profits, which will depend, to a certain extent, on the accounting policies adopted by the firm with respect to such items as stock valuation, the treatment of depreciation and research and development, etc.

## (c) Discounted cash flow techniques (DCF)

Before discounted cash flow techniques can be fully described it is necessary to consider in more detail the timing of cash flows.

## The time value of money

One of the main disadvantages of both the payback and accounting rate of return methods is that they ignore the fact that it is preferable to receive money earlier rather than later, because of the opportunity to invest in the meantime, i.e. money has a time-value.

The future value of £1000 invested at a constant rate of interest say ten per cent per annum can be found by using the compound interest formula:

$$F = P(1 + i)^t$$

where F = future value, P = sum invested now (year 0), and i = number of years for which the money is invested.

Year 1     $F = £1000 (1 + 0.10)^1 = £1100$
Year 2     $F = £1000 (1 + 0.10)^2 = £1210$
Year 2     $F = £1000 (1 + 0.10)^3 = £1331$

The above compounding technique converts a present value into a future value.

Discounting is the opposite of compounding. Discounting converts cash to be received in the future into a value at the present time.

The formula for calculating future values can be rearranged to provide one for determining present values.

$$P = \frac{F}{(1 + i)^t}$$

Using the sum of £1331 received at the end of year 3 its present value

$$P = \frac{£1331}{(1 + 0.1)^3} = £1000$$

£1210 received at the end of year 2

$$P = \frac{£1210}{(1 + 0.1)^2} = £1000$$

£1100 received at the end of year 1

$$P = \frac{£1100}{(1 + 0.1)^1} = £1000$$

This discounting technique which converts cash inflows and outflows for different years into their respective values at the same point of time (now), allows for the time value of money.

Discounted cash flows are cash flows which have been converted into a common value (present value), and can be treated in a like manner.

## The rate of interest (discount rate)

The economic theory of a firm operates via the principle that the firm should operate at a level where marginal revenue is equal to marginal

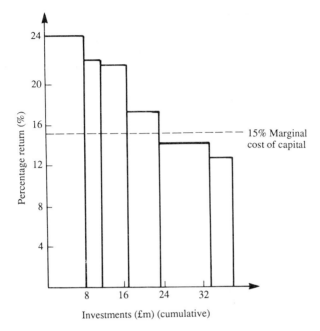

Figure 9.1

costs. When this is applied to capital investment decisions shareholders' wealth is maximized. Figure 9.1 illustrates this principle.

The marginal revenue is denoted by the percentage return on investment and the marginal cost by the firm's marginal cost of capital. The term cost of capital represents the cost of the capital to finance the investments. In the above diagram it can be seen that investment 1 involves expenditure of £8m and yields a 25 per cent rate of return, whereas investment 2 requires expenditure of £3m and yields a return of 22.5 per cent. This diagram illustrates that the firm should invest in projects 1, 2, 3 and 4 because their returns exceed the firm's cost of capital. Projects 5 and 6 will be rejected.

The cost of capital is a market determined rate of interest, and is the discount rate (or required rate of return) which is used for discounting cash flows in investment appraisal calculations. In this chapter it is assumed that:

1  The discount rate is constant over the life of an investment; and
2  all cash flows can be predicted withs certainty so that a risk premium need not be added to the discount rate in order to compensate for risk. The unadjusted rate represents the risk free rate and is the discount rate used to allow for time value of money.

The DCF model has two variations; net present value (NPV) and internal rate of return (IRR). Both approaches take into account the timing of cash flows.

## Net present value method

The net present value (NPV) of an investment is the difference between the present value (PVs) of the predicted cash receipts (cash inflows) and predicted cash outlays (cash outflows).

A positive NPV arises when the present values of the receipts exceeds those of the outlays, and will indicate that the investment should be accepted.

*Example 4*
A firm can invest £10,000 in a project with a life of three years. The forecasted cash inflows are as follows:

Year 1   £4000
Year 2   £5000
Year 3   £4000

The cost of capital is ten per cent per annum. Should the investment be made?

The investment outlay is at its present value of £10,000 and the present values of the cash inflows can be found by using the discounted formula, mentioned earlier:

$$P = \frac{F}{(1+i)^t}$$

$$\frac{4000}{(1.10)^1} + \frac{5000}{(1.10)^2} + \frac{4000}{(1.10)^3} = 10{,}700 \text{ PV of inflows}$$

$$(10{,}000) \text{ PV of outflows}$$

$$\text{NPV} = +770$$

This positive NPV indicates that the investment should be made.

If the discounting formula $P = \dfrac{F}{(1 + i)^t}$ is rearranged

it can be expressed as   $P = F \times \dfrac{1}{(1 + i)^t}$

$\dfrac{1}{(1 + i)^t}$ is called the discount factor

This discount factor can be found in tables published by CIMA.

To use the table the discount factors are found by referring to each year of the cash flows and the relevant interest rate. For example using a ten per cent interest rate, the discount factor for year 1 is 0.909, and for years 2 and 3 the factors are 0.826 and 0.751. These discount factors are then multiplied by the estimated cash flows (F) in order to find the present values of the cash flows.

Using example 4 the calculation is as follows:

| Year | Cash flow (£) | Discount factor | Present value (£) |
|------|---------------|-----------------|-------------------|
| 0 | (10,000) | 1 | (10,000) |
| 1 | 4,000 | 0.909 | 3,636 |
| 2 | 5,000 | 0.826 | 4,130 |
| 3 | 4,000 | 0.751 | 3,004 |
| | | NPV | +770 |

Students will observe the following:

Firstly the discount factors found in the table have been based on £1 received in t years time, e.g.

$$\text{Year } 1 = \frac{£1}{(1.10)} = 0.909$$

$$\text{Year } 2 = \frac{£1}{(1.10)^2} = 0.826$$

$$\text{Year } 3 = \frac{£1}{(1.10)^3} = 0.751$$

Secondly the year column in the above calculation is based on year-ends.

In this chapter the tables will be used whenever possible. Obviously for a particular year or rate of interest not given in the table it will be necessary to resort to the basic discounting formula, e.g. discounting a future cash flow in year 27 to a present value at an interest rate of 15.5 per cent.

$$P = \frac{F}{(1.155)^{27}} = 0.020F$$

## Relevant cash flows

So far in this chapter all the inflows and outflows used in the NPV calculations have been assumed to be relevant. The following points should be noted when assessing the information which should be included in a discounted cash flow computation under both techniques (NPV and IRR):

1   Shareholders' wealth is based upon the movement of cash, and therefore accounting concepts and policies have no effect upon the firm's wealth. Non-cash flow accounting or book entries must therefore be excluded from discounting calculations. The most common of these entries is the non-cash item, depreciation.

2   Variable overheads will be relevant for decisions which involve a change in the activity level. However, fixed overhead which has been allocated or apportioned are irrelevant. It is only if total fixed costs increase or are avoidable as a result of the decision that the incremental or avoidable fixed costs are included as a relevant cash flow.

3　Costs which have been incurred (sunk costs) cannot affect future decisions and are therefore irrelevant to such decisions.
4　An opportunity cost, i.e. the greatest future benefit foregone or sacrifice made, as a result of using a particular resource or choosing a particular alternative, should be included in the DCF model.

*Example*
A firm has spent £5000 on research concerning an investment in machinery (with a five year life) which would cost £100,000 and have a nil residual value. If the machinery is purchased it will be depreciated on a straight line basis, and estimated cash inflows arising from the investment, over its five year life are £30,000 per annum after deducting depreciation on the machinery, but before deducting operating costs.

These operating costs include variable costs, £10,000 pa, allocated fixed costs, £15,000 pa; additional supervisor, £12,000 pa; indirect material needed to operate the machinery is in stock and has a resale value of £3000 pa. Its original cost was £6000 pa.

Advise the firm. Its cost of capital is 10 per cent.

*Solution*
Points to consider:

1　The £5000 research cost is a sunk cost and is therefore irrelevant.
2　The annual depreciation of £20,000, being a non-cash item must be excluded from the calculation, and is therefore added to the estimated cash inflows £20,000 + £30,000 = £50,000 pa.
3　The allocated fixed costs are irrelevant, but the additional supervisor at £12,000 pa represents an incremental fixed costs and is therefore relevant.
4　The resale value of the indirect material is an opportunity cost of using that material and will be included in the computation. Its original book cost is a sunk cost and is therefore excluded.
5　Both the cost of the machinery and its variable operating costs are future costs, relevant to this decision.
6　Relevant operating costs amount to £10,000 + £12,000 + £3000 = £25,000 pa.

| Year | Outflows | Inflows | Net Cash flow | Discounted factor | Present values |
|---|---|---|---|---|---|
| 0 | (100,000) | | (100,000) | 1 | (100,000) |
| 1 | (25,000) | 50,000 | 25,000 | 0.909 | 22,725 |
| 2 | (25,000) | 50,000 | 25,000 | 0.826 | 20,650 |
| 3 | (25,000) | 50,000 | 25,000 | 0.751 | 18,775 |
| 4 | (25,000) | 50,000 | 25,000 | 0.683 | 17,075 |
| 5 | (25,000) | 50,000 | 25,000 | 0.621 | 15,525 |
| | | | | NPV = | (5,250) |

The negative NPV of £5250 would indicate rejection of this investment.

## Annuities

When the annual cash flows are constant (an annuity) it is possible to find the present values by either discounting the cash flows individually, as in the earlier examples or by multiplying the annual cashflow by an annuity factor.

The annuity factor is simply the sum of the present value factor for each year of an annuity.

For an annuity starting in year 1 and finishing in year t the annuity factor is:

$$\frac{1 - (1 + i)^{-t}}{i}$$

where i = interest rate, t = year.

*Example 6*
Find the present value of an annuity of £5000 payable at the end of each year for four years at an interest rate of 12 per cent using:

(a)  discount factors,
(b)  an annuity factor,
(c)  the annuity formula.

*Solution*
(a)  Present value = £5000 × 0.983 + £5000 × 0.797 + £5000 × 0.712
+ £5000 × 0.636
= £15,185

(b)  Present value = £5000 × 3.037 = £15,185

(c)  Annuity factors = $\dfrac{1 - (1.12)^{-4}}{0.12}$ = 3.037

   PV = £15,185

If an annuity does not start at year 1, then the calculation using an annuity factor is modified.

*Example*
Find the present value of an annuity of £5000 starting in year 5 and finishing in year 10, if the interest rate is 8 per cent.

*Solution*
PV = £5000 × (annuity factor for year 10 − annuity factor for year 4)*
   = £5000 × (6.710 − 3.312) = £16,990

* The year before the first cash flow arises.

## Perpetuities

A perpetuity is an annuity which continues to infinity. The present value of a perpetuity which starts in year 1 is the cashflow $\times 1/i$ where $i$ is the interest rate.

The present value of a perpetuity of £2000 at an interest rate of 15 per cent

$$= £2000 \times \frac{1}{0.15} = £13,333$$

If the perpetuity commences at a later year, say, year 7

$$\text{then PV} = £2000 \times \frac{1}{0.15} \times \text{discount factor for the previous year} - \text{year 6}$$

$$= £2000 \times \frac{1}{0.15} \times 0.432 = £5760$$

## The internal rate of return (IRR) method

The internal rate of return is that rate of interest at which the present value of an investment is zero.

*Example 4*
A firm can invest £10,000 in a project with a life of three years, estimated cash inflows are as follows:

Year 1   £4000
Year 2   £5000
Year 4   £4000

It is not necessary to know the firm's cost of capital in order to calculate the IRR.

The IRR is found by a trial and error process, using a number of discount factors until the NPV is zero.

An 8 per cent discount factor produces a positive NPV of £1165. A 12 per cent discount factor produces a positive NPV of £405. It is therefore necessary to apply a higher percentage until zero is reached. A 15 per cent discount factor gives a negative NPV of £108. Once a positive and negative NPV have been calculated the IRR is found by using an interpolation method.

The interpolation formula is as follows:

$$\text{Lower interest rate} + \frac{\text{NPV of lower rate}}{\text{NPV of lower rate} - \text{NPV of higher rate}} \times (\text{Higher rate} - \text{Lower rate})$$

$$12\% + \frac{405}{405 - (-108)} \times (15\% - 12\%)$$

$$= 14.37\% \text{ (IRR)}$$

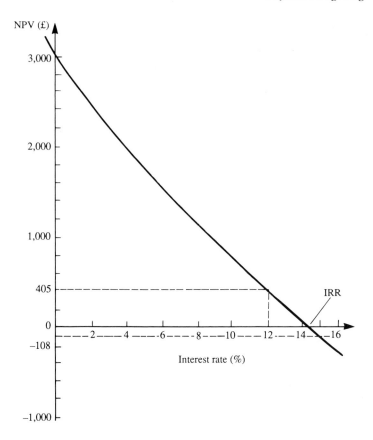

Figure 9.2

The interpolation method only gives an approximate IRR because it assumes a linear relationship between NPVs and interest rates. The greater distance between any two interest rates producing positive and negative NPVs the less accurate is the IRR. Students would be advised when engaged on the trial and error process of selecting arbitrary interest rates to ensure that the gaps between the rates chosen are not too large.

The calculation of the internal rate of return is illustrated in Figure 9.2.

Although the firm's cost of capital is not required to calculate the IRR, it is necessary to compare the two rates in order to decide whether to make the investment. If the IRR exceeds the cost of capital as in the above example, 14.4 per cent is greater than 10 per cent, then the investment will yield a positive NPV and should be accepted.

When management rank mutually exclusive projects, the higher the IRR of a project the greater the priority in its ranking.

The calculation of the IRR is simplified when an annuity arises.

*Example 7*
A firm is considering an investment of £11,000 which will yield cash inflows of £5000 for three years. Cost of capital is 10 per cent. Calculate the IRR.

*Solution*
The IRR will be where the annual cash flow × annuity factor, less the investment outlay = zero.

$$\text{Annuity factor} = \frac{\text{Cost of investment}}{\text{Annual cash flow}} = \frac{£11,000}{£5,000} = 2.2$$

In the annuity table, for year 3, 2.2 lies between 17 per cent and 18 per cent.

The IRR is between 17 per cent and 18 per cent which being greater than the cost of capital makes the project acceptable.

## Comparison of the internal rate of return and net present value methods

In most situations the NPV method will result in the same decisions as the IRR method. However, the next example will show that conflict can arise between the methods.

*Example 8*
Project A and project B are mutually exclusive.

| Year | | Project A Cash flow (£) | Project B Cash flow (£) |
|---|---|---|---|
| 0 | Capital investments | 1,000 | 10,000 |
| 1 | Inflows | 240 | 2,300 |
| 2 | Inflows | 288 | 2,640 |
| 3 | Inflows | 346 | 3,040 |
| 4 | Inflows | 414 | 3,500 |
| 5 | Inflows | 498 | 4,020 |

Cost of capital is 10 per cent

Which investment should be made?

*Solution*

| | IRR | NPV |
|---|---|---|
| Project A | 20% | +£309 |
| Project B | 15% | +£1441 |

The IRR ranks project A higher, whereas the NPV ranks project B first. Because these projects are mutually exclusive it is essential to rank them correctly.

The conflict arises because B is ten times the size of A. This gives a higher NPV but in relative terms it is less profitable with a lower percentage return. Obviously B is preferable since it gives the greatest increase in shareholders' wealth.

A method which can be used to check the IRR ranking is called the incremental yield calculation.

The incremental yield is the internal rate of return of the difference in cashflows between the two project.

| Year | Cash flows (B–A) (£) |
|------|----------------------|
| 0    | (9000)               |
| 1    | 2060                 |
| 2    | 2353                 |
| 3    | 2694                 |
| 4    | 3086                 |
| 5    | 3522                 |

IRR = 14.4%

The additional investment of £9000 in project B is worthwhile, as it yields a return of 14.4 per cent which is greater that the firm's cost of capital of 10 per cent. This is in accord with the ranking given by the NPV method.

### Advantages of internal rate of return

1 This method gives a percentage rate of return as a measure of performance and managers find this easy to comprehend as it can be related to the current interest rates.
2 It is not necessary to know the required rate of return, which can be difficult to determine.

### Advantages of net present value

1 This method gives an absolute measure of profitability and shows the change in shareholders' wealth.
2 The NPVs of investments are additive, i.e. double the cash flows and the NPV is doubled.
3 The NPV always gives the correct ranking, for mutually exclusive projects whereas the IRR may not. However the IRR ranking can be checked using the incremental yield technique.
4 The NPV gives clear accept/reject decisions whereas the IRR can give multiple solutions when the cash flows involve a multiple change in sign.

    e.g. Year 0  (£1200)
        Year 1   £4000
        Year 2  (£3000)

See Figure 9.3.

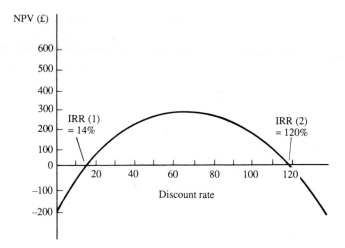

Figure 9.3

5　The NPV method assumes that the reinvestment of interim cash flows will be at the cost of capital. This is a realistic assumption as the costs of capital should be in line with current market rates of interest. However, the IRR assumes that interim cash flows will be reinvested at a rate of interest equal to the IRR. This is a rate of interest peculiar to the investment and unlikely to be similar to market rates.

Although the net present value approach is technically superior to the internal rate of return method the latter is more widely used in practice. Recent surveys indicate that some firms use both variations of the DCF model.

## Advantages of discounted cash flow techniques

1　They consider the timing of cash flows and allow for the time value of money.
2　They recognize all the years involved in the life of a project, unlike the payback method.
3　Definite decisions are made in accept/reject situations, unlike the other investment appraisal techniques which depend upon arbitrary targets.
4　They are based on cash flows, not profits, and are therefore unaffected by accounting conventions. Also the firm can exercise greater control over the liquidity aspect of investments.
5　Risk can be incorporated into DCF computations by adjusting the discount rate (NPV method) or cut-off rate (IRR method).

## Disadvantages of discounted cash flow techniques

1  There may be difficulty in accurately establishing rates of interest of the cash flow period.
2  Lack of adequate expertise in order to properly apply the techniques and interpret results.
3  These techniques are based on cash flows, whereas reported earnings are based on profits. The inclusion of DCF analysis may cause projected earnings to fluctuate considerably and thus have an adverse effect on share prices. A project's cash flow and its contribution to the profit and loss account in a particular year will differ substantially for the following reasons:

(a)  Capital expenditure affects the cash flow in the year in which it occurs, but in the profit and loss account it is spread over a period of years.
(b)  Receipt of cash may occur at a different time to that when sales are made.
(c)  The period in which cash grants and depreciation allowances are credited to the profit and loss account often differs from the period when they are received.

In this chapter we have described the procedures involved in the capital investment process and the various investment appraisal techniques.

Although discounted cash flow techniques are technically superior to other methods because they incorporate the time value of money, Pike in his comprehensive survey of some of the largest UK companies found that payback is the mosts widely employed method of evaluation. His findings are as follows:

Evaluation methods used by UK companies

|  | 1975 (%) | 1980 (%) |
|---|---|---|
| Payback period | 71 | 79 |
| Accounting rate of return | 51 | 51 |
| Internal rate of return | 42 | 54 |
| Net present value | 32 | 38 |

The Pike survey also revealed that 90 per cent of the firms used multiple evaluation criteria. This might indicate that managers select the technique which best flatters a particular project, or that no single method is sufficiently ideally suited to appraise all types of proposals.

## Examination questions

### *Question 1 (CIMA)*

A company is considering investing in a new manufacturing facility with the following characteristics:

A   initial investment £350,000 – scrap value nil;
B   expected life 10 years;
C   sales volume 20,000 units per year;
D   selling price £20 per unit;
E   variable direct costs of £15 per unit;
F   fixed costs excluding depreciation £25,000 per year.

The project shows an internal rate of return (IRR) of 17 per cent. The managing director is concerned about the viability of the investment as the return is close to the company's hurdle rate of 15 per cent. He has requested a sensitivity analysis.
    You are required to:

(a)   Recalculate the internal rate of return (IRR) assuming each of the characteristics A to F above, in *isolation*, varies adversely by 10 per cent.
(b)   Advise the managing director of the most vulnerable area likely to prevent the project meeting the company's hurdle rate.
(c)   Explain what further work might be undertaken to improve the value of the sensitivity analysis undertaken in (a).
(d)   Re-evaluate the situation if another company, already manufacturing a similar product, offered to supply the units at £18 each; this would reduce the investment required to £25,000 and the fixed costs to £10,000.

*Answer 1*

| | | (£) |
|---|---|---|
| Sales | 20,000 × £20 | 400,000 |
| Variable cost | 20,000 × £15 | 300,000 |
| Contribution | 20,000 × £5 | 100,000 |
| Fixed cost | | 25,000 |
| Profit (cash flow) | | 75,000 |

(a)

| | Investment (£) | Life (Years) | DCF Factors* | Cash flow (£) | IRR (%)[†] |
|---|---|---|---|---|---|
| A | 385,000 a | 10 | 5.133 | 75,000 | 14.5 |
| B | 350,000 | 9 | 4.669 | 75,000 | 15.5 |
| C | 350,000 | 10 | 5.385 | 65,000 b | 13.0 |
| D | 350,000 | 10 | 10.000 | 35,000 c | 1.0 |
| E | 350,000 | 10 | 7.778 | 45,000 d | 5.0 |
| F | 350,000 | 10 | 4.828 | 72,500 e | 16.0 |

*Notes*

* Investment/cash flow
[†] From cumulative tables. Using A as an example:

10 years at 14% = 5.22 DCF; 10 years at 15% = 5.02 DCF

a   £350,000 + £35,000 (10%) = £385,000

b   Drop in volume of 10% = 2,000 units × £5 contribution
        = £10,000
    Net = 75,000 − £10,000 = £65,000
c   Drop in price of 10% = £2 × 20,000 units = £40,000
    Net = £75,000 − £40,000 = £35,000
d   Increase in variable cost of £0% = £1.50 × 20,000 units
        = £30,000
    Net = £75,000 − £30,000 = £45,000
e   Increase in fixed costs of 10% = £2,500
    Net = £75,000 − £2,500 = £72,500

(b)   The most vulnerable areas, in descending order of risk are:

|   |   | Effect on IRR |
|---|---|---|
| D | Fall in selling price | Disastrous drop |
| E | Increased variable cost | Substantial drop |
| C | Fall in sales volume | Somewhat below cut-off |
| A | Increased investment | Marginally below cut-off |

Changes in characteristics B and F keep the IRR above the cut-off level.

(c)   *Further work*
The value of the sensitivity analysis could be improved by:

● Using different rates of change from the single rate of 10 per cent.
● Examining the results of favourable as well as adverse changes.
● Testing the outcomes of combinations of changes, e.g. price reductions with volume increases, higher capital expenditure with longer life, higher variable cost with lower sales volume, etc.
   Calculating expected values for each element by using probabilities.

(d)   *New position*

|   |   | (£) |
|---|---|---|
| Sales | 20,000 × £20 | 400,000 |
| Variable cost | 20,000 × £18 | 360,000 |
| Contribution | 20,000 × £2 | 40,000 |
| Fixed cost |   | 10,000 |
| Profit (cash flow) |   | 30,000 |

New investment is £25,000 which would be repaid within the first year and thus has a negative discount.

Unless there are special commercial or logistic, as opposed to financial, reasons for not using the other company as a sub-contractor, the idea should be adopted.

## Question 2 (CIMA)

A local government department is proposing to purchase a mechanical hedge-cutting machine to replace existing manual work. Manpower savings are greatest when using a machine with the largest cutting blade but the initial purchase cost increases more than proportionately to the width of the cut achieved.

The relevant cost details are:

| Cutter size: | 12in (£000) | 18in (£000) | 24in (£000) | 30in (£000) | 36in (£000) |
|---|---|---|---|---|---|
| Purchase cost | 20 | 30 | 45 | 70 | 100 |
| Annual operating cost saving after deduction of depreciation | 8 | 10 | 11 | 8 | 6 |

Depreciation: straight-line method over ten years.
Taxation, assume no tax allowances or tax payment.

The local council will not authorize any proposed investment which does not yield a discounted cash flow (DCF) return of 15 per cent per annum. All proposals meeting this target are further subject to an overall total investment limit.
You are required to:

(a) Calculate the discounted cash flow (DCF) yield for each of five machines.
(b) State the largest sized machine which could be purchased and meet the 15 per cent investment criterion.
(c) List five factors that would influence the decision on this particular investment if there are more investment projects than funds available; at least two should be in favour of proceeding with it and at least two supporting deferment.

*Answer 2*
(a)

| Cutter size | 12in (£000) | 18in (£000) | 24in (£000) | 30in (£000) | 36in (£000) |
|---|---|---|---|---|---|
| Year 0 | −20 | −30 | −45 | −70 | −100 |
| Annual gross savings | 8 | 10 | 11 | 8 | 6 |
| Add back: | | | | | |
| Depreciation | + 2 | + 3 | + 4.5 | + 7 | + 10 |
| Net Savings | 10 | 13 | 15.5 | 15 | 16 |
| DCF index | 2 | 2.31 | 2.9 | 4.67 | 6.25 |
| Cum. factor for 10 yrs | 40% 2.40 | As | 30% 3.09 | 16% 4.83 | 9% 6.42 |
| | 50% 1.98 | 12in | 40% 2.4 | 17% 4.64 | 10% 6.14 |
| Difference | 0.42 | 0.42 | 0.69 | 0.19 | 0.28 |
| | 0.02 | 0.09 | 0.19 | 0.03 | 0.11 |
| Difference % | 0.42 | 0.42 | 0.69 | 0.19 | 0.28 |
| | 1% | 21% | 28% | 15% | 39% |
| Yield (approx) | 50% | 42% | 33% | 17% | 10% |

(b)  *Present value*
15% × 10 years = 4.97

| Cutter size | 12in | 18in | 24in | 30in | 36in |
|---|---|---|---|---|---|
| PV | 49.7 | 64.61 | 77.04 | 74.55 | 79.52 |

|  | PV | Capital expenditure |
|---|---|---|
| 18in | 64.61 | 30 |
| 12in | − 49.70 | − 20 |
| Extra | 14.91 | 10 |

Therefore 18in preferred

|  | | |
|---|---|---|
| 24in | 77.04 | 45 |
| 18in | − 64.61 | − 30 |
| Extra | 12.43 | 15 |

Therefore 18in preferred

By inspection 30in and 36in are worse than 24in.
Therefore 18in is the largest size to be purchased.

(c)  *In favour of proceeding*

- It meets the investment criteria.
- It is the best of the opportunities.
- There is a possible increase in manual labour cost over time, thus the savings may well be even greater (in opportunity cost terms).
- DCF return of some 42 per cent seems attractive.
- Inflation – equipment costs are increasing and may continue to do so.
- Safety – operating conditions may be safer with the new equipment as workers will be less exposed in dangerous traffic conditions.

*In favour of deferment*

- If we wait there may be an improvement in the economics of a larger machine, e.g. lower capital cost for the same savings.
- There might be some technological breakthrough or improvement for the whole range of machines.
- Alternative investment – funds might be used in alternative projects yielding greater savings or other benefits.
- Purchase of the machine might lead to redundancies with loss of job opportunities in an area of high unemployment.

## Question 3 (CIMA)

You have just been appointed management accountant to a company that markets three products. These are sold to a wide range of industries and marketing is done through three geographical areas: South, Midland and North.

For the year ending 31 December 1988 the company presents you with the following budget:

| | *Area* | | | |
|---|---|---|---|---|
| | *South (£000)* | *Midland (£000)* | *North (£000)* | *Total (£000)* |
| Sales | 1100 | 440 | 660 | 2200 |
| Cost of goods sold | 575 | 230 | 345 | 1150 |
| | 525 | 210 | 315 | 1050 |
| Warehousing cost | | | | |
| Freight | 77 | 33 | 52.8 | 162.8 |
| Supplies | 44 | 17.6 | 26.4 | 88 |
| Wages and salaries | 74 | 29.6 | 44.4 | 148 |
| | 195 | 80.2 | 123.6 | 398.8 |
| Selling costs | | | | |
| Salesmen's salaries | 30 | — | — | 30 |
| Salesmen's commissions | 22 | — | 52.8 | 74.8 |
| Salesmen's expenses | 23 | — | — | 23 |
| Agents' commissions | — | 22 | — | 22 |
| Sales office and management | 24.5 | 9.8 | 14.7 | 49 |
| Advertising | 95 | 38 | 57 | 190 |
| | 194.5 | 69.8 | 124.5 | 388.8 |
| Administration cost | 120 | 48 | 72 | 240 |
| Total | 509.5 | 198 | 320.1 | 1037.6 |
| Net profit (or lost) | 15.5 | 12 | (5.1) | 22.4 |

Your investigations into budgeted figures reveal the following:

*Sales and cost of goods*

| Products | D | E | F |
|---|---|---|---|
| Units sold in thousands: | | | |
| Area: South | 33.0 | 44.0 | 33.0 |
| Midland | 13.2 | 17.6 | 13.2 |
| North | 19.8 | 26.4 | 19.8 |
| Per unit | (£) | (£) | (£) |
| Standard selling price | 12 | 10 | 8 |
| Standard variable production costs | 5 | 4.50 | 4 |

Fixed production overhead included in cost of goods sold, is £160,000 per annum.

Warehousing costs (packaging and despatch are done in each area).

| Area | South (£) | Midland (£) | North (£) |
|---|---|---|---|
| Freight costs, negotiated rates per unit of product sold | 0.70 | 0.75 | 0.80 |
| Warehouse: | | | |
| Supplies per unit | 0.40 | 0.40 | 0.40 |
| Wages per unit | 0.65 | 0.45 | 0.45 |
| Supervision salaries, per annum | 14,000 | 4,000 | 9,000 |

*Selling costs*

In South area there are six salesmen each paid a basic wage of £5000 per annum with a commission of two per cent of sales. Their fixed expenses are £2000 per annum each and variable expenses one per cent of sales.

In Midland area, manufacturers' agents are used. They receive a commission of five per cent of sales from which they have to meet all their expenses. However, they can also sell products of other manufacturers provided these are not directly competitive.

In North area there are three salesmen paid solely by a commission of eight per cent of sales. From this they have to meet all their expenses.

The salaries of the company sales manager and his assistant together with expenses, total £25,000 per annum. Of the total advertising £130,000 is national advertising under the direction of the company sales manager.

*Other sales office and advertising costs*

| Area | South (£) | Midland (£) | North (£) |
|---|---|---|---|
| Local sales office costs | 12,000 | 4,000 | 8,000 |
| Local advertising | 40,000 | 5,000 | 15,000 |

*Administration costs, per annum*

Fixed costs relating to the whole company are £140,000.

The remainder varies with the number of orders which are budgeted at: South 32,000; Midland 6000; North 12,000.

The company uses a cut-off rate of 14 per cent annum in deciding capital expenditure projects.

You are to deal with each of the following four requirements independently of one another. Assume that items that are not affected by the suggested changes stay the same; ignore taxation and inflation.

(a) State, with reasons, whether, in view of the loss shown in the budget presented to you, you agree with a proposal to close the North area.

(b) Calculate what extra sales value would need to be made in the Midland area to cover additional local advertising of £15,000 there and provide an extra profit of £10,000. Assume that the average value per order remains constant.

(c)   Calculate the benefits or otherwise of a proposal to change the Midland area from manufacturers' agents to a salaried sales force of three salesmen paid on the same basis as those in South area if an increase in sales of 15 per cent were achieved (representing an increase of 10 per cent of the number of orders) as a result of the change.

(d)   Explain, with supporting calculations, whether you would approve of a proposal to change the basis of remuneration of salesmen in the North area to that operating in the South area. The change would require the immediate payment of £3500 to each salesmen in the North area as compensation, and, as a result of the change, sales would alter as follows:

|  | Proportion of 1988 budget | |
|---|---|---|
|  | Sales | Number of orders received |
| Year | (%) | (%) |
| 1988 | 95 | 98 |
| 1989 | 100 | 100 |
| 1990 | 105 | 105 |

## Answer 3

(a)   The budgeted loss for the North is £5100. On the assumption that all regional costs will not be removed by closure, the North region contribution must be established.

| Product | D | E | F | Total |
|---|---|---|---|---|
| Units sold | 19,800 | 26,400 | 19,800 | 66,000 |
|  | (£) | (£) | (£) | (£) |
| Sales | 237,600 | 264,000 | 158,400 | 660,000 |
| Variable product costs | 99,000 | 118,800 | 79,200 | 297,000 |
| Production contribution | 138,600 | 145,200 | 79,200 | 363,000 |

| Other variables | |
|---|---|
| Freight, supplies and wages 1.65 unit | (108,900) |
| Salesmen's commissions | (52,800) |
| Administration £2 order | (24,000) |
|  | 177,300 |

| Costs saved upon closure: | |
|---|---|
| Warehouse supervision | (9,000) |
| Local advertising | (15,000) |
| Local sales office costs | (8,000) |
|  | 145,300 |

Note, wages should be 66,000 units at £0.45 = £29,700 + £9000 supervision = £38,700. However the figure given in the budget is £44,400, a discrepancy of £5700.

The proposed closure of the North region could not be supported since some £145,300 contribution could be lost. This does assume however that sales lost in the North would not be picked up in the Midlands or South, and further, that savings in capital employed (warehouse premises, stocks, customer credit, etc.) do not justify the lost contributions.

(b)  Midlands

| Product | D | E | F | Total |
|---|---|---|---|---|
| Units sold | 13,200 | 17,600 | 13,200 | 44,000 |
| | (£) | (£) | (£) | (£) |
| Sales | 158,400 | 176,000 | 105,600 | 440,000 |
| Variable product costs | 66,000 | 79,200 | 52,800 | 198,000 |
| Production contribution | 92,400 | 96,800 | 52,800 | 242,000 |

| Other variables | |
|---|---|
| Freight, supplies and wages 1.65 unit | (70,400) |
| Salesmen's commissions | (22,000) |
| Administration £2 order | (12,000) |
| | 137,600 |

| Additional margin required: | |
|---|---|
| Profit | 10,000 |
| Local advertising | 15,000 |
| | 25,000 |

Extra sales value required is: $\dfrac{25,000}{137,600} \times 440,000 = £79,942$

(c)

| | (£) |
|---|---|
| Margin from workings in (b) | 137,600 |
| Additional margin 15% | 20,640 |
| Add back sales commissions £22,000 × 1.15 | 25,300 |
| Add variable order costs saved | |
| (15% − 10%) = 5% of £12,000 | 600 |
| | 46,540 |

| Salesmen's costs: | (£) |
|---|---|
| Salaries 3 × £5000 | 15,000 |
| Commission 2% on £440,000 × 1.15 | 10,120 |
| Expenses 3 × £2000 | 6,000 |
| Variables 1% on £440,000 × 1.15 | 5,060 |
| | 36,180 |
| Additional profit | 10,360 |

(d)  Part (a) of the answer showed that as a continuing area the North produces a contribution of £177,300. The proposal in (d) must be measured against this.

| Proposal | 1988 (£) | 1989 (£) | 1990 (£) |
|---|---|---|---|
| Sales | 627,000 (95%) | 660,000 | 693,000 (105%) |
| Margin | | 177,300 | |
| Add back commission | | 52,800 | |
| Add back order costs | | 24,000 | |
| | 241,395 (95%) | 254,100 | 266,805 (105%) |
| Order costs | 23,520 (98%) | 24,000 | 25,200 (105%) |
| | 217,875 | 230,100 | 241,605 |
| Selling costs: | | | |
| Fixed salaries | | | |
| and expenses | (21,000) | (21,000) | (21,000) |
| Variable commission | | | |
| and expenses 3% | (18,810) | (19,800) | (20,790) |
| | 178,065 | 189,300 | 199,815 |

The incremental profits (and therefore cash flows) are:

| | (£) | 14% discount | (£) |
|---|---|---|---|
| 1988 | 765 | 0.88 | 673 |
| 1989 | 12,000 | 0.77 | 9,240 |
| 1990 | 22,515 | 0.67 | 15,085 |
| | | | 24,998 |

This figure of £24,998 exceeds the immediate compensation payable which is £10,500. The proposed change can therefore be recommended.

### Question 4 (CIMA)

Due to competition from low-priced imports a large company has decided that it must close one of its factories which is an important employer of labour in a country town. This closure will displace 600 people at present employed there.

After consultation with relevant trade unions the board of the company is considering offering the following options to employees at the factory.

1  To relocate them at another of the company's factories some 100 miles away.
2  To retrain them for jobs at other plants, each some 20–25 miles away.
3  To allow early retirement for a limited category of employee.
4  To declare redundant those who do not accept, or are not eligible for, the above three options.

The board has, however, made a qualification to its offer. This is that the average cost per employee of the proposed scheme, capitalized in present value terms, should not exceed twice the average redundancy cost if all employees were to be made redundant.

The board has therefore asked you, the management accountant, to:

(a) Calculate the expected average cost per employee of the proposed scheme and say whether or not it exceeds the criterion set.
(b) List what non-financial benefits might accrue to:

    (i)   the company's present employees;
    (ii)  the company itself;

    if the board's offer were to be accepted.

Your investigations of the situation reveal the following:

1 *Relocation*

It is proposed that each employee taking up this option should receive a £1000 interest-free loan towards new housing, repayable at the end of five years, and a relocation grant of £750. The extra personnel department expenses to deal with the administration of this work will amount to £15,000 during the year following the closure.

These costs will to some extent be offset by the fact that at the new location there is a shortage of relevantly skilled labour. It is assessed that each person who relocates will save the company recruiting costs of £50 and make available increased production (compared with unskilled employees) over the first twelve months of employment worth £120 per month in terms of contribution and a reduction in rejects of £80 per month for the first six months. However, it is expected that ten per cent of employees who relocate will have left their job of their own accord by the end of the year, by which time they will have repaid their £1000 loans. Savings for that proportion of employees should be ignored for the whole period.

2 *Retraining*

Costs of a two month retraining course payable by the company will be £180 per employee selecting this option. During this time they will each be on full salary which can be taken as an average of £350 per month. Additional administration costs of £5000 will be incurred.

Offsetting these costs will be benefits at the plants from the work on which retraining is being done. These comprise £50 recruitment cost saving and avoidance of loss of production from labour turnover amounting to £100 per person per month in terms of contribution for the first six months. However, it is expected that after retraining only 70 per cent of those doing the course will take up work with the company, the balance leaving the company of their own accord.

3 *Early retirement*

This would offer half-pay (i.e. an average of £2500 per annum). It can be assumed that employees in this group have, on average, five years to go before normal retirement.

## 4　Redundancy

This varies with the age and service of each individual employee. For calculation purposes employees may be placed into two categories. Those in category P can be regarded as averaging 12 years' service and those in category Q as averaging four years' service. The entitlement of pay for each year of service will average $1\frac{1}{4}$ weeks for the first category with an average wage of £90 per week; for the second category it is one week's pay for each year of service with an average wage of £80 per week. However, the Government will refund 41 per cent of this cost to the company.

*Employee intentions*

Preliminary enquiries indicate the following intentions.

|  | Number in each category choosing the option | |
| --- | --- | --- |
| Option | P | Q |
| 1　Relocate | 88 | — |
| 2　Retrain | 198 | 136 |
| 3　Retire early | 40 | — |
| 4　Redundancy | 70 | 68 |

*Other information*

For purposes of this calculation the company wishes to capitalize its annual expenditure at 12 per cent annum.

You should work to the nearest whole number and ignore taxation.

### Answer 4

(a)　Since the decision criterion relates to a comparison of scheme cost with redundancy cost, the latter will be calculated first, on the assumption that all costs would be immediate.

| Category | Employees | Average service years | Weeks due | Rate | Cost per employee (£) | For total employees (£) |
| --- | --- | --- | --- | --- | --- | --- |
| P | 396 | 12 | 15 | £90 | 1,350 | 534,600 |
| Q | 204 | 4 | 4 | £80 | 320 | 65,280 |
|  | 600 |  |  |  |  | 599,880 |
| Government refund (assume immediate) 41% | | | | | | 245,951 |
| Net cost to the company | | | | | | 353,929 |

$$\text{Average cost per redundant employee} = \frac{£353,929}{600} = £590$$

Therefore the average cost per employee for the alternative scheme must not exceed $2 \times £590 = £1180$

*Evaluation of the alternative scheme*
*Relocations*
88 employees are selecting this option

|  | (£) |
|---|---|
| Interest free loan | 88,000 |
| Relocation grant | 66,000 |
| Personnel costs (discounted at 12%) 0.89 | 13,350 |
| Loan repayment | (8,010) |
| Leavers (say 9) 9,000 × 0.89 | (45,030) |
|  | 114,310 |

Benefits:
(To be based on 79 employees only)

|  | (£) | (£) |
|---|---|---|
| Recruiting costs at £50 |  | 3,950 |
| Increased production 79 × 12 × 120 | 113,760 |  |
| Reduced rejects      79 × 6 × 80 | 37,920 |  |
|  | 151,680 |  |
| at 0.89 |  | 134,995 |
|  |  | 138,945 |
| Net benefit from relocation |  | 24,635 |

*Retraining*
334 employees are selecting this option

|  | (£) |
|---|---|
| Cost of training course | 60,120 |
| Administration costs | 5,000 |
| Salary 334 × 350 × 2 | 233,800 |
|  | 298,920 |

Benefits:

|  | (£) |
|---|---|
| 70% × 334 = 234 × £50 recruitment costs |  |
| (treat as immediate saving) | 11,700 |
| 234 × £100 × 6 months £140,000 discounted at 0.89 | 124,956 |
|  | 136,656 |
| Net cost of retraining | 162,264 |

*Early retirement*
40 employees are selecting this option

40 × 2,500 × 5 years (assume payment at the commencement of each year)
£100,000 × 4.04                                        £404,000

*Redundancy*
138 employees are selecting this option

| Category | Employees | Average service years | Weeks due | Rate | Cost per employee (£) | For total employees (£) |
|---|---|---|---|---|---|---|
| P | 70 | 12 | 15 | £90 | 1,350 | 94,500 |
| Q | 68 | 4 | 4 | £80 | 320 | 21,760 |
| | | | | | | 116,260 |

Government refund (assume immediate) 41%  245,951

Net cost to the company  68,593

*Summary of scheme cost*

| | (£) |
|---|---|
| Relocation | (24,635) |
| Retraining | 162,264 |
| Retirement | 404,000 |
| Redundancy | 68,593 |
| | 610,222 |

$$\text{Average cost per scheme employee} = \frac{£610,222}{600} = £1017$$

The scheme cost falls within the constraints set by the Board.

(b)  *Non-financial benefits to:*
1   The Company's present employees

(a)  They will benefit from the knowledge that at least they have been given a personal choice from four options.
(b)  Since the proposals emanate from consultation with their trade unions, employees will perhaps feel that the procedure has been proper and considerate. This can be reassuring in what are clearly unhappy circumstances.
(c)  The employee who relates strongly to the company, e.g. family tradition of employment with the company, has options which will allow the links to continue, although not necessarily in the same area.
(d)  Family pressures and relationships may not be so strained as under a direct closure/redundancy operation. For example, the personal sense of being discarded may be avoided by the retraining and relocation options.

2   The Company itself

(a)  Since the scheme, as indicated earlier emanates from the trade union discussion, the industrial relations environment on a group basis may not be so disturbed as under imposed closure/redundancy.
(b)  There is likely to be a lower level of adverse publicity. It is particu-

larly noted that the Company is an important employer in a country town where employment alternatives may not exist.

(c)  The Scheme provides some evidence of, and indeed, basis for, manpower planning. This should offer managerial benefits.

(d)  Closure and redundancy represents a discarding of known and unknown human asset attributes and skills. This is avoided, at least in part, by the scheme.

## Further reading

Lumby, S., *Investment Appraisal*, 2nd edn, Van Nostrand Reinhold (UK), 1984.

Pike, R.H., *Capital Budgeting in the 1980's: A Major Survey of the Investment Practices in Large Companies*, CIMA, 1982.

Van Horne, J.C., *Financial Management and Policy*, Prentice Hall, 1983.

# 10 Further aspects of capital budgeting

## The effect of inflation on capital budgeting

The cash flows of investments may be expressed at contemporary price levels, i.e. ones which include the effects of future inflation and are the actual money amounts estimated to be spent or received in the future.

These *money cash flows* must be discounted by a *money interest rate*. A money interest rate is the market interest rate, which is comprised of three elements: a percentage to compensate for the time value of money, plus premiums for risk and anticipated inflation.

However, cash flows can also be stated in terms of current prices, i.e. excluding inflation. These *real cash flows* are not present values, but just exclude the effects of future inflation. Real cash flows must be discounted by a *real interest rate*, which will compensate for the time value of money and risk, but exclude a premium for inflation.

## The relationship between the interest rates

The money interest rate is equal to the real interest rate plus the rate of inflation. However this is an approximate relationship. For a more accurate relationship, let the following be considered:

$$\frac{\text{Money cash flow at time t}}{(1 + M)^t} = \text{Present value}$$

where M = money discount rate, t = year.

A money cash flow first discounted by the inflation rate will equal a real cash flow, which when discounted by the real discount rate gives the present value.

$$\frac{\text{Money cash flow at time t}}{(1 + I)^t (1 + R)^t} = \text{Present value}$$

where I = inflation rate, R = real discount rate, t = year.

Therefore

$$\frac{\text{Money cash flow at time t}}{(1 + M)^t} = \frac{\text{Money cash flow at time t}}{(1 + I)^t (1 + R)^t}$$

i.e. $(1 + M) = (1 + I)(1 + R)$

Therefore $1 + R = \dfrac{1 + M}{1 + I}$

Therefore $R = \dfrac{1 + M}{1 + I} - 1$

*Example*

If the money interest rate is 15 per cent, and anticipated inflation is 10 per cent, find the real interest rate

$$\text{Real interest rate} = \frac{1 + 0.15}{1 + 0.10} - 1 = 4.55\%$$

The money rate is equal to a little more than the real rate plus the inflation rate.

This means that if £1000 is invested (assuming zero inflation) at the real rate of 4.55 per cent, then at the end of the year £1045.50 is obtained to compensate for the time value of money. To maintain this return in real terms this amount must grow by 10 per cent (inflation rate) to £1045.50 × 1.10 = £1150. Therefore with 10 per cent inflation a return of 15 per cent is required, which consists of 4.55 per cent to compensate for the time value of money, and a premium of 10.46 per cent to maintain the investment's purchasing power.

*Comprehensive example*

An investment with a life of three years will cost £15,000 and has an estimated scrap value at the end of its life of £3000. The annual cash inflows, including the effects of inflation, are expected to be:

Year 1   £12,000
Year 2   £16,000
Year 3   £19,000

Annual cash outflows will be £7000 in the first year and remain constant over the three years in real terms.

If the market discount rate (money rate) is 15 per cent and the general rate of inflation is 8 per cent find the net present value of the investment using computations based in:

(a)  money terms; and
(b)  real terms.

*Solution*

(a)  It is important for students to note that, unless otherwise stated, cash flows can be assumed to be expressed in money terms. In this example, therefore, the investment, its scrap value, and the cash flows are stated in money terms, and only the cash outflows must be converted to money cash flows.

Year 1                              = £7000
Year 2    £7000 ×   1.08    = £7560
Year 3    £7000 × $(1.08)^2$ = £8165

In the following NPV computation money cash flows are discounted by a money rate of interest.

| Years | Inflows (£) | Outflows (£) | Net cash flow (£) | Discount factor (Money rate 15%) | Present value (£) |
|---|---|---|---|---|---|
| 0 |  | (15,000) | (15,000) | 1.000 | (15,000) |
| 1 | 12,000 | (7,000) | 5,000 | 0.870 | 4,350 |
| 2 | 16,000 | (7,560) | 8,440 | 0.756 | 6,381 |
| 3 | 19,000 | (8,165) | 10,835 | 0.658 | 7,129 |
|  | 3,000 |  | 3,000 | 0.658 | 1,974 |
|  |  |  |  | NPV = | £4,834 |

(b)  Cash flows are now expressed in real terms as follows: Annual cash outflows (which include one year – first year – of inflation).

$$£7000 \times \frac{1}{1.08} = £6481 \text{ annum}$$

$$\text{Scrap value} = £3000 \times \frac{1}{(1.08)^3} = £2382$$

$$\text{Annual cash inflows, Year 1}\quad £12,000 \times \frac{1}{(1.08)} \quad £11,111$$

$$\text{Annual cash inflows, Year 2}\quad £16,000 \times \frac{1}{(1.08)^2} = £13,717$$

$$\text{Annual cash inflows, Year 3}\quad £19,000 \times \frac{1}{(1.08)^3} = £15,083$$

In this NPV calculation real cash inflows are discounted by a real rate of interest.

$$\text{The real discount rate is: } \frac{1.15}{1.08} - 1 = 6.48\%$$

| Years | Inflows (£) | Outflows (£) | Net cashflow (£) | Discount factor (Real rate 6.48%) | Present value (£) |
|---|---|---|---|---|---|
| 0 | | (15,000) | (15,000) | 1.000 | (15,000) |
| 1 | 11,111 | (6,481) | 4,630 | $\dfrac{1}{1.0648}$ | 4,348 |
| 2 | 13,717 | (6,481) | 7,236 | $\dfrac{1}{(1.0648)^2}$ | 6,382 |
| 3 | 15,083 | (6,481) | 8,602 | $\dfrac{1}{(1.0648)^3}$ | 7,125 |
| | | 2,382 | 2,382 | $\dfrac{1}{(1.0648)^3}$ | 1,973 |
| | | | | NPV = | £4,828 |

## Inflation rates

So far in this chapter it has been assumed that all cash flows increase at the same rate of inflation. However, in reality one finds that different cash flows, e.g. those relating to wages, material and plant will increase at different rates.

When DCF calculations are in money terms each cash flow includes its specific inflation rate, rather than the general inflation rate, and will be discounted at the money rate of interest as before.

However, calculations in real terms are more complex as they must ensure that the real cash flows exclude their specific rates of inflation rather than the general inflation rate. A real discount rate must therefore be calculated individually for each cash flow with a different rate of inflation.

*Example*
An investment with a life of three years requires cash expenditure of £20,000. There will be no residual value. The annual cash inflows and outflows at current price levels are £25,000 and £15,000 respectively. The general rate of inflation is eight per cent. Cash outflows will rise in line with the general rate of inflation but the cash inflows are estimated to increase at seven per cent. The money rate of interest is 17.7 per cent.

Find the NPV of the investment using a calculation based in real terms.

*Solution*
If this calculation was required in money terms it would involve simply inflating the cash inflows and outflows at seven per cent and eight per cent and then discounting them by 17.7 per cent.

However, in real terms the cash flows will be unadjustsed as they are already expressed in current (real) terms and must be discounted by real interest rates.

The real rates are as follows:

$$\text{Cash inflows} = \frac{1.177}{1.07} - 1 = 10\%$$

$$\text{Cash outflows} = \frac{1.177}{1.08} - 1 = 9\%$$

| Years | Cash flow (£) | Discount factor (Real rates) | Present values (£) |
|-------|---------------|------------------------------|--------------------|
| 0 | (20,000) | 1.0 | (20,000) |
| 1–3 | 25,000 | 2.487* | 62,175 |
| 1–3 | (15,000) | 2.531† | (37,965) |
| | | NPV = | £4,210 |

*Annuity factor at 10 per cent for 3 years.
†Annuity factor at 9 per cent for 3 years.

## Risk

In the last chapter it was assumed that the future cash flows of projects were known with certainty. In reality the cash flows are uncertain and may vary. This variation of cash flows about some central or expected value is known as risk. The larger the likely variation the greater the risk, if there is no variation then there is no risk i.e. we know the outcome with certainty.

The most widely used measure of risk is the *standard deviation* of the cash flows (or its square the *variance*). Given two projects with approximately equal expected NPVs but the first with a standard deviation of £6000 and the second project with a standard deviation of £9000, the first project would be accepted in preference to the second as the standard deviation (and hence risk) is lower.

One of the problems with using the standard deviation as a measure of risk is that the standard deviation does not distinguish between projects of different size. A project with a large investment and corresponding large cash flows will tend to have a larger standard deviation than a project with much smaller cash flows, due to the size of the projects and not due to the true risk of the projects. To overcome this problem of size we replace the standard deviation by the coefficient of variation. This is the standard deviation divided by the expected value and the result is expressed as a percentage.

The main objection to the use of the standard deviation as a measure of risk is that most investors are concerned about obtaining a very low return (downside risk) rather than a higher than average return (upside risk). J.C.T. Mao in a survey of a range of medium and large companies in the USA showed that managers were relating risk to the possibility of a bad outcome and this was influencing their investment policy. This downside risk can be measured by the *semivariance* rather than variance. It is calculated in the same manner as the variance but only for values below the expected return. However, this measure has conceptual problems as well as difficulties in developing the theory further, particularly as the variance fits in with sampling theory used in portfolio theory. Hence the standard deviation is still more widely used.

## Calculation of the mean and standard deviation of the net present value of a project

*Example*
Investment: £100,000

|  | Possible cash flows (£1000) | Probability |
|---|---|---|
| 1st year | 30 | 0.2 |
|  | 50 | 0.3 |
|  | 80 | 0.5 |
|  |  | 1.0 |
| 2nd year | 50 | 0.1 |
|  | 90 | 0.3 |
|  | 110 | 0.6 |
|  |  | 1.0 |

Cost of capital 12 per cent per annum.

*Solution*
Expected return 1st year $= 30 \times 0.2 + 50 \times 0.3 + 80 \times 0.5 = 61$
Expected return 2nd year $= 50 \times 0.1 + 90 \times 0.3 + 110 \times 0.6 = 98$

$$NPV = -100 + \frac{61}{1.12} + \frac{98}{(1.12)^2} = 30.99$$

Now variance $= \Sigma x^2 p(x) - (\bar{x})^2$ for each year.

Variance for investment is zero (cash flow is certain at £100,000)

Variance for 1st year $= 30^2 \times 0.2 + 50^2 \times 0.3 + 80^2 \times 0.5 - 61^2 = 409$

Variance for 2nd year $= 50^2 \times 0.1 + 90^2 \times 0.3 + 110^2 \times 0.6 - 98^2 = 336$

$$\text{Variance (NPV)} = 0 + \frac{409}{1.12^2} + \frac{336}{1.12^4}$$

$$= 539.59$$

Therefore standard deviation $= 23.23$.

*Note*, assuming the early cash flows are independent of each other, the variances have to be added together (do not add the standard deviations). However, the variances occur at different points in time so they must be discounted by the appropriate yearly discount factor. Now the variances are square measures therefore they have to be discounted by the squares of the normal yearly discount factors. Hence the discount factor for the variance of 336 in year two is the square of $1/(1.12)^2$ i.e. $1/(1.12)^4$.

The project has a NPV of £30,990 with a standard deviation of £23,230.

The coefficient of variation is $\dfrac{23.23}{30.99} \times 100 = 75.0\%$

This is very high. Most risk adverse decision makers would be unhappy with coefficients of variation greatly in excess of ten per cent.

*Example 2*

A project requires an initial investment of £300,000. The yearly cash inflows follow normal distributions with the following means and standard deviations:

|          | Mean     | Standard deviation |
|----------|----------|--------------------|
| 1st year | £150,000 | £30,000            |
| 2nd year | £200,000 | £34,000            |
| 3rd year | £ 80,000 | £16,000            |

The cost of capital is eight per cent per annum.

*Solution*

NPV = $-300 + 150 \times 0.9259 + 200 \times 0.8573 + 80 \times 0.7938$

$\qquad$ = 73.85

i.e. £73,850

Variance = $0 + 30^2 \times 0.9259^2 + 34^2 \times 0.8573^2 + 16^2 \times 0.7938^2$

$\qquad$ = 1782

Standard deviation = 42.22

The NPV of the project is £73,850 with a standard deviation of £42,220.

The cash flows followed normal distributions therefore the overall project follows a normal distribution. Hence the probability that the project will obtain a positive NPV can be determined.

$$Z = \frac{0 - 73.85}{42.22} = -1.75$$

From normal tables, the area to the left of the mean but right of our zero value = 0.4599.

Therefore probability of a positive NPV is 0.5 + 0.4599 = 0.9599, about 96 per cent, only a 4 per cent chance of netting a negative NPV.

## Analysing risk using simulation

The previous section methods for analysing risk can only be used if the cash flows follow well known distributions such as the normal or poisson and are independent from year to year. It may not be used if:

1  there are many sources of cash flow all varying in their distribution, or
2  the time horizon may vary, and is a random variable, or
3  the independence assumption does not hold then a more robust approach is required.

Computer simulation enables the management accountant to analyse complex investments for which direct mathematical methods do not exist or are inadequate for the purpose. Because of the power of modern micro-computers simulation involving hundreds of complex, repetitive calculations can be carried out. It examines a wide range of different scenarios eventually leading to a rational decision to accept or reject the project.

Simulation is also ideally suited to answer such questions as, 'What happens if ...?' and hence sensitivity analysis can be applied.

*Example*
Should the following project be undertaken?

Initial cash outflow £8000
Length of project 3 years
Cost of capital 12 per cent per annum
Likely cash flows:

| Year 1 cash inflow | Prob. | Year 2 cash inflow | Prob. | Year 3 cash inflow | Prob. |
|---|---|---|---|---|---|
| 2000 | 0.2 | 4000 | 0.3 | 1000 | 0.5 |
| 4000 | 0.5 | 8000 | 0.4 | 3000 | 0.3 |
| 7000 | 0.3 | 9000 | 0.3 | 4000 | 0.2 |
|  | 1.0 |  | 1.0 |  | 1.0 |

The first step is to assign random numbers to each cash flow according to the probabilities. To achieve the correct allocation, first determine the cumulative probability distributions for each of the three years and then use the cumulative probabilities to allocate the random numbers as follows:

Year 1
  Cash flows

| (£1000) | Probability | Cumulative probability | Random numbers |
|---|---|---|---|
| 2 | 0.2 | 0.2 | 0–1 |
| 4 | 0.5 | 0.7 | 2–6 |
| 7 | 0.3 | 1.0 | 7–9 |
|  | 1.0 |  |  |

Year 2
  Cash flows

| (£1000) | Probability | Cumulative probability | Random numbers |
|---|---|---|---|
| 4 | 0.3 | 0.3 | 0–2 |
| 8 | 0.4 | 0.7 | 3–6 |
| 9 | 0.3 | 1.0 | 7–9 |
|  | 1.0 |  |  |

Year 3
  Cash flows

| (£1000) | Probability | Cumulative probability | Random numbers |
|---|---|---|---|
| 1 | 0.5 | 0.5 | 0–4 |
| 3 | 0.3 | 0.8 | 5–7 |
| 4 | 0.2 | 1.0 | 8–9 |
|  | 1.0 |  |  |

*Notes*

As the probabilities are given to one decimal place only one digit random numbers, i.e. 0 to 9, are needed.

The first cumulative probability is 0.2, this means allocating the first two random numbers, 0–1, to the first cash flow to £2,000. Notice the allocation is up to but including the number 3 which corresponds with the cumulative probability of 0.3. This is the first random number to be allocated to the next cash flow. The second cumulative probability is 0.7 which means allocating from 3 up to 6. Proceeding in this way the last set of random numbers for the first year are 7,8,9. Years 2 and 3 have been treated in the same manner.

All that is needed is a source of random numbers. A calculator or a computer can be used to generate random numbers. In this example computer generated random numbers are to be used. A table of computer generated numbers is given in the appendix.

Three random numbers are needed for the first simulation, one for each yearly cash flow. The random number table gives 0,9,1. These correspond to cash flows respectively of £2000; £9000 and £1000.

Remembering the initial cash outflow of £8000 and discounting at 12 per cent

$$\text{NPV} = -8 + 2 \times 0.8929 + 9 \times 0.7972 + 1 \times 0.7118$$

$$= 1.6724$$

The expected NPV of £1672 is positive indicating that the project should be undertaken.

However the main value of simulation is that it can be repeated a large number of times and a distribution of NPVs can be obtained giving a clearer estimate of the risk factor.

The simulation results are best shown in the form of a table. The following table contains ten simulations (using the first thirty random numbers in column one of the random number table) along with the mean, standard deviation and range for the NPVs and the cumulative probability distribution of the NPVs.

Simulation table

| Simulation number | Cash outflows £1000 | Year 1 | | Cash inflows Year 2 | | Year 3 | | NPV |
|---|---|---|---|---|---|---|---|---|
| | | rn | cf | rn | cf | rn | cf | |
| 1 | 8 | 0 | 2 | 9 | 9 | 1 | 1 | 1.672 |
| 2 | 8 | 1 | 2 | 5 | 8 | 1 | 1 | 0.875 |
| 3 | 8 | 8 | 7 | 6 | 8 | 3 | 1 | 5.339 |
| 4 | 8 | 5 | 4 | 1 | 4 | 2 | 1 | −0.528 |
| 5 | 8 | 2 | 4 | 5 | 8 | 3 | 1 | 2.661 |
| 6 | 8 | 7 | 7 | 5 | 8 | 9 | 4 | 7.475 |
| 7 | 8 | 1 | 2 | 3 | 8 | 6 | 3 | 2.299 |
| 8 | 8 | 7 | 7 | 2 | 4 | 0 | 1 | 2.151 |
| 9 | 8 | 2 | 4 | 1 | 4 | 1 | 1 | −0.528 |
| 10 | 8 | 3 | 4 | 3 | 8 | 3 | 1 | 2.661 |

| | | |
|---|---|---|
| Mean NPV | = | 2.406 |
| Standard deviation | = | 2.464 |
| Minimum NPV | = | −0.528 |
| Maximum NPV | = | 7.475 |

Probability distribution

| Class interval | Probability | Cumulative probability |
|---|---|---|
| >−1 and <0 | 0.2 | 0.2 |
| > 0 and <1 | 0.1 | 0.3 |
| > 1 and <2 | 0.1 | 0.4 |
| > 2 and <3 | 0.4 | 0.8 |
| > 3 and <4 | 0 | 0.8 |
| > 4 and <5 | 0 | 0.8 |
| > 5 and <6 | 0.1 | 0.9 |
| > 6 and <7 | 0 | 0.9 |
| > 7 and <8 | 0.1 | 1.0 |

The mean and standard deviation of the NPVs can be determined using the simulated NPVs in the simulation table. In addition if the NPVs are grouped into class intervals a probability distribution and a cumulative probability distribution can be determined for the project.

The cumulative probability distribution can be used to estimate that the probability of getting a negative NPV is 0.2. Note this is only an estimate based on a sample of size 10, too small a sample in practice.

The simulation was run on a computer one hundred times giving the following results:

| | |
|---|---|
| Number of simulation | 100 |
| Mean NPV | £2910 |
| Standard Deviation | £2358 |
| Minimum NPV | −£2314 |
| Maximum NPV | £8272 |

Probability distributions

| Class interval | Probability | Cumulative probability |
|---|---|---|
| >−3 and <−2 | 0.01 | 0.01 |
| >−2 and <−1 | 0 | 0.01 |
| >−1 and < 0 | 0.09 | 0.10 |
| > 0 and < 1 | 0.19 | 0.29 |
| > 1 and < 2 | 0.09 | 0.38 |
| > 2 and < 3 | 0.17 | 0.55 |
| > 3 and < 4 | 0.17 | 0.72 |
| > 4 and < 5 | 0.08 | 0.80 |
| > 5 and < 6 | 0.07 | 0.87 |
| > 6 and < 7 | 0.04 | 0.91 |
| > 7 and < 8 | 0.07 | 0.98 |
| > 8 and < 9 | 0.02 | 1.00 |

The probability of getting a negative NPV based on a sample size of a hundred is 0.10. The distribution is slightly positively skewed hence reducing the probability of rejecting the project. In this case where there is an asymmetric distribution the coefficient of variation is misleading.

$$\text{Coefficient of variation} = \frac{2.358}{2.910} \times 100 = 81.0\%$$

The high value of the coefficient of variation is to some extent inconsistent with the probability of 0.10 of rejecting the project.

## Sensitivity analysis

Another approach to risk which can be used with or without simulation is sensitivity analysis. This approach is usually used in ongoing situations where there is a need to identify which facts are most critical to a current project. When the critical factors have been identified they can be monitored to act as an early warning system before the project begins to show a loss. There can also be benefits in identifying the 'not so critical' factors because less time needs to be paid to them.

*Example*
A new project requires an initial investment of £8500 which it is estimated will generate net end of year cash flows of £3000 over a five year period. The companies cost of capital is estimated at 12 per cent per annum.

*Solution*
NPV under assumptions given $= -8{,}500 + 3{,}000 \times 3.605$

$$= £2{,}315$$

(See annuity table in appendix, annuity factor over 5 years at 12 per cent is 3.605)

Clearly the project should be undertaken as the NPV is positive. A sensitivity analysis on each factor is now carried out.

### Initial investment

As the NPV is £2315, if the initial cost rose by £2315 to £10,815, an increase of 27.2 per cent, the NPV would reach zero and the project would not be worth undertaking.

### Net annual cash inflow

For the NPV to be zero, the net annual cash inflows would have to be £C where

$$0 = -8500 + C \times 3.605$$

which leads to

$$C = \frac{8500}{3.605} = 2358$$

Which means if the net cash flows drop below £2358, a change of 21.4 per cent, the project should not be undertaken.

### The cost of capital

If the cost of capital is greater than the internal rate of return the project should be rejected.
At the IRR the NPV is zero. Let the annuity factory be A, then:

$$0 = -8500 + 3000 \times A$$

Therefore $A = \dfrac{8500}{3000} = 2.833$

Looking through the annuity table for a five year project the nearest is 2.86 at 22 per cent. The IRR is approximately 22 per cent. A percentage increase over the estimated cost of capital (12 per cent) of 83 per cent.

### Life of the project

4 years  NPV = −8500 + 3000 × 3.037 = £611
3 years  NPV = −8500 + 3000 × 2.402 = −£1294

Hence if the life of the project drops below four years it should not be undertaken. A change of 20 per cent.

### Sensitivity analysis summary

| Factor | Current value | Critical value | % change |
|---|---|---|---|
| Investment | £8,500 | £10,815 | +27.2 |
| Annual | | | |
| Cash flow | £3,000 | £2,358 | −21.4 |
| Cost of capital | 12% | 22% | +83 |
| Life of project | 5 years | 4 years | −20 |

It can be seen from our analysis that none of the factors analysed is particularly critical. There are no factors with a percentage change less than 20. The cost of capital is the least critical, showing that for this project the cost accountant does not have to be too concerned about the accuracy of our cost of capital calculation.

The problem with sensitivity analysis is that it only considers changing one variable at a time. Parametric analysis which considers more than one variable changing at a time is not very far advanced and is difficult to interpret. Sensitivity analysis is a ranking method.

## Multiple project selection

Now consider the selection of a group of projects (either at one time or over a fixed time period) which if accepted contain sequential sub-decisions over time.

## Decision trees

*Example*
A strawberry grower has sufficient acreage at the moment to meet the demand over the next year for his product. However, a well known cider maker is considering producing a new cocktail 'the strawberry

stinger' and has approached our grower to supply the necessary straw-
berries starting in two years' time (at the end of the second season). To
meet the new demand it will be necessary for the grower to increase his
acreage in time to put in more strawberry plants.

The new acreage can be obtained immediately for an outlay of
£100,000, or in one year's time when the price is estimated to be either
£105,000 with a probability of 0.3 or £120,000 with a probability of 0.7.
If at any time the grower has excess acreage there is a probability of 0.2
that his current customer will take the surplus and increase his net
earnings by 10 per cent. This higher level of sales will be maintained as
long as the extra acreage is being used for the normal market.

His current net operating profit is £30,000 a year. The new contract, if
taken, will add £8000 to the net operating profit.

The farmer's current cost of capital is 10 per cent per annum. Assume
all cash flows take place at the year end.

*Solution*
The current net operating profit of £30,000 can be ignored as it is not an
incremental cash flow. However the 10 per cent increase of £3000 is an
incremental cash flow.

It is assumed that if the extra acres are used in the first year they will
also be used in the second year and then used for the strawberry stinger
in future years. Cash flows from the contract will not start until the end
of the third year. (See Figure 10.1.)

*Calculations of discounted cash flows.*
1  *Extra acres purchased now*
(a)  Increase in current net profit in both years.

> Extra cash inflows:  £3000 at the end of 1st year
> £3000 at the end of 2nd year
> £8000 from end of 3rd year (Annuity)

$$\text{NPV} = 3000 \times 0.9091 + 3000 \times 0.8264 + \frac{8000}{0.10} \times 0.8264$$

$$= £71,319$$

(b)  Increase in current net profit only in second year.

> Extra cash inflows: £3000 at the end of 2nd year
> £8000 from the end of 3rd year (Annuity)

$$\text{NPV} = 3000 \times 0.8264 + \frac{8000}{0.10} \times 0.8264$$

$$= £68,591$$

(c)  No increase in current net profit in first two years.

> Cash inflows: £8000 from end of 3rd year (Annuity)

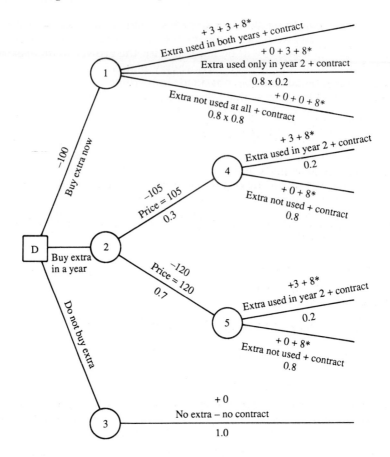

8* = An annuity of £8,000 1 year in perpetuity (in text)

Figure 10.1

$$NPV = \frac{8000}{0.10} \times 0.8264$$

$$= £66,112$$

Expected value at node 1:
0.2 × £71,319 + 0.8 × 0.2 × £68,591 + 0.8 × 0.8 × £66,112
= £67,550

Therefore expected incremental NPV to buy extra acres now is:
− £100,000 + £67,550
= − £32,450

2  *Extra acres purchased in one year's time*

Extra cash inflows: same as 1 (b)
NPV = £68,591

Extra cash inflows: same as 1 (c)
NPV = £66,112

Expected value at node 4 and 5:
= 0.2 × £68,591 + 0.8 × £66,112
= £66,608

Expected value at node 2:
= 0.3 × (−£105,000 + £66,608) + 0.7 × (−£120,000 + £66,608)
= −£48,892

Therefore expected incremental NPV for delaying buying decision for one year is −£48,892

3  *No extra acres at any time*

Extra cash inflows: None.
NPV = 0

Therefore expected incremental NPV if contract not taken = £0

| | |
|---|---|
| EV under buy now policy is | −£32,450 |
| EV under buy later policy is | −£48,892 |
| EV under do not buy policy is | £0 |

Therefore the optimal policy is not to take on the extra acreage and hence not to accept the new project. The expected NPV of this decision is

$$\frac{£30,000}{0.10} = £300,000$$

## The profitability index

The profitability index is defined as the present value of the cash flows (excluding the initial cash outflow) divided by the initial investment

$$PI = \frac{PV}{I}$$

This measure can be used for ranking projects which have sub-stantially different levels of investments.

As NPV = PV − I

Therefore dividing through by I

$$\frac{NPV}{I} = \frac{PV}{I} - \frac{I}{I}$$

$$\frac{NPV}{I} = PI - 1.$$

The NPV criteria is to invest in a project only when the NPV is greater than zero, therefore the right hand side must also be greater than zero if the project is to be selected. Hence;

$$PI - 1 > 0$$

i.e. PI > 1 is the new criteria for project selection.

If the projects being compared are independent projects then decisions using the profitability index are the same as would be made using the present value approach. The appeal of the profitability index is that it is a relative measure, which may be easily converted into a percentage, and can be used to compare projects with different investment levels.

Consider two projects A and B with the following information:

| Project | Investment (£) | PV (£) | NPV (£) |
|---|---|---|---|
| A | 100 | 136 | 36 |
| B | 500 | 548 | 48 |

Therefore PI (A) $= \dfrac{136}{100} = 1.36$

and PI (B) $= \dfrac{548}{500} = 1.096$

Both projects have a PI greater than 1 and should be selected (note both NPVs are greater than zero). However if the projects are mutually exclusive then using an NPV criteria project, B would be selected, having the highest NPV.

Using a PI criteria project A would be selected as it shows a return, in present value terms, of 36 per cent compared with A's 9.6 per cent. If there are a number of other projects with the same investment and NPV as A and the maximum amount that could be invested is £500, then five project type As could be producing a total NPV of 5 × £36, i.e. £180 compared to B's £48.

The PI criteria does lead to the correct decision in the single period capital rationing situation if the total capital can be fully used.

However, if there is more than one period then the profitability index may not lead to the correct decision.

## Multi-period capital rationing

Consider the following investment opportunities available to a company assuming the company's cost of capital is 10 per cent.

Cash available for investment in addition to the project cash inflows in year 0 is £100,000 and in year 1 £50,000. Any cash not invested at the

| Project | Year 0 | Cash flows (£1000) Year 1 | Year 2 | Year 3 | NPV | PI |
|---------|--------|--------|--------|--------|-------|-------|
| A | −60 | 20 | 80 | 50 | 61.86 | 2.03 |
| B | −50 | 30 | 70 | 30 | 57.66 | 2.15 |
| C | | −80 | 100 | 60 | 55.00 | 1.75* |

* all cash inflows discounted to year 0

beginning of a year may be invested in the money market for a year at eight per cent per annum.

There is insufficient capital to invest in all three projects. The PI criteria indicates that as much as possible should be invested in project B as it has the largest PI, and then in project A and so on.

The result is:

| Project | Investment | NPV |
|---------|-----------|-------|
| B | 50 | 57.66 |
| A | 50 | 51.55 |
| C | 80 | 55.00 |
| NPV of unused cash invested at 8% pa | | −0.30* |
| | | 163.91 |

*As only 83 per cent of project A is taken up, cash inflow in year 1 is 30 + 0.83 × 20 = 46.7

Therefore total available for investment is 46.7 + 50 = 96.7.

Project C requires 80 leaving 16.7 to be invested in year 1 in the money market.

Therefore cash flows associated with the surplus cash including interest are:

| Year | Cash flow | Discount factor | NPV |
|------|-----------|-----------------|--------|
| 1 | −16.7 | 0.9091 | −15.18 |
| 2 | 18.0 | 0.8264 | 14.88 |
| | | | − 0.30 |

An alternative approach is to formulate this investment problem as a linear programming model to maximize the net present value of the cash flows.

## Linear programming model

Let $x_1$ be the proportion of project A taken up, and similar definitions for $x_2$ and $x_3$ for B and C.

First year constraint:

$$60 x_1 + 50 x_2 + s_1 = 100$$

where $s_1$ is the surplus cash not invested put on deposit at 8 per cent per annum.

Second year constraint:

$$80 x_3 + s_2 = 50 + 20 x_1 + 30 x_2 + 1.08 s_1$$

where $s_2$ is the surplus cash put on deposit in year 2.

Note the surplus cash from year 1 with interest and the cash inflows from projects A and B are now available for investment.

Re-arrange the equation:

$$- 20 x_1 - 30 x_2 + 80 x_3 - 1.08 s_1 + s_2 = 50$$

In addition the variables $x_1$, $x_2$, and $x_3$ must be restricted to lie between 0 and 1, ensuring that the projects cannot be invested in more than once.

$$x_1 < = 1, x_2 < = 1, x_3 < = 1$$

The objective function is the net present value of all the cash flows:

$$z(\max) = 61.86 x_1 + 57.66 x_2 + 55.00 x_3 - 0.0182 s_1 - 0.165 s_2$$

Surplus cash flows

| Year | 0 | 1 | 2 |
|------|-----|----------|----------|
|      | $-s_1$ | $1.08s_1 - s_2$ | $1.08s_2$ |
| DF   | 1 | 0.9091 | 0.8264 |

Therefore

$$NPV = (-1 + 1.08 \times 0.9091)s_1 + (-0.9091 + 1.08 \times 0.8264)s_2$$

$$= -0.0182s_1 - 0.0165s_2$$

The negative coefficients reflect the fact that the company is investing its surplus cash flows at 8 per cent, while borrowing money at 10 per cent.

The problem was solved using a linear programming computer package which gave the following optimal solution.

Variables

$x_1 = 0.833$
$x_2 = 1$
$x_3 = 1$
$s_1 = 0$
$s_2 = 0$
$z(\max) = 164.21$

Shadow prices

| Constraint | Shadow price |
|------------|--------------|
| 1 | 1.031 |
| 2 | 0 |
| 3 | 0 |
| 4 | 6.11 |
| 5 | 55.00 |

The linear programming solution gives (in this case the some NPV (164.21) as the PI approach apart from founding errors.

Optimum solution is invest in 0.833 of project A, i.e. invest £50,000 out of the £60,000 available but invest fully in projects B (£50,000) and C (80,000).

In general the linear programming approach will always give the optimum solution, the PI method may not.

## Examination questions

### Question 1 (CIMA)

You have been appointed as chief management accountant of a well established company with a brief to improve the quality of information supplied for management decision making. As a first task you have decided to examine the system used for providing information for capital investment decisions. You find that discounted cash flow techniques are used but in a mechanical fashion with no apparent understanding of the figures produced. The most recent example of an investment appraisal produced by the accounting department showed a positive net present value of £35,000 for a five year life project when discounted at 14 per cent which you are informed was the range charged on the bank loan raised to finance the investment. You note that the appraisal did not include consideration of the effects of inflation nor was there any form of risk analysis.

You are required to:

(a) Explain the meaning of a positive net present value of £35,000.
(b) Comment on the appropriateness or otherwise of the discounted rate used.
(c) State whether you agreed with the treatment of inflation, and, if not, explain how you would deal with inflation in investment appraisals.
(d) Explain what is meant by 'risk analysis' and describe ways this could be carried out in investment appraisals and what benefits (if any) this would bring.

### Answer 1

(a) The net present value of £35,000 is the amount by which the present values of the cash inflows of the project exceed the present values of cash outflows. Present value means the discounted value of such cash flows, recognizing that money has a time value. The net present value of a project, if positive as in this instance, can be explained as the potential increase in consumption made possible by the project valued in present-day terms.

(b) In calculations of net present value the choice of a discounting rate is super-important. Controversy has raged for years on the subject of which is the best rate to use. This rate is usually known as the cost of capital, the calculation of which is a complex subject involving consideration of the company's financial structure, methods of financing and capital gearing.

If one uses 'the rate charged on the bank loan' one is using the incremental cost of capital, and it may be useful to have a 'snapshot' of the project performance on this basis.

But it is generally agreed that the prime snapshot must be taken using the weighted average cost of capital, in other words, the average of the cost of each individual source of capital (whether it be share capital, retained profits, long- and medium-term loans), weighted according to its proportion of the total amount of capital in use.

It would make sense in this case to recalculate the net present value of the project using discount rates based on the weighted average cost of capital, since the maximization of profit is likely to be the main objective.

(c)   To fail to consider the effects of inflation in investment appraisal is dangerous, since, according to the type of project, its fixed or working capital intensity and the profile of cash flows, both in and out, over the life of the project, inflation can have a significant effect on performance.

The approach to dealing with inflation is either on the basis of the residual net cash flows or on the basis of the detailed estimates of cash inflows and outflows. In other words, assume that future increases in costs will be passed on in prices so that the net cash flow will be increased by the general rate of inflation, or estimate the inflation rates likely to apply to each input and output so that a recalculation of net cash flow can be effected on a more meaningful basis.

The latter approach is to be recommended since a bland assumption of all costs and prices going up or down with, say the retail price index is naïve. On the other hand, let us have no doubts about the difficulties of forecasting inflation rate.

(d)   Virtually all investment decisions are made under conditions which involve uncertainty and it is necessary for the ultimate decision-taker, explicitly or implicitly, to attempt to assess this uncertainty, convert it into known risks and decide whether the probabilities of these risks render the project acceptable or not. This is risk analysis. Uncertainty could be treated as a function of time by calculating the payback period, but this ignores returns after the payback period.

A higher discounting rate than the organization's cost of capital could be used, obviously resulting in relatively heavier discounting of the more distant cash flows.

A more sensible approach is a probabilistic analysis, either on the basis of the residual net cash flows or, better still, on the basis of the forecast items in detail. The approach would be to ask for say three estimates of the various project cash flows (optimistic, pessimistic, most likely) then to assign probabilities to each, thus giving a probability distribution of the cash flows. The benefit of this approach is the knowledge of likely variations in the result due to the estimated variations in the cash flows, which allow the effects of uncertainty to be more clearly seen, hopefully resulting in a more informed decision.

### Question 2 (CIMA)

Wyemark Electronics plc has been offered a fixed price contract to manufacture 12 specialized robotic work stations at £102,732 each. Four work stations would be made and sold each year and the contract would run for three years from 1 July 1987. The following estimates have been made for the contract.

*Equipment*  Special equipment will have to be bought and paid on 1 July 1987. The minimum amount required for the contract costs £150,000 and this could be resold on 30 June 1990 for £50,000. Ideally, Wyemark wishes to keep initial investment as low as possible but work studies show that additional equipment would reduce semi-skilled labour costs by one per cent for each additional £1000 of equipment. Equipment, over and above the minimum, can only be purchased in increments of £1000, has no resale value and must be paid for on 1 July 1987.

*Labour*  Each of the work stations will require 2000 hours of skilled labour and 4000 hours of semi-skilled labour with current rates of £6 and £4 per hour respectively. During the first year it is expected that skilled labour will be in short supply and that skilled labour for the contract will have to be redeployed from existing work where there is a contribution of £8 per hour, net of labour costs. If the contract is accepted an existing technical manager, who has to have been made redundant, will continue to be employed on a permanent basis. His current salary is £18,000 per annum and his redundancy terms were to have been a £30,000 lump sump payable on 1 July 1987 and a pension of £4000 per annum (not inflation-proofed).

*Overheads*  Overheads are absorbed at the rate of £20 per skilled labour hour as follows:

|  | (£) |
|---|---|
| Fixed overhead | 13 |
| Variable overhead | 7 |
|  | 20 |

Wages, salaries and overheads are expected to increase at 10 per cent per annum compound.

*Materials*

| Material | Quantity per work station units | Current stock units | Original cost per unit (£) | Current purchases per unit (£) | Current realizable value per unit (£) |
|---|---|---|---|---|---|
| X | 20 | 170 | 600 | 850 | 650 |
| Y | 15 | 60 | 500 | 550 | 200 |

Material X is used regularly by Wyemark for its existing production but Y is used rarely and if not used for the new contract would have to be disposed of immediately. In addition to the two materials mentioned, the work stations each require ten microchip circuits which would have to be bought in. No price is yet available but Wyemark is confident that it will be able to obtain a price that will be fixed for the duration of the contract. Replacement prices and current realizable values of X and Y are expected to increase at the rate of 15 per cent per annum compound.

Wyemark has a cost of capital of 16 per cent in money terms and it can be assumed that all payments and revenues arise on the last day of the year to which they relate unless otherwise stated. Price changes are deemed to take place annually at midnight on 30 June and because of its wish to enter this market, Wyemark is prepared to accept this contract on a breakeven basis.

You are required to:

(a)   Calculate the maximum price per circuit that Wyemark should pay assuming that the circuits are purchased in three batches, payment is made at the end of each year and the minimum amount of equipment is purchased.
(b)   Calculate the minimum amount of additional equipment which should be purchased assuming that it is discovered that the microchip circuits cannot be bought at less than £1200 each.

### Answer 2

Working

| | 30 June 1988 (£) | 30 June 1989 (£) | 30 June 1990 (£) |
|---|---|---|---|
| Receipts | 102,732 × 4 | | |
| Work stations | 410,928 | 410,928 | 410,928 |
| Sale of equipment | | | 50,000 |
| Lump sum 1 July 1987 | 30,000 | | |
| | | | |
| Payments | | | |
| Equipment 1 July 1987 | 150,000 | | |
| Skilled labour | | | |
| (2000 hrs × £6 × 4 weeks) | 48,000 +10% | 52,800 +10% | 58,080 |
| Semi-skilled labour | | | |
| (4000 hrs × £4 × 4 weeks) | 64,000 +10% | 70,400 +10% | 77,400 |
| Skilled labour opportunity cost | | | |
| (2000 hrs × £8 × 4 weeks) | 64,000 | | |
| Technical manager | | | |
| Salary | 18,000 +10% | 19,800 +10% | 21,780 |
| Pension | 4,000 | 4,000 | 4,000 |
| | 14,000 | 15,800 | 17,780 |
| Overhead variable only | 56,000 +10% | 61,600 +10% | 67,760 |
| (2000 hrs × £7 × 4 weeks) | | | |
| Material X | | | |

| | | | |
|---|---|---|---|
| (20 units × 4 weeks × £850) | 68,000 +15% | 78,200 +15% | 89,930 |
| Material Y | | | |
| 15 units × 4 weeks × £200) | | 60 units × £550 +15% | |
| | 12,000 | 37,950 +15% | 43,642 |
| Wages, salaries | | | |
| Overheads, material | 326,000 | 316,750 | 354,632 |

## (a) Discount cash flow at 16%

| | 30 June 1988 (£) | 30 June 1989 (£) | 30 June 1990 (£) |
|---|---|---|---|
| Sundry inflows | | Equipment | |
| Technical manager | | 50,000 × | |
| £30,000 × 1.000 | 30,000 | 0.641 | 32,050 |
| Outflows | | | |
| Equipment | | | |
| £150,000 | (150,000) | | |
| Other (£326,000) | 316,750 | (354,632) | |
| × 0.862 | (281,012) × 0.743 | (235,345) × 0.641 | (227,319) |
| | (431,012) | (235,345) | (227,319) |
| Net Outflow | (401,012) | (235,345) | (195,269) |

| | |
|---|---|
| Total net outflows | (£831,626) |
| Inflows from work stations | |
| £410,928 × 2.242 | 921,301 |
| Net inflow | 89,675 |

| | |
|---|---|
| Cost per 40 circuits, fixed on 1 July 1988: | |
| £89,675/2.242 | £39,998 |
| Therefore cost per circuit £39,998/40 | £1,000 |

## (b)

| | | (£) |
|---|---|---|
| Purchase price | | 1,200 |
| Breakeven price | | 1,000 |
| Difference | | 200 |
| | × | 40 circuits |
| Annual difference | × | 2.242 |
| Additional discounted cost | | 17,936 |

This amount must be saved from semi-skilled labour

| Discount semi-skilled labour costs: | (£) |
|---|---|
| Year 1  £64,000 × 0.862 = | 55,168 |
| Year 2  £70,400 × 0.743 = | 52,307 |
| Year 3  £77,440 × 0.641 = | 49,639 |
| | 157,114 |

| PV effect of 1% reduction in semi-skilled labour | (£) |
|---|---|
| Labour cost reduction = £157,114 × 1% | 1,571 |
| Capital cost increase | 1,000 |
| Net PV saving | 571 |

Total saving required = 17,936
Net saving per £1,000 equipment = £571
Therefore, equipment required to generate total saving required

$$= \frac{£17,936}{£571} \times £1,000 = £31,412$$

Rounded up = £32,000

### Question 3 (CIMA)

The managers of a dairy are planning to launch a new range of real cream ices and the marketing department has produced the following information:

Project horizon:    6 years

Annual total contribution of new range (undiscounted) and estimated probabilities:

|  | Years 1–3 | Years 4–6 | Probabilities |
|---|---|---|---|
| If demand is high | £40,000 | £30,000 | 0.75 |
| If demand is low | £15,000 | £10,000 | 0.25 |

If the present range of ice creams is continued and the new range is not introduced it is expected that sales will decline and the present contribution of £30,000 per annum will reduce by 5 per cent per annum, meaning that contribution in year 1 is expected to be £28,500.

It is possible to commission a market research survey, at a cost of £12,000 to assess likely demand. The market research company has been used before and its reliability can be summarized as follows:

| Outcome of survey | Subsequent sales performance | |
|---|---|---|
|  | High | Low |
| 'High' forecast | 70%* | 20% |
| 'Low' forecast | 30% | 80% |

*this means that when sales were high the survey had forecast this 70 per cent of the time.

It has been decided that if the survey predicts high demand for the new range then £15,000 will be invested in new equipment and there will be increased marketing effort which it is estimated will increase contributions by £20,000 per annum if demand is high and by £10,000 per annum if demand is low. However if the survey predicts low demand then it has been decided that the company will continue with the old range of ice creams. The dairy has a cost of capital of 20 per cent per annum.

Using decision tree analysis, you are required to:

(a)  Calculate the expected value of the new project without a market research survey.

(b) ·Calculate the expected present value of continuing with the old range.
(c) Calculate the expected present value of the new project if the market research survey is carried out:
(d) Recommend a course of action to the firm.

## Answer 3

(See Figure 10.2.)

(a) *Cash flows for new project without market research*

|  | High demand | | Low demand | |
|---|---|---|---|---|
| Year | Cash flow (£000) | Present value (£000) | Cash flow (£000) | Present value (£000) |
| 1 | 40 | 33.333 | 15 | 12.500 |
| 2 | 40 | 27.778 | 15 | 10.417 |
| 3 | 40 | 23.148 | 15 | 8.681 |
| 4 | 30 | 14.468 | 10 | 4.823 |
| 5 | 30 | 12.056 | 10 | 4.019 |
| 6 | 30 | 10.047 | 10 | 3.349 |
| NPV | | 120.830 | | 43.788 |

Expected NPV = $(0.75 \times 120.830 + 0.25 \times 43.788) \times £1000$
          = £101,569

(b) *Cash flows for old products range*

| Year | Cash flow (£000) | Present value (£000) |
|---|---|---|
| 1 | 28.500 | 23.750 |
| 2 | 27.075 | 18.802 |
| 3 | 25.721 | 14.885 |
| 4 | 24.435 | 11.784 |
| 5 | 23.213 | 9.329 |
| 6 | 22.053 | 7.385 |
| NPV | | 85.938 |

Expected NPV = £85,938

(c)  There are three branches here, but the figures for only two need to be calculated since if the survey forecast is low then the company will continue with the old range for which the present value was calculated in (b).

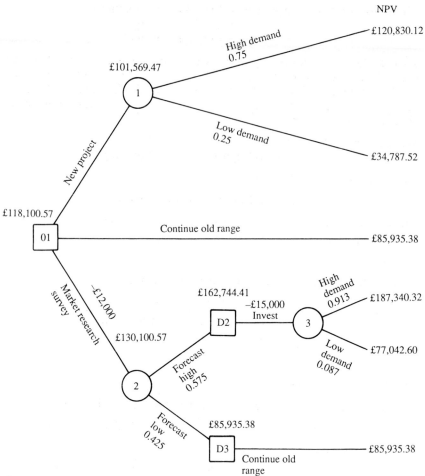

Figure 10.2

## Cash flows for the new project after survey

| | Forecast high | | | |
|---|---|---|---|---|
| | Result high | | Result low | |
| Year | Cash flow (£000) | Present value (£000) | Cash flow (£000) | Present value (£000) |
| 1 | 60 | 50.000 | 25 | 20.833 |
| 2 | 60 | 41.667 | 25 | 17.362 |
| 3 | 60 | 34.722 | 25 | 14.468 |
| 4 | 50 | 24.113 | 20 | 9.645 |
| 5 | 50 | 20.094 | 20 | 8.038 |
| 6 | 50 | 16.745 | 20 | 6.698 |
| NPV | | 187.341 | | 77.044 |

Therefore total present values = £187,340 ('high'-high)
= £77,042 ('high'-low)
= £85,935 ('low')

To calculate the required present value one must allow for the cash expenditures and also attach probabilities to the chance branches. We need to calculate p ('high'), the probability that the forecast will be 'high' and p (high/'high'), the probability that demand is actually high given that the forecast is 'high'.

We may then obtain p ('low') = 1 − p ('high') and
p (low/'high') = 1 − p (high/'high')

By conditional probabilities:

p('high') = p('high'/high)p(high) + p('high'/low) p(low)

All the values of the right-hand side are given so that:

p('high') = (0.7 × 0.75) + (0.2 × 0.25) = 0.575
p('low') = 1 − 0.575 = 0.425

To calculate p (high/'high'), we use Bayes theorem.

$$p(high/'high') = \frac{p('high'/high)p(high)}{p('high'/high)p(high) + p('high'/low)p(low)}$$

$$= \frac{0.7 \times 0.75}{0.575} = 0.913$$

Therefore p(low/'high') = 1 − 0.913 = 0.087

So that the expected present value if the forecast is 'high' is

£(0.913 × 187,340) + (0.087 × 77,042) − (15,000) = £162,744

and the expected present value with the survey is

£(0.575 × 162,744) + (0.425 × 85,935) − 12,000 = £118,100

(d) If the objective of the dairy is to maximize the expected present value from this project, then the survey should be carried out and the extra investment made if the forecast is high, for an expected present value of £118,100.

### Question 4 (CIMA)

A company is considering an investment in an overseas project which will involve the investment (in 1980 money terms) of £1 million in plant, divided evenly over 1981 and 1982. This investment will yield a gross income of £800,000 per annum from 1983 to 1986 inclusive, but will incur costs of £200,000 per annum in the same period, both figures in 1980 money terms

Inflation for the period in question (with 1980 as 100; is forecast as 20 per cent per annum for plant and 10 per cent per annum for income and costs. the projected local consumer price index, affecting income, plant investment and other costs, is an increase of 12 per cent per annum. Taxation can be ignored.

You are required to:

(a)   Calculate for the project:

    (i)   the discounted cash flow (DCF) (internal rate of return) in real terms to the nearest whole number;

    (ii)   the net present value (NPV) if the cost of capital is 10 per cent real.

(b)   List any four tests of sensitivity analysis that could be applied to help management in its decision on this proposed investment.

(c)   (i)   Calculate, using a simulation method based on random numbers and working upwards cumulatively from the lowest levels of expenditure, income and costs at 00 to the highest levels at 99, the NPV of the project at 100 per cent real if the random numbers appearing were 35 06 93.

An analysis of the possible levels of plant investment, income and costs shows the following:

| Plant investment | | Income | | Costs | |
|---|---|---|---|---|---|
| Level in 1980 money per annum (£000) | Probability of that level | Level in 1980 money per annum (£000) | Probability of that level | Level in 1980 money per annum (£000) | Probability of that level |
| 450 | 0.10 | 650 | 0.10 | 170 | 0.10 |
| 500 | 0.50 | 700 | 0.15 | 185 | 0.20 |
| 550 | 0.30 | 750 | 0.25 | 200 | 0.40 |
| 600 | 0.07 | 800 | 0.35 | 215 | 0.20 |
| 650 | 0.03 | 850 | 0.15 | 230 | 0.10 |
| | 1.00 | | 1.00 | | 1.00 |

    (ii)   Explain, very briefly, what advantages, if any, you see in this method of risk analysis (if a sufficiently large number of calculations were carried out) as compared with sensitivity analysis.

## Answer 4

In part (a) the examiner asks for a yield in real terms and a net present value using a real 10 per cent as the discount rate. Since the cash flows are given in 1980 money terms the inflation rates in question would not appear to be required and the calculation would be:

| | (£000) | 10% | | 30% | |
|---|---|---|---|---|---|
| 1981 | (500) | 0.91 | (445) | 0.77 | (385) |
| 1982 | (500) | 0.83 | (415) | 0.59 | (295) |

| 1983 | 600 | 0.75 | 450 | 0.46 | 276 |
|------|-----|------|-----|------|-----|
| 1984 | 600 | 0.68 | 408 | 0.35 | 210 |
| 1985 | 600 | 0.62 | 372 | 0.27 | 162 |
| 1986 | 600 | 0.56 | 336 | 0.21 | 126 |
|      | 1400 |     | NPV 696 |  | 94 |

This indicates an NPV at 10 per cent of £696,000 and a DCF yield or internal rate of return in excess of 30 per cent.

However, in this question there are differential inflation rates and this fact must be considered in calculating the real return.

|      | Plant | Local | Income | Costs local |
|------|-------|-------|--------|-------------|
| 1980 | 100   | 100   | 100    | 100         |
| 1981 | 120   | 112   | 110    | 112         |
| 1982 | 144   | 125   | 121    | 125         |
| 1983 |       |       | 133    | 140         |
| 1984 |       |       | 146    | 157         |
| 1985 |       |       | 161    | 176         |
| 1986 |       |       | 177    | 197         |

Therefore, adjusting the present values from the earlier workings:

|      | 10% | 30% |
|------|-----|-----|
| 1981 | $(455) \times \dfrac{120}{112}$ (488) | $(385) \times \dfrac{120}{112}$ (412) |
| 1982 | $(415) \times \dfrac{144}{125}$ (478) | $(295) \times \dfrac{144}{125}$ (340) |
| 1983 | $450 \times \dfrac{133}{140}$ 427 | $276 \times \dfrac{133}{140}$ 262 |
| 1984 | $408 \times \dfrac{146}{157}$ 379 | $210 \times \dfrac{146}{157}$ 195 |
| 1985 | $372 \times \dfrac{161}{176}$ 340 | $162 \times \dfrac{161}{176}$ 148 |
| 1986 | $336 \times \dfrac{177}{197}$ 302 | $126 \times \dfrac{177}{197}$ 113 |
|      | NPV 10% Real  482 | (34) |

(a)(i)  *DCF rate estimate*
NPV has moved 482 + 34 = 516 for a change of 20 per cent in the discount rate, i.e. 25.8 per one per cent.

Yield estimate therefore $30\% - \dfrac{34}{25.8} = 29\%$

This result is marginally affected by the wide range of discount rates used (10–30 per cent).

(ii)   As above calculation £482,000

(b)   Sensitivity analysis is the process of testing the variation in project acceptability in response to variation in selected project variables. A listing only is asked for in the question.

1   Effect of delays in bringing the project to production, e.g. construction over three years instead of two years.
2   Effect of escalation in plant costs.
3   Effect of variation in the commercial life of the entire project.
4   Effect of cost inflation which does not result in a corresponding income increase.

(c)(i)   Since the question tells us to work upwards cumulatively from lowest to highest values the random numbers will correspond to probability groupings, e.g. for plant investment, random numbers 00–09 inclusive will identify a plant investment of £450,000, numbers 10–59, an investment of £500,000, and so on.

Thus:

|  |  |  | (£) |
|---|---|---|---|
| Plant investment |  | RN35 | 500,000 |
| Income |  | RN 06 | 650,000 |
| Costs |  | RN 93 | 230,000 |
|  |  |  | 420,000 |

|  | (£,000) | 10% factor |  |
|---|---|---|---|
| 1981 | (500) | 0.91 | $(455) \times \dfrac{120}{112}$ (488) |
| 1982 | (500) | 0.83 | $(415) \times \dfrac{144}{125}$ (478) |
| 1983 | 420 | 0.75 | $315 \times \dfrac{133}{140}$ 299 |
| 1984 | 420 | 0.68 | $286 \times \dfrac{146}{157}$ 266 |
| 1985 | 420 | 0.62 | $260 \times \dfrac{161}{176}$ 238 |
| 1986 | 420 | 0.56 | $235 \times \dfrac{177}{197}$ 211 |
|  |  |  | 48 |

Therefore NPV at 10 per cent real is £48,000

(c)(ii)  If the suggested procedure is repeated many times a distribution of internal rates of return for the project can be computed, thus providing management with additional guidance in decision making. The distribution of each variable must be known in order that random samples can be selected from each, and the values combined to produce an internal rate of return. Such an internal rate of return is a project simulation whereas sensitivity analysis is selective in identifying the impact on project return of change in a single variable.

## Question 5

A company is considering a project involving the outlay of £300,000 which it estimates will generate cash flows over its two year life at the probabilities shown in the following table.

Cash flows for project year 1

| Cash flow (£) | Probability |
|---|---|
| 100,000 | 0.25 |
| 200,000 | 0.50 |
| 300,000 | 0.25 |
| | 1.00 |

Year 2

| *If cash flow in year 1 is:* (£) | *there is a probability of:* | *that cash flow in year 2 will be:* (£) |
|---|---|---|
| 100,000 | 0.25 | Nil |
| | 0.50 | 100,000 |
| | 0.25 | 200,000 |
| | 1.00 | |
| 200,000 | 0.25 | 100,000 |
| | 0.50 | 200,000 |
| | 0.25 | 300,000 |
| | 1.00 | |
| 300,000 | 0.25 | 200,000 |
| | 0.50 | 300,000 |
| | 0.25 | 325,000 |
| | 1.00 | |

Note, all cash flows should be treated as being received at the end of the year.

It has a choice of undertaking this project at either of two sites (A or B) whose costs are identical and are included in the above outlay. In terms of the technology of the project itself, the location will have no effect on the outcome.

If the company chooses site B it has the facility to abandon the project at the end of the first year and to sell the site to an interested purchaser for £150,000. This facility is not available at site A.

The company's investment criterion for this type of project is to use a discount rate of ten per cent per annum. Its policy would be to abandon the project on site B and to sell the site at the end of year 1 if its expected cash flows for year 2 were less than the disposal value.

You are required to:

(a)  Calculate the NPV of the project on site A.
(b)  (i)  Explain, based on the data given, the specific circumstances in which the company would abandon the project on site B.
     (ii)  Calculate the NPV of the project on site B taking account of the abandonment facility.

(c)  Calculate the financial effect of the facility for abandoning the project on site B, stating whether it is positive or negative.

Ignore tax and inflation.

## Answer 5

(See Figure 10.3.)

| | | Expected value (£000) | |
|---|---|---|---|
| Year 0 | (300) | (300) | (300) |
| Year 1 | 91 | 182 | 273 |
| Year 2 | 83 | 166 | 238.625 |
| | (126) | 48 | 211.625 |
| Probability | 0.25 | 0.50 | 0.25 |
| NPV for each option | (31.5) | 24 | 52.906 |
| Overall NPV = 45.406 | | | |

NPV of project on site A is £45,406.

(b)(i)   The specific circumstance in which the company would abandon the project on Site B is when the expected NPV of cash receipts in year 2 is less than the NPV of the £150,000 selling price.

This would happen when the income in year 1 is at the £100,000 level. The expected value of the income in year 2 has an NPV of £83,000 whereas the £150,000 selling price has an NPV of £136,500. At the £200,000 level the NPV of year 2 income is £166,000 and financially better than the NPV of the selling price.

(ii)   *NPV of project on Site B with abandonment facility*
Calculation is as part (a) except for £150,000 income possibility.

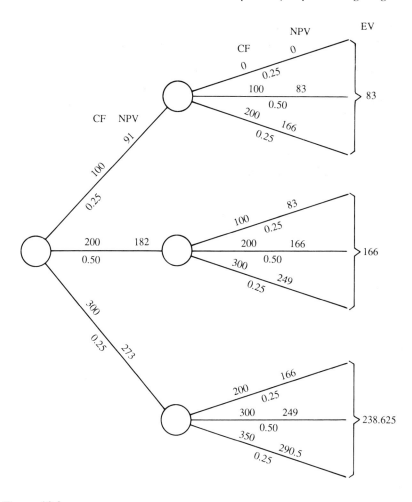

Figure 10.3

| | | Expected value (£000) | |
|---|---|---|---|
| Year 0 | (300) | (300) | (300) |
| Year 1 | 91 | 182 | 273 |
| Sales Year 1 150×0.91 | 136.5 | — | — |
| Year 2 | — | 166 | 238.625 |
| | (72.5) | 48 | 211.625 |
| Probability | 0.25 | 0.50 | 0.25 |
| NPV for each option | (18.125) | 24 | 52.906 |
| Overall NPV = | | 58.781 | |

NPV of project on site B is £58,781.

(c)   Seen as a cash flow in time, the NPV of the project with abandonment facility is greater by £58,781 − £45,406, i.e. £13,375. As it is in excess of the 10 per cent investment criterion it is positive.

## Further reading

Bhaskar, K., Linear programming and capital budgeting, in *Journal of Business Finance and Accounting*, Summer 1978.

Herbst, A.F., *Capital Budgeting: Theory, Quantitative Methods, and Applications*, Harper and Row, 1982.

Levy, H. and Sarnat, M., *Capital Investment and Financial Decisions*, 3rd edn, Prentice Hall, 1986.

Lucey, T., *Investment Appraisal; Evaluating Risk and Uncertainty*, CIMA, 1975.

# 11 Cost, profit and investment centres

An organization may be divided into cost, profit and investment centres for control, performance evaluation and motivation purposes.

## Cost centres

'A cost centre is a location, function or items or equipment in respect of which costs may be ascertained, and related to cost units for control purposes.' *Management Accounting: Official Terminology*, CIMA, 1982.

Cost centres only relate to costs and do not include revenues or investments.

The most common measure of cost centre performance is budgetary control, whereby actual costs are compared with budgeted costs which are flexed to actual levels of activity.

## Profit centres

'A profit centre is a segment of the business entity by which both revenues are received and expenditures are caused or controlled, such revenues and expenditures being used to evaluate segmental performance.' *Management Accounting: Official Terminology*, CIMA, 1982.

Profit centres do not necessarily mean that decentralization exists. However managers should have sufficient authority to make decisions about selling prices and transfer prices.

Net profit, budgetary control and the contribution to sales (C/S ratio) are all commonly used measures of profit centres' performance.

## Investment centres

'An investment centre is a profit centre in which inputs are measured in terms of expenses, and outputs are measured in terms of revenues, and in which assets employed are also measured – the excess of revenue over expenditure then being related to assets employed.' *Management Accounting: Official Terminology*, CIMA, 1982.

The managers of investment centres are therefore responsible for costs, revenues and assets employed.

The performance of an investment centre is normally measured by:

(a)   return on capital employed (ROCE) which is sometimes referred to as return on investment (ROI),
(b)   residual income (RI).

These two measures of performance are described as follows:

## Return on investment (ROI)

$$ROI = \frac{Net\ profit}{Capital\ employed} \times 100$$

The ratio can be divided into other ratios, i.e. the net profit margin and the asset turnover. The net profit margin is determined by the firm's pricing policy and its cost control. The asset turnover shows the amount of sales generated by the capital available and whether a firm has over- or under-utilized its assets.

$$ROI = \frac{Net\ profit}{Capital\ employed} \times 100$$

(Net profit margin)          (Asset turnover)

$$ROI = \frac{Net\ profit}{Sales} \times 100 \times \frac{Sales}{Capital\ employed}$$

### Advantages of ROI

1   It relates a return to a level of investment.
2   The ROI can be analysed into other ratios which are useful for analytical purposes.
3   It can be used for inter-firm comparison, providing the firms, whose results are being compared, are of comparable size and of the same industry.

### Limitations of ROI

1   Problems in defining the profit and capital employed.
     Should capital employed be valued at net or gross book value?

Should capital employed be valued at historic or current cost?
Should capital employed include or exclude intangible assets?
Is the profit arrived at before or after deducting tax?
Is the profit arrived at after deducting *uncontrollable* or *controllable* allocated head office expenses?
Usually capital employed will be valued at net book value, and the fixed assets are indexed to provide a current cost. Profit is usually calculated before deducting tax and after charging *controllable* allocated head office expense.

2  The ROI of company X can only be compared with the ROI of company Y if the accounts of both companies are based on similar accounting policies. The policies relate to the following: depreciation, stock and fixed asset valuation and the treatment of research and development expenditure.

3  The ROI may influence a divisional manager to select only investments with high rates of return (i.e. rates which are in line or above his target ROI). Other investments which could increase the value of the business may be rejected. These types of decisions are sub-optimal and result in a manager under-investing in order to preserve his ROI.

# Residual income (RI)

Residual income is the net operating income of a division less an imputed interest charge on the divisional assets.

*Example*
Division A has capital employed of £100,000, net income of £30,000 and a cost of capital of 12 per cent.

| | | |
|---|---|---|
| Net income | = £30,000 | |
| Interest charge | = (12,000) | (12% of £100,000) |
| Residual income | 18,000 | |

## Advantages

1  Unlike the ROI the RI approach is not concerned with preserving a relative measure. It strives to maximize an absolute figure, the RI thereby increasing shareholders' wealth. This is achieved by accepting opportunities which earn a rate of return which is in excess of the cost of capital. Sub-optimal decisions should not therefore arise.

2  The cost of capital charge on divisional investments ensure that managers are aware of the opportunity cost of funds.

3  If each division is charged with a common group cost of capital then decisions taken at divisional level should be compatible with the interest of the organization as a whole.

### Disadvantages

1 There may be difficulties in defining the net operating income and the value of the divisional investments.
2 Identifying controllable and uncontrollable factors at divisional level may be difficult.
3 There can be problems in calculating an accurate cost of capital. Should the firm use a simple group cost of capital to enhance goal congruency, or individual divisional costs of capital which reflect each division's level of risk?

*Example*
Divisions X and Y are currently considering an outlay on new investment projects.

|  | Division X | Division Y |
|---|---|---|
| Investment outlay | £200,000 | 200,000 |
| Net annual return | 32,000 | 22,000 |
| Target ROI | 18% | 11% |

The group's cost of capital is 13%

Should the projects be accepted or rejected?

*Solution*

$$\text{ROI} = \frac{32,000}{200,000} \times 100 = 16\%$$

$$\text{ROI} = \frac{22,000}{200,000} \times 100 = 11\%$$

*Using the ROI*
The ROI for the projects is 16 per cent for X and 11 per cent for Y. Project X would therefore be rejected because it is less than the target ROI of 18 per cent. Project Y would be accepted as its percentage return of 11 per cent is not less than its target ROI.

*Using RI*

|  | Division X | Division Y |
|---|---|---|
| Net return | £32,000 | £22,000 |
| Imputed *interested* (13% of £200,000) | (£26,000) | (£26,000) |
| Residual income | £6,000 | (£4,000) |

Using RI Project X would therefore be accepted.

This method is similar to the NPV approach in DCF in that they are both based on a cost of capital calculation and are expressed in absolute terms.

$$\text{Project X} \quad \text{NPV} = (\pounds200{,}000) + \frac{\pounds32{,}000}{0.13} \quad \text{(in perpetuity)}$$

Gain £46,154

In the majority of situations the ROI method and the NPV method will result in the same decision being made.

$$\text{Project Y} \quad \text{NPV} = (\pounds200{,}000) + \frac{\pounds33{,}000}{0.13} \quad \text{(in perpetuity)}$$

$$\text{Loss} = (\pounds30{,}770)$$

A typical divisional residual income statement is as follows:

Divisional performance statement

|  | (£) | (£) |
|---|---|---|
| Revenue |  | X |
| Less variable costs |  | X |
| Contribution |  | X |
| Less controllable fixed costs |  | X |
| Controllable profit |  | X |
| Less interest on controllable investment |  | X |
| Controllable residual income |  | X |
| Less uncontrollable cost (allocated head office charges) | X |  |
| Less interest on uncontrollable investment | X | X |
| Net residual income |  | X |

Let us consider a comprehensive example which relates to these two measures of performance.

*Comprehensive example*

The head office of WT plc receives regular financial statements from its divisions. Although non-controllable overhead and an apportionment of centrally incurred costs are charged in these, the divisional income statements identify divisional controllable profit.

Since the divisions are given the status of investment centres, there is emphasis on return on divisional investment and the company, having regard to the cost of capital figure used in major investment decisions, has set a target of 12 per cent for this.

For the quarter ended 31 March the summarized returns of two of the divisions are as follows:

Division income statements

| | Southern Division | | Northern Division | |
|---|---|---|---|---|
| | (£) | (£) | (£) | (£) |
| Sales | | | | |
| External | | 100,000 | | 650,000 |
| Internal (to other divisions) | | 200,000 | | 50,000 |
| | | 300,000 | | 700,000 |
| Cost of goods sold | | | | |
| Direct material | 50,000 | | 100,000 | |
| Direct labour | 100,000 | | 120,000 | |
| Controllable overheads | 50,000 | | 80,000 | |
| | | 200,000 | | 300,000 |
| Selling and distribution expenses | | 10,000 | | 50,000 |
| | | 210,000 | | 350,000 |
| Controllable profit | | 90,000 | | 350,000 |
| Noncontrollable | | | | |
| Divisional overhead | 11,000 | | 30,500 | |
| Central overhead (Apportioned on basis of sales volume) | 9,000 | | 21,000 | |
| | | 20,000 | | 51,500 |
| Divisional net profit | | 70,000 | | 298,500 |
| Divisional investment | | £350,000 | | £2,000,000 |
| Return on divisional investment | | 20% | | 15% |

It is considered appropriate to compare the performance of these two divisions since both manufacture the same range of products selling at similar prices. Intra group transfers are made at market price.

Although the Northern Division has a more modern plant than the Southern Division and a larger profit, there is some concern at the comparatively low rate of return that it is earning.

As the newly appointed management accountant, you have been asked to draft a report for the financial controller of WT plc commenting on and comparing the performance of the two divisions. In your report consider the transfer pricing method used by the company and the use of the rate of return on investment as a measure of operating performance. Make suggestions for improving the divisional performance appraisal system, if you consider that there is room for improvement. Consider the role that residual income might play in a revised performance measurement system.

*Solution*

Draft report to the Financial Controller on the operating performance of Southern and Northern Divisions

Expenses and profit as a percentage of sales value

|  | Southern Division | Northern Division |
|---|---|---|
| Direct material | 17% | 14% |
| Direct labour | 33 | 17 |
| Controllable overhead | 17 | 12 |
|  | 67 | 43 |
| Selling and distribution | 3 | 7 |
| Non-controllable divisional overhead | 4 | 4 |
| Central charge | 3 | 3 |
| Profit | 23 | 43 |
|  | 100% | 100% |

The more modern plant used by the Northern Division may account for the lower level of controllable expenses for that division when such expenses are expressed as a percentage of sales revenue.

Selling expenses of the Southern Division are three per cent of sales value whereas they are seven per cent for the Northern Division. The reason for this may be the high proportion of intra company transfers in the Southern Division's sales. These transfers are made at market price. This is usually appropriate as a basis but here it could be appropriate to use a lower price if there are considerable savings in selling and distribution costs on intra-company transfers. It could be appropriate for such savings to be shared between the transferor and transferee divisions, this is likely to assist with achieving goal congruence between divisions.

Return on investment is a commonly used measure of divisional operating performance but there are obvious problems in determining appropriate values for both the numerator and the denominator in the calculation. In the current case, to achieve a meaningful comparison, it may be necessary to recalculate the investment values on a common basis as it seems that the amount stated for the Southern Division may well be the written down book value of plant acquired some years ago.

It might be appropriate to consider residual income as an alternative (or supplement) to return on divisional investment. Even with the existing values for divisional investment, the comparison achieved by using residual income is helpful. The calculations given below demonstrate that the Northern Division has a higher surplus than the Southern Division even when charged with interest at the cost of capital rate (12%).

### Residual Income Calculations

|  | Southern Division (£) | (£) | Northern Division (£) | (£) |
|---|---|---|---|---|
| Controllable profit | | 90,000 | | 350,000 |
| Interest on (controllable?) | | | | |
| Investment in division at 12% | | 42,000 | | 240,000 |
| Divisional residual income | | 48,000 | | 110,000 |

| | | | | |
|---|---|---|---|---|
| Non-controllable divisional overhead | 11,000 | | 30,500 | |
| Apportionment of general overhead | 9,000 | | 21,000 | |
| | | 20,000 | | 51,500 |
| Divisional net residual income | | 28,000 | | 58,500 |

If the return on investment calculations are used to appraise the worthwhileness of the recent investments by Northern Division in new plant, then caution must be exercised. Comparisons of rates of return must be undertaken with care. In addition to the problem of ensuring that the values for divisional investments are stated on a common basis there is the further point that it is more logical to encourage divisions to adopt investment policies that will maximize divisional residual income than it is for them to attempt to maximize divisional rate of return. Attempts by a division to maximize its rate of return can lead to the rejection of good investment opportunities.

Firms have become increasingly large, resulting in the need to decentralize. It is vital in a decentralized organization to clearly define cost, profit and investment centres and to establish their measures of performance.

## Examination questions

### Question 1 (CIMA)

You have recently been appointed as management accountant attached to the headquarters of the Alphabet Group plc, with special responsibility for monitoring the performances of the companies within the group. Each company is treated as an investment centre and every month produces an operating statement for the group headquarters. Summaries of the statements for companies X and Y, which make similar products at similar prices, for the last month show a typical situation.

Extract from company monthly operating statements

| | X (£000) | Y (£000) |
|---|---|---|
| Sales | 600 | 370 |
| Less variable costs | 229 | 208 |
| Contribution | 371 | 162 |
| Less controllable fixed overheads (including depreciation on company assets) | 65 | 28 |
| Controllable profit | 306 | 134 |
| Less apportioned group costs | 226 | 119 |
| Net profit | 80 | 15 |

| | | |
|---|---|---|
| Company assets | £6.4m | £0.9m |
| Estimated return on capital employed (on annual basis) | 15% | 20% |

Although both companies are earning more than the target return on capital of 12 per cent there is pressure on interest rates which means that this rate must be increased soon and the board is concerned at the relatively low return achieved by X.

You are required to:

(a) Compare the discuss the relative performance of the two companies as shown in the summarized operating statements.
(b) Redraft the operating statements using an alternative performance measurement to return on capital employed and interpret them against a background of rising interest rates.
(c) Critically compare the use of return on capital employed and the alternative performance measures used in (b) to assess the performance of investment centres.

## Answer 1

(a)

$$\text{ROCE} = \frac{\text{Profit}}{\text{Capital employed}} \times 100$$

| | X | Y |
|---|---|---|
| Estimate ROCE (annual basis) | 15% | 20% |
| Monthly profit | £80,000 | £15,000 |
| | ×12 | ×12 |
| Annualized profit | £960,000 | £180,000 |

Actual ROCE (annual basis) $\dfrac{£0.06m}{£6.4m} \times 100 = 15\%$   $\dfrac{£0.18m}{£0.9m} \times 100 = 20\%$

| | (£000) | (%) | (£000) | (%) |
|---|---|---|---|---|
| Sales | 600 | 100 | 370 | 100 |
| Less: variable costs | 229 | 38 | 208 | 56 |
| Contribution | 371 | 62 | 162 | 44 |
| Less controllable fixed costs | 65 | 11 | 28 | 8 |
| Controllable profit | 306 | 51 | 134 | 36 |
| Less apportioned group costs | 226 | 38 | 119 | 32 |
| Net profit | 80 | 13 | 15 | 4 |

| | | |
|---|---|---|
| Actual ROCE (annual basis) | 15% | 20% |

$$\text{ROCE} = \frac{\text{Profit}}{\text{Capital employed}} \times 100 = \frac{\text{Sales}}{\text{Capital employed}} \% \times \frac{\text{Profit}}{\text{Sales}} \%$$

Use annualized sales and profits

X

$$\frac{£7.2m}{£6.4m} \times \frac{£0.96m}{£7.2m} = 112.5\% \times 13.5\%$$
$$= 15\%$$

Y

$$\frac{£4.44m}{£0.9m} \times \frac{£0.18m}{£4.44m} = 493.3\% \times 4.1\%$$
$$= 20\%$$

1  On an ROCE basis, Y *appears* to out-perform X: 20 per cent ROCE compared to 15 per cent ROCE
2  Both companies earn more than the target cost of capital of 12 per cent.
3  However, both X and Y have an actual ROCE which meets the estimated ROCE.
4  Compared to X, Y generates relatively large sales from a relatively small investment base, but sales yield a relatively low profit.
5  Group costs are probably apportioned on a fairly arbitrary basis, therefore the resultant net profit is not entirely related to divisional performance.
6  X has a higher contribution/sales ratio than, Y 62 per cent to 44 per cent.
7  X has higher controllable profits than Y, 51 per cent to 36 per cent and has lower controllable costs:

|                          | X   | Y   |
|--------------------------|-----|-----|
| Variable costs           | 38% | 56% |
| Controllable fixed costs | 11% | 8%  |
| Total controllable costs | 49% | 64% |

X may well be a more modern plant than Y.
Given Y's extremely high sales/capital employed ratio, Y's assets may be almost completely depreciated and thus have a very low written-down value. X's modern plant is included in the accounts at recent cost levels.
Y's depreciation charge is thus relatively low, whereas X's is relatively high.
8  As noted in 1 above, Y appears to out-perform X as it has a higher ROCE but, given points 2–6, this is not necessarily a true reflection of real financial performance.

(b)  The two major categories of divisional financial performance are:

(i)   those based on relative values, e.g. ROCE;
(ii)  those based on absolute values, e.g. residual profit.

Operating statements – residual profit basis

|  | X (£000) | Y (£000) |
|---|---|---|
| Sales | 600 | 370 |
| Less variable costs | 229 | 208 |
| Contribution | 371 | 162 |
| Less controllable fixed overheads (including depreciation) | 65 | 28 |
| Controllable profit | 306 | 134 |
| Less imputed interest | 64* | 9† |
| Controllable residual profit | 242 | 125 |
| Less apportioned group costs | 226 | 119 |
| Net residual profit | 16 | 6 |

\* £6.4m × 12% p.a. × 1/12 = £64,000 per month
† £0.9m × 12% p.a. × 1/12 =  £9,000 per month

As interest rates rise, the imputed interest charges will rise. This will affect X particularly since its assets have a book value of £6.4 m compared with Y's book value of £0.9 m. Revaluation of assets at current cost will facilitate comparisons.

(c)

1  ROCE uses relative values whereas residual profit uses absolute values.
2  Residual profit highlights the need for managers to make capital investments which will yield a return greater than the imputed interest charge calculated on a cost of capital.
3  ROCE can act as a disincentive to investment; managers may not accept investments at a return lower than current ROCE, even though these investments yield a return higher than the current cost of capital.
4  Residual profit has a sounder theoretical basis, but ROCE is more popular in practice. However, to obtain full benefits, ROCE should be used in conjunction with other performance measures.

### Question 2 (CIMA)

A new company formerly a public sector organization, is considering what control systems to adopt. In order to increase its effectiveness it wishes to develop a system of inter-departmental comparisons. It is considering whether this aim would best be served by establishing cost centres, profit centres, or investment centres.

You are required, in the context of enabling the company to obtain valid comparisons of inter-departmental performance, to explain under the following headings in respect of each type of centre

(a)  its distinguishing characteristics;
(b)  what conditions need to exist for its adoption;
(c)  the nature of the difficulties that the management accountant would have in assembling and using relevant data required for its operation.

## Answer 2

(a)  *Distinguishing characteristics*
A cost centre is a location, function or item of equipment in respect of which costs may be ascertained and related to cost units for control purposes. Thus its distinguishing feature is that it relates to costs only.

A profit centre is a segment of the business entity by which both revenue and expenditures are controlled. It thus differs from a cost centre in that the revenue also is accumulated and thereby a profit (or loss) established within the given segment.

An investment centre is a profit centre controlling revenues and costs but in which, in addition, the profit is related to the assets employed in earning the profit.

(b)  *Conditions needed for the adoption of each type of centre.*
Cost centres are relatively simple and consist mainly of locations at which costs can be separately identified and collected. They are the most widespread basis for cost control and can consist of a single person or machine. Provided a cost number or job number is allocated costs can be booked thereto and separately recorded. For interdepartmental performance comparison a unit of measurement of output is normally required although in its absence the absolute total cost can be compared. It is necessary at each cost centre to separate those costs directly accountable by the person responsible and those costs which may be apportioned to the centre, e.g. computer costs, canteen expenses.

In a profit centre the prime need is for there to be an ability to segregate a definable amount of sales for the particular segment to produce a sales income. The person responsible for a profit centre should have control over both the sales policy and the production facilities. This indicates a limitation to a decentralized unit or a clearly defined product line within a factory.

For control purposes the sales revenue could be 'imputed' insofar as a profit centre's 'sales' may be exclusively to the other profit centres within the organization. It would be necessary, however, for the person held accountable to be able to influence the 'sales' volume and price to afford an incentive for managerial effort.

Profit centres generally are likely to be larger than cost centres and may include a number of cost centres for internal control purposes.

For an investment centre the general conditions already detailed relating to the segregation of revenues and costs are a prerequisite. In addition it must be possible to identify the assets employed in the particular business segment or product line. It is, therefore, only generally satisfactorily employed where a manager has control over the investment policy of his particular area.

As many assets may be in common use by several profit centres, for example the factory buildings, utilities, transport, material and tool stores, investment centres are likely to be even larger than profit centres. An investment centre may comprise several profit centres giving control at a higher stage in the management structure.

### (c) *Difficulties in assembling and using relevant data*
In a cost centre, as indicated in part (a), a system is necessary to identify the costs. This would necessitate issuing a code book to provide unique numbers for identifying each cost centre. A second difficulty would be segregating directly controllable costs from those only indirectly controllable.

Other problems include:

- deciding output units which are easily recordable and readily understood;
- designing a system such that the costs centre costs can be aggregated into departments;
- relating the cost centres to productive output;
- producing results quickly enough to be useful;
- being required to produce standards or prepare budgets for pre-approval and later comparison.

For a profit centre, the difficulties include those already described under cost centres on the expenditure side. In addition the revenue needs to be segregated and difficulties will arise on factors such as goods returned, goods on approval, warranties and guarantees, obsolescent stock, stock valuations and quantity discounts.

There are likely to be some difficulties in segregating sales by product lines if customers take several products and of identifying individual sales if all invoicing is done by a national head office.

On the cost side there will be the need to apportion corporate advertising, research expenses and general administrative costs.

One significant problem is the pricing of interdepartmental transfers when components or products are supplied between profit centres.

To effect a closed-loop control system the total of all individual profit centres should aggregate to the corporate whole.

For an investment centre the difficulties will first relate to those already specified in establishing revenue allocations and the related costs. In addition it is first necessary to allocate all fixed assets in use. It will then be necessary to decide, in establishing a base to relate profit for interdepartmental comparison, whether the fixed assets should be:

at cost,
at written down value;
at replacement value.

Other difficulties will be decisions such as:

How will joint assets be allocated, e.g. boiler plants, canteen and sports facilities?
Will assets include idle plant and incomplete construction?
Will working capital be included?
In making comparisons, will all segments be expected to make the same return on whatever asset base is chosen?

The selection of measures of comparison of centres' results should be such as to promote goal congruence between the company as a whole and the executives in charge of the investment centres.

### Question 3 (CIMA)

A company selling a wide range of equipment and products for wood and metal preservation has expanded rapidly in the last few years. A new marketing manager has been appointed who has asked what assistance in his work he could expect from the management accountant. The marketing manager's first sales budget is due to be prepared in the next two months and he has suggested that a cost reduction programme should be organized in conjunction with the introduction of budgets.
   You are required to:

(a)  list the areas of information where you feel the management accountant could offer help to the marketing manager;
(b)  (i)   discuss briefly the merits and disadvantages of the suggestion for a cost reduction programme concurrent with the budget preparation;
     (ii)  state your recommendations with reasons.

### Answer 3

(a)  *How the management accountant can help the marketing manager*

- Analysis of cost and profitability (contribution per product).
- Analysis by product/product group to arrive at minimum group size.
- Analysis of costs by market/type of customer (e.g. direct sales as compared to through agents) to arrive at minimum account size.
- Analysis of costs of different distribution methods (e.g. by mail/road/van salesman etc.).

- Assessment of validity of using own warehouse.
- Comparison of cost of different distribution channels (e.g. wholesalers, retailers, agents).
- Comparison of profitability by size of order or size of customer.
- Analysis of salesmen's costs compared with their performance – development of control system for these costs.
- Help in compilation of sales budget and marketing costs budget.
- Calculation of expected costs for any marketing changes being considered.

(b)(i)  *Merits and disadvantages of concurrent cost reduction programme*
Merits:

- Makes the budgeting process an opportunity for a real review (compared with zero base budgeting) rather than a 'mechanical' (routine) exercise.
- Would yield figures against which comparisons of actuals would be more relevant than if changes are made after the budget which would be based on the old organization.
- Shows the marketing manager's intentions clearly and at an early stage both to top management and to his own department.
- Gives opportunity to other departments likely to be affected by the proposed change to object and/or adjust their own budgets/plans.

Disadvantages:

- Not much time for consideration of alternatives or for detailed work on the new routines or for consultation with others
- May result in excessive guesswork and estimates of figures being built into the budget which might invalidate the usefulness of the budget.
- There are differences between cost reduction and budgeting. They may require different attitudes and involve different people (e.g. technologists/specialists as compared with accountants) and thus do not necessarily go well together.

(ii)  *Recommendations*
It depends largely on the adequacy of time between now and final budget submission for the cost reduction programme to be set in motion. If there is enough time, then it would be acceptable concurrently. If not, then the cost reduction programme should be introduced separately. The indicated period of two months is probably insufficient.

**Question 4 (CIMA)**

Financial data for the past year for two subsidiary companies X Ltd and Y Ltd are given below:

|  | X Ltd (£000) | Y Ltd (£000) |
|---|---|---|
| Sales | 735 | 690 |
| Depreciation | 140 | 100 |
| Other costs | 400 | 320 |
| Fixed assets at cost | 1400 | 1200 |
| Accumulated depreciation | 980 | 400 |
| Working capital | 160 | 100 |

Depreciation is calculated by the straight-line method.

The directors of the holding company assess managerial performance on the return achieved on capital employed. For a management review it has been decided that fixed assets should be revalued to replacement cost using these price indices, assuming cost price equals 100: X Ltd 160; Y Ltd 120.

In addition the following adjustments are to be made to Y Ltd's results to equate with the treatment given by X Ltd.

(i) X Ltd purchased computer equipment last year for £70,000 (seven-year life). Y Ltd leased identical equipment at an annual rental of £12,000.

(ii) X Ltd spent £10,000 on a plant overhaul which Y Ltd will not need to do for at least three years.

(iii) X Ltd and Y Ltd both spent £30,000 on advertising; X Ltd charged all to last year's accounts, but Y Ltd carried forward 50 per cent to the current year.

(iv) X Ltd and Y Ltd both spent £20,000 in each of the past two years on research; X Ltd charged each year's expense as incurred. Y Ltd spread each charge equally over four years.

You are required to:

(a) Calculate and compare the initial returns of the two companies, analysing differences due to profitability on sales and intensity of asset use.

(b) Recalculate the results for both companies after undertaking the fixed assets revaluation and adjusting Y Ltd's figures for the other factors given, commenting briefly on the results.

(c) Calculate the residual income of each company for the year, after the adjustments, based on a 12 per cent investment return, commenting briefly on the results.

(d) State the likely reactions of the chief executive of each company on being offered a new investment project costing £200,000 and giving a 16 per cent return, on the assumption that his overall performance is assessed on

(i) return on capital employed;
(ii) residual income.

Ignore taxation.

### Answer 4

(a) Profit (all calculations are £000)

|  | X Ltd | | Y Ltd | |
|---|---|---|---|---|
| Sales | | 735 | | 690 |
| Less costs: | | | | |
| Depreciation | 140 | | 100 | |
| Other | 400 | | 320 | |
|  | 540 | | 420 | |
| Profit | | 195 | | 270 |
| Capital employed | | | | |
| Fixed assets | 1400 | | 1200 | — |
| Less depreciation | 980 (7 years) | | 400 (4 years) | |
|  | 420 | | 800 | |
| Working capital | 160 | | 100 | |
|  | | 580 | | 900 |

$$\text{ROCE} = \frac{195}{580} = 33.62\% \qquad \frac{270}{900} = 30\%$$

$$\text{Profit/Sales} = \frac{195}{735} = 26.5\% \qquad \frac{270}{690} = 39.1\%$$

$$\text{Sales/CE} = \frac{735}{580} = 1.27 \qquad \frac{690}{900} = 0.77 \text{ times}$$

Comparison:
X Ltd's ROCE is somewhat higher (nearly 4 per cent) than that of Y Ltd.

This slight superiority is achieved by a very much higher intensity of capital use (1.27 times compared with 0.77 times) though substantially offset by a lower profitability on sales (26.5 per cent compared with 39.1 per cent).

(b) Revaluation adjustments (all calculations are £000)

|  | X Ltd | | Y Ltd | |
|---|---|---|---|---|
| Original profit | | 195 | | 270 |
| Less depreciation (extra) | | | | |
| $140 \times (1.6 - 1) =$ | | 84 | $100 \times (1.2 - 1) =$ | 20 |
| New profit | | 111 | | 250 |
| CE Fixed assets $(1400 \times 1.6) = 2240$ | | | $(1200 \times 1.2)$ | $= 1440$ |
| Less depreciation $(980 \times 1.6) = 1568$ | | | $(400 \times 1.2)$ | $= 480$ |
| | | 672 | | 960 |
| New CE | $672 + 160 =$ | 832 | $960 + 100$ | $= 1060$ |

Other adjustments (all calculations are £000)

Y Ltd                           Profit                    Capital employed

|  | | Profit | | | Capital employed |
|---|---|---|---|---|---|

(i)  Add rental              12                          70
Less depreciation          10                          10
                                            +2                                        +60
(ii)                                        −10                                      —
(iii)                                       −15                                      −15
(iv)          Actual cost      Should be     Actual cost Should be
Last year but one  (5)   (20)                    (15)     (NIL)
Last year      (5+5=10)  (20)          −10      (15+10)   (NIL)    −25
                                            −33                                      +20
From revaluation section − extra    +250                          +1060
                                            217                                      1080

Y Ltd

New ROCE        $= \dfrac{217}{1080} = 20.1\%$

New Profit/Sales  $= \dfrac{217}{690} = 31.4\%$

New Sales/CE      $= \dfrac{690}{1080} = 0.639$ times

X Ltd

New ROCE        $= \dfrac{111}{832} = 13.34\%$

New Profit/Sales  $= \dfrac{111}{735} = 15.1\%$

New Sales/CE      $= \dfrac{735}{832} = 0.883$ times

Comments:

- Both ROCE ratios have dropped, particularly X Ltd's (which is now less tnan half of what it previously was), and Y Ltd's is now the higher. Y Ltd's profitability on sales is lower than it was before (in (a)) but is twice that of X Ltd whereas previously it was 1.5 times that of X Ltd.
- X Ltd's intensity of capital use has dropped substantially and is now comparable to Y Ltd's which has risen.
- X Ltd's ROCE has particularly suffered from the larger adjustment for fixed assets which are much older than Y Ltd's. This was somewhat offset by the notional value of X Ltd's leased computer.

(c)  Residual income is the net income of an investment less the imputed interest on the investment capital used by each company.

|  | X Ltd<br>(£) | Y Ltd<br>(£) |
|---|---|---|
| Profit | 111,000 | 217,000 |
| Investment (£832,000 × 12%) |  | (£1,080,000 × 12%) |
|  | 99,840 | 129,600 |
|  | £11,160 | £87,400 |

Y Ltd's result shows up very much better (roughly eight times) than that of X Ltd.

It achieves nearly double the profit whilst using only 30 per cent more cost of investment.

(d)   Return on capital employed

|  | X Ltd | | Y Ltd | |
|---|---|---|---|---|
|  | (£) | (£) | (£) | (£) |
| New profit | 111,000 |  | 217,000 |  |
| Plus extra | 32,000 |  | 32,000 |  |
|  |  | 143,000 |  | 249,000 |
| New CE | 832,000 |  | 1,080,000 |  |
| Plus extra | 200,000 |  | 200,000 |  |
|  |  | 1,032,000 |  | 1,280,000 |
| ROCE | = 13.86% |  | = 19.45% |  |
|  | (cf 13.34%) |  | (cf 20.1%) |  |
| | Better, therefore Accept | | Worse, therefore Reject | |

Note, A 16 per cent project must improve X Ltd's overall ROCE and worsen Y Ltd's.

(ii)   Residual income

|  | X Ltd<br>(£) | Y Ltd<br>(£) |
|---|---|---|
| New profit | 143,000 | 249,000 |
| Less (£1,032,000 × 12%) | | (£1,280,000 × 12%) |
|  | 123,840 | 153,600 |
| Residual income | £19,160 | £95,400 |
| This is larger than | £11,160 | £87,400 |
| Therefore accept | accept | |

Note, they must both accept a project yielding 16 per cent for which they would be 'charged' 12 per cent.

The extra income will be £8,000 in each case (£200,000 × (16% − 12%)). This is a much larger percentage of X Ltd's income than Y Ltd's and therefore more significant.

## Further reading

Bromwich, M., Measurement of divisional performance: A comment and extension, in *Readings in Accounting and Business Research*, Spring, 1977.

Coates, J.B., Smith, J.E., and Stacey, R.J., Results of a preliminary survey into the structure of divisionalized companies, divisionalized performance appraisal and the associated role of management accounting, in Cooper, D., Scapens, R. and Arnold, J., *Management Accounting Research and Practice*, CIMA, 1983.

Lee, T.A., *Income and Value Measurement*, 3rd edn, Van Nostrand Reinhold, 1985.

# 12 Standard costing and variance analysis

Standard costing involves the setting of predetermined cost estimates in order to provide a basis for comparison with actual costs. A standard cost is a planned cost for a unit of product or service rendered. Although the terms budgeted and standard cost are sometimes used interchangeably, budgeted costs normally describe the total planned costs for a number of products.

*Example of a standard cost card for a unit of product*

| Direct materials | (£) | |
| --- | --- | --- |
| x − 5 kilos at £1 per kilo = 5 | | |
| y − 3 kilos at £2 per kilo = 6 | | |
| | 11 | |
| Direct labour | | |
| 7 hours at £5 per hr | 35 | |
| Variable production overheads | | |
| 7 hours at £1 per hr | 7 | |
| Fixed production overheads | | |
| 7 hours at £2 per hr | 14 | |
| Standard full production cost | 67 | |

The selling price and the contribution or profit may also be shown. Some firms include non-production costs in the standard cost per unit.

## Setting standards

### Costs

Direct material costs per unit of raw material are estimated by the purchasing department after considering the quality of material to be used, suppliers' prices, inflation and the availability of bulk purchase discounts.

Direct labour rates per hour are set by reference to the type of skills to be used, union agreements, inflation and the market rates.

### Quantity

The standard quantity of material is determined by the quality of material to be used, normal loss requirements and the skill of labour involved.

The standard time for a job is the time in which a task should be completed at standard performance. Standard performance is the rate of output which motivated skilled workers can achieve as an average over the working day if they comply with the specified method. Work study and the learning curve are useful techniques for determining standard hours. It is important to note that the standard hour is not just a measure of time, but a common measure of work content, e.g. 200 chairs at 5 hours per chair and 100 desks at 10 hours per desk can be expressed as 2000 hours of output.

## Types of standard

1 *Current standards*   These are standards established for use over a short period of time, related to current conditions, i.e. with current wastage and inefficiencies. The problem with this type of standard is that it does not try to improve on current levels of efficiency.

2 *Basic standards*   These are standards which have been established for use over a long period of time. The main disadvantage of this type of standard is that because it has remained unaltered over a long period of time it may be out of date. Its main advantage is in showing the changes in trend of price and efficiency from year to year.

3 *Ideal standards*   These are standards which are based on perfect operating conditions, i.e. they assume no wastage, no normal loss, no machine breakdowns, no idle time, no periods of relaxation, materials are obtained at the cheapest possible prices and labour is paid at the lowest possible rates. Variances from ideal standards are useful for highlighting areas where a close examination might result in large cost savings. However, ideal standards are not often used in practice because they are perceived by the employees as being unrealistic and may have an adverse motivational impact on the workforce.

4 *Attainable standards*   These are standards which are based on normal operating conditions, i.e. allowances are made for wastage and some inefficiency. If correctly set, attainable standards are the best type of standard to use, since they provide employees with a realistic challenging target. Attainable standards have the greatest motivational impact on the workforce.

## Advantages of standard costing

A standard costing system has many advantages which include the following:

1　Budgets are compiled from standards.
2　Standard costing highlights areas of strength and weakness.
3　Actual costs can be compared with standard costs in order to evaluate performance.
4　The setting of standards should result in the best resources and methods being used and thereby increase efficiency.
5　Standard costs can be used to value stock and provide a basis for setting wage incentive schemes.
6　Standard costing simplifies bookkeeping, as information is recorded at standard, instead of a number of historic figures.
7　It operates via the management by exception principle, where only those variances (differences between actual and expected results) which are outside certain tolerance limits are investigated, thereby economizing on managerial time and maximizing efficiency.
8　Control action is immediate, e.g. as soon as material is issued from stores to production it can be compared with the standard material which should have been used for the actual production.
9　Transfer prices are based on standard rather than actual costs. If the latter were used inefficiencies in the form of excess costs might be passed on from one division to another division.

## Problems in standard costing

1　A lot of input data is required which can be expensive.
2　Standard costing is usually confined to organizations whose processes or jobs are repetitive.
3　Unless standards are accurately set any performance evaluation will be meaningless.
4　Uncertainty in standard costing can be caused by inflation, technological change, economic and political factors, etc. Standards therefore need to be continually updated and revised.
5　It may be difficult to set standards at a level which both motivates the workforce and achieves the corporate goals.
6　The maintenance of the cost data base is expensive.

## Variance analysis

Variances explain the differences between actual results and expected results, and will therefore be either favourable variances (F) or adverse variances (A). If actual is as expected then there will be no variance.

　　Standard operating statements represent a list of variances reconciling budgeted profit or contribution with actual profit. Standard operating statements can be prepared using either absorption or marginal costing principles.

Students will note that cost variances are recorded in the cost account books, but sales variances do not appear in the books. This is because sales are entered in the accounts at actual selling price and the sales variances are only shown in management reports in order to help reconcile budgeted profit or contribution to actual profit.

### Sales variances

(a)  The sales price variance represents the difference between the actual selling price per unit and the standard selling price per unit, multiplied by the actual quantity of units sold, i.e. did the units sell for more or less than their standard selling price?
(b)  The sales volume variance represents the difference between the actual units sold and the budgeted quantity, multiplied by either the standard profit per unit or the standard contribution per unit. In absorption costing standard profit per unit is used, but in marginal costing, standard contribution per unit must be used.

### Formula

Sales price variance = (Actual selling price per unit − Standard selling price per unit) Actual quantity sold.

Sales volume variance = (Actual sales quantity − Budgeted sales quantity) Standard profit per unit or Standard contribution per unit.

### Material cost variances

(a)  The material price variance is the difference between the standard price and the actual purchase price for each unit of material, multiplied by the actual quantity of material purchased.
It is preferable to base the price variance on the actual quantity of material purchased and not on the actual quantity used in order that price variances can be reported for control purposes as soon as possible, i.e. when the materials are purchased.
(b)  The material usage variance is the difference between the actual quantity of material used and the standard quantity of material that should be used for actual production, multiplied by the standard price per unit of material.

### Formulae

Material price variance = (Actual price per unit of material − Standard price per unit of material) Actual quantity purchased.

Material usage variance = (Actual quantity of material used − Standard quantity for actual production) Standard price per unit of material.

### Labour cost variances

(a)  The labour rate variance is the difference between the actual direct labour rate per hour and the standard direct labour rate per hour, multiplied by the actual hours paid, i.e. was the rate per hour paid to the direct labour force more or less than standard?

(b)  The labour efficiency variance is the difference between the actual hours taken to produce the actual output and the standard hours that this output should have taken, multiplied by the standard rate per hour.

(c)  The idle time variance represents the difference between hours paid and hours worked, i.e. idle hours multiplied by the standard wage rage per hour.

### Formulae

Labour rate variance = (Actual rate per hour − Standard wage rate per hour) Actual hours paid.

Labour efficiency variance = (Actual hours worked − Standard hours for actual production) Standard wage rate per hour.

Idle time variance = (Hours paid − Hours worked) Standard wage rate per hour.

### Variable overhead variances

(a)  The variable overhead expenditure variance is the difference between the actual variable overhead rate per hour and the standard variable overhead rate per hour multiplied by the actual hours worked.

The actual hours worked must be used not the actual hours paid because the latter may include ideal time and it is usually assumed that variable overheads will not be recovered in idle time.

(b)  The variable overhead efficiency variance is the difference between actual hours worked and the standard hours for actual production multiplied by the standard variable overhead rate per hour.

### Formulae

Variable overhead expenditure variance = (Actual variable overhead rate per hour − Standard variable overhead rate per hour) Actual hours worked.

Variable overhead efficiency variance = (Actual hours worked − Standard hours for actual production) Standard variable overhead rate per hour.

### Fixed production overhead variances

The total fixed production overhead costs variances represents the under/over absorbed fixed production overhead in the period.

This under/over absorbed overhead may be due to differences between actual and budgeted fixed overheads, i.e. expenditure variances, and/or differences between the actual and budgeted levels of activity, i.e. volume variances.

(a)   The fixed overhead expenditure variance is simply the difference between the actual and budgeted fixed production costs. It can arise in both marginal and absorption costing.

(b)   The fixed overhead volume variance represents the difference between the actual units produced and the budgeted units, multiplied by the standard fixed cost per unit. If expressed in hours it is the difference between the budgeted hours and the standard hours for actual production, multiplied by the standard fixed overhead rate per hour.

The fixed overhead volume variance can never arise in marginal costing because under this technique all the fixed costs are charged to the period irrespective of the actual level of activity.

### Formula

Fixed overhead expenditure variance = Actual fixed overheads − Budgeted fixed overheads.

Fixed overhead volume variance in units = (Actual units produced − Budgeted units) Standard fixed cost per unit.

Fixed overhead volume variance in hours = (budgeted hours − Standard hours for actual products) Standard fixed overhead rate per hour.

The fixed overhead volume variance can be analysed into the following variances:

1   The fixed overhead efficiency variance = (Actual hours worked − Standard hours for actual production) Standard fixed overhead rate per hour.

2   The fixed overhead capacity variance = (Budgeted hours − Actual hours paid) Standard fixed overhead rate per hour.

3   The fixed overhead idle time variance = (Actual hours paid − Actual hours worked) Standard fixed overhead rate per hour.

This analysis of the fixed overhead volume variance shows the effects on fixed production costs of efficiency/inefficiency and of the under/over utilization of capacity.

Figure 12.1 shows most of the variances which need to be studied and their inter-relationships.

Students will note that the sales mix and quantity variances and the material mix and yield variances are dealt with in the next chapter.

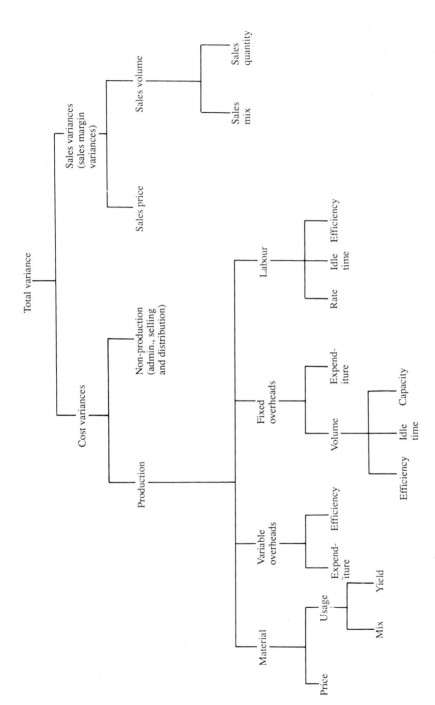

Figure 12.1 *Summary of variances*

## Reasons for variances occurring

The following list of possible causes of variances is not exhaustive, but does provide many of the common reasons found in practice.

| | |
|---|---|
| Labour rate variance | Use of higher/lower grade of skilled workers than planned or wage inflation. |
| Labour efficiency variance | Use of higher/lower grade of skilled workers than planned or the quality of material used, errors in allocating time to jobs. |
| Idle time variance | Illness, machine breakdown, hold-ups on the production line because of lack of material. |
| Material price variance | Good/bad purchasing, or the quality of material purchased or material price inflation, unforeseen discounts received. |
| Material usage variance | Use of higher/lower quality of material than planned, or efficiency of workforce, theft, stricter quality controls. |
| Overhead expenditure variance | Inflation or greater/less economical use of services, change in type of service used. |
| Overhead capacity variance | Over/under utilization of plant capacity, excessive idle time. |
| Overhead efficiency variance | Efficiency of workforce and plant, and technological change. |

*A comprehensive example*
Data

Standard cost
Production                    Requirements per item of product
Direct material               20 kilos at £1.50 per kilo
Direct wages                  30 hours at £2.10 per hour

|  | (per month) |
|---|---|
| Overhead fixed | £40,000 |
| variable | £160,000 |
| Normal capacity | 120,000 hours |

Marketing

|  | (per month) |
|---|---|
| Sales | 4,000 items at £175 each |

Actual for the month of October 19XX                    Cost
                                                        (£000)

Production
Direct material   purchase   80,000 kilos                     128
                  issued     78,000 kilos
Direct wages                 116,000 hours                    232
Overhead   fixed                                               42
           variable                                           150
Output (3800 items)

|  | Value (£000) |
|---|---|
| Marketing | |
| Sales (3500 items) | 623 |

There was no stock at the beginning of the month.

Required:

(a)  Standard cost per kilo.
(b)  A schedule of variances.
(c)  Verification of actual profit.
(d)  (i)  A standard absorption operating statement.
     (ii) A standard marginal operating statement.

*Solution*
(a)  *Standard cost and profit per unit*

|  | (£) |
|---|---|
| Direct labour 30 hours at £2.10 per hour | 63 |
| Direct materials 20 kilos at £1.50 per kilo | 30 |
| Prime cost | 93 |

Variable overhead $\dfrac{£160,000}{120,000 \text{ hrs}}$ = £1.33 per hr × 30 hrs    40

Fixed overhead $\dfrac{£40,000}{120,000 \text{ hrs}}$ = £0.33 per hr × 30 hrs    10

| | |
|---|---|
| Standard cost | 143 |
| Selling price | 175 |
| Standard profit | £32 per unit |

Standard contribution = £42/unit

(b)  *Schedule of variances*
Sales variances:

Price variance   = (Actual price per unit − Standard price per unit)
                   Actual quantity of units sold.
                 = (178 − 175) 3500 units
                 = £10,500 favourable

Volume variance = (Actual quantity of units sold − Standard quantity of units sold) Standard profit or contribution per unit

= (3500 units − 4000 units) £32 or £42

= £16,000   adverse if based on profit

or   £21,000   adverse if based on contribution.

Cost variances:

1   Material variances:

Price variance   = (Actual price per kilo − Standard price per kilo) Actual quantity of kilos purchased

= (1.60 − £1.50) 80,000 kilos

= £8000   adverse

Usage variance   = (Actual quantity of kilos issued − standard quantity of kilos) Standard price per kilo

For actual production

= (78,000 kilos − 76,000 kilos) £1.50

required to         38,000 units × 20 kilos/unit
produce 3800 units
=£3000   adverse

2   Labour variances:

Rate variance = (Actual wage rate per hr − Standard wage rate per hr) Actual hours paid

= (£2 − £2.10) 116,000 hrs

= £11,600   Favourable

Efficiency variance = (Actual Hours worked − Standard hours for actual production) Standard wage rate per hour

= (116,000 − 114,000 hours) £2.10

required to         3800 units × 30 hrs/unit
produce 3800 units
= £4200   adverse

Idle time variance = (Hours paid − hours worked) Standard wage rate per hour

= (116,000 hours − 116,000 hours) £2.10

= nil

Overhead variances

1  Variable overhead:

Efficiency variance = (Actual hours worked − Standard hours for actual production) Standard variable overhead rate per hour
= (116,000 hrs − 114,000 hrs) £1.33 per hr
= £2667  adverse

Expenditure variance = (Actual variable overhead rate per hr − Standard variable overhead rate per hr) Actual hours worked
= (1.1931 − £1.3333) 116,000 hrs
= £4667  Favourable

2  Fixed overhead:

Expenditure variance = Actual fixed overhead − Budgeted fixed overheads
= £42,000 − £40,000
= £2000  adverse

Volume variance = (Budgeted hours − Standard hours for actual production) Standard fixed overhead rate per hour
= (120,000 hrs − 114,000 hrs)
£0.33 per hr
= £2000  adverse

(Budgeted units − Actual units produced) fixed cost per unit

(4000 units − 3800 units)  £10 = £2000  adverse

The volume variance can be analysed into an efficiency and capacity variance.

Efficiency variance = (Actual hours worked − Standard hours) Standard fixed overhead rate per hr. For actual production
= (116,000 hrs − 114,000 hrs) £0.33 per hr
= £667  adverse

Capacity variance (Actual hours paid − Budgeted hours) Standard fixed overhead

= (116,000 hrs − 120,000 hrs) £0.33 per hr
= £1333  adverse

(c)  *Verification of actual profit*

|  | (£) | (£) | (£) |
|---|---|---|---|
| Revenue |  |  | 623,000 |
| Less costs |  |  |  |
| Material | 128,000 |  |  |
| Labour | 232,000 |  |  |
| Variable overhead | 150,000 |  |  |
| Fixed overhead | 42,000 |  |  |
|  |  | 552,000 |  |
| Less closing stocks |  |  |  |
| Material (2000 kilos × £1.50) | 3,000 |  |  |
| Finished units* |  |  |  |
| (3000 units × £143) | 42,900 |  |  |
|  |  | (45,900) |  |
| Cost of sales |  |  | (506,100) |
| Net profit |  |  | £116,900 |

*In the above computation the finished units are valued at the full standard cost of £143 per unit.

However if this stock of finished goods is valued at the standard marginal cost of £133 per unit then the cost of sales would increase by 300 units (£143 − £133) = £3,000, resulting in an actual profit of £113,900

(d)(i)  *Standard absorption operating statement*

|  | (£) |
|---|---|
| Budgeted profit | 128,000 |
| Sales volume variance (based on profit) | (16,000) |
| Sales price variance | 10,500 |
|  | 122,500 |

| | Favourable | Cost variance | Adverse | |
|---|---|---|---|---|
| Material price |  |  | 8,000 | |
| Material usage |  |  | 3,000 | |
| Labour rate | 11,600 |  |  | |
| Labour efficiency |  |  | 4,200 | |
| Variable overhead |  |  |  | |
| Expenditure | 4,667 |  |  | |
| Efficiency |  |  | 2,667 | |
| Fixed overhead |  |  |  | |
| Expenditure |  |  | 2,000 | |
| Volume |  |  | 2,000 | (5,600) |
| Actual profit |  |  |  | = 116,900 |

Note, the fixed overhead volume variance can be shown in its constituent parts, i.e. as the fixed overhead efficiency and capacity variances.

(d)(ii)  *Standard marginal operating statement*

|  | (£) |
|---|---|
| Budgeted profit | 128,000 |
| Sales volume variance (based on contribution) | (21,000) |
| Sales price variance | 10,500 |
|  | 117,500 |

| | Favourable | Cost variance | Adverse | |
|---|---|---|---|---|
| Material price | | | 8,000 | |
| Material usage | | | 3,000 | |
| Labour rate | 11,600 | | | |
| Labour efficiency | | | 4,200 | |
| Variable overhead | | | | |
| Expenditure | 4,667 | | | |
| Efficiency | | | 2,667 | |
| Fixed overhead | | | | |
| Expenditure | | | 2,000 | |
| | | | | (3,600) |
| Actual Profit | | | | = 113,900 |

An alternative standard marginal operating statement can be used which reconciles budgeted contribution with actual profit as follows:

|  | (£) |
|---|---|
| Budgeted contribution | 168,000 |
| Sales volume variance (based on contribution) | (21,000) |
| Sales price variance | 10,500 |
|  | 157,500 |

| | Favourable | Variable cost variance | Adverse | |
|---|---|---|---|---|
| Material price | | | 8,000 | |
| Material usage | | | 3,000 | |
| Labour rate | 11,600 | | | |
| Labour efficiency | | | 4,200 | |
| Variable overhead | | | | |
| Expenditure | 4,667 | | | |
| Efficiency | | | 2,667 | (1,600) |
| Actual contribution | | | | = 155,900 |
| Less budgeted fixed costs | | | | |
| | | | 40,000 | |
| Expenditure variance | | | 2,000 | |
| Actual fixed cost | | | | (42,000) |
| Actual profit | | | | 113,900 |

### Important points concerning the above operating statements

1 *Sales volume variance*  In the absorption operating statement it is based on standard profit per unit, whereas in the marginal operating statement it is based on standard contribution per unit, regardless of whether the marginal statement commences with budgeted profit or budgeted contribution.

2 *Fixed overhead variance*  The fixed overhead *expenditure* variance occurs in both the marginal and absorption statements. However, the fixed overhead *volume* variance cannot appear in any type of marginal statement, because in marginal costing fixed costs are not absorbed into the units, but are all charged to the period irrespective of actual level of activity.

## Network analysis

Budgetary control methods have been employed in some form on most project work but have normally suffered from a number of weaknesses. The result has been that the traditional unit costing methods have not prevented costs of projects rising.

Project cost control is an extension of budgetary control methods and it enables some of these weaknesses to be overcome. It provides a reliable basis for comparison with incurred costs and hence provides for the calculation of variances. These variances in turn permit management by exception. It provides a method of controlling both costs and physical progress. Unit costing methods are complementary to, and not an alternative to, project cost control.

Most projects that companies undertake which involve capital expenditure will incur costs over a reasonable period of time lasting between about six months to ten years. The project may involve hundreds of activities each of which may take longer or shorter to complete than previously estimated. The management of such projects is crucial if the company does not want to risk large costs that occur if deadlines are not met, or wish to make substantial savings by good planning and cost effective scheduling of projects costs.

Two associated methods, CPM (critical path method) and PERT (program evaluation and review technique), have been devised to help the management accountant plan and control the projects.

There are six steps that need to be carried out when applying these methods.

1 Define the project and split the project into distinct activities and tasks.
2 Determine the relationships between the activities, and list all precedence relationships.
3 Draw a network diagram showing the precedence relationships between the activities.
4 Determine the duration and cost of each activity.

5 Calculate the critical path and its duration for the network.
6 Use the network to help plan, schedule, monitor and control the project.

The critical path is the longest pathway through the network. Any delay to activities on this pathway will delay completion of the project. Hence the management accountant must pay particular attention to this pathway, and other pathways whose durations are close to the critical path duration, if he is to effectively control the project. Reducing the time on the critical path by allocating additional resources will allow project deadlines to be revised. Flexibility can be obtained by identifying non-critical activities and replanning, rescheduling and reallocating resources such as manpower, machinery and finance.

## The CPM approach

Consider the following maintenance project which has to be undertaken by Smid Industries.

The company has identified five activities A to E, along with their associated duration and cost, which have to be completed within 25 weeks.

| Activities | Precedence | Duration (weeks) | Direct cost (£) |
|---|---|---|---|
| A | None | 5 | 800 |
| B | None | 3 | 420 |
| C | A | 8 | 560 |
| D | B | 6 | 240 |
| E | C,D | 7 | 700 |

Steps 1, 2 and 4 of the project analysis have been carried out. Steps 3, drawing the network, and 5, calculating the critical path have now to be done.

Each activity is represented in Figure 12.2 by a line (not to scale) with an arrow to show order of precedence. At the beginning and end of each activity arrow there is a node representing an event. Event nodes are numbered in sequence, in this example in steps of ten, from the beginning of the network to the end. The activities A and B with no preceding activities start from the start node zero. Using the precedence conditions C follows A after node 10, and D follows B after node 20. Note node 10 is the event concerned with the end of activity A and the start of activity C. Node 20 here guarantees that activity C cannot start until activity A has been completed, hence satisfying one of the project requirements. Activity E then follows both activities C and D after node 30, with node 40, the end node, completing the diagram.

To calculate the critical path the earliest and latest event times at each node have to be determined. Starting from node 0, the earliest time activities A and B can start is zero (measuring time from the start of the project). This number is inserted in the left-hand corner of node 0. The

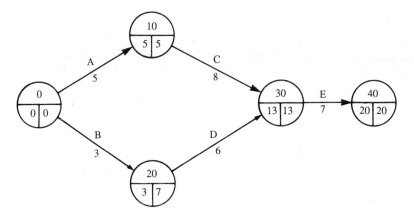

Figure 12.2

earliest time that C can start is when A has been completed which is 5
weeks after the start (i.e. 0 + 5), this is the earliest start time at node 10.
Similarly the earliest start time at node 20 is 3. The start of activity E,
node 30, depends upon the completion of activities C (5 + 8) and D (3 +
6). The latest to be completed is C at 13 weeks, giving an earliest time
for node 40 of 13 + 7 = 20. The total project time is therefore 20 weeks.

To determine the latest event times work backwards through the
network starting at the end node 40. If the project is to be completed at
the earliest possible time, which is currently 20 weeks, the latest time
event 40 can take place is at 20 weeks.

Moving back down the network to node 30, the latest time event 30
can take place if the project is to be completed in 20 weeks is 20 − 7 =
13. (Insert this on the diagram at the bottom right-hand side of node
30.) Similarly latest event time at node 20 is 13 − 6 = 7, and at node 10
is 13 − 8 = 5. At node 0 there is a choice between 5 − 5 = 0 and 7 − 3 =
4. The lowest value is always selected giving zero in this case.

The critical path can be determined as that path which joins all the
nodes with zero slackness. Zero slackness occurs at all nodes where the
earliest and latest event times are the same, i.e. nodes 0, 10, 30, and 40.
The critical path must pass through these nodes as these are the nodes
at which no delay can occur in the starting of the next activity once all
preceding activities have been completed. The critical activities are
therefore A, C and E and the project duration is 20 weeks. Activities B
and D are not critical.

The total direct cost of the project is £800 + 420 + 560 + 240 + 700 =
£2720.

The maintenance project for Smid Industries can be completed within the required time of 25 weeks without the need to use additional
resources.

## Float

All activities not lying on the critical path contain total float. Total float is the time by which an activity may be delayed or extended without increasing the overall project time. The total float for an activity can be calculated using the formula:

Total float = Latest time of head event − Earliest time of tail event
− Duration

Note, the tail event occurs before the head event.

The total float on activity D is 13 − 3 − 6 = 4, i.e. activity D can be delayed by up to 4 weeks without extending the time of the project beyond 20 weeks.

Other types of float used are free float and independent float defined as:

Free float = Earliest time of head event − Earliest time of tail event
− Duration

Independent float = Earliest time of head event − Latest time of tail
event − Duration

The identification of float in a project provides opportunity to make greater use of existing resources. This very process stresses to management the necessity to make resources more flexible wherever possible and should lead in the longer run to a more efficient use of resources and hence reduce costs.

## Use of dummy activities

Sometimes the precedence requirements cause problems in the drawing of a network, and dummy activities have to be incorporated. These dummy activities do not have a physical reality, they are given a zero duration, but are only included in the diagram as a dashed line, to preserve the precedence logic.

For example assume that Smid Industries required in the maintenance project that activity D is to be preceded by both activities A and B. The network diagram will need adjusting by incorporating a dummy activity between node 10 and node 20 (see Figure 12.3).

Recalculating the earliest and latest event times still gives the critical path as ACE of duration 20 weeks. However the flexibility has been reduced as the earliest event time for node 20 is now 5 instead of 3.

## Project cost control

Project cost control can be applied in a number of ways. One way is to use the network to plan and schedule the timing of costs and then use these budgeted costs to monitor and control the project.

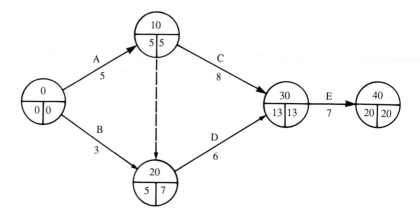

Figure 12.3

The stages in the budgeting process are:

1 Identify all costs associated with each of the activities. Add them together to get one estimated cost for each activity.
2 Calculate from the estimated cost per activity the estimated cost per time period.
3 The earliest and latest start times should be used, to determine the costs during each time period in order to complete the project within the target period.

For simplicity, assume that the cost of an activity is incurred uniformly over the duration of the activity. In certain situations this assumption would not be valid and a more comprehensive analysis would have to be adopted.

Apply this budgeting process to the Smid Industries project and assume step 1 has been completed and the net costs for each activity are the direct costs. Calculate the direct cost per week for each activity.

| Activity | Direct cost (£) | Duration (weeks) | Direct cost per week (£) |
|---|---|---|---|
| A | 800 | 5 | 160 |
| B | 420 | 3 | 140 |
| C | 560 | 8 | 70 |
| D | 240 | 6 | 40 |
| E | 700 | 7 | 100 |

Using the earliest start times, activity A has the earliest start time of zero and a duration of 5 weeks, therefore the budget contribution from A will be £160 for each of the first five weeks. Activity D has an earliest

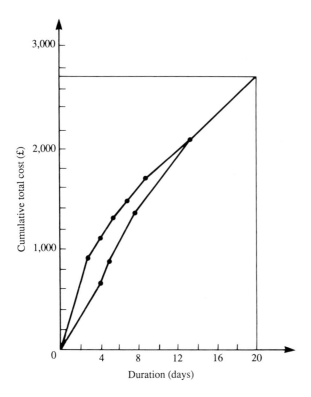

Figure 12.4

start time of 3 weeks (original problem without the dummy) and a duration of 6 weeks making a budget contribution of £40 during each week from week 4 to week 9 inclusive.

Applying this approach to all of the activities leads to the table of budget contributions shown. The table shows the budget contributions for each activity week by week. These are accumulated to give the total budget for the entire project for each week. The weekly totals have been accumulated to determine the total amount that should have been spent to date.

The critical activities must spend their budgeted amount at the time given in the table. The non-critical activities may however be delayed until the latest start times.

Using the latest start times we get the revised table for the budgeted costs.

By comparison the budget with the latest start times uses less finance in the first few weeks than the budget with the earliest start times. Thus the two budgets show the earliest and latest times that the funds can be spent and therefore the management accountant can choose any budget that falls within these two tables. This can be illustrated by Figure 12.4.

Budget contributions

| Activity | | | | | | | | | | | Week | | | | | | | | | | |
|---|---|---|---|---|---|---|---|---|---|---|---|---|---|---|---|---|---|---|---|---|---|
| | 1 | 2 | 3 | 4 | 5 | 6 | 7 | 8 | 9 | 10 | 11 | 12 | 13 | 14 | 15 | 16 | 17 | 18 | 19 | 20 | Total |
| A | 160 | 160 | 160 | 160 | 160 | | | | | | | | | | | | | | | | 800 |
| B | 140 | 140 | 140 | | | | | | | | | | | | | | | | | | 420 |
| C | | | | | | 70 | 70 | 70 | 70 | 70 | 70 | 70 | 70 | | | | | | | | 560 |
| D | | | | 40 | 40 | 40 | 40 | 40 | 40 | | | | | | | | | | | | 240 |
| E | | | | | | | | | | | | | | 100 | 100 | 100 | 100 | 100 | 100 | 100 | 700 |
| Total | 300 | 300 | 300 | 200 | 200 | 110 | 110 | 110 | 110 | 70 | 70 | 70 | 70 | 100 | 100 | 100 | 100 | 100 | 100 | 100 | 2720 |
| Cumulative total | 300 | 600 | 900 | 1100 | 1300 | 1400 | 1520 | 1630 | 1740 | 1810 | 1880 | 1950 | 2020 | 2120 | 2220 | 2320 | 2420 | 2520 | 2620 | 2720 | |

Budget contributions

| Activity | | | | | | | | | | | Week | | | | | | | | | | |
|---|---|---|---|---|---|---|---|---|---|---|---|---|---|---|---|---|---|---|---|---|---|
| | 1 | 2 | 3 | 4 | 5 | 6 | 7 | 8 | 9 | 10 | 11 | 12 | 13 | 14 | 15 | 16 | 17 | 18 | 19 | 20 | Total |
| A | 160 | 160 | 160 | 160 | 160 | | | | | | | | | | | | | | | | 800 |
| B | | | | | 140 | 140 | 140 | | | | | | | | | | | | | | 420 |
| C | | | | | | 70 | 70 | 70 | 70 | 70 | 70 | 70 | 70 | | | | | | | | 560 |
| D | | | | | | | | 40 | 40 | 40 | 40 | 40 | 40 | | | | | | | | 240 |
| E | | | | | | | | | | | | | | 100 | 100 | 100 | 100 | 100 | 100 | 100 | 700 |
| Total | 160 | 160 | 160 | 160 | 300 | 210 | 210 | 110 | 110 | 110 | 110 | 110 | 110 | 100 | 100 | 100 | 100 | 100 | 100 | 100 | 2720 |
| Cumulative total | 160 | 320 | 480 | 640 | 940 | 1150 | 1360 | 1470 | 1580 | 1690 | 1800 | 1910 | 2020 | 2120 | 2220 | 2320 | 2420 | 2520 | 2620 | 2720 | |

## Monitoring costs

Budgets are normally produced before the project is undertaken and are then used to monitor and control the project costs to ensure that the project is progressing as far as possible on schedule and as close to the budget as can be achieved.

Assume that the Smid Industries maintenance project, working on the earliest start times, has just completed the tenth week with activities A and B completed, C being ahead of schedule with only two weeks to complete, and D being behind schedule with one more week needed, E has not yet started.

The costs to date of each activity has been:

| Activity | Direct cost (£) |
|----------|-----------------|
| A        | 1000            |
| B        | 370             |
| C        | 400             |
| D        | 250             |
| E        | 0               |
|          | 2020            |

The value of work completed can be calculated using the formula:

Value of work = Total budget per activity × percentage of work completed.

The analysis can be summarized in the following table:

| Activity | Total cost (£) | Percentage completed | Value of work completed (£) |
|----------|----------------|----------------------|------------------------------|
| A        | 800            | 100                  | 800                          |
| B        | 420            | 100                  | 420                          |
| C        | 560            | 75                   | 420                          |
| D        | 240            | 83                   | 200                          |
| E        | 700            | 0                    | 0                            |
|          | 2720           |                      | 1840                         |

The budgeted cost to date is £1810 (see cumulative total at week 10 in the earliest start table).

The difference between the costs incurred and the budgeted expenditure is known as the current budget variance. Hence the current budget variance is £2020 − 1810 = £210 showing that the incurred cost is greater than the budgeted costs to date.

The current budget variance can be split into two component variances, the performance variance and the efficiency variance defined as:

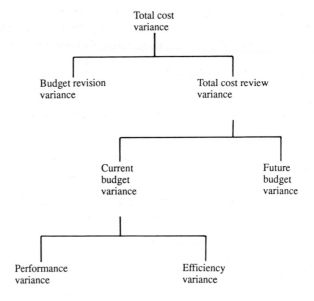

Figure 12.5

Performance variance = budget value of work done − budgeted
                      expenditure
                    = £1840 − 1810 = £30

Efficiency variance = incurred cost − budget value of work
                    = £2020 − 1840 = £180

The positive performance variance shows that the work is ahead of schedule whereas the positive efficiency variance shows that over-spending has occurred.

As C requires two more weeks and D one more week and assuming that E will still take its estimated time of seven weeks, the project will require nine weeks to complete, a total project time of nineteen weeks. This is a saving of one week on the estimated project time. Hence there is a slight overrun on the cost, but a potential saving of one week in total time.

There are a number of variances that may be used in project cost control, which are components of the total cost variance. Their relationship is shown in Figure 12.5.

### Projecting crashing with CPM

Suppose that Smid Industries have to complete the maintenance project within 15 weeks instead of 25 weeks. The critical path is 20 weeks, hence the deadline cannot be met unless more resources can be obtained to shorten the times of some of the activities. This shortening of the activities is called crashing. The introduction of new resources will involve extra expenditure and the management accountant needs to determine which activities to crash in order to achieve the minimum extra cost.

The project crashing procedure is as follows:

1 Determine the critical path
2 Calculate the crash cost per unit time period for each activity in the network where:

$$\text{Crash cost/unit time period} = \frac{\text{Crash cost} - \text{normal cost}}{\text{Normal time} - \text{crash time}}$$

3 Identify the activity on the critical path with the smallest crash cost/unit time period. Crash this activity as much as possible until:

(i) another path becomes critical as well, or
(ii) the deadline has been met; or
(iii) no more crashing of this activity can be done.

Stop whenever any one of these conditions has been fulfilled.

4 If condition 3(ii) is met the task has been completed. If condition 3(i) is met return to step 3 crashing on both critical paths simultaneously. If condition 3(iii) is met return to step 3 ignoring any activities previously fully crashed.

The following information was obtained for the Smid Industries project.

| | *Time* *(weeks)* | | *Cost* *(£)* | |
|---|---|---|---|---|
| *Activity* | Normal | Crash | Normal | Crash |
| A | 5 | 3 | 800 | 900 |
| B | 3 | 2 | 420 | 500 |
| C | 8 | 5 | 560 | 740 |
| D | 6 | 3 | 240 | 540 |
| E | 7 | 4 | 700 | 910 |

The crash times per week are:

A $(900 - 800)/(5 - 3) =$ 50
B $(500 - 420)/(3 - 2) =$ 80
C $(740 - 560)/(8 - 5) =$ 60
D $(540 - 240)/(6 - 3) =$ 100
E $(910 - 700)/(7 - 4) =$ 70

Now proceed to crash

| Activity cut | Project duration (weeks) | Cost (£) | Cumulative cost (£) |
|---|---|---|---|
| None | 20 | 0 | 2720 |
| A by 2 | 18 | 100 | 2820 |
| ACE is still critical | | | |
| C by 2 | 16 | 120 | 2940 |
| ACE and BDE are now critical. It is a choice between cutting C and B at £60 + 80 = £140 or E or £70. | | | |
| E by 1 | 15 | 70 | 3010 |

The target of 15 weeks has been achieved at a total additional cost of £3010 − 2720 = £290.

### The PERT approach

The CPM method assumes that the activity durations are certain. The PERT approach was developed to deal with activities where there is uncertainty in the duration times of the activities. For a PERT activity three estimates of the duration are required.

Optimistic time (a) = the shortest time the activity will take if everything goes well.

Most likely time (m) = the model time, i.e. the time that most would estimate.

Pessimistic time (b) = the longest time the activity will take assuming everything does not go well.

PERT assumes that these time estimates follow a beta probability distribution giving the expected activity time as

$$t = \frac{a + 4m + b}{6}$$

and the standard deviation as

$$s = \frac{b - a}{6}$$

The expected activity times can be used, as in CPM, to find the expected project duration, and the activity standard deviations can be used to examine the likely variability in the expected project duration.

Assume that PERT is to be applied to the Smid Industries project and the following time estimates are provided, assuming the same logic as previously.

| Activity | a | m (week) | b |
|----------|---|----------|---|
| A | 2 | 5 | 8 |
| B | 2 | 2.5 | 6 |
| C | 4 | 7 | 16 |
| D | 5 | 6 | 7 |
| E | 1 | 8 | 9 |

Calculate the expected times, the standard deviation and the variance (standard deviation squared) of the activities.

| Activity | t | s (weeks) | V |
|----------|---|-----------|---|
| A | 5 | 1 | 1 |
| B | 3 | 0.667 | 0.444 |
| C | 8 | 2 | 4 |
| D | 6 | 0.333 | 0.111 |
| E | 7 | 1.333 | 0.778 |

The expected durations are the same as in the CPM example and hence the critical path in ACE with duration 20 weeks as before. The variance for the project duration is the same as the variance of the critical path which is the sum of the variances of the *critical activities*:

Project variance = 1 + 4 + 1.778
= 6.778

As the standard deviation is the square root of the variance:

Project standard deviation = 2.60 weeks

PERT assumes that the project times are independent of each other and that the total project time follows a normal distribution.

Hence the probability of the project time exceeding 25 weeks can be determined using normal tables:

$$Z = \frac{25 - 20}{2.6} = 1.92$$

From normal tables, table area = 0.4726
Therefore tail area = 0.5 − 0.4726
= 0.0274

Just under a 3 per cent chance that the project will exceed the deadline.

A 95 per cent confidence interval for the project time could also be calculated.

95% CI = Mean ± 1.96 × Standard deviation
= 20    ± 1.96 × 2.6 weeks
= 20    ± 5.1 weeks

The probability is 0.95 that the time estimates would have come from a project whose duration is between 14.9 and 25.1 weeks.

### Advantages of project cost control over traditional methods

A sound logical analysis is the fundamental approach of CPM and PERT which leads to a better initial plan and better control. Project cost control encourages close cooperation between estimation, planning, and accounting functions from the outset. This leads to a more realistic budget in which financial responsibilities can be clearly allocated. The evidence suggests that where project cost control has been introduced substantial savings have been made.

## Examination questions

### Question 1 (CIMA)

Uniproduct Ltd manufactures a single product for which the following information is available:

| Standard cost data | |
|---|---:|
| Monthly production (units) | 20,000 |
| | (£) |
| Direct materials | |
| 20,000 kgs at £2 per kg | 40,000 |
| Direct labour | |
| 25,000 hours at £4 per hour | 100,000 |
| Variable overhead | 100,000 |
| Fixed overhead | 60,000 |
| Total cost | 300,000 |
| Sales 20,000 units at £18 | 360,000 |
| Profit | 60,000 |

The following extracts were taken from the actual results and reports produced for two consecutive accounting periods.

| Period 1 extracts | Period 2 extracts |
|---|---|
| Production 18,000 units | Production 18,000 units |
| | Sales 17,000 units at £20 each |
| Direct material price variance £3800 (F) | Direct labour efficiency variance £10,000 (F) |
| Direct materials usage variance £2000 (A) | Variance overhead expenditure variance £1000 (F) |
| Direct labour rate variance £4100 (A) | Fixed overhead volume variance £6000 (A) |
| Direct labour efficiency variance £8000 (F) | Fixed overhead expenditure variance £1000 (A) |

(F indicates a favourable variance and A an unfavourable variance.)
You are required to:

(a)  Explain and interpret every variance in extract 1 showing the underlying calculations.

(b) Calculate any additional variances that can be derived from the period 2 extracts assuming that a suggestion is followed that the company should change to a standard marginal system.

(c) Calculate the sub-variances of the fixed overhead volume variance assuming that an alternative suggestion is adopted that such a sub-division would aid management control.

(d) Comment on how far the sub-variances mentioned in (c) and other overhead variances do aid management control.

### Answer 1

(a) Direct materials cost

The flexed budget for these would be 18,000 kg × £2 per kg = £36,000
Actual consumption was 19,000 kg × £1.80 per kg = £34,200
Therefore material price variance = 19,000 kg × 20 p per kg (F)
= £3800 (F)
Material usage variance = 1000 kg × £2 kg (A) = £2000 (A)

The material price variance represents the difference between the standard price and the actual price for the actual quantity of material. The material usage variance represents the difference between the standard quantity specified for the actual production and the actual quantity used at the standard purchase price.

Direct labour costs

The flexed budget for these would be 22,500 hours at £4 per hour = £90,000
The actuals were 20,500 hrs at £4.20 per hour = £86,100.
Therefore direct labour rate variance = 20,500 hrs at 20p per hour (A) = £4100 (A)
Direct labour efficiency variance = 2000 hrs at £4 per hour (F) = £8000 (F)

The direct labour rate variance represents the difference between the standard and actual direct labour rate per hour for the actual hours worked.

The direct labour rate efficiency variance represents the difference between the standard hours for the production achieved and the hours actually worked valued at the standard labour rate.

(b) In a sense, the company already has a 'marginal' system in that fixed and variable costs are differentiated, but a standard marginal layout would show:

|  | (£) |
|---|---|
| Original budget contribution | 120,000 |
| Flexed budget contribution | 136,000 |
| Contribution variance (F) | 16,000 |

which is in part due to sales volume (3,000 units at £6 per unit) = £18,000 (A) and in part due to sales price (17,000 units at £2 per unit) = £34,000 (F)

(c) The presence of a direct labour efficiency variance of £10,000 indicates a saving of 2500 hours at a fixed overhead cost rate of £2.40 per hour = fixed overhead efficiency variance of £6000 (F). But this has reduced capacity utilization by

5000 direct labour hours at £2.40 per hour = fixed overhead capacity variance of £12,000 (A).

(d) Analysing the reasons for income, cost and profit differences and passing on this information in a timely and intelligible fashion to those managers who are responsible and accountable must be good. Whether or not it is effective in management control terms depends upon the zest of managers, their abilities, and the absence of restriction from taking appropriate corrective action.

Taking the variances in (c) specifically, labour efficiency should obviously be encouraged not only because of the labour cost advantages but also because of the impact on fixed cost recovery. Unfavourable capacity variances make the point that capacity is available and is not being used: it is then a question of pinpointing the reason for this and taking action. Furthermore, those overhead variances which arise merely because of the conventions of overhead absorption are not controllable by managers.

### Question 2 (CIMA)

The ideal standard cost for Product 22 based on a monthly output of 50,000 units is given below:

| Variable cost per unit | |
|---|---|
| Direct material A | 5 lbs at £2.00 per lb |
| Direct material B | 3 lbs at £4,00 per lb |
| Direct labour M | 2 hours at £3.60 per hr |
| Direct labour N | 1.5 hours at £2.50 per hr |
| Indirect labour | 0.5 hours at £2.50 per hr |
| Maintenance labour and expense | 0.1 hours at £2.50 per hr |
| Other overhead | 15% of direct material cost and 10% of direct labour cost |

| Fixed cost | per month |
|---|---|
| Supervisory salaries | £95,000 |
| Other overhead | £109,000 |

For the month of April 1986 the following adjustments were agreed as the basis for that month's attainable standard costs:

- Material A to be given a superior finish by the supplier incurring a 10 per cent surcharge.
- Material B to be purchased in larger consignments at a 12.5 per cent discount but this increases the variable overhead cost to 20 per cent for this type of material.
- Labour cost per hour increased under a trade union agreement by 20 p for labour N and 10 p for indirect and maintenance labour.
- Labour element N increased to 1.6 hours per unit because of problems with a major jig.
- Labour turnover necessitates employing some inexperienced workers

      10 per cent type M with 50 per cent efficiency and
      25 per cent type N with 60 per cent efficiency.

Actual results for April 1986 were:

| Production | 49,000 units |
|---|---|
| Direct material A | 247,000 lbs at £2.16 per lb |
| Direct material B | 149,000 lbs at £3.60 per lb |
| Direct labour M | 104,000 hours at £3.80 per hr |
| Direct labour N | 87,000 hours at £3.15 per hr |
| Indirect labour | 24,000 hours at £2.60 per hr |
| Maintenance | 4,500 hours at £5.10 per hour |
| Variable overhead | £251,000 |
| Supervisory salaries | 97,000 |
| Other fixed overhead | £110,000 |

You are required for Product 222 to:

(a) Calculate:

    (i) the ideal standard cost per unit;
    (ii) the attainable standard cost per unit for the month of April 1986;
    (iii) the total variance between the ideal and attainable standards for the April output;
    (iv) the total variance between actual costs for April and the attainable standard.

(b) Analyse the total variance under (a) (iv) to show the elements applicable to:

    (i) direct material price and usage for material A;
    (ii) direct labour rate and efficiency for labour type M.

(c) From the calculations at (a) (iii) and (a) (iv) above, comment on the benefits of following a policy of setting both ideal and attainable standards.

(d) Comment on the results obtained in part (b) above.

**Answer 2**

(a) *Ideal standard cost per unit*

| | | (£) | (£) |
|---|---|---|---|
| Direct materials | | | |
| A | 5 lbs × £2.00 | 10.00 | |
| B | 3 lbs × £4.00 | 12.00 | |
| | | | 22.00 |
| Direct labour | | | |
| M | 2.0 hours × £3.60 | 7.20 | |
| N | 1.5 hours × £3.00 | 4.50 | |
| | | | 11.70 |
| Indirect labour | 0.5 hours × £2.50 | 1.25 | |
| Maintenance | 0.1 hours × £5.00 | 0.50 | |
| Variable overhead | | | |
| Direct materials | 15% × £22.00 | 3.30 | |
| Direct labour | 10% × £11.70 | 1.17 | |
| | | | 6.22 |
| Total variable cost | | | 39.92 |

| | (£) | |
|---|---|---|
| Fixed overhead | | |
| Supervisory salaries | | |
| £95,000/50,000 | 1.90 | |
| Other | | |
| £109,000/50,000 | 2.18 | |
| | | 4.08 |

Ideal standard cost per unit      44.00

(ii) *Attainable standard cost per unit*

| | | (£) | (£) |
|---|---|---|---|
| Direct materials | | | |
| A | £10.00 + 10% | 11.00 | |
| B | £12.00 − 12.5% | 10.50 | |
| | | | 21.50 |
| Direct labour | | | |
| M | (see note below) | 8.00 | |
| N | (see note below) | 5.60 | |
| | | | 13.60 |
| Indirect labour | 0.50 hours × £2.60 | 1.30 | |
| Maintenance | 0.10 hours × £5.10 | 0.51 | |
| Variable overhead | | | |
| Direct material A | 15% × £11.00 | 1.65 | |
| Direct material B | 20% × £10.50 | 2.10 | |
| Direct labour | 10% × £13.60 | 1.36 | |
| | | | 6.92 |
| Total variable cost | | | 42.02 |
| Fixed overhead | | | 4.08 |
| Attainable standard cost per unit | | | 46.10 |

| Note | Workers | Hours | Units | Average hours per unit |
|------|---------|-------|-------|------------------------|
| M | 9 × 2 | 18 | 9.0 | |
| | 1 × 2 | 2 | 0.5 | |
| | | 20 | 9.5 | 20/9.5 = 2.105 |
| | | | | 2.105 × £3.80 = £80 |
| | | | | |
| N | 7.5 × 1.6 | 12 | 7.5 | |
| | 2.5 × 1.6 | 4 | 1.5 | |
| | | | | 16/9 = 1.778 |
| | | | | 1.778 × £3.15 = £5.60 |

(iii)

| | (£ per unit) | | Units | | Total (£) |
|---|---|---|---|---|---|
| Ideal standard cost = | 44.00 | × | 49,000 | = | 2,156,000 |
| Attainable standard cost = | 46.10 | × | 49,000 | = | 2,258,900 |

Variance = 2.10 × 49,000 = 102,900 A

(iv)
Actual costs for April

| | | (£) | (£) |
|---|---|---|---|
| Direct materials | | | |
| A | 247,000 × £2.16 = | 533,520 | |
| B | 149,000 × £3.60 = | 536,400 | |
| | | | 1,069,920 |
| Direct labour | | | |
| M | 104,000 × £3.80 = | 395,200 | |
| N | 87,000 × £3.15 = | 274,050 | |
| | | | 669,250 |
| Indirect labour | 24,000 × £2.60 = | 62,400 | |
| Maintenance | 4,500 × £5.10 = | 22,950 | |
| Variable overhead | | 251,000 | |
| | | | 336,350 |
| Fixed overhead | | | |
| Supervisory salaries | | 97,000 | |
| Other | | 110,000 | |
| | | | 207,000 |
| Total actual cost | | | 2,282,520 |
| Less: | | | |
| Attainable standard | 49,000 × £46.10 = | | 2,258,900 |
| Total variance | | | 23,620A |

(b) *Analysis of variances*

Actual compared to attainable
(£)

(i) Direct materials
A: 247,000 lbs − (49,000 × 5) lbs × 2.20
= (247,000 − 245,000) lbs × £2.20

$= 2200 \text{ lbs} \times £2.20$        $= \text{(Adverse)}$    4400 Usage
$247,000 \text{ lbs} \times £(2.20 - 2.16)$    $= \text{(Favourable)}$    9880 Price
$= 247,000 \text{ lbs} \times £0.40$

(ii)  Direct labour
M:   $104,000 \text{ hours} - (49,000 \times 2.105) \times £3.80$
$= (104,000 - 103,158) \text{ hours} \times £3.80$
   $= \quad 842 \text{ hours} \times £3.80$        $= \text{(Adverse)}$      3200
Efficiency
$104,000 \text{ hours} \times £*3.80 - 3.80) =$        Nil       Rate

(c)  *Benefits of setting attainable and ideal standards*
*Direct material A*  Management were prepared for a price rise on a steeper scale than that which actually occurred. The favourable price variance is thus realistic and praiseworthy.

Note, in the above case, the setting of an attainable standard has eliminated a 'spurious' element in the variances that would otherwise have been present. There is no need for management to inquire into differences of which they are aware in advance. Moreover, management can alter their action at the earliest opportunity, should any alternation be practicable, and they can alter it beforehand rather than afterwards.

*Direct labour*  The rise in the direct labour rate was known in advance.
*Variable overhead*  The actual was less than the ideal standard. However, since the attainable standard had been prepared, this drop in costs was expected.
*Other costs*  Again, there was advance indication of what was likely to happen.

In conclusion, the benefit of preparing the attainable standard cost was the foreknowledge of what was likely to happen, the opportunity of making changes earlier than might have otherwise been possible and the elimination of the need to search for reasons for some parts of the variances that occurred.

(d)  *Comments on the results in part (b)*
*Direct material A*  Poor usage of materials – is this related to slightly altered specification?
*Direct labour type M*  No wage rate variances – increases are already catered for. Type M has an adverse efficiency of 4.5 per cent.
*Variable overhead*  In total, these favourable variances broadly compensate for the adverse direct labour variances.

### Question 3 (CIMA)

A company with two cost centres 1 and 2, manufactures two products K and P whose standard variable costs of production per article are:

Product K

| Cost centre | Quantity (units) | Price/rate (£ per unit) | Total (£) |
|---|---|---|---|
| 1 Direct materials 101 | 12 | 5 | 60.00 |
| 2 Direct materials 102 | 4 | 15 | 60.00 |
| | (hours) | (£ per hour) | (£) |
| 1 Direct labour Grade A | 10 | 3.40 | 34.00 |
| 1 Direct labour Grade B | 6 | 2.40 | 14.40 |
| 2 Direct labour Grade C | 16 | 1.80 | 28.80 |
| 1 Variable overhead | 16 | 0.60 | 9.60 |
| 2 Variable overhead | 16 | 0.50 | 8.00 |
| | | | £214.80 |

Product P

| Cost centre | Quantity (units) | Price/rate (£ per unit) | Total (£) |
|---|---|---|---|
| 1 Direct materials 101 | 16 | 5 | 80.00 |
| 2 Direct materials 102 | 6 | 4 | 24.00 |
| | (hours) | (£ per hour) | (£) |
| 1 Direct labour Grade A | 14 | 2.40 | 33.60 |
| 1 Direct labour Grade B | 12 | 1.80 | 21.60 |
| 2 Direct labour Grade C | 12 | 1.80 | 21.60 |
| 1 Variable overhead | 14 | 0.60 | 8.40 |
| 2 Variable overhead | 12 | 0.50 | 6.00 |
| | | | £173.60 |

Budgeted data for a period of four weeks each of 40 hours are:

| | Product K | Product P |
|---|---|---|
| Standard selling prices per article | £315 | £270 |
| Budgeted output on which standard costs are based | 330 articles | 570 articles |
| Budgeted sales for period No. 10 | 320 articles | 620 articles |

Fixed production overhead

| Cost Centre 1 | £26,250 |
|---|---|
| Cost Centre 2 | £18,180 |

Marketing and administration costs total £18,000 per period and are treated as fixed period costs.

Actual data for period No. 10 were:

|  | Number of articles | |
|---|---|---|
|  | Product K | Product P |
| Actual output | 300 | 600 |
| Actual sales   at standard price | 290 | 500 |
| at £360 each | 50 | Nil |
| at £255 each | Nil | 60 |

Costs:

Centre 1

| Direct materials 101 | 15,600 units at £4.60 per unit |
|---|---|
| Direct materials 102 | Nil |
| Direct materials 103 | Nil |
| Direct labour Grade A | 2,880 hours at £3.70 per hour |
| Direct labour Grade B | 11,000 hours at £2.20 per hour |
| Direct labour Grade C | Nil |
| Overhead:   variable | £7,680 |
| fixed | £28,200 |

Centre 2

| Direct materials 101 | Nil |
|---|---|
| Direct materials 102 | 1,120 units at £15.00 per unit |
| Direct materials 103 | 4,160 units at   £4.20 per unit |
| Direct labour Grade A | Nil |
| Direct labour Grade B | Nil |
| Direct labour Grade C | 12,720 hours at £1.80 per hour |
| Overhead:   variable | £7,360 |
| fixed | £17,000 |

The company absorbs fixed production overhead into product costs by means of cost centre direct labour hour rates. All variances are transferred to the profit and loss account. Marketing and administration costs were are the budget level.

You are required in respect of period No. 10 to:

(a) Calculate the cost variances marked with a '?' in the following table.

| Cost variances | Cost centre 1 (£) | Cost centre 2 (£) |
|---|---|---|
| (i)    Direct materials price | 6,240 (F) | ? |
| (ii)   Direct materials usage | 12,000 (A) | ? |
| (iii)  Direct labour efficiency | ? | 1,296 (A) |
| (iv)   Direct labour rate | ? | Nil |
| (v)    Production overhead efficiency | ? | 1,440 (A) |
| (vi)   Production overhead expenditure | 1,032 (A) | ? |
| (vii)  Production overhead volume | ? | 900 (F) |

(b) Present a profit and loss statement for the company that incorporates the cost variances by cost centre.

(c) Comment on the relative performance of the two cost centres.

## Answer 3

*Workings*

Fixed production overhead

| Cost centre | 1 | | 2 |
|---|---|---|---|
| Total costs | £26,520 | | £18,180 |
| Direct labour hours | | | |
| Product K 16 × 330 | 5,280 | 16 × 330 | 5,280 |
| P 14 × 570 | 7,980 | 12 × 570 | 6,840 |
| | 13,260 | | 12,120 |
| Rate per hour | £2.00 | | £1.50 |

| Product | K (£) | | P (£) |
|---|---|---|---|
| CC1 16 hours at £2.00 | 32 | 14 hours at £2.00 | 28 |
| CC2 16 hours at £1.50 | 24 | 12 hours at £1.50 | 18 |
| | 56 | | 46 |

Total production overhead

| Cost centres | 1 (£) | 2 (£) |
|---|---|---|
| Fixed – as above | 2.00 | 1.50 |
| Variable | 0.60 | 0.50 |
| | 2.60 | 2.00 |

Standard costs

| Product | K (£) | | P (£) |
|---|---|---|---|
| Selling price | 315.00 | | 270.00 |
| Less: | | | |
| Direct materials | 120.00 | 104.00 | |
| Direct labour | 77.20 | 55.20 | |
| Variable overhead | 17.60 | 14.40 | |
| Fixed overhead | 56.00 | 46.00 | |
| | | 270.80 | 219.60 |
| Profit | | 44.20 | 50.40 |

### (a) Cost variances

| | (£) Favourable (Adverse) |
|---|---|
| (i) Cost centre 2 – direct material price | |
| DM 102 1120 units × £15.00 − £15.00) | 0 |
| DM 103 4160 units × £4.00 − £4.20) | (832) |
| | (832) |
| (ii) Cost centre 2 – direct material usage | |
| DM 102 [(4 × 300) − 1120] units × £15.00 | 1200 |
| DM 103 [(6 × 600) − 4160] units × 4.00 | (2240) |
| | (1040) |

(iii)   Cost centre 1 − direct labour efficiency

| | |
|---|---:|
| DL A [(10 × 300) − 2880] hours × £3.40 | 408 |
| DL B [(6 × 300) + (14 × 600)−11,000] hours × £2.40 | (1920) |
| | (1512) |

(iv)   Cost centre 1 − direct labour rate

| | |
|---|---:|
| DL A   2880 hours × (£3.40 − £3.70) | (864) |
| DL B 11,000 hours × (£2.40 − £2.20) | 2200 |
| | 1336 |

(v)   Cost centre 1 − production overhead efficiency

DL A  10 × 300 ⎤
DL B   6 × 300 ⎬  13,200−13,880 hrs = 680 hrs × £2.60                (1768)
       + 14 × 600 ⎦

(vi)   Cost centre 2 − production overhead expenditure
[£18,180 + (12,720 × £0.50)] − (£7360 + 17,000)                180

(vii)   Cost centre 1 − production overhead volume
[(2880 + 11,000) hours × £2.60] −
            [£26,520 + (13,880 hours × £0.60)]                1240

(b)   *Profit and loss statement – period 10*
(Adverse variances in brackets)

|  | | | | (£) |
|---|---|---:|---:|---:|
| Budget profit product   K 320 at   44.20 each 14,144 | | | | |
|                         P 620 at £50.40 each 31,248 | | | | |
| | | | | 45,382 |

Sales variances
Product K

| | | |
|---|---:|---:|
| Volume + 20 at £44.20 | 884 | |
| Price        50 at + £45 | 2,250 | |
| | | 3,134 |

Product P

| | | | |
|---|---:|---:|---:|
| Volume − 60 at £50.40 | (3,024) | | |
| Price        60 at − £15 | (900) | (3,924) | |
| | | | (790) |
| Standard operating gross profit | | | 44,602 |

Production variances:

Cost Centre 1

| | | |
|---|---|---:|
| (i) | Direct material price | 6,240 |
| (ii) | Direct material usage | (12,000) |
| (iii) | Direct labour efficiency | (1,512) |
| (iv) | Direct labour rate | 1,336 |
| (v) | Production overhead efficiency | (1,768) |

|       |                                              |         |         |          |
| ----- | -------------------------------------------- | ------- | ------- | -------- |
| (vi)  | Production overhead expenditure              | (1,032) |         |          |
| (vii) | Production overhead volume                   |         | 1,240   |          |
|       |                                              |         |         | (7,496)  |

**Cost Centre 2**

|       |                                              |         |         |          |
| ----- | -------------------------------------------- | ------- | ------- | -------- |
| (i)   | Direct material price                        |         | (832)   |          |
| (ii)  | Direct material usage                        |         | (1,040) |          |
| (iii) | Direct labour efficiency                     |         | (1,296) |          |
| (iv)  | Direct labour rate                           |         | —       |          |
| (v)   | Production overhead efficiency               |         | (1,440) |          |
| (vi)  | Production overhead expenditure              | 180     |         |          |
| (vii) | Production overhead volume                   |         | 900     |          |
|       |                                              |         |         | (3,528)  |
|       |                                              |         |         | (11,024) |

| | |
| --- | --- |
| Actual operating gross profit | 33,578 |
| Less: Marketing and administration costs | 18,000 |
| Actual net profit | £15,578 |

**(c)  *Comparative performance of cost centres***

Cost centre 1 (CC1) and cost centre 2 (CC2) both overspent compared with budget by £7496 and £3528 respectively. This may indicate that factors outside the immediate control of managers may be reflected in the results. CC1's overspending was 5.3 per cent compared with CC2's 4.3 per cent, so to that extent CC2 did better.

Additionally CC1 had a large favourable material price variance which may not be directly controllable at departmental level; whereas CC2's was an adverse £832. If this item was eliminated the total variances become:

CC1  £13,736 up 9.6%
CC2  £3696 up 3.3%

This more clearly shows CC2 to have done better. This trend is also indicated by an aggregation of the efficiency variances.

|                      | CC1        | CC2       |
| -------------------- | ---------- | --------- |
|                      | (£)        | (£)       |
| Material usage       | (12,000)   | (1,040)   |
| Labour efficiency    | (1,512)    | (1,296)   |
| Overhead efficiency  | (1,768)    | (1,440)   |
|                      | (15,280)   | (3,776)   |

It would, therefore, appear that of the two poor performances CC2 was the more acceptable. However, without further information, the situation cannot be fairly evaluated because, for example CC1 material usage excess may have been due to the purchase of cheap and unsatisfactory material.

## Question 4 (CIMA)

Sciento Products Ltd manufactures complex electronic measuring instruments for which highly skilled labour is required. Conventional standard costing has been used for some time but problems have been experienced in setting realistic standards for labour costs.

Analysis of production times has shown that there is a learning curve effect on the labour time required to manufacture each unit and it has been decided to allow for this in establishing standard times and in the subsequent variance analysis. Records have been kept of the production times for the Electronometer, an extract of which follows.

| Cumulative production units | Cumulative time hours | Average time per unit |
|---|---|---|
| 1 | 200 | 200 |
| 2 | 360 | 180 |
| 4 | 648 | 162 |
| 8 | 1166 | 145.8 |

The labour time analyses have shown that the learning curve follows the general form:

$$y = ax^b$$

where y = average labour hours per unit, a = number of labour hours for first unit, x = cumulative number of units, b = the learning index.

During period 11 the following data were recorded.

| | |
|---|---|
| Cumulative production at start of period | 526 units |
| Production in period | 86 units |
| Wages paid | £71,823 for 6,861 actual hours |
| Materials actual costs | £20,850 |
| Actual overheads for period | £152,600 |

Budgeted and standard cost data for Electronometers:

| | |
|---|---|
| Budgeted production | 86 units |
| Budgeted overheads | £150,903 |
| Standard labour cost | £10 per hour |
| Standard material cost per unit | £250 |

You are required to:

(a) Calculate and analyse where possible the materials, labour and overhead cost variances.
(b) Calculate a total standard cost for Electronometers
(c) Discuss the usefulness or otherwise of allowing for the learning effect in establishing labour standards.

**Answer 4**

*Workings*

| Cumulative production units | Cumulative time (hours) | Average (hours) |
|---|---|---|
| 1 | 200 | 200 |
| 2 | 360 | 180  (200×90%) |
| 4 | 648 | 162  (180×90%) |
| 8 | 1166 | 145.8 (162×90%) |

Thus a 90 per cent learning curve is in operation.

$$y = ax^b$$

$$b = \frac{\log(1-0.1)}{\log 2} = \frac{0.04576}{0.30103} = -0.152$$

Now x = 526 +86 = 612

| | |
|---|---|
| Average hours per unit, at end = $200 \times 612^{-0.152}$ | = 75.413 |
| Total hours at end = 75.413 × 612 | = 46,153 |
| Average hours per unit at start = $200 \times 526^{-0.152}$ | = 77.169 |
| Total hours at start = 77.169 × 526 | = 40,591 |
| Standard hours per batch of 86 = 46,153 − 40,591 | = 5,562 |
| Average standard hours per unit = 5562/86 | = 64.67 |

$$\text{Standard OAR} = \frac{£150,903}{5562} = £277 \text{ (approx.)}$$

(b)  *Electronmeters standard cost schedule*

| | per unit £ |
|---|---|
| Direct material | 250 |
| Direct labour 64.67 × £10 per hour | 647 |
| | 897 |
| Overheads 64.67 × £27 per hour | 1,746 |
| Total | 2,643 |

(a)  *Variance analysis*

(i)   Total cost

| | (£) | (£) |
|---|---|---|
| Standard £2643 × 86 | | 227,298 |
| Actual | | |
| Direct materials | 20,850 | |
| Direct labour | 71,823 | |
| Overheads | 152,600 | |
| | | 245,273 |
| | | 17,975 |

(ii)  Direct labour cost variance

| | |
|---|---|
| Standard £647 × 86 | 55,642 |
| Actual | 71,823 |
| | 16,181A |

(a)  Direct labour rate variance
     AHW (SR − AR)
     (6861 × £10) − £71,823                                       3,213A

(b)  Direct labour efficiency variance
     SR (SHP − AHW)
     £10 (5562 − 6861)                                            12,990A

(iii)  Direct materials cost variance
       Standard £250 × 86                                         21,500
       Actual                                                     20,850
                                                                    650F

(iv)  Overhead variance
      Total
      Standard £27 × 5562                                        150,174
      Actual                                                     152,600
                                                                   2,426A

(a)  Expenditure
     BC − AC
     £150,174 − 152,600                                           2,426A

(b)  Volume
     OAR (Budgeted hours − AHW)
     = BC − (OAR × AHW)
     = £150,174 − (£27 × 6861)                                   35,073F

(c)  Efficiency
     OAR (SHP − AHW)
     = £27 (5562 − 6861)                                         35,073A

(c)  *Use of the learning curve in establishing labour standards*
- Useful where work is labour intensive rather than capital intensive.
- Useful in dealing with new products.
- Use of learning curve may lead to:

     1  improved planning, e.g. production scheduling;
     2  improved standard setting and, therefore, control and motivation;
     2  improved standard setting and, therefore, control and motivation;
     3  improved product pricing.

- It should be recognized that eventually a 'steady state' period will be reached and the learning curve will no longer apply.
- Learning curves are likely to be approximate only, but an approximate guide is better than none at all.

### Question 5 (CIMA)

The managers of a company have analysed a project, and the coded activities have been listed below with their durations and immediate predecessors.

| Activity code | Immediate predecessor | Duration (days) |
|---|---|---|
| A | — | 13 |
| B | A | 2 |
| C | A | 6 |
| D | B | 20 |
| E | B | 5 |
| F | C | 2 |
| G | E,F | 4 |
| H | F | 3 |
| I | D | 5 |
| J | D | 10 |
| K | C | 5 |
| L | G,I | 2 |
| M | G,I,J | 3 |
| N | G,I,J,H,K | 15 |
| O | L,M,N | 2 |

You are required:

(a) Draw up and analyse the project planning diagram to show the duration of the project and the critical path.

(b) Present the results you have obtained in (a) above in the form of a bar chart and Gantt chart based on earliest start dates.

(c) Calculate when the project should begin and when it will finish, assuming the estimated hours are adhered to and using the calendar printed below. Note that the company operates on a five day week basis and that G, H, I, J and K must be completed by Friday 26 June.

Calendar

| | April | May | June | July |
|---|---|---|---|---|
| Monday | 20 27 | 4 11 18 25 | 1 8 15 22 29 | 6 13 20 27 |
| Tuesday | 21 28 | 5 12 19 26 | 2 9 16 23 30 | 7 14 21 28 |
| Wednesday | 22 29 | 6 13 20 27 | 3 10 17 24 | 1 8 15 22 29 |
| Thursday | 23 30 | 7 14 21 28 | 4 11 18 25 | 2 9 16 23 30 |
| Friday | 24 | 1 8 15 22 29 | 5 12 19 26 | 3 10 17 24 31 |

## Answer 5

(a) Figure 12.6 shows the project planning diagram.

(b) Figure 12.7 shows the results obtained presented in the form of a bar chart.

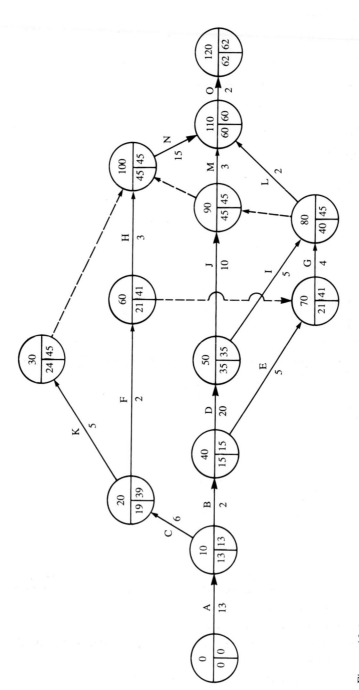

Figure 12.6

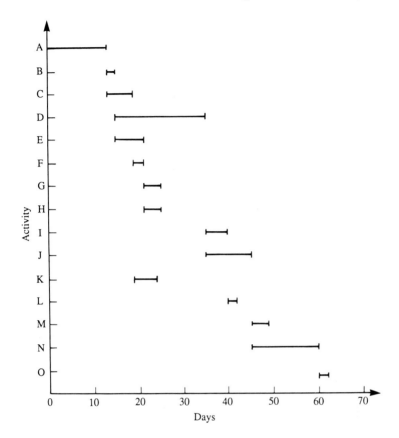

Figure 12.7

(c)

|   | EST (Days) | LST (Days) |
|---|---|---|
| G | 40 | 45 |
| H | 45 | 45 |
| I | 40 | 45 |
| J | 45 | 45 |
| K | 45 | 45 |

GHIJK must be completed by Friday 26 June. 45 workings must be allowed for the completion of GHIJK before any subsequent activities can be started. Therefore,

   project starting date is Monday 27 April.

After completion of GHIJK, a further 17 working days are required (N = 15, 0 = 2). Therefore,

   project completion date is Tuesday 21 July.

## Further reading

Barnes, K. and Targett, P., Standard costing in distribution, *Management Accounting*, (May, 1984).

Harvey, D.W. and Soliman, S.Y., Standard cost variance analysis in a learning environment, *Accounting and Business Research*, Summer, 1983.

Staffurth, C., *Project Cost Control*, 2nd edn, CIMA/Heinemann, 1980.

# 13 Further aspects of variance analysis

## Material mix and yield variances

When the proportions of materials in a mixture are changeable and controllable it is useful to sub-analyse the material usage variance. The materials mix variance should only be calculated where the materials in the mix are interchangeable items, e.g. a desk may be comprised of wood, glue, nails, etc. These materials are separate items whose usage must be controlled separately, i.e. they are not interchangeable and it would be inappropriate to calculate a mix variance.

## Material mix variance

This variance arises when the materials are not mixed in standard (i.e. planned) proportions, and it shows whether the actual mix is more expensive or cheaper than the standard mix. A favourable mix variance will arise if a greater proportion of cheaper materials is used. Whereas there will be an adverse mix variance if a greater proportion of dearer materials is used.

### Formula

(Actual mixture of input − Actual mixture of input in standard proportions) × (Standard price i.e. the standard mixture).

## Material yield variance

This variance arises when the actual output or yield differs from the expected yield. It shows the efficiency of the usage of all the materials together in the mix.

### Formula

(Standard input for the actual output − Actual mixture in standard proportions) Standard Price

or (Actual yield − Expected yield) Standard weighted average cost per unit of all materials in the mix

*Example*
ABC is a cleaning fluid produced by mixing three chemicals A, B and C in the proportions 5:3:2 respectively. The production process does not always mix the chemicals in these proportions, but the fluid can be sold if the mixture is within certain limits. The standard prices for the chemicals are:

  A   £2.40 per litre
  B   £2.00 per litre
  C   £2.80 per litre

There is a 10 per cent normal loss during the process, so that the expected yield is 90 per cent.

During the last period the output of ABC was 184,000 litres.

The inputs were   92,000 litres of A at £2.52 per litre
                  68,000 litres of B at £1.88 per litre
                  42,000 litres of C at £2.92 per litre

Calculate the appropriate variances

*Solution*
*Material price variance*
(Actual price − Standard price) Actual quantity purchased.

  A   (£2.52 − £2.40) 92,000 litres  = £11,040 Adverse
  B   (£1.88 − £2.00) 68,000 litres  =  £8,160 Favourable
  C   (£2.92 − £2.88) 42,000 litres  =  £1,680 Adverse

  Price variance                     =  £4,560 Adverse

*Material mix variance*
(Actual mixture of input − Actual mixture of input in standard proportions i.e. the standard mix) × Standard Price.

  5/10 A  (92,000 − 101,000) £2.40 = £21,600 Favourable
  3/10 B  (68,000 −  60,600) £2.00 = £14,800 Adverse
  2/10 C  (42,000 −  40,400) £2.88 =  £4,608 Adverse
  Mix variance                     =  £2,192 Favourable

*Material yield variance*
(Standard input for actual output − Actual mixture in standard proportions) Standard Price

5/10 A (102,222 — 101,000) £2.40 = £2,933 Favourable
3/10 B ( 61,333 — 60,600) £2.00 = £1,466 Favourable
2/10 C ( 40,889 — 40,000) £2.88 = £1,408 Favourable
*204,444 ltrs 202,000 ltrs
Material yield variance = £5,807 Favourable

or (Standard Input — Actual Input) Standard weighted average price per litre

$$(204{,}444 \text{ litres} - 202{,}000 \text{ litres} \times \frac{£23.76/\text{litres}}{10 \text{ litres of input}} = £5{,}807 \text{ favourable}$$

A 5 litres at £2.40 = £12.00
B 3 litres at £2.00 = £6.00
C 3 litres at £2.88 = £5.76

| | | |
|---|---|---|
| Standard input | 10 litres | £23.76 |
| Normal loss | (1) | |
| Standard output | 9 litres | |

Therefore standard input for actual output $= \dfrac{10}{9} \times 184{,}000$ litres

= *204,444 litres

The material yield variance can also be found by comparing the actual yield with the expected yield at the standard weighted average price per litre.

(Actual yield — Expected yield) Standard average price per litre of output

$$= (184{,}000 - {}^{*}181{,}800)\frac{£23.76}{9 \text{ litres}} = £5{,}807 \text{ approximately}$$

* 202,000 litres    Input
   20,200 litres less 10% Normal loss
181,800 litres

*Material usage variance*
(Standard input for actual output — Actual mixture) Standard price

A (102,222 — 92,000) £2.40 = £24,533 Favourable
B ( 61,333 — 68,000) £2.00 = £13,334 Adverse
C ( 40,889 — 42,000) £2.88 = £3,200 Adverse

Usage variance                    £7,999 Favourable

The usage variance of £7999 favourable is equal to the sum of the favourable mix and yield variances £2192 + £5807 = £7999.
In the above example a favourable mix variance has arisen because less of chemical A, (a relatively expensive chemical was used than planned. The favourable yield variance is due to the actual yield being greater than the expected yield, for the given inputs.

## Sales mix and quantity variances

Where management can control the proportions of the products sold it is useful to sub-analyse the sales volume variance into a sales mix variance and a sales quantity variance.

## Sales mix variance

This variance occurs when the products are not sold in a mix which is the same as the standard, i.e. (planned) mix. The variance shows whether the actual proportions of each product sold are a more or less profitable mix than the budgeted proportions. The sales mix variance is calculated in a similar way to the material mix variance.

### Formula

(Actual mix − Actual mix in standard proportions) Standard profit per unit proportions i.e. standard mix

## Sales quantity variance

This variance is the total sales volume variance of all the products combined, and is valued at the weighted average standard profit per unit

### Formula

(Actual quantity − Budgeted quantity) Weight average standard profit per unit.

### Example
A small company manufactures and sells three products. Its sales budget for a quarter is as follows:

| Product | Price (£) | Cost (£) | Profit Margin (£) | Quantity (£) | Profit (£) | Turnover (£) |
|---|---|---|---|---|---|---|
| 1 | 30 | 16 | 14 | 3,000 | 42,000 | 90,000 |
| 2 | 10 | 9 | 1 | 7,000 | 7,000 | 70,000 |
| 3 | 20 | 18 | 2 | 2,000 | 4,000 | 40,000 |
| | | | | 12,000 | £53,000 | £200,000 |

Actual results for the quarter are:

| Product | Profit margin (£) | Quantity | Profit (£) | Turnover (£) |
|---|---|---|---|---|
| 1 | 15 | 2,200 | 33,000 | 68,200 |
| 2 | 1 | 10,400 | 10,400 | 104,000 |
| 3 | 4 | 2,200 | 8,800 | 48,400 |
| | | 14,800 | £52,200 | £220,600 |

The company is concerned over the fact that its profit has fallen, yet turnover has increased. Calculate the relevant variances in order to explain the situation.

*Solution*
*Sales price variance*
(Actual price − Standard price) Actual quantity sold

1  (£31 − £30)  2,200 = £2,200 Favourable
2  (£10 − £10) 10,400 = Nil
3  (£22 − £20)  2,200 = £4,400 Favourable

Price variance        = £6,600 Favourable

*Sales volume variance*
(Actual quantity − Budgeted quantity) Standard profit per unit

1  ( 2,200 − 3,000)  £14 = £11,200 Adverse
2  (10,400 − 7,000)   £1 = £ 3,400 Favourable
3  ( 2,200 − 2,000)   £2 = £  400 Favourable

Volume variance       = £ 7,400 Adverse

The sales volume variance can be analysed into sales mix and quantity variances.

*Sales mix variance*
(Actual mix − Actual mix in standard proportions i.e. standard mix) Standard profit per unit

3/12* 1  (2200 − 3700)      £14 = £21,000 Adverse
7/12* 2  (10,400 − 8633)     £1 =  £1,767 Favourable
2/12* 3  (2200 − 2467)       £2 =   £534 Adverse
         ‾‾‾‾‾‾   ‾‾‾‾‾‾          = £19,767 Adverse
         14,800   14,800 mix variance

* Standard proportions.

*Sales quantity variance*
(Actual quantity − Budgeted quantity) Weighted average standard profit per unit

$$= (14,800 - 12,000) \ \frac{£53,000}{12,000 \ \text{units}}$$

Quantity variance = £12,367 Favourable

Sales volume variance = Sales mix variance + Sales quantity variance

£7400 adverse = £19,767 adverse + £12,367 favourable

In the above example the adverse sales volume variance is due to the adverse sales mix variance. The latter has arisen because less of product 1 (the most profitable product) was sold than planned.

However, the adverse sales mix variance has been offset to a certain extent by the favourable sales quantity variance, as a result of selling more units than budgeted.

This small company has sold more units, overall, than planned but in unprofitable proportions.

## The revenue method for calculating sales mix and quantity variances

There is another method of calculating sales mix and quantity variances based on sales value rather than on the number of units.

Students should note the following points concerning this method:

1 The sales volume variance is the same under both methods. However the sales mix and quantity variance calculated by the revenue method will be totally different from the variances calculated by the previous method.
2 In the revenue method the actual sales revenue is based on standard sales price, i.e. the actual sales revenue is actual sales units at the standard sales price per unit.

### Formulae

Sales mix variance = (Actual mix in revenue at standard price − Actual mix in standard proportions i.e. standard mix in revenue) Standard profit/sales ratio

Sales quantity variance = (Actual revenue at standard price − Budgeted revenue) Weighted average standard profit/sale ratio

### Example
Brown Ltd sells two products X and Y. The following information is provided.

Budgeted data

|  | Units | Price (£) | Revenue (£) | Profit (£) | Profit/sales ratio |
|---|---|---|---|---|---|
| X | 12,000 | 10 | 120,000 | 24,000 | 20% |
| Y | 16,000 | 5 | 80,000 | 20,000 | 25% |
|  |  |  | 200,000 | 44,000 |  |

Actual data

|  | Units | Revenue (£) |
|---|---|---|
| X | 9,400 | 96,000 |
| Y | 20,000 | 96,000 |
|  |  | 192,000 |

Calculate the sales volume variance and analyse it into sales mix and quantity variances by the revenue method.

*Solution*

*Sales mix variance*
(Actual mix at standard price – Actual mix in standard proportions i.e. standard mix) × Standard profit/sales ratio

$$
\begin{array}{lll}
 & (£) & (£) \\
X & ( 94,000 - 116,400)^* & \times\ 20\% = £4,480A \\
Y & \underline{100,000} - \underline{77,600)^*} & \times\ 25\% = £5,600F \\
 & 194,000 \quad 194,000 &
\end{array}
$$

Sales mix variance                 = £1120F

* Note standard proportions are 6:4.

Therefore 6/(6+4) × 194,000 = 116,400

and 4/(6+4) × 194,000 = 77,600

*Sales quantity variance*
(Actual revenue at standard price – Budgeted revenue) × Weighted average standard profit/sales ratio

$$
\begin{array}{ll}
 & (£) \qquad\quad (£) \\
X & ( 94,000 - 120,000) \\
Y & \underline{(100,000 - \quad 80,000)} \\
 & (194,000 - 200,000) \times 22\%^* = £1320A
\end{array}
$$

Sales quantity variance = £1320A

* (44,000/200,000) × 100% = 22%

*Sales volume variance*
(Actual revenue at standard price − Budgeted revenue) × Standard profit/sales ratio

$$
\begin{array}{llll}
 & (\pounds) & (\pounds) & \\
X & (\ 94{,}000 - & 120{,}000) \times 20\% & = \pounds5200A \\
Y & (100{,}000 - & 80{,}000) \times 25\% & = \pounds5000F \\
\end{array}
$$

Sales volume variance            = £  200A

Sales volume variance = Sales mix variance + Sales quantity variance

£200A                     = £1120F            + £1320A

In the above example the sales volume variance is adverse because of the adverse quantity variance, i.e. the actual revenue at standard price was less than the budgeted revenue. However the favourable sales mix variance indicates that if the standard revenue of £194,000 had been obtained from planned proportions of X and Y, then the profit would have been £1120 lower than the profit from the actual sales mix.

## Planning and operational variances

The main problem with conventional variance analysis for budgetary control reporting purposes is that its emphasis on comparison between actual and planned performance results in a disregard for changes in these planned results. Because standards become out-of-date and un-realistic the traditional accounting model does not serve as an oppor-tunity cost system.

Professors Joel Demski and Michael Bromwick have suggested a different approach towards variance analysis, in which the total vari-ance (traditional variance) is analysed into planning and operational variances.

This modern approach involves establishing two types of standards, an 'ex-ante' and an 'ex-post' standard. The ex-ante is the original stan-dard or budget used in the traditional model, whereas the ex-post standard is one based on actual conditions; that is, one which would have been incorporated in the original plan if the actual conditions had been known in advance. It is a revised standard, based on hindsight.

## The operational variance

The operational variance measures management's operating efficiency by comparing actual results with a revised standard/budget (i.e. the ex-post standard). This variance reflects opportunity costs, i.e. cash flows gained or lost as a result of actual performance differing from a realistic standard. Operational variances tend to be controllable.

**Formula**

Operational variance = Actual − Revised standard


## The planning variance

The planning variance tests management's forecasting skills by comparing the original budget (ex-ante), with the revised budget (ex-post). This variance reflects planning error, not operating efficiency, and therefore unlike operational variances, does not show the opportunity costs of cash flows gained or lost. Planning variances may be avoidable, depending on whether there is a perfect substitute for the resource actually used.


**Formula**

Planning variance = Original standard − Revised standard

Note:
    Total traditional variance
    (Actual − original standard)

    Operational variance
    (Actual − Revised standard)

    Planning variance
    (Original standard − revised standard)


*Example*
At the beginning of 1988 Wasp Ltd established a standard for its marginal costs of £50 per unit. Actual production costs during September 1988 were £608,000 when 8000 units were made.

With the benefit of hindsight the management of Wasp Ltd realizes that a more realistic standard cost for current conditions would be £80 per unit. Calculate the planning and operational variances.


*Solution*
*Total (traditional) variance*
Standard cost (ex-ante) of 8000 units at £50 = £400,000
Actual cost of 8000 units                    = £608,000
                    Total variance = £208,000 (Adverse)

*Operational variance*
8000 units should have cost           =
    (realistically, ex-post) at £80   = £640,000
Actual cost of 8000 units             = £608,000
                    Operational variance   £ 32,000 (Favourable)

*Planning variance*

| | |
|---|---|
| 8000 units at the original standard cost at £50 (ex ante) | = £400,000 |
| 8000 units at the revised standard cost at £80 (ex post) | = £640,000 |
| | £240,000 (Adverse) |

The planning variance was adverse because the original standard was too optimistic, i.e. the standard cost was understated thus over-estimating expected profits.

Traditional variance = Operational    + Planning Variances

£208,000 = £32,000 favourable + £240,000 Adverse

*Comprehensive example*

Kemp Ltd's budgeted production and sales were 1000 units. The original estimated sales price and standard costs for new products were:

| | (£) | (£) |
|---|---|---|
| Standard sales price per unit | | 100 |
| Standard costs per unit | | |
| Raw materials Aye 10 lb at £5 | 50 | |
| Labour 6 hours at £4 | 24 | 74 |
| Standard contribution per unit | | 26 |

Actual results were:

First year's results

| | (£000s) | (£000s) |
|---|---|---|
| Sales 1000 units | | 158 |
| Production costs 1,000 units | | |
| Raw materials Aye 10,800 lb | 97.2 | |
| Labour 5800 hours | 34.8 | 132 |
| Actual contribution | | £26 |

'Throughout the year we attempted to operate as efficiently as possible, given the prevailing conditions,' stated the Managing Director. 'Although in total the performance agreed with budget, in every detailed respect, except volume, there were large differences. These were due, mainly, to the tremendous success of the new insulating material which created increased demand both for the product itself and all the manufacturing resources used in its production. This then resulted in price rises all round.'

'Sales were made at what was felt to be the highest feasible price but, it was later discovered, our competitors sold for £165 per unit and we could have equalled this price. Labour costs rose dramatically with increased demand for the specialist skills required to produce the product and the general market rate was £6.25 per hour – although Kemp always paid below the general market rate whenever possible.'

'Raw material Aye was chosen as it appeared cheaper than the alternative material Bee which could have been used. The costs which were expected at the time the budget was prepared were, per lb, Aye, £5, and Bee, £6. However, the market prices relating to efficient purchases of the materials during the year were:

Aye £8.50 per lb, and
Bee £7.00 per lb.

Therefore it would have been more appropriate to use Bee, but as production plans were based on Aye it was Aye that was used.'

'It is not proposed to request a variance analysis for the first year's results as most of the deviations from budget were caused by the new product's great success and this could not have been fully anticipated and planned for. In any event the final contribution was equal to that originally budgeted so operations must have been fully efficient.'

Required:

(a) Compute the traditional variances for the first year's operation.
(b) Prepare an analysis of variances for the first year's operations which will be useful in the circumstances of Kemp Ltd. The analysis should indicate the extent to which the variances were due to operational efficiency or planning causes.

*Solution*
(a) *Traditional variances (actual compared with the original budget)*

| | |
|---|---|
| Sales price variance | = (Actual price − Standard price) × Actual quantity sold |
| | = (£158 − £100) × 1000 units |
| | = £58,000 Favourable |
| | |
| Material price variance | = (Actual price − Standard price) × Actual quantity purchased |
| | = (£9 − £5) × 10,800 lb |
| | = £43,200 Adverse |
| | |
| Material usage variance | = (Actual quantity used − Standard quantity) × Standard price |
| | = (10,800* − 10,000$^\dagger$) × £5 |
| | = £4,000 Adverse |

* Required to produce 1000 units.
$^\dagger$ Required by 1000 units.

| | |
|---|---|
| Labour rate variance | = (Actual rate − Standard rate) × Actual) hours paid |
| | = (£6 − £4) × 5800 hours |
| | = £11,600 Adverse |
| | |
| Labour efficiency variance | = (Actual hours worked − Standard hours) × Standard rate |
| | = (5800 hr* − 6000 hr$^\dagger$) × £4 |
| | = £800 Favourable |

The sum of the traditional variances is equal to nil, and therefore the operational and planning variances are, in total, nil.

*(b)(i)   Operational variances (actual compared with revised standard)*

| | |
|---|---|
| Sales price variance | = (Actual price − Standard price) × Actual quantity sold |
| | = (£158 − £165) × 1000 units |
| | = £7000 Adverse |
| Labour rate variance | = (Actual rate − Standard rate) × Actual hours paid |
| | = (£6 − £6.25) × 5800 hours |
| | = £1450 Favourable |
| Labour efficiency variance | = (Actual hours worked − Standard hours) × Standard rate revised |
| | = (5800 hr − 6000 hr) × £6.25 |
| | = £1250 Favourable |
| Material price variance | = (Actual price − Standard price) × Actual quantity purchased |
| | = (£9 − £8.50) × 10,800 lb |
| | = £5.400 Adverse |
| Material usage variance | = (Actual quantity used − Standard quantity) × Standard price revised |
| | = (10,800 − 10,000) × £8.50 |
| | = £6800 Adverse |

The sum of the operational variances is £16,500 Adverse.

*(b)(ii)   Planning variances (original standard compared with revised standard)*

| | |
|---|---|
| Sales price variance (uncontrollable) | = (Original standard − revised standard) × Standard quantity |
| | = (£100 − £165) × 1000 units |
| | = £65,000 Favourable |
| Labour rate variance (uncontrollable) | = (Original standard − revised standard) × Standard quantity |
| | = (£4.0 − £6.25) × 6000 hr |
| | = £13,500 Adverse |
| Material price variance | = (Original standard − revised standard) × Standard quantity |
| Uncontrollable | = (£5.0 − £7.0) × 10,000 lb |
| | = £20,000 Adverse |
| Controllable | = (£7.0 − £8.5) × 10,000 lb |
| | = £15,000 Adverse |
| | £35,000 Adverse |

Note, in the above example the material price variance is split into a controllable and uncontrollable planning variance. The difference between the revised standards for Bee and Aye is deemed to be controllable because management is to blame for selecting the wrong material. Aye was used, whereas the substitute Bee should have been used as its revised standard cost is cheaper.

## Limitations of planning and operational variances

Although planning and operational variances provide a better idea of why actual results fail to reach original budget than the traditional variances they have the following limitations:

1 It may not be practical to find all the possible perfect substitutes for the resources actually used.
2 It can be difficult to obtain accurate revised standard costs for the resources actually used and their substitutes.
3 Most companies still use the traditional approach, i.e. there is a general resistance towards change.

## Standard process costing

Standard process costing can be used instead of the first-in first-out (FIFO) and weighted average costing methods used in process costing.

All finished output and work on progress is valued at standard cost. In the case of work in progress it is the equivalent units which are costed at standard cost.

There will be no losses or gains in standard process costing as these are replaced by variances.

The efficiency and usage variances are evaluated by using the equivalent units of production in the period as the actual output in the period. The equivalent units are calculated in the same manner as the FIFO method.

The labour efficiency and material usage variances are recorded in the process account, whereas the other cost variances are more likely to appear in their respective accounts, e.g. material price, labour rate and all the overhead variances will be shown in the materials, labour and overheads account.

*Example*
Manning Ltd manufactures a chemical in a single process. The standard cost per kilo of the chemical is:

|  | (£) |
|---|---|
| Direct materials 3 kilos at £10 per kilo | 30 |
| Direct labour 1 hour at £8 per hr | 8 |
| Fixed overhead 1 hour at £12 per hr | 12 |
| Standard cost per kilo | 50 |

Budgeted output per period is 2000 kilos of chemical and the budgeted fixed costs are therefore £24,000.

Actual costs and production details in the period under review are as follows:

Opening stock 400 kilos, 100 per cent complete for direct materials, and 60 per cent complete for labour and overhead.

Total finished output of chemical in the period is 2200 kilos.

Closing stock 800 kilos, 100 per cent complete for direct materials, and 20 per cent complete for labour and overhead.

|  |  | (£) |
|---|---|---|
| Direct materials purchased and used 3000 kilos |  | 29,400 |
| Direct labour hours 1140 hours |  | 9,600 |
| Fixed overhead |  | 11,600 |
|  | Actual costs | 50,600 |

Required:

(a) The total cost of finished output
(b) The total cost of work in progress WIP (closing and opening).
(c) The variances for the period.

*Solution*
*Workings*
    Statement of equivalent units

| | Total units | Material | Labour and overhead | |
|---|---|---|---|---|
| Opening WIP | 400 | 0 | (40% added) | 160 |
| Other finished output | 1800 | 1800 | | 1800 |
| Total finished output | 2200 | 1800 | | 1960 |
| Closing WIP | 800 | 800 | (20% complete) | 160 |
| Equivalent units | | 2600 | | 2120 |

(a) Total cost of finished output is valued at standard cost

   2200 kilos at £50 per kilo = £110,000

(b) Cost of closing WIP is valued at the standard cost of its equivalent units.

|  |  | (£) |
|---|---|---|
| Direct materials 800 units | at £30 = | 24,000 |
| Direct labour 240 units | at £ 8 = | 1,280 |
| Fixed overheads 240 units | at £12 = | 1,920 |
|  |  | 27,200 |

Cost of opening WIP

|  |  | (£) |
|---|---|---|
| Direct materials 400 units at £30 = | 12,000 |
| Direct labour 240 units | at £ 8 = | 1,920 |
| Fixed overheads 240 units at £12 = | 2,880 |
|  | 16,800 |

(c)  *Variances*

Materials price variance

| | |
|---|---|
| 3000 kilos of material actually cost | £29,400 |
| It should cost 3000 kilos × £10/K | £30,000 |
| | 600 Favourable |

Materials usage variance

| | |
|---|---|
| 2600 equivalent units used | 3000 kilos |
| It should use 2600 units at 3 kilos per unit | 7800 kilos |
| | 4800F |

Standard cost per kilo £10 = £48,000 Favourable

Direct labour rate variance

| | |
|---|---|
| 1140 hours actually cost | £9600 |
| It should cost 1140 hours at £8 per hour | 9120 |
| | 480 Adverse |

Direct labour efficiency variance

| | |
|---|---|
| 2120 equivalent units did take | 1140 hours |
| It should take 2120 units at 1 hour per unit | 2120 hours |
| | 980 Favourable |

Standard cost per hour £8 = £7840 Favourable

Fixed overhead expenditure variance

| | (£) |
|---|---|
| Budgeted fixed overheads (2000 kilo at £12.00) | 24,000 |
| Actual fixed overheads | 11,600 |
| | 12,400 Favourable |

Fixed overhead volume variance

| | |
|---|---|
| Budgeted output of equivalent units | 2000 kilos |
| Actual equivalent units | 2120 kilos |
| | 120 kilos F |

at £12 per kilo = £1440 Favourable

This variance can be sub-analysed into an efficiency and capacity variance.

Fixed overhead efficiency variance

Labour efficiency hours − 980 hours at £12 = 11,760 F

Fixed overhead capacity variance

| | |
|---|---|
| Budgeted hours (2000 kilos at 1 hour) = | 2000 hours |
| Actual hours                            = | 1140 hours |
| | 860 hours A |

at £12 = £10,320 Adverse

*Summary of variances*

| | (£) | (£) |
|---|---|---|
| Standard cost of output in period | | |
| 2600 equivalent units of material at £30 | 78,000 | |
| 2120 equivalent units of labour | | |
| and overhead (£8 + £12) at £20 | = 42,400 | |
| | | 120,400 |

*Variances*

| | (£) | |
|---|---|---|
| Direct material price | 600F | |
| Direct material usage | 48,000F | |
| Direct labour rate | 480A | |
| Direct labour efficiency | 7,840F | |
| Fixed overhead expenditure | 12,400F | |
| Fixed overhead volume | 1,440F | |
| | | 69,800F |
| Actual costs | | £50,600 |

## The interpretation and investigation of variances

### Introduction

Variance analyses highlights areas of strength and weakness, but does not indicate what action, if any should be taken. A manager must be able to correctly interpret the significance of variances before he can initiate control action.

### Problems encountered in the interpretation of variances

1　Because of the various pressures on a budgetary control system inaccuracies can arise in the recording of actual results (material, labour and machine time used). This undermines the credibility of the variances reported.

2　Efficiency variances will depend on the tightness or looseness of the standards set, and therefore any decisions regarding these variances must be taken in the light of the standard used.

3　There may be interdependence between variances, e.g. buying cheaper material will result in a favourable price variance, but may adversely affect the material usage and labour efficiency variances.

4　Inflation poses a problem. If standard average price levels have been set, then in the first half of the year actual prices will be below standard prices, resulting in favourable price variances. However, in the second half of the year actual will exceed standard causing adverse price variances. If the standards are based on current price levels, they will have to be continually revised otherwise adverse price variances will arise.

5 Some variances are controllable, so that action can be taken, and the system is brought back on course. Other variances may be uncontrollable resulting in the revision of budget.

6 The size of a variance is important. Tolerance limits are set so that only variances which exceed these limits are reported.

Small favourable and adverse variances should cancel each other out over a number of control periods.

Tolerance limits can be either subjectively or statistically established.

*Statistical control charts*

Historical data is used to calculate the standard deviation which determines the confidence limits in the chart.

*Example*

It has been estimated that the mean time (taken as the standard time) to complete and operation is 120 minutes, with a standard deviation of 24 minutes. Management have decided to set warning limits at mean $\pm 1.96$ standard deviations, and action limits at mean $\pm 2.57$ standard deviations. These limits have been set subjectively, being the five per cent and one per cent probability limits with regard to the estimated likelihood of the process being set out of control.

The warning and action limits would therefore be:

Warning limits : Upper $120 + (1.96 \times 24) = 167.04$ minutes
: Lower $120 - (1.96 \times 24) = 72.68$ minutes
Action limits : Upper $120 + (2.57 \times 24) = 181.68$ minutes
: Lower $120 + (2.57 \times 24) = 58.32$ minutes

The crosses in Figure 13.1 indicate the actual results as they become available. A represents an adverse variance, B a favourable variance. C indicates a warning that the situation is perhaps starting to get out of control, bringing management's attention to what may turn out to be a case for investigation. D shows that action is now required to correct the process. Management should therefore resort to comparing the expected costs and benefits of investigation.

The problem with this technique is that the wider the tolerance limits set the greater the risk of controllable variances being undetected. However, if narrow control limits are set too many uncontrollable variances may be investigated.

A cumulative (multiple period) approach can be employed which detects trends earlier than existing-period variances.

7 Costs of investigation

A cost-/benefit approach can be used as follows:

Investigate the variance if $C < (1 - P)L$, where C = cost of investigation L = benefits derived from control action, P = probability of variance being uncontrollable. (Hence $1 - P$ is the probability of variance being controllable)

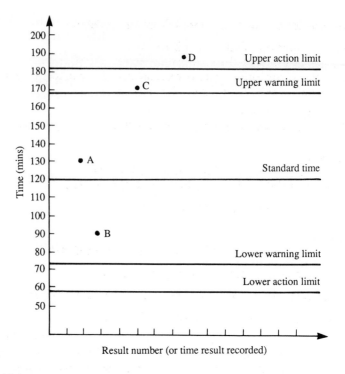

Figure 13.1

*Example*
A £2000 adverse labour efficiency variance is reported. Costs of investigation are £500 and estimated savings are £2000 per annum. Costs of corrective action if variance is controllable will be £600. Probability of the variance being controllable is 0.4. Should the variance be investigated?

*Solution*
From $C < (1-P) L$

$$500 < (1-0.4) (2000 - 600)$$
$$500 < 840$$

Therefore investigate.

Also the expected value can be calculated:

|  |  |  | (£) |
|---|---|---|---|
| Uncontrollable | 0.4 × (500) | = | (200) |
| Controllable | 0.6 × 900* | = | 540 |
| Expected value |  | = | 340 |

*£2,000 − (£500 + £600)
As positive, investigate.

The limitations of this approach are as follows:

(i) estimation of the probabilities;
(ii) estimation of the saving;
(iii) the assumption that investigation of a controllable variance leads to its immediate elimination.

8 Composite variances
This is concerned with who is responsible for a particular variance.

*Example*
Standard per unit 5 kilos of material at £4/kg
Actual 100 units, 550 kilos of material, at £5/kg.

Who is responsible for the variances?

*Solution*
Price variance = (£5 − £4) 550 kilos    = £550 Adverse

(The purchasing manager's responsibility).

Usage variance = (550 kg − 500 kg) £4 = £200 Adverse

(The production manager's responsibility.)

However, there is a composite variance (not reported in traditional methods) which shows that in addition to the above the production manager should be responsible for some of the price variance – the extra usage at the excess price.

50 kg × £1 = £50 Adverse

9 Some managers feel that a standard represents an average, therefore variances will inevitably arise and should not be taken seriously.
10 The traditional approach towards variance analysis fails to distinguish between those variances which are due to errors in planning and variances arising as a result of operating efficiency.

The above list of problems regarding the interpretation of variances is not exhaustive. Management will have to consider these problems deeply before initiating control action.

## Examination questions

### Question 1 (CIMA)

Country Preserves produce jams, marmalades and preserves. All products are produced in a similar fashion; the fruits are low temperature cooked in a vacuum process and then blended with glucose syrup with added citric acid and pectin to help setting.

Margins are tight and the firm operates a system of standard costing for each batch of jam.

The standard cost data for a batch of raspberry jam are:

Fruit extract        400 kg at £0.16 per kg
Glucose syrup    700 kg at £0.10 per kg
Pectin                  99 kg at £0.332 per kg
Citric acid            1 kg at £2.00 per kg
Labour              18 hrs at £3.25 per hour
Standard processing loss 3%

The summer of 1987 proved disastrous for the raspberry crop with a late frost and cool, cloudy conditions at the ripening period, resulting in a low national yield. As a consequence normal prices in the trade were £0.19 per kg for fruit extract although good buying could achieve some savings. The impact of exchange rates on imports of sugar has caused the price of syrup to increase by 20 per cent.
The actual results for the batch were:

Fruit extract        429 kg at £0.18 per kg
Glucose syrup    742 kg at £0.12 per kg
Pectin               125 kg at £0.328 per kg
Citric acid            1 kg at £0.95 per kg
Labour              20 hrs at £3.00 per hour

Actual output was 1164 kg of raspberry jam.
    You are required to:

(a)  Calculate the ingredients' planning variances that are deemed uncontrollable.
(b)  Calculate the ingredients' operating variances that are deemed controllable.
(c)  Comment on the advantages and disadvantages of variance analysis using planning and operating variances.
(d)  Calculate the mixture and yield variances.
(e)  Calculate the total variance for the batch.

### Answer 1

Original standard

|  |  | (£) |
|---|---|---|
| 400 × 0.16 |  | 64 |
| 700 × 0.10 |  | 70 |
| 99 × 0.332 |  | 32.868 |
| 1 × 2.00 |  | 2 |
| 1200 |  | 168.868 |
|  | Labour | 58.500 |
| 1200 |  | 227.368 |
| 36 |  | — |
| 1164 |  | 227.368 |

Revised standard

|  | (£) |
|---|---|
| 400 × 0.19 | 76 |
| 700 × 0.12 | 84 |
| 90 × 0.332 | 32.868 |
| 1 × 2.00 | 2 |
| 1200 | 194.868 |
| Labour | 58.500 |
| 1200 | 253.368 |
| 36 | — |
| 1164 | 253.368 |

Actual

|  | (£) |
|---|---|
| 428 × 0.18 | 77.04 |
| 742 × 0.12 | 89.04 |
| 125 × 0.328 | 41.008 |
| 1 × 0.95 | 0.95 |
| 1296 | 208.03 |
| Labour | 60.000 |
| 1296 | 268.038 |
| 132 | — |
| 1164 | 268.038 |

(a)  Planning variances

£227.368 − £253.368 = £26.00 Adverse

| Analysis | (£) |
|---|---|
| Fruit | 12.00 Adverse |
| Glucose syrup | 14.00 Adverse |

(b)  Ingredients, operating variances

£194.868 − £208.03 = £13.162 Adverse

1  Price

| AQP(SP − AP) | (£) |
|---|---|
| 428(0.19 − 0.18) = | 4.28 Favourable |
| 742(0.12 − 0.12) = | — |
| 125(0.332 − 0.328) = | 0.50 Favourable |
| 1(2.00 − 0.95) = | 1.05 Favourable |
|  | − £5.83 Favourable |

2  Usage

Note, standard usage = standard input in standard mix for actual output.

Standard usage − Actual usage × Standard price

|  |  |  | (£) | (£) |  |
|---|---|---|---|---|---|
| 400 | − | 428 | × 0.19 = | 5.32 | Adverse |
| 700 | − | 742 | × 0.12 = | 5.04 | Adverse |
| 99 | − | 125 | × 0.332 = | 8.632 | Adverse |
| 1 | − | 1 | × 2.00 = | — |  |
| 1200 |  | 1296 |  |  |  |
| 36 |  | 132 |  |  |  |
| 1164 |  | 1164 |  | 18.992 | Adverse |

3  Memorandum
Labour

|  | (£) |  |
|---|---|---|
| Standard cost | 58.50 |  |
| Actual cost | 60.00 |  |
| Variance | 1.50 | Adverse |

Check: £5.83 Favourable − £18.992 Adverse − £1.50 Adverse
= £14.662 Adverse

£253.368 − £268.03 = £14.662 Adverse

(c)  The advantages of variance analysis using planning and operating variances are that:

1  It ensures that standards do not become outdated, given changing business conditions.
2  Isolation of operational variances helps responsibility accounting; factors under control of managers are identified and reported upon.
3  Realistic standards and variances improve management motivation.
4  It helps in the revision of standards and provides feedback on the accuracy of original standards.

The disadvantages are that:

1  It may be difficult to establish a revised standard
2  There is a heavier workload for accounting and managerial staff.
3  There will be management pressure to analyse variances as planning/uncontrollable.

(d)
1  Mixture
Actual usage in standard mix − Actual usage in actual mix × Standard price

|  |  | (£) | (£) |  |
|---|---|---|---|---|
| 432 | 428 | × 0.19 | = 0.76 | F |
| 756 | 642 | × 0.12 | = 1.68 | F |
| 106.92 | 125 | × 0.332 | = 6.003 | A |
| 1.08 | 1 | × 2.00 | = 0.16 | F |
| 1296 | 1296 |  | 3.403 | A |

2   Yield
    Standard usage/Standard mix/Standard price
    1164/0.97 1200

    | (£) | (£) |
    |---|---|
    | 400 × 0.19 = | 76.00 |
    | 700 × 0.12 = | 84.00 |
    | 99 × 0.322 = | 32.868 |
    | 1 × 2.00 = | 2.00 |
    | 1200 | 194.868 |

    Actual usage/Standard mix/Standard price
    1164 → 1296

    | (£) | = | (£) |
    |---|---|---|
    | 432 | × 0.19 = | 82.08 |
    | 756 | × 0.12 = | 90.72 |
    | 106.92 | × 0.322 = | 35.497 |
    | 1.08 | × 2.00 = | 2.16 |
    | 1200 | | 210.457 |

    £194.868 − £210.457 = £15.589 Adverse
    Check: Usage = Mix + Yield

    £18.992 Adverse = £3.403 Adverse + £15.589 Adverse

(e)   Total variance = Original standard − Actual
$$= £227.368 − £268.03$$
$$= £40.662 \text{ Adverse}$$

(£)
Check: Planning variance  = 26.000 Adverse
         Operating variance = 14.662 Adverse
                                          40.662 Adverse

## Question 2 (CIMA)

A firm produces a plastic feedstock using a process form of manu-facture. The firm operates in an industry where the market price fluctuates and the firm adjusts output levels period by period in an attempt to maximize profit which is its objective. Standard costing is used in the factory and the following information is available.

Process 2 receives input from process 1 and, after processing transfers the output to finished goods. For a given period, the opening work-in progress for process 2 was 600 barrels which had the following values;

| | Value (£) | Percentage complete |
|---|---|---|
| Input material (from process 1) | 3,000 | 100 |
| Process 2 material introduced | 6,000 | 50 |
| Process 2 labour | 1,800 | 30 |
| Process 2 overhead | 2,700 | 30 |
| | 13,500 | |

During the period 3700 barrels were received from process 1 and at the end of the period, the closing work in process was at the following stages of completion.

|  | Percentage completion |
|---|---|
| Input material | 100 |
| Process 2 material introduced | 50 |
| Process 2 labour | 40 |
| Process 2 overhead | 40 |

The following standard variable costs have been established for process 2.

|  | Standard variable cost per barrel |
|---|---|
| Input material (standard cost process 1) | 5 |
| Process material | 20 |
| Labour | 10 |
| Overhead | 15 |
|  | £50 |

During the period, actual costs for process 2 were:

|  | (£) |
|---|---|
| Material | 79,500 |
| Labour | 39,150 |
| Overhead | 60,200 |
|  | 178,850 |

In addition you are advised that the following theoretical functions have been derived.

Total cost (£) = 100,000 + 20Q + 0.005Q²
Price per barrel (£) = 76 − 0.002 Q

where Q represent the number of barrels.
You are required to:

(a)   Determine the theoretical production level which will maximize profit.
(b)   Prepare the process 2 account assuming that the calculated production level is achieved.
(c)   Prepare the accounts for process 2 material, labour and overhead showing clearly the variance in each account.

**Answer 2**

(a)   Demand function P = 76 − 0.002Q
        Total revenue    TR = Q(76 − 0.002Q)
                = 76Q − 0.002Q²
Therefore marginal revenue MR = 76 − 0.004Q

Total cost function            TC = 100,000 + 20Q + 0.005Q²
Therefore marginal cost:      MC = 20 + 0.01Q

To maximize profit, MR = MC
Therefore 76 − 0.004Q = 20 + 0.01Q

56 = 0.014Q
Q = 4000 barrels

(b)
*Workings*

| | |
|---|---|
| Opening work-in-progress | 600 barrels |
| Input from process 1 | 3700 barrels |
| | 4300 barrels |
| Production, as per (a) | 4000 barrels |
| Closing work-in-progress | 300 barrels |

| Cost item | Closing work-in-progress | | | | |
|---|---|---|---|---|---|
| | units | (%) | Equivalent units | Completed units | Total |
| Input material | 300 | 100 | 300 | 4000 | 4300 |
| Material introduced | 300 | 50 | 150 | 4000 | 4150 |
| Labour | 300 | 40 | 120 | 4000 | 4120 |
| Overhead | 300 | 40 | 120 | 4000 | 4120 |

| Cost item | Opening work-in-progress | | | |
|---|---|---|---|---|
| | units | (%) | Equivalent units | Period effective units |
| Input material | 600 | 100 | 600 | 3700 |
| Material introduced | 600 | 50 | 300 | 3850 |
| Labour | 600 | 30 | 180 | 3940 |
| Overhead | 600 | 30 | 180 | 3940 |

Note, the question states that 'standard costing is used in the factory'. Entries in the process account are thus valued as standard.

Valuations at standard cost
Completed production 4,000 × £50 = £200,000
Closing work in progress:

| | (£) | (£) |
|---|---|---|
| Input material | 300 × 5 = | 1500 |
| Material introduced | 150 × 20 = | 3000 |
| Labour | 120 × 10 = | 1200 |
| Overhead | 120 × 15 = | 1800 |
| | | 7500 |

Transfers to process 2 account:

| | (£) | (£) |
|---|---|---|
| Material | 3850 × 20 = | 77,000 |
| Labour | 3940 × 10 = | 39,400 |
| Overhead | 3940 × 15 = | 59,100 |
| | | 175,000 |

Transfer from process 1
3700 × 5 = £18,500

*Process 2 account*

| | barrels | (£) | | barrels | (£) |
|---|---|---|---|---|---|
| Opening work in progress | 600 | 13,500 | Transfer to finished goods | 4000 | 200,000 |
| Transfer from process 1 | 3700 | 18,500 | Closing work in progress | 300 | 7,500 |
| Materials introduced | | 77,000 | | | |
| Labour | | 39,400 | | | |
| Overhead | | 59,100 | | | |
| | 4300 | 207,500 | | 4300 | 207,500 |

(c)  *Process 2 materials account*

| | | | |
|---|---|---|---|
| Stores | 79,500 | Process 2 | £77,000 |
| | | Material variance a/c | 2,500 |
| | 79,500 | | 79,500 |

*Process 2 labour account*

| | | | |
|---|---|---|---|
| Wages | 39,150 | Process 2 | 39,400 |
| Labour variance a/c | 250 | | |
| | 39,400 | | 39,400 |

*Process 2 overhead account*

| | | | |
|---|---|---|---|
| Overheads | 60,200 | Process 2 | 59,100 |
| | | Overhead variance a/c | 1,100 |
| | 60,200 | | 60,200 |

## Question 3 (CIMA)

From the data given below, relating to the manufacture of a special lubricant you are required to:

(a)  Calculate the operating profit variance for the month of October 1988.
(b)  Analyse this difference into its sub-variance covering sales and production changes.
(c)  Explain briefly what you consider to be the main problem indicated by the figures and how this could be overcome.

Budget – operations for one month.
  Input, 20 batches of 500 litres each

| Direct materials | % of quantity | Price per litre (£) |
|---|---|---|
| X | 30 | 0.60 |
| Y | 20 | 0.30 |
| Z | 50 | 0.45 |

| Direct labour | % of hours | Rate per hour (£) |
|---|---|---|
| Blending | 60 | 2.50 |
| Filtering | 30 | 2.25 |
| Packing | 10 | 2.00 |

| Total labour hour | 8,000 |
| Overhead cost variable | £0.06 per litre |
| fixed | £5750 |
| Output | 10,000 litres |
| Selling price | £3.55 per litre |

Actual results for the month of October 1988

| Direct materials used | (litres) | Price per litre (£) |
|---|---|---|
| X | 2200 | 0.80 |
| Y | 2500 | 0.35 |
| Z | 4800 | 0.65 |

| Direct labour | (hours) | Rate per hour (£) |
|---|---|---|
| Blending | 5000 | 2.60 |
| Filtering | 2000 | 2.20 |
| Packing | 700 | 2.00 |

| Overhead cost variable | £655 |
| fixed | £5800 |

The output of 9500 litres from 19 batches processed was all sold at an average price of £3.71 per litres.

**Answer 3**

(a)  Budget: 20 batches × 500 litres = 10,000 litres

|  | (litres) | (£/litre) | (£) |
|---|---|---|---|
| Direct material |  |  |  |
| X | 3,000 | 0.60 | 1,800 |
| Y | 2,000 | 0.30 | 600 |
| Z | 5,000 | 0.45 | 2,250 |
|  | 10,000 |  | 4,650 |

|  | (hours) | (£/hour) | (£) |
|---|---|---|---|
| Direct labour |  |  |  |
| Blending | 4,800 | 2.50 | 12,000 |
| Filtering | 2,400 | 2.25 | 5,400 |
| Packing | 800 | 2.00 | 1,600 |
|  | 8,000 |  | 19,000 |
| Variable overhead |  |  | 600 |
| Fixed overhead |  |  | 5,750 |
| Total cost |  |  | 30,000 |
| Standard cost per litre |  |  | 3.00 |
| Selling price per litre |  |  | 3.55 |
|  |  |  | 0.55 |
| Budgeted profit for month 10,000 × £0.55 |  |  | 5,500 |

Actual results for October 1988

| | (litres) | (£/litre) | (£) |
|---|---|---|---|
| Direct material | | | |
| X | 2200 | 0.80 | 1760 |
| Y | 2500 | 0.35 | 875 |
| X | 4800 | 0.65 | 3120 |
| | 9500 | | 5755 |

| | (hours) | (£/hour) | (£) |
|---|---|---|---|
| Direct labour | | | |
| Blending | 5000 | 2.60 | 13,000 |
| Filtering | 2000 | 2.20 | 4,400 |
| Packing | 700 | 2.00 | 1,400 |
| | 7700 | | 18,800 |

| | | | |
|---|---|---|---|
| Variable overhead | | | 655 |
| Fixed overhead | | | 5,800 |
| | | | 6,455 |
| Total cost | | | 31,010 |
| Sales 9500 litres at £3.71 | | | 32,345 |
| Actual profit | | | 4,235 |
| Profit variance | | | 1,265A |

(b) *Sub-variance analysis*

| | Adverse (£) | Favourable (£) |
|---|---|---|
| Profit volume 10,000 − 9500 | | |
| = 500 litres × £0.55 | 275 | |
| Sales price 9500 × (£3.71 − £3.55) | | 1520 |
| Direct material price | | |
| X 2200 litres × 20p | 440 | |
| Y 2500 litres × 5p | 125 | |
| Z 4800 litres × 20p | 960 | |

Direct material usage/mix

| | Standard mix % | Standard | Actual | (£) | (£) | (£) |
|---|---|---|---|---|---|---|
| X | 30 | 2850 | 2200 | 650×0.60 | | 390 |
| Y | 20 | 1900 | 2500 | 600×0.30 | 180 | |
| Z | 50 | 4750 | 4800 | 50×0.45 | 22.5 | |
| | | 9500 | 9500 | | | |

Direct labour rate

| | | |
|---|---|---|
| Blending 5000 hrs × 10p | 500 | |
| Filter 2000 hrs × 5p | | 100 |

Direct labour mix for 19 batches standard hrs $= \dfrac{19}{20} \times 8000$

$\qquad\qquad\qquad\qquad\qquad\qquad\qquad = 7600$ hours

|  | Standard hours | Actual hours | Difference | (£/hr) | (£) | (£) |
|---|---|---|---|---|---|---|
| Blending 60% | 4560 | 5000 | 440 | 2.50 | 1100 | |
| Filtering 30% | 2280 | 2000 | 280 | 2.25 | | 630 |
| Packing 10% | 760 | 700 | 60 | 2.00 | | 120 |
| | 7600 | 7700 | | | | |

Variable overhead spending

|  | (£) | |
|---|---|---|
| Standard 9500 × 0.06 | 575 | |
| Actual | 655 | |
| | | 85 |

Fixed overhead expenditure

|  | | |
|---|---|---|
| Budget | 7750 | |
| Actual | 5800 | |
| | | 50 |

Fixed overhead volume

|  | | | |
|---|---|---|---|
| 95% absorption × £5750 | 5462.6 | | |
| Budget | 5750 | | |
| | | 287.5 | |
| | | 4025 | 2760 |
| | | £1265A | |

(c) The main problem evidenced by the variance analysis appears to be the price increase of certain inputs – in particular, direct material X and Z, and blending labour rates. Some of this cost has been recovered in a selling price increase, but product production and sales are down and this could be the result of the price increase.

Efforts should be made to identify the reason for the substantial material price increases. It may be that alternative suppliers could be identified.

## Question 4 (CIMA)

A company's control system involves providing the following data for a three-month period:

- budget for months 1, 2 and 3.
- A first update made at the end of month 1 for months 2 and 3.
- A second update made at the end of month 2 for month 3.
- Actual for months 1, 2 and 3.

The following data relate to month 3 of period:

|  | Sales volume (000 units) | Selling price (£) | Contribution on selling price (%) | Total overhead (£000) |
|---|---|---|---|---|
| Budget | 120 | 3.1 | 20 | 55 |
| First update | 96 | 3.1 | 20 | 48 |
| Second update | 108 | 2.9 | 18 | 43 |
| Actual | 100 | 3.0 | 19 | 47 |

You are required to:

(a) Calculate the following variances for month 3:

    (i)   profit variance;
    (ii)  sales mix profit variance;
    (iii) sales volume profit variance;
    (iv)  overhead total variance.

in respect of:

●  actual as compared with budget;
●  second update as compared with first update.

(b) Comment briefly on the implications of the results of (a) above, briefly explaining what help they can provide to management.

(c) Explain briefly (but do not calculate) what extra value for control purposes management might obtain if it were to compare each of the following:

    (i)   first update with budget;
    (ii)  second update with budget;
    (iii) actual with second update.

## Answer 4

(a) *Variance for month 3 – actual as compared with budget*

| Sales volume (000) | Selling price (£) | Sales price (£000) | Contribution on selling price (%) | Contribution (£000) | Average contribution per unit | Overhead (£000) | Profit (£) |
|---|---|---|---|---|---|---|---|
| Actual |  |  |  |  |  |  |  |
| 100 | 3.0 | 300 | 19 | 57 | 0.57 | 47 | 10,000 |
| Budget |  |  |  |  |  |  |  |
| 120 | 3.1 | 372 | 20 | 74.4 | 0.6 | 55 | 19,400 |

(i) Profit variance (9400) Adverse

(ii) Sales mix profit variance
    100,000 units × £(0.57 − 0.62) = (5000) Adverse

(iii)  Sales volume profit variance
(100,000 − 120,000) units × £0.62 = (£12,400) Adverse

(iv)  Overhead total variances £55,000 − 47,000 = £8000 Favourable

*Variances for month 3 − second update compared with first update*

| | Sales volume update (000) | Selling price (£) | Sales price (£000) | Contribution on selling price (%) | Contribution (£000) | Average contribution per unit | Overhead (£000) | Profit (£) |
|---|---|---|---|---|---|---|---|---|
| 2nd | 108 | 2.9 | 313.2 | 18 | 56.376 | 0.522 | 43 | 13,376 |
| 1st | 96 | 3.1 | 297.6 | 20 | 59.520 | 0.62 | 48 | 11,520 |

(i)  Profit variance 1,856 Favourable

(ii)  Sales mix profit variance
108,000 units × £(0.522 − 0.62) = (10,584) Adverse

(iii)  Sales volume profit variance
(108,000 − 96,000) units × £0.62 = £7440 Favourable

(iv)  Overhead total variances £48,000 − 43000 = £5000 Favourable

(b)  The actual results compared with budget are unfavourable. The volume sold is only 83 per cent of budget and the average price received dropped by over 3 per cent. The total contribution was accordingly down by £17,400 (23 per cent).

The overhead costs were down by £8000 but without knowing the division between fixed and variable it is difficult to comment on the efficiency achieved.

For management there is an indication of the need to review the basis of the budget sales volumes and also prices, if the variances do not entirely reflect changes in the product mix. An analysis also needs to be made to check if there is a continuing adverse trend.

*The second update compared with the first update* shows an increase in sales expectations from 98,000 to 108,000 units. This compares with 12,000 units in the budget. These seem significant changes month by month, i.e. down 20 per cent then up to 12 per cent.

Expected average prices have fallen from £3.1 to £2.9 per unit. This is possible in the expectation of selling more of the cheaper products.

Overhead costs, however, drop by £5000 although sales are expected to rise by 12,000 units.

The indications are that management should review the basis of the sales forecasts to ensure that the changes in volume are backed by action plans to meet the targets. A check should also be made on the overhead cost calculation − it could be right, for example, if there had been a dramatic fall in interest rates.

(c)   *Value for control purposes of further comparisons*
(i)   First update with budget
The budget in most companies is treated as the real benchmark against which actual results should be judged. If repeated updates are undertaken then by inference the actuals should be near the final forecast.

However, if the variances, first update versus budget, are calculated and excluded it does eliminate some repetition and comment. It may also show areas where real action is needed and what would happen if no action were taken.

(ii)   Second update with budget
The value of this comparison is to see if the revisions are bringing the new update more in line with budget. Otherwise it is best to see it as a combination of:

Budget versus first update    In total budget
First update versus second    versus second update.

The two individual exercises are worthwhile as they represent progressive steps and give financial data on variances made in the physical planning.

(iii)   Actual with second update
This is useful because it gives comparison of actuals with the plan formulated just prior to the month of action, that is, whether the new actions have achieved the desired results. If the budget is regarded as a planners' document then the second update is seen as the operating management's guidelines. They may only need to concern themselves with the final analysis.

Overall, therefore, there is some significance in these comparisons:

Budget versus first update
First update versus second update
Second update versus actual

Each is hopefully a progressive step towards the actual results. Budget versus actual will be a summation of all three.

### Question 5 (ACA)

Equinox is the main product of the Solstice Chemical Corporation. The product is manufactured in two processes with all the output from process 1 (chemical C) being transferred to process 2. Additional raw material (chemical D) is added at the start of processing in process 2 and the finished product is packed, in standardized containers, and dispatched to the finished goods store. A standard costing system is used and this is integrated with the company's financial accounting system.

The following standards apply:

| Process 1<br>Standard specification for<br>1000 kilos of C | (£) | Process 2<br>Standard specification for<br>1000 kilos of Equinox | (£) |
|---|---|---|---|
| Direct material | | Direct material | |
| 400 kilos of A at 0.36 | 144 | 1,050 kilos of C at £0.70 | 735 |
| 700 kilos of B at £0.08 | 56 | 50 kilos of D at £0.50 | 25 |
| Direct labour | | Direct labour | |
| 25 hours at £4.00 per hour | 100 | 5 hours at £4.00 per hour | 20 |
| Variable overhead | | Variable overhead | |
| 25 direct labour hours | | 5 direct labour hours at | |
| at £8.00 | 200 | £9.20 | 46 |
| Fixed overhead | | Fixed overhead | |
| 25 direct labour hours | | 5 direct labour hours at | |
| at £8.00 | 200 | £14.00 | 70 |
| | | Packing material | 4 |
| | £700 | | £900 |

The standards allow for a normal loss in volume of 10 per cent of the good output in each process; this loss occurs at the *beginning* of the process.

The following details apply for the operations of a particular week:

| | (£) |
|---|---|
| Purchase of raw materials | |
| 8000 kilos of A at £0.39 per kilo | 3120 |
| 16,000 kilos of B at £0.05 per kilo | 800 |
| 1500 kilos of D at £0.54 per kilo | 810 |

### Process 1

| | | |
|---|---|---|
| Direct material issued<br>to production | | |
| | A | 8,000 kilos |
| | B | 17,000 kilos |
| Direct labour | 530 hrs at £4.10 = £2173 | |
| Variable overhead | £4134 | |
| Fixed overhead | £4900 (actual) | |
| | £5000 (budgeted) | |

| | (kilos) | Degree of completion |
|---|---|---|
| Packing material | — | |
| Production and WIP | | |
| Opening WIP | 2,100 | 50% |
| Output (completed<br>production) | 22,000 | 100% |
| Closing WIP | 2,675 | 30% |

### Process 2

Direct material issued
to production

|  |  |  |
|---|---|---|
| C |  | 22,000 kilos |
|  |  | (transferred from process 1) |
| D |  | 930 kilos |

| Direct labour | 110 hrs at £3.80 = £418 |
|---|---|
| Variable overhead | £912 |
| Fixed overhead | £1510 (actual) |
|  | £1660 (budgeted) |
|  | £95 |

Packing material

| Production and WIP | (kilos) | Degree of completion |
|---|---|---|
| Opening WIP | 1,050 | 50% |
| Output (completed production) | 17,000 | 100% |
| Closing WIP | 3,225 | 25% |

Direct material price variances are calculated when the material is purchased. Raw material stocks are, therefore, recorded at standard cost and issued to production at standard cost. All other production expenses are charged at 'actual' from the expense accounts to the process accounts and any variances are transferred from the process accounts to appropriate variance accounts. Such transfers are made weekly. Output transferred from process 1 to process 2 is transferred at standard cost and work in process is valued on this basis.

You are required:

(a)  Write up the process accounts for process 1 and process 2.
(b)  Comment on the mix of raw materials used in process 1 during the week.
(c)  Comment on the profitability of process 2 if chemical C can be sold at £0.90 per kilo and the market price of Equinox is £1.05 per kilo.

### Answer 5

*Workings for process account 1*

Calculation of equivalent units

|  | Units | Materials | Equivalent units labour and overheads |  |
|---|---|---|---|---|
| Opening WIP | 2,100 | 2,100 | 1,050 | (50%) |
| Opening WIP completed | 2,100 | 0 | 1,050 | (50%) |
| Other completed work (22,000 − 2,100) | 19,900 | 19,900 | 19,900 |  |

| | | | |
|---|---|---|---|
| Output of C to process 2 | 22,000 | 19,900 | 20,950 |
| Closing WIP | 2,675 | 2,675 | 802.5 (30%) |
| Equivalent units of work done | | 22,575 | 21,752.5 |

As the degree of completion of materials is not given in the question, then it is assumed that opening and closing WIP are 100 per cent complete as to materials.

Stock valuation (at standard cost)

(£)

| | | |
|---|---|---|
| Opening stock | 2100 equivalent units of material at £(144 + 56) = £200 per 1000 units | = 420 |
| | 1050 equivalent units of labour and overhead at *£500 per 1000 units | = 525 |
| | | 945 |

*£(100 + 200 + 200)

| | | |
|---|---|---|
| Closing stock | 2675 equivalent units of material at £200 per 1000 units | = 535 |
| | 802.5 equivalent units of labour and overhead at £500 per 1000 units | = 401.25 |
| | | £936.25 |

| | | |
|---|---|---|
| Finished output | 22,000 kilos of C at £700 per 1000 units | = £15,400 |

*Workings for process account 2*

Calculation of equivalent units

| | Units | Materials | Equivalent units labour and overheads |
|---|---|---|---|
| Opening WIP | 1,050 | 1,050 | 525 (50%) |
| Opening WIP completed | 1.050 | 0 | 525 (50%) |
| Other completed work (17,000 − 1.050) | 15,950 | 15,950 | 15,950 |
| Output of Equinox | 17,000 | 15,950 | 16,475 |
| Closing WIP | 3,225 | 3,225 | 806.25 (25%) |
| Equivalent units of work done | | 19,175 | 17,281.25 |

It is assumed that opening and closing WIP are 100 per cent complete as to materials.

Stock valuation (at standard cost)
Stock are not packed and therefore their standard cost will exclude packing material. Standard material costs is (£25 + £375) = £760 per 1000 equivalent units, and the standard labour and overhead costs are (£20 + £46 + £70) = £136 per 1000 equivalent units.

|  |  | (£) |
|---|---|---|
| Opening stock | 1050 equivalent units of material at £760 per 1000 units | = 798.0 |
|  | 525 equivalent units of labour and overhead at £136 per 1000 units | |
|  |  | = 71.4 |
|  |  | £869.4 |
| Output of Equinox – | 17,000 kilos at £900 per 1000 kilos | = £15,300 |
| Closing stock – | 3225 equivalent units of material at £760 per 1000 units | = £2,451 |
|  | 806.25 equivalent units of labour and overhead at £136 per 1000 units | = 109.65 |
|  |  | £2560.65 |

*Calculation of variances*
Material
Price variance does not appear in the process account.
Usage variance = (Actual quantity − Standard quantity) × Standard price

For C $\quad$ = (22,000 − 20,133.75*) × 0.7
$\qquad$ = £1306.38A

For D $\quad$ = (930 − 958.75)[†] × 0.5
$\qquad$ = £14.38F

* $19,175 \times \dfrac{1050}{1000}$

[†] $19,175 \times \dfrac{50}{1000}$

Labour
Rate variance = (Actual rate − Standard rate) × Actual hours paid
$\qquad$ = (£3.80 − 4.00) × 110
$\qquad$ = £22.00F

Efficiency variance = (Actual hours worked − Standard hours)
$$\times \text{ Standard Rate}$$
$$= (110 - 86.406^*) \times £4$$
$$= £94.38A$$

$$^* 17,281.25 \times \frac{5}{1000}$$

Variable overhead
Efficiency variance = (Actual hours worked − Standard hours)
$$\times \text{ Standard rate}$$
$$= (110 - 86.406) \times £9.20$$
$$= £217.06A$$

| Expenditure | 110 hours actually cost | £912 |
|---|---|---|
| | 110 hours should have cost (110 × £9.2) | £1012 |
| | | £100F |

Material
Price variance does not appear in the process account but rather in the raw material account.

Usage variance
= (Actual quantity − Standard quantity) × Standard price

| For A | = (8000 − 9030*) × 0.36 |
|---|---|
| | = £370.8F |

| For B | = (17,000 − 15,802.5)† × 0.08 |
|---|---|
| | = £95.8A |

$$^* 22,575 \times \frac{400}{1000}$$

$$^† 22,575 \times \frac{700}{1000}$$

Labour
Rate variance    = (Actual rate − Standard rate) × Actual hours
paid
$$= (£4.10 - 4.00) \times 530$$
$$= £53.00A$$

Efficiency variance = (Actual hours worked − Standard hours)
$$\times \text{ Standard rate}$$
$$= (530 - 543.8125^*) \times £4$$
$$= £55.25F$$

$$^* 21,752.5 \times \frac{25}{1000}$$

Variable overhead
Efficiency variance = (Actual hours worked − Standard hours)
  × Standard overhead rate
  = (530 − 543.8125) × £8
  = £110.50 F

Expenditure       530 hours actually cost       4134
                  530 hours should have
                    cost (530 × £8)             £4240
                                                £106F

Fixed overhead
Expenditure variance = (Actual fixed overheads − Budgeted fixed
                        overheads)
  = £4900 − 5000
  = £100 F

Efficiency variance = (Actual hours worked − Standard hours)
  × Standard fixed overhead rate
  = (530 − 543.8125) × £8
  = £110.50 F

Capacity variance  = (Actual hours paid − Budgeted hours)
  × Standard fixed overhead rate
  = (530 − 625*) × £8
  = £760 A

  * £5000/£8

Process Account 1

| | (£) | | (£) |
|---|---|---|---|
| Opening WIP | 945.00 | Output of C to P2 | 15,400.00 |
| Direct labour | 2,173.00 | Adverse variances | |
| Variable overhead | 4,134.00 | Material B usage | 95.80 |
| Fixed overhead | 4,900.00 | Labour rate | 53.00 |
| Material A | | Fixed overhead capacity | 760.00 |
| (8000 kg at £0.36) | 2,880.00 | | |
| Material B | | | |
| (17,000 kg at £0.08) | 1,360.00 | | |
| | (£) | | (£) |
| Favourable variances | | | |
| Material A usage | 370.80 | | |
| Labour efficiency | 55.20 | | |
| Variable overhead | | | |
| efficiency | 110.50 | | |
| Variable overhead | | | |
| expenditure | 106.60 | | |
| Fixed overhead | | | |
| efficiency | 110.50 | | |
| Fixed overhead | | Closing WIP | 936.20 |
| expenditure | 100.00 | | |
| | £17,245.00 | | £17,245.00 |

Fixed overhead

Expenditure variance = (Actual fixed overheads − Budgeted fixed
                          overheads)
                      = £1,510 − 1,660
                      = £150 F

Efficiency variance     = (Actual hours worked − Standard hours)
                          × Standard fixed overhead rate
                      = (110 − 86.40625) × £14
                      = £330.31A

Capacity variance       = (Actual hours worked − Budgeted hours)
                          × Standard fixed overhead rate
                      = (110 − 118.571*) × £14
                      = £120A

  * £1660/£14

Packing materials variance − only finished units are packed therefore
the actual costs relate to the 17,000 kilos of Equinox.

17,000 kilos cost £95, but should cost $17,000 \times \dfrac{4}{1,000}$ = £68

Variance = £95 − £69 = £27 Adverse

Process account 2

| | (£) | | (£) |
|---|---|---|---|
| Opening WIP | 869.40 | Output of Equinox | 15,300.00 |
| Direct labour | 418.00 | Adverse variances | |
| Variable overhead | 912.00 | Usage Material C | 1,306.38 |
| Fixed overhead | 1,510.00 | Labour efficiency | 94.38 |
| Packing materials | 95.00 | Variable overhead | |
| | | efficiency | 217.06 |
| Material C (17,000 | | Fixed overhead | |
| kilos from Process 1) | 15,400.00 | efficiency | 330.31 |
| Material D (930) | | Fixed overhead | |
| kilos at £0.50) | 465.00 | capacity | 120.00 |
| Favourable variances | | Packing material cost | 27.00 |
| Material C usage | 14.38 | | |
| Labour rate | 22.00 | | |
| Variable overhead | | | |
| expenditure | 100.00 | | |
| Fixed overhead | | Closing WIP | 2,560.65 |
| expenditure | 150.00 | | |
| | £19,995.78 | | £19,955.78 |

(b)(i) The mix variance = (Actual mix − Actual mix in standard
proportions) × Standard price

$$(\pounds)$$

4/11   Material A [8,000 − 9,090.9] £0.36 =   392.72F
7/11   Material B[17,000 − 15,909.1] £0.08 =   87.27A

       25,000    25.000               £305.45F

(ii)  The yield variance
22,575 equivalent units did use 25,000 kilos

but should use $\left( 22{,}575 \times \dfrac{1100}{1000} \right)$ = 24,832.5 kilos

                                167.5 kilos

Standard weighted average price per kilo of A and B is £200/1000 kilos

Therefore yield variance = 167.5 kilos $\times \dfrac{\pounds 200}{1000}$ = £30.45A

Total usage variance                     = £275.00F

The favourable mix variance is a result of buying less of the more expensive material A than planned (the actual cost of A was £0.03 per kilo above the standard price).

However, if the output from process 1 (chemical C) is of low quality because of its content being mainly that of material B, the cheaper material, then the labour efficiency and material usage variances in process 2 may be adversely affected.

(c)  Decisions about further processing should be based on a comparison between the incremental revenue and incremental costs of further processing, e.g.

$$(\pounds)$$

Sales of Equinox = (1000 kilos × £1.05 = 1050
Sale of C        = (1050 kilos × £0.90 =  945
Incremental revenue              =  105

Incremental costs

|                    | (£) |
|--------------------|-----|
| Material D         | 25  |
| Direct labour      | 20  |
| Packing material   | 4   |
| Variable overhead  | 46  |
|                    | (95) |

(Further processing) Incremental gain =     £10

It is therefore more profitable to produce Equinox than chemical C, assuming that fixed overheads are not incremental.

# Further reading

Bromwich, M., Standard costing for planning and control, in Arnold, J., Carsberg, B., Scapens, R., *Topics in Management Accounting*, Philip Allan, 1980.

Harvey, M., Thompson, T., Planning and operational variances, *Accountancy*, February 1978.

Kennedy, A., Mixes in variance analysis, *Management Accountant*, February 1982.

Martindale, A., Stirring the variances mix, *Management Accounting*, November 1982.

# 14

# Computerized accounting information systems (CAIS) and the cost and management accountant

## Introduction

Management accounting like most business areas is experiencing a revolution. The pace of development of information technology (IT), and particularly its availability to all sizes of companies, is putting the management accountant under pressure. Only those management accountants who are prepared to meet this challenge, not only in keeping up with current technological developments but in foreseeing their applications, will have a chance of success in the future.

Studies in the mid-1980s by Collier the (*The Impact of Information Technology on the Management Accountant*, CIMA, 1984), by Carr (*Information Technology and the Accountant*, ACCA, 1985), by Bhaskar and Williams (*The Impact of Microprocessors on the Small Accounting Practice*, ICAEW, 1984) and by Cooper and Lybrand (*The Chartered Accountant in the Information Technology Age*, ICAEW, 1985) show the concern by the major accounting bodies in the UK that the accountant needs to be not only aware of IT but also up-to-date in its application.

Management accounting is concerned with decision making, planning and control in an increasingly complex environment. Hence there is a need to analyse a large amount of data drawn from many sources relatively quickly. Computer software can be used to hasten routine aspects of planning, budgeting, and forecasting. Other software is designed to enhance the management accountants' analytical, interpretive, and communication skills.

The Collier study showed that most management accountants have access to a wide range of computers which support the financial and management accounting applications, as well as having some decision support software. They were involved with the selection, development, and implementation of the computerized system. The level of involvement varied between participating in the selection of accounting soft-

362

ware at the minimum level to writing programs and adapting readily available system. There clearly is a new career path opening up for the person prepared to work in the interface area between cost and management accounting and information technology.

## Necessary knowledge

An effective cost accountant must possess an adequate understanding of the potential usefulness of IT in an information age. To achieve this he should have a sound knowledge of information technology management as studied at stage II of the CIMA examinations.

This means knowing:

(i)   Systems theory, the nature of information and information systems;
(ii)  how to design, select and install a system;
(iii) The computing side;
      The different types of computers available, with an idea of the advantages and limitations of each, a general knowledge of their architecture and the principles on which they work; Other computer hardware available and input/output/storage devices;
      general principles of programming and a knowledge of program language levels, e.g. operating systems, program language translators, utility routines, and applications packages;
(iv)  The nature of data and its collection and storage.

The above knowledge should not be purely of a theoretical nature but must be applied. For example it is insufficient to know generally about operating systems. The student should have had some experience, however limited, with an operating system such as DOS on the IBM-PC (or compatible computer). He should be familiar with utility routines such as FORMAT, for formatting discs, or COPY, for copying files from one disc to another. He should know the general nature but not necessarily have experience of accounting application programs such as general ledger programs, payroll programs, or accounts receivable packages.

The up-to-date management accountant must also be familiar with some special purpose software which is increasingly being used in management accounting:

Word-processing, spreadsheets, financial modelling, graphics, data base management, and statistical packages.

There are a number of packages available now which integrate several of these areas, e.g. Symphony contains a spread sheet, a data base and a word processor. Data can easily be transferred between the various utilities. It is also a useful skill to be able to write small pseudo-programs called 'macros' to automate the use of several packages in a management accounting application.

## Computerized accounting information system (CAIS)

A major role of an accounting information system within an organization is to aid the collecting, recording, and storing of financially orientated data as well as converting the data into meaningful decision making information for management. To achieve integration of accounting functions many companies employ a computerized data base.

Conceptually, an accounting information system data base is a *central* collection of facts and figures that serves the accounting information needs of the various organizational subsystems.

Most companies, when initially moving from a manual accounting system to a computerized system, computerize first one and then another of its manual accounting tasks until all operations are automated. The computer files needed to support each application are developed independently of each other, with only a partial coordination of the information stored on the files. Consequently a number of files hold duplicate information. This means that extra work is required to maintain the data files, and in some cases there may be inconsistencies if different files containing common data are updated at different times. Therefore data redundancy and inconsistencies will be reduced if all the data is pooled from all the accounting sources into a common body of information called a data base. This data base is accessed by one or more application programs for the purposes of data processing.

The advantages of a data base approach is that the data base makes efficient use of computerized storage space while continuing to serve the informational needs of all users. Also when various departments pool their data, each department has access to the full data base.

With the use of a computerized data base system it is possible to integrate the performance of accounting processes on the computer, therefore contributing to data processing efficiency.

Consider the system flowchart in Figure 14.1 where the financial statement preparation and budgetary planning and control processing has been integrated. The 'financial statement program' carries out the necessary accounting to prepare the company's financial statements as well as updating the general ledger file from the old general ledger file and journal transactions file. The 'create budget file program' uses data input from the terminal to create a budget file. The 'budget report program' uses the budget file in conjunction with the actual operating results to produce weekly budget exception reports and year to date budget reports. The 'projections program' using the budget file produces long and short term planning budgets as well as the projected financial statements. This is the budgetary planning and control side of the system. Hence we have a small example of the integration of the financial and management accounting activities within a computerized accounting information system (CAIS).

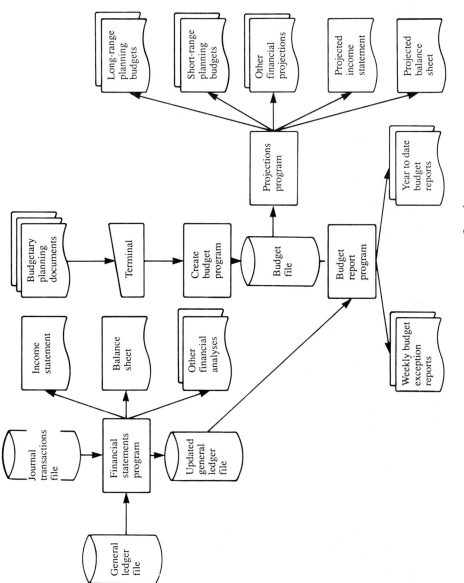

Figure 14.1 *Financial statements and budget processing: system flowchart*

## Decision support systems

A decision support system (DSS) is any system, application, or program that provides information to help the user make an informed decision. In practice, it is usually a computer based system which is orientated towards decision making rather than information processing. However the CAIS, illustrated earlier, is an example of a DSS that also handles information processing. DSS tend to support the decision maker rather than providing a unique decision by incorporating some aspect of sensitivity analysis. This may be in the form of a 'what if' question. DSS are used most frequently with semi-structured to unstructured problems and involve several disciplines, e.g. accounting and finance, computer science, operational research, and management.

A wide variety of decision support software is available to the cost and management accountant ranging from simple programs using a single algorithm, to expert systems.

## Simple program

These programs are usually written in well known computer language like Pascal, Basic or Cobol. This makes them easily portable between computers. A simple example would be a program which calculates the economic order quantity given the annual demand, the order cost per order and the stock-holding cost per item per year. Additionally it may calculate the total annual cost of the optimal policy and compare it with a given non-optimal order level.

Example   Annual demand equals 2000 items a year.
          Order cost per order is £20.
          Stockholding cost per item per year is £2.
Then the package would use the formula:

$$Q = \sqrt{\frac{2 \times D \times C}{H}}$$

$$\text{giving } Q = \sqrt{\frac{2 \times 2000 \times 20}{2}}$$

$$Q = 200$$

i.e. Order in quantities of 200, ten times a year.
The minimum total cost (T) is given by:

$$T = \sqrt{2 \times 2000 \times 20 \times 2}$$

$$T = £400$$

The package could calculate costs for different order levels from 50 to 500 in steps of 50. This would allow the decision maker to see what the cost saving would be if the company changed from a current order level to the optimal order level.

'What if' questions can be dealt with by changing the input variables.

## Data bases

Data bases used as computerized accounting information systems were covered previously. However there are relational data base packages available on micro-computers that are increasingly being used to aid decision making. One example is DBASE4 which has a comprehensive control centre menu which guides the user through the necessary steps to create, amend or search the databases.

The major power of this type of package is that data base programs may be written by the user to automate the use of the data base. This is a higher level language than Cobol or Basic and hence is much easier to use. This means that a competent DBASE4 programmer, who could easily be a management accountant, can set up data bases along with their associated programs which will maintain the data base and generate information upon request. For example the details of a dentist's patients could be stored in a data base. Then a DBASE4 program could be written to generate on a weekly basis a list of those patients who have not attended in the last six months, and to print out the address labels for the reminder cards.

## Spreadsheets

A spreadsheet is a blank worksheet that consists of horizontal rows and vertical columns. Each intersection of a row and a column forms a cell in which data can be stored. The data can either be numeric or text. Spreadsheets like Lotus 1−2−3 contain thousands of rows and hundreds of columns, so that large amounts of data can be stored within the spreadsheet.

The power of the spreadsheet comes from its ability to handle 'what if' questions, and like the data base packages, programs called 'macros' can be written to automate the use of the spreadsheet.

*Example*
Trade United Ltd has been asked to bid to supply units of Zeta over a three year period to the French government. The contract requires that the company securing the bid will supply the following units:

| Year | 1 | 2 | 3 |
|------|------|------|------|
| Units | 20,000 | 15,000 | 10,000 |

To produce these quantities new production facilities will be required costing £100,000. The cost of goods sold is estimated to be 60 per cent of sales. Other fixed costs are:

| | Year 0 | Year 1 | Year 2 | Year 3 |
|---|---|---|---|---|
| Demand | | 20,000 | 15,000 | 10,000 |
| Investment | 100,000 | | | |
| Contract price (£) | | 20.00 | 20.00 | 20.00 |
| Sales | | 400,000 | 300,000 | 200,000 |
| Cost of goods sold | | 240,000 | 180,000 | 120,000 |
| Gross margin | | 160,000 | 120,000 | 80,000 |
| Other expenses | | 40,000 | 45,000 | 50,000 |
| Profit before tax | (100,000) | 120,000 | 75,000 | 30,000 |
| Tax | | 48,000 | 30,000 | 12,000 |
| Profit after tax | (100,000) | 72,000 | 45,000 | 18,000 |
| | | | | |
| Internal rate of return | | | 21.32% | |
| Net present value (10%) | | | 16168.29 | |

Figure 14.2   *Zeta Company Ltd – spreadsheet example*

| Year | 1 | 2 | 3 |
|---|---|---|---|
| Other costs excluding depreciation (£) | 40,000 | 45,000 | 50,000 |

Assume a tax rate of 40 per cent (assume for simplicity that the tax cash flows occur at the end of each year in which the profit is generated, and ignore the tax position of the initial investment).

What should the break-even contract bid price be if the company want to achieve at least a 10 per cent return on its investment?

*Solution*

The problem's cashflows on a year by year basis have been entered into a Lotus 123 spreadsheets (see Figure 14.2) using initially a price of £20. The internal rate of return is 21.32 per cent showing that the initial chosen price of £20 is too high. When the £20 price is replaced by a lower price of, say £19, the whole spreadsheet is recalculated giving a new IRR. This new IRR is still above the target IRR of 10 per cent. Replacing the price by successive lower values, leads to the contract price of £18.24 giving an IRR of 10.06 per cent (see Figure 14.3).

The spreadsheet displays values which are the result of formulae relating the various cells. Figure 14.4 shows the formulae used in the spreadsheet. For example the formula in cell D12 is +D8 * D10. This means take the value of 20,000 stored in D8 and multiply it by the value of £20 stored in D10. This will be the sales in year 1, which is displayed and stored in D12. Similarly the profit after tax in year 1 in cell D21 is given by the formula +D18 − D19. The values stored in D18 and D19 are themselves calculated from formulae. The spreadsheet has special function formulae for the internal rate of return (IRR) and the net

|  | Year 0 | Year 1 | Year 2 | Year 3 |
|---|---|---|---|---|
| Demand |  | 20,000 | 15,000 | 10,000 |
| Investment | 100,000 |  |  |  |
| Contract price (£) |  | 18.24 | 18.24 | 18.24 |
| Sales |  | 364,800 | 273,600 | 182,400 |
| Cost of goods sold |  | 218,880 | 164,160 | 109,440 |
| Gross margin |  | 145,920 | 109,440 | 72,960 |
| Other expenses |  | 40,000 | 45,000 | 50,000 |
| Profit before tax | (100,000) | 105,920 | 64,440 | 22,960 |
| Tax |  | 42,368 | 25,776 | 9,184 |
| Profit after tax | (100,000) | 63,552 | 38,664 | 13,776 |
| Internal rate of return |  | 10.06% |  |  |
| Net present value (10%) |  | 78.37716 |  |  |

Figure 14.3　*Zeta Company Ltd – spreadsheet example*

| | A | B | C | D | E | F | G |
|---|---|---|---|---|---|---|---|
| 1 | | | | | | | |
| 2 | | | | | | | |
| 3 | | | | | | | |
| 4 | | | | | | | |
| 5 | | | | Year 0 | Year 1 | Year 2 | Year 3 |
| 6 | | | | | | | |
| 7 | | | | | | | |
| 8 | Demand | | | | 20,000 | 15,000 | 10,000 |
| 9 | Investment | | | 100,000 | | | |
| 10 | Contract price (£) | | | | 20.00 | +E10 | +E10 |
| 11 | | | | | | | |
| 12 | Sales | | | | +E8 * E10 | +F8 * F10 | +G8 * G10 |
| 13 | Cost of goods sold | | | | +E12 * 0.6 | +F12 * 0.6 | +G12 * 0.6 |
| 14 | | | | | | | |
| 15 | Gross margin | | | | +E12−E13 | +F12−F13 | +G12−G13 |
| 16 | Other expenses | | | | 40,000 | 45,000 | 50,000 |
| 17 | | | | | | | |
| 18 | Profit before tax | | | −D9 | +E15−E16 | +F15−F16 | +G15−G16 |
| 19 | Tax | | | | +E18 * 0.4 | +F18 * 0.4 | +G18 * 0.4 |
| 20 | | | | | | | |
| 21 | Profit after tax | | +D18−D19 | | +E18−E19 | +F18−F19 | +G18−G19 |
| 22 | | | | | | | |
| 23 | | | | | | | |
| 24 | | | | | | | |
| 25 | | | | | | | |
| 26 | Internal rate of return | | | | @IRR (0.1,D21..G21) | | |
| 27 | Net present value (10%) | | | | +D21 + @NPV (0.1,E21..G21) | | |

Figure 14.4　*Zeta Company Ltd – spreadsheet example*

present value (NPV) as can be seen in cells D26 and D27. The IRR is calculated on the cash flows stored in cells in row 21 from C21 to F21.

## Modelling software

Some modelling software may appear similar to a spreadsheet to the naïve user as many models use a matrix format consisting of rows and columns. Each row represents a variable and each column represents a line so that a cell contains the value of a variable at one point in time. The relationship between the variables is defined in mathematical terms containing variable names rather than cell references. For example if the spreadsheet problem was solved using a modelling package then the calculation of the profit for all four years (0 to 3) would be defined by the program line:

Profit after tax = Profit before tax − Tax

This instruction would be applicable to all the four columns as specified in an earlier program line. The output to the problem would look similar to the spreadsheet output and could even be identical.

The package will have a 'what if' option in the menu which will allow the user to amend either the model or the input data, e.g. change the tax rate or the initial price of £20. The same approach could be used as in the spreadsheet in order to obtain the contract at an IRR of 10 per cent. However, most modelling packages have a 'goal seeking' option where the program finds the optimal solution directly. The user specifies the goal: IRR = 10 per cent and specifies the variable to be changed as price. The program will then determine the optimal price as £18.24.

The major advantage of modelling software over spreadsheets is that it is easier to modify the model using modelling software rather than spreadsheets. The user with modelling software can include uncertainty in the definition of any variable.

There are a number of specialized modelling packages which do not use a matrix structure but use a range of specialist techniques. Forecasting packages such as TIMESTAT or WIZARD contain a range of forecasting techniques. Stochastic modelling packages such as @RISK contain routines for decision trees, simulation, inventory control, markov chains and dynamic programming. @RISK will also accept data from Lotus 123 spreadsheets.

## Expert systems

An expert system is a package that uses knowledge generally possessed by an expert to solve a problem. It is designed to copy the problem solving techniques of the human expert. For example, the forecasting package FORECAST PRO uses an expert system that examines the data

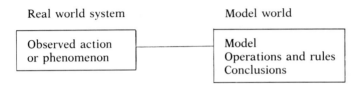

Figure 14.5

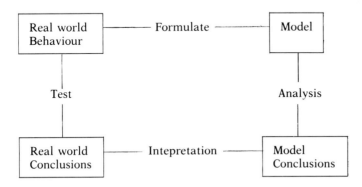

Figure 14.6

and chooses the optimal forecasting procedure and calculates the optimal parameters to be used.

The user can follow the recommendation or use an alternative method. For example the package might decide that there is a time series element in the data and recommend that the method of moving averages should be used. The user could override the recommendation and insist that a linear regression approach should be used.

The expert system is a powerful tool representing a new approach to problem solving. It is still to be exploited in the field of cost and management accounting.

## The modelling process

To gain an understanding of the processes involved in modelling, consider the two 'worlds' in Figure 14.5. Suppose we want to understand some action or phenomenon in the real world. For example, we might want to control departmental costs. To study these costs we might calculate various cost variances. These variances would form the model. Using the model the variance values would be determined and then interpretated in terms of the costs centres. These stages are represented by Figure 14.6.

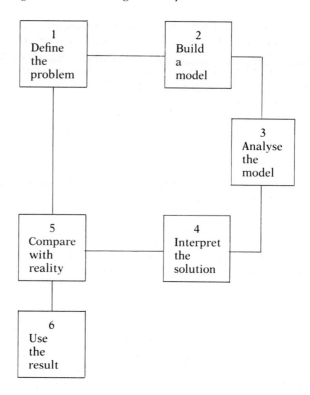

Figure 14.7

The interpretation drawn from the model must be compared with the real world to see if they fit the real world. Are the right variances being used, or are the interpretations correct? Some simplifying assumption may have been made which is not valid. If the model needs correcting or remodelling the whole process is repeated again. The whole process involves repeating the modelling cycle until the conclusions drawn from the model are consistent with our knowledge of the real world.

The full modelling cycle is represented in Figure 14.7.

The steps in the modelling process are therefore:

1   *Define the problem*
What is to be done or found out? Problem definition requires setting limits or boundaries to the problem which will help define the model content and the detail of analysis.

2   *Build a model*
Not all the factors in a problem situation can be incorporated in a model. Hence there is a need for simplification by making assumptions and reducing the number of factors under consideration. Studies have

shown that it is better to start with a simple model and then gradually complicate the model in small steps to the level of complexity required, rather than starting with too complex a model and then simplifying until it can be solved. Each stage of the model development can then be tested against reality before proceeding to the next level of complexity.

The relationships between the variables needs to be determined before the model structure can be built. A knowledge of possible model types should be known if an appropriate model is to be built. Questions that should be asked:

- Are the possible outcomes known with certainty?
  If the outcomes are certain then a deterministic model can be developed, if not then a stochastic approach using probabilities would be required.
- Is it a static or dynamic situation?
- Can an optimal solution be found?
  If it can be found then an algorithmic approach should achieve the solution. Otherwise a rule of thumb method (an heuristic) should lead to a good solution but not necessarily an optimal solution.

### 3   Analyse the model
Substitute the data derived from the real world and the simplifying assumptions and solve the resulting problem. This may require the use of a sophisticated mathematical analysis, e.g. linear programming using specialized software (e.g. LINDO) or a 'what if' analysis using a spreadsheet or modelling package to do variance analysis. If the model is too complicated to solve it will be necessary to go back a stage and simplify the model until a solution technique can be found.

### 4   Interpret the solution
What are the implications of the model solution on the real problem?

If the model solution is reduce stock levels by 50 per cent, how is it to be implemented? Can it be done instantaneously or will it take a few weeks? What is the effect on existing warehouse staff and warehouse space? Can we utilize the space and staff for some other product, if not what additional costs might be incurred which was not included in the model?

### 5   Compare with reality
If the solution is implemented will the outcome be as predicted by the model? Are the simplifying assumptions still valid, or has the problem changed? Are the predicted results precise enough? Can you test the model by using data in which you know the outcome?

### 6   Use the result
When the model has satisfied all the appropriate tests then the result can be implemented. Careful consideration should be given to this stage. Personel who are likely to be affected by the outcome should be involved in all stages of the model development. Any computer software

involved in the implementation must be user friendly, otherwise it will soon be used incorrectly, or not at all.

The model must be maintained. It was initially constructed from the initial problem. Have any of the parameters changed? For example, in a forecasting problem have the values of the seasonal factors changed from the initial problem? Have the values previously taken as constants now become variables? Has the size of the problem changed so that variables which could previously be taken as insignificant now become critical?

## Queueing

In a situation where the arrival of materials cannot be controlled exactly it is often naïvely assumed that if the material arrive rate doubles then the total time from the time of arrival to the completion of loading doubles given no change in the number of loaders. The situation is far more complex. Operational researchers have shown that the total time is dependent upon the arrival rate, the queue discipline, and the service rate. If the arrival rate is close to the service rate then the system will tend to clog up and long queues will result. The analysis of some of the simple queuing systems can be analysed using the queuing theory. If the situation is complex then a simulation approach may be necessary.

### The simple queue model

*Arrival pattern*
If the material arrival is at random then there is a reasonable chance that the arrival distribution follows a poisson distribution. (This is the more often observed pattern in practice.)

To check if the arrival rate in practice follows a poisson distribution a chi-squared goodness of fit test can be applied.

*Example*
Assume that the inter-arrival times of 100 items of stock was recorded as follows:

| Inter-arrival time (minutes) | Frequency |
|:---:|:---:|
| 0 | 4 |
| 1 | 12 |
| 2 | 19 |
| 3 | 24 |
| 4 | 18 |
| 5 | 11 |
| 6 | 7 |
| 7 | 4 |
| 8 | 1 |
| | 100 |

Take as our null hypothesis ($H_0$) that the observed times follow a poisson distribution, i.e. The distribution is a good fit to a poisson distribution.

Hence: $H_1$: The distribution does not fit a poisson distribution.

To apply the chi-squared test, the expected frequencies assuming $H_0$ need to be calculated. To calculate poisson expected values or poisson probabilities the mean is required.

From the above data

mean = 327/100
     = 3.27

Calculate poisson probabilities:

$$P(0) = e^{-3.27} \qquad\qquad\qquad = 0.0380$$
$$P(1) = e^{-3.27} \times 3.272^1/1! \qquad = 0.1234$$
$$P(2) = e^{-3.27} \times 3.272^2/2! \qquad = 0.2032$$
$$P(3) = e^{-3.27} \times 3.272^3/3! \qquad = 0.2215$$
$$P(4) = e^{-3.27} \times 3.272^4/4! \qquad = 0.1811$$
$$P(5) = e^{-3.27} \times 3.272^5/5! \qquad = 0.1184$$
$$P(6) = e^{-3.27} \times 3.272^6/6! \qquad = 0.0645$$
$$P(7) = e^{-3.27} \times 3.272^7/7! \qquad = 0.0301$$
$$P(8) = e^{-3.27} \times 3.272^8/8! \qquad = 0.0123$$

Multiplying each probability by 100 (the sum of the observed frequencies) gives the expected frequencies:

$E(0) = $     3.88
$E(1) = $    12.43
$E(2) = $    20.32
$E(3) = $    22.15
$E(4) = $    18.11
$E(5) = $    11.84
$E(6) = $     6.45
$E(7) = $     3.01
$E(8) = $     1.23

Note 1 the sum of the expected frequencies does not sum to 100 as the balance of 0.58 is the expected frequency for 9 or more.

Note 2 for the chi-squared test only a tail end expected frequency can be less than 5 but must be greater or equal to 1. The end frequencies need to be combined until these conditions are satisfied.

Hence:

| Time | Observed frequency 0 | Expected frequency E |
|---|---|---|
| 0 | 4 | 3.88 |
| 1 | 12 | 12.43 |
| 2 | 19 | 20.32 |
| 3 | 24 | 22.15 |
| 4 | 18 | 18.11 |

| | | |
|---|---|---|
| 5 | 11 | 11.84 |
| 6 | 7 | 6.45 |
| 7 or more | 5 | 4.82 |
| | 100 | 100.00 |

The chi-squared statistic is given by:

$$\chi^2 = \varepsilon(0 - E)^2/E$$

The full calculation is:

| O | E | O−E | $(O-E)^2$ | $(O-E)^2/E$ |
|---|---|---|---|---|
| 4 | 3.88 | 0.12 | 0.0144 | 0.004 |
| 12 | 12.43 | 0.43 | 0.1849 | 0.015 |
| 19 | 20.32 | 1.30 | 1.7424 | 0.086 |
| 24 | 22.15 | 1.85 | 3.4224 | 0.155 |
| 18 | 18.11 | 0.11 | 0.0121 | 0.001 |
| 11 | 11.84 | 0.84 | 0.7056 | 0.060 |
| 7 | 6.45 | 0.55 | 0.3025 | 0.047 |
| 5 | 4.82 | 0.18 | 0.0324 | 0.007 |
| Sample chi-squared | | | | 0.383 |

Degrees of freedom (V) = Number of rows − (1 for each parameter used) −1 (for total)

$$V = 8 - 1 - 1 = 6$$

Lose one degree of freedom as the mean of the data was used to calculate the expected values.

Lose one degree of freedom as the total of 100 was used

From chi-squared tables the test chi V=6 at the 5 per cent level = 12.59

Hence as the sample chi-squared is less than the test value, accept $H_0$.

The arrival pattern is poisson.

Hence the assumption of a poisson arrival pattern of the simple queuing model is satisfied.

   This implies that the arrivals are occurring at random and that the probability of an item arriving in a fixed period is constant and independent of the number of previous arrivals and the length of the queueing time.

### Queue discipline

The simple queue model assumes a first-in, first-out (FIFO) discipline, i.e. the items are served in the same order they arrive. This is not inconsistent with normal practice.

### Service pattern

Usually when stock is loaded the time taken is not a constant but varies due to a number of factors. The simple queue model assumes the service pattern is a negative exponential distribution which fits a large number of practical situations. In any particular situation the chi-squared goodness of fit could be applied to observed service times to test if the negative exponential distribution is the most appropriate distribution to apply in the case.

The simple queue model assumes a single server but multi-server systems have been analysed.

### Analysis of a simple queue

Formula for the simple queue are expressed in terms of three variables: the arrival rate $\lambda$; the service rate $\mu$ and the traffic intensity p. The traffic intensity is also a measure of the utilization of the server and is given by:

$$p = \frac{\lambda}{\mu}$$

Note, p must be less than 1 otherwise the arrival rate would be higher than the service rate and queues would become infinite.

### Some queueing formula

Average time spent in system (queue + service) $= \dfrac{1}{\mu - \lambda}$

Average number of items in the system $= \dfrac{\lambda}{\mu - \lambda}$

Average time spent in queue $= \dfrac{p}{\mu - \lambda}$

Average number of items in the queue $= \dfrac{p\lambda}{\mu - \lambda}$

Probability of n items in the system $= (1 - p)\, p^n$

Probability of more than n items in the system $= p^{n+1}$

### Application

Various cartons are arriving at the packaging department at a rate of 40 cartons per hour. Due to the different types of cartons the packaging time varies, but the average packing time per carton is one minute. The company want to determine the amount of room to leave for storing the cartons before they are packed.

This will involve determining the average number of items in the queue which is given by:

$$\frac{p\lambda}{\mu - \lambda}$$

Now $\lambda$ = 40 per hour, and as the average service time is one minute $\mu$ = 60 per hour (note same time period must be used in the formula).

Hence  $p = \dfrac{40}{60} = 0.667$

Therefore average number in queue $= \dfrac{0.667 \times 40}{60 - 40}$

$$= 1.33 \text{ items}$$

This is insufficient information for the design of the storage area as the average number will be exceeded a large amount of the time. Strictly there is no upper limit for the queue length as in theory it could be infinite. The usual approach is to determine the queue length that will only be exceeded a small percentage of the time, say five per cent.

This cannot be determined directly but we can approach the solution using the formula for the probability of more than n items in the system.

Let n = 5 then:

$P(x > 5) = 0.667^6 = 0.0881$ which is too large so try n = 6 and n = 7

$P(x > 6) = 0.0587, P(x > 7) = 0.0392$

This means that for only 3.9 per cent of the time there will be more than 7 cartons in the system. As one of these cartons will be being serviced the number in the queue will not exceed 6, therefore design the queueing area to take 6 cartons.

The times that items spend in the queue and in the system were not needed to solve this problem but they can be determined as follows:

Average time in system $= \dfrac{1}{60 - 40} = 0.0500$ hours = 3 minutes

Average time in queue $= \dfrac{0.667}{60 - 40} = 0.0333$ hours = 2 minutes

## Examination questions

### Question 1 (CIMA)

The budgeting procedures in your organization involve considerable manual effort. Computer facilities are now available and it is proposed that a financial modelling system be introduced to improve the quality of information with less accounting effort.

You are required to:

(a)  Explain what is meant by financial modelling.
(b)  State how financial modelling could be applied to budget procedures.

(c)   List three advantages that you would expect from its application to preparing budgets.

### Answer 1

(a)   *Definition of finance modelling*
Financial modelling involves the use of computer programs that contain a model of the relationships between all or some of the elements of a financial system of an organization. When data concerning an actual or projected change in one element of the system are fed into the computer, the program will demonstrate the effects on all other elements that have been included in the program.

To give a simple example, if a model of the system is built into the program on the assumption that debtors pay in six weeks, by entering any given level of monthly sales for a period, the computer program would show the level of debtors at the end of the month. It would also show the monthly cash to be received from debtors for any period.

(b)   *Application to budget procedures*
In the case of standard costing, the program would convert unit standard quantities and prices (previously entered) into totals when multiplied by actual outputs/inputs (entered, for example, monthly). It would calculate variances from standard when actual data for the month were either cumulated from entries during the month or entered separately. The program would calculate these variances in respect of quantities (e.g. material quantity variances) and values (e.g. direct labour rate variances).

In the case of other budget data, such as departmental administration or selling costs, the budget data for the year (entered previously) would be cumulated and when actual cost data was entered (monthly, for example) the budget data would be flexed, where relevant, compared with actual and variances shown according to the degree of analysis entered into the program.

The program could be written so as to project the outcome of the current month's data and variances on the cost and profit for the remainder of the year.

In situations where changes to the budget become necessary, these could be entered at the appropriate point and the program would adjust the relevant budget totals, perhaps show new variances based on the new budget and perhaps project the year-end cost and profit resulting from the change.

(c)   *The advantages*
Any three from the following:

- It would cut out tedious manual calculations of variances.
- It usually allows print-outs to be produced directly from the program (as a by-product) rather than by separate typing/preparation.

- It enables projections resulting from current variances or from changes in budget to be made easily.
- It speeds up the preparation of monthly figures.
- It can be linked to show results of changes on areas outside budgeting, e.g. cash flow, etc.
- The process of building the model will contribute significantly to a better understanding of the budgeting procedure.
- It will provide a framework for examining problems and enabling management to predict what would happen if certain events were to take place.

## Question 2 (ACA)

(a)  Describe what is meant by a data base management system
(b)  With examples describe the following:

> (i)   a relational data base management system;
> (ii)  a hierarchical data base management system;
> (iii) a network data base management system.

(c)  Discuss the advantages and disadvantages of installing a data base system, using examples to support your case.

## Answer 2

(a)  *Description of a data base management system*
A data base management system (DBMS) is a software package for creating, updating and extracting information from a data base. In order to describe a DBMS more fully it is necessary to explain the term 'data base'. (The descriptions in subsequent sections are just as inevitably linked with descriptions of different types of data base).

A simple explanation of a data base is a file of information which is not designed to satisfy a single, specific, limited application but rather designed to serve the needs of several functions in an organization. This could be expanded to call a data base a generalized integrated collection of data which is structured on natural data relationships so that it provides all necessary access paths to each unit of data in order to fulfil the differing needs of all users. Unfortunately the term has slowly become corrupted so that it is now also used to denote any data file even if used for a single application. (Data base sounds more impressive than file!)

A classic example of an application of a data base system might be with regard to wages information. This might be needed by the personnel department (to note current wage rates and any changes), the wages department (to pay staff) and the production department (to update work in progress records). Rather than each department having their own files of data with problems of duplication and also information becoming out of phase between files, one single file of wages information could be constructed to serve the needs of all three departments.

The essential feature of a DBMS is to allow the various 'applications programs' of the different users to operate against a background of changing file structure for the data being stored. This is achieved by means of two pieces of software – a data description language (DDL) and a data manipulation language (DML). The former provides the DBMS with a description of records and fields of data stored and their relationships (sometimes called a data dictionary). The latter allows programs using the data base to store, modify, access or delete data records. In addition to these simple essential functions, the DBMS will also allow logs to be maintained of data usage and provide security against attempts at unauthorized access, against data corruption, and recovery and restart facilities after hardware or software failure.

### (b) *Different types of DBMS*

The three data base management systems are distinguished by the different view that they give to the user as to how data is stored. For a particular DBMS, this user's view (referred to in some circles by the unpleasant piece of jargon an 'external model') may well differ from one user to another and will probably differ again from the actual way in which data is physically stored in the computer system (sometimes called an 'internal model'). The relationships between each user's view of stored data and the physical method of storage are called 'mappings'. These are organized by the data base management system.

### (i) *Relational data base management systems*

When using a relational DBMS, data is seen to be stored in a series of tables (sometimes, somewhat confusingly, referred to as 'relations'). For instance, information concerning clients of a firm supplying large-scale corporate finance might be set out in three tables:

Client details

| Number | Name | Address | Assets (£m) | Liabilities (£m) | Credit rating |
|--------|------|---------|-------------|------------------|---------------|
| 1001 | AA Co | 1 High St | 100 | 75 | B |
| 1002 | AB Ltd | 10 New St | 50 | 45 | D |

Loan details

| Account number | Name | Interest (%) | Amount (£000) | Repayments (pa) | Type |
|----------------|------|--------------|---------------|-----------------|------|
| 123 | AB Ltd | 13.40 | 100 | 4 | 2 |
| 134 | PQ Plc | 12.25 | 40 | 12 | 1 |

Payment details

| Account number | Payment (£000) | Date |
|----------------|----------------|------|
| 123 | 6.957 | 010186 |
| 134 | 0.667 | 100186 |

These tables resemble the files of records relating to accounts that might be kept on a conventional accounting system. Rather than call each row on the table a record, they are called 'tables'; each column is not called a field but rather an 'attribute'. In order to establish connections between tables, some tables must keep some common fields or attributes.

The relational DBMS presents the user with a simple picture of stored data. The use of separate tables does not imply that there is a particular relationship or dependency between data in one table and another. This means that deleting information about one loan account when settled would not automatically mean losing the standing information about that client. (This is not the case in other types of DBMS.)

### (ii)   *Hierarchical data base management systems*

The hierarchical (or tree) data base management systems recognize that there are certain dominant elements of data and in respect of each dominant element of data one or more subordinate elements of data. Such data could be represented as a form of family tree (analogies used often relate to trees with roots and branches of family trees with children and parents). For instance a firm of private tutors keeping details of students and their performance on courses in preparation for exams might show information as follows:

| | |
|---|---|
| Examination | PEII Dec X5 |
| Course | Intro, Interim, Final |
| Class | A,B,C,D... |
| Firm | AB Co, CD Co, EF Co |
| Student | Adams, Brown, Cleese |

A firm will wish to accumulate certain data regarding each examination (dates of exam, dates results published, dates of oral tuition courses, number of students enrolled, study material to be issued). In respect of each oral course certain details will be needed (dates, numbers enrolled and attending, test papers sat, material issues). For each class information about course tutors, rooms used, average marks achieved will be recorded. Further information will then be maintained of firms and students in each class, their marks and attendance.

In a hierarchical system certain records must exist before others can be created, details of an examination must be established before courses can be scheduled for that exam. Conversely when deleting records, data relating to a student can be deleted without deleting any more dominant information, such as firm, class or course details; but if the data relating to a course is deleted the subordinate data relating to classes firms and students may well also be deleted. Another problem with hierarchical DBMS is that data may be stored more than once and, depending on the relationship between records, if such data requires updating, each instance of the appropriate record may need to be sought and updated.

(iii)   *Network data base management systems*

Network (or graph) data base management systems operate in a similar fashion to hierarchical systems though now the concept of dominant and subordinate is expanded. This results from the fact that relationships between records need not simply be 'one to one' or 'one to many'. One student is attached to one firm with a firm's students in one class; also one class contains many students with the relationships implied in (ii). However it is likely that a firm will have students in different courses in different classes at the same time, in which case the simple tree structure becomes too simplistic since 'branches' need to move both upwards and downwards. The logical relationship between different types of records is referred to as a 'set'.

(c)   *Advantages and disadvantages of DBMS*

(i)   Advantages include:

1   The availability to management of a comprehensive collection of data about an enterprise rather than the limited information available from separate files of data prepared for a single application.
2   Data is in general recorded only once, not several times, with the inherent advantages that:

- less storage space is required;
- data can be updated by single input; and
- there are no discrepancies between similar data kept on different files.

3   The DBMS handles the construction and processing of files saving programming time. There are several DBMS packages widely available and it is possible to write programs to perform data handling tasks with such packages with little programming knowledge.
4   It is easy to introduce new applications that make use of the existing data base.

(ii)   Disadvantages:

1   Initial cost – although the sort of data base packages available for micro-computers have come down in price over the past few years, installing a DBMS on a larger computer is a much costlier exercise. The initial cost will be increased by time taken to organize and transfer data and time spent testing the new system.
2   Security – although any DBMS will attempt to ensure that access to data and the ability to alter data is controlled to ensure authorized access only, there is always the possibility of breaches of such security.
3   Political – the database needs to serve the needs of several users. Difficulties are often encountered in getting all users to agree on what data needs to be stored, the method of storage and the general requirements from the DBMS.
4   Privacy – with a greater amount of data readily available to man-

agement, particularly data about personnel, individuals may feel that their privacy suffers. Such views are one factor behind the recent Data Protection Act.

### Question 3 (CIMA)

A and B are competing importers of a lightweight industrial pick-up truck, the 'Gamma'. Market research suggests that there is demand for such vehicles of about 1200 per year, evenly spread over the year and that, bearing in mind the facilities available on the truck, its price should be around £11,000, but discounts may be available. The price to the dealer is about £8000 depending upon exchange rates. The management accountants at A have the task of determining the price to charge for the vehicle that will give the greatest monthly profit from the sale of Gammas.

Past experience suggest that A's market share and profit depends not only on the price A charges, but on the price that B charges. The following pattern seems to have merged.

If both companies charge the same price, than A secures about 45 per cent of the market and B, 55 per cent. When B has a lower price, then A losses about 3 per cent market share for every £200 price difference.

On the other hand, when B has a higher price, then A gains about 2 per cent market share over and above the 45 per cent per £200 price difference.

From A's point of view, B normally changes its price monthly.

A's management accountants have ruled out trial and error pricing and have decided to develop a simulation model to investigate price behaviour patterns based on monthly periods.

You are required to:

(a)   Develop a simulation model from A's point of view, using algebra, showing:

  (i)   an expression for monthly profit;
  (ii)  an expression for market share when B's price is the same as A's;
  (iii) an expression for market share when B's price is higher than A's;
  (iv)  an expression for market share when B's price is lower than a's

(b)   Draw a flow diagram to show how the model would be used to simulate pricing/demand behaviour using a computer

(c)   Prepare a statement for the management accountants showing the strengths and weaknesses of simulation as a management technique.

**Answer 3**

(a)  d = total demand (monthly)
  a = A's market share %
  b = B's market share %
  p = price (per Gamma)
  p1 = A's price (per Gamma)
  p2 = B's price (per Gamma)
  c = Cost (per Gamma)
  x1 = A's profit (monthly)

(i)  $x1 = (a \times d)(p1 - c)$

(ii)  if $p1 = p2$, $a = 0.4d$

(iii)  if $p1 > p2$, $a = 0.45d - 0.3d \times \dfrac{p1 - p2}{200}$

(iv)  if $p1 < p2$, $a = 0.45d + 0.2d \times \dfrac{p2 - p1}{200}$

(b)  See Figure 14.8. Note, it is assumed that the values of d, p1 and p2 are already stored in the computer.

(c)
  To:    Management Accountants, A.
  From:   A Consultant
  Subject:  Simulation as a management technique

*Strengths*
- It can be applied where other management techniques would be inappropriate or too complex.
- The simulation model enables management to obtain a simple representation of a complex, real-life problem.
- In developing the simulation model, management will gain a greater understanding of the problem.
- The model can be used to assess the outcome of alternative business scenarios.

*Weaknesses*
- Almost invariably, access to computing facilities is required, although in today's environment this does not represent a great barrier to use.
- Substantial inputs of management and staff time may be required to construct the model.
- Models can become overly complex.
- Finally, it should be noted that the simulation model only provides information to managers who must make the ultimate decisions.

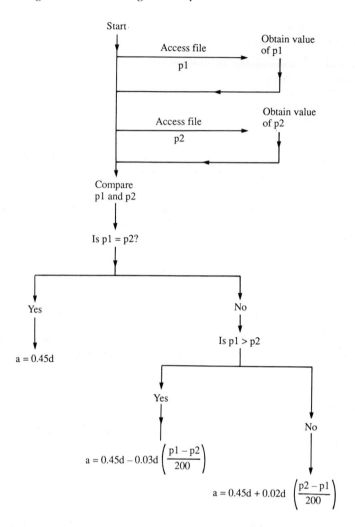

Figure 14.8

### Question 4 (CIMA)

A company which has a range of profitable products is experiencing serious cash flow problems. The management accountant has decided to analyse the data relating to debtors, for she suspects that those debtors who owe more to the company are the ones who are taking longer to settle. A sample of 400 debts is produced and is analysed under the following headings.

(i)  Period outstanding beyond the normal credit period
    1–2 weeks slow

3–4 weeks very slow
5–6 weeks warning letter
7–8 weeks legal action

(ii) Amount of debt
£1000–1999 small
£2000–2999 medium
£3000–3999 large
£4000–4999 substantial

The clerks in the department have undertaken an examination of the 400 debts, and have produced the table below:

|  | Slow | Very slow | Warning letter | Legal action |
|---|---|---|---|---|
| Small | 12 | 15 | 16 | 17 |
| Medium | 15 | 17 | 21 | 27 |
| Large | 17 | 26 | 26 | 41 |
| Substantial | 26 | 32 | 37 | 55 |

You are required to:

(a) Use the chi-squared test or refute the suspicion of the management accountant.
(b) Explain carefully what is meant by the term 'significance' in the present context, and how a 'hypothesis test' differs from a 'test of significance'.

## Answer 4

(a) The chi-squared test is used to compare an observation distribution, O, with an expected distribution, E.

$$\chi^2 = \varepsilon \frac{(O - E)^2}{E}$$

O:

|  | Small | Medium | Large | Substantial | Total | % |
|---|---|---|---|---|---|---|
| Slow | 12 | 15 | 17 | 26 | 70 | 17.5 |
| Very slow | 15 | 17 | 26 | 32 | 90 | 22.5 |
| Warning letter | 16 | 21 | 26 | 37 | 100 | 25.0 |
| Legal action | 17 | 27 | 41 | 55 | 150 | 35.0 |
|  | 60 | 80 | 110 | 150 | 400 | 100.0 |

E:

|  | % | Small | Medium | Large | Substantial | Total |
|---|---|---|---|---|---|---|
| Slow | 17.5 | 11 | 14 | 19 | 26 | 70 |
| Very slow | 22.5 | 13 | 18 | 25 | 34 | 90 |
| Warning letter | 25.0 | 15 | 20 | 27 | 38 | 100 |
| Legal action | 35.0 | 21 | 28 | 39 | 52 | 140 |
|  | 100.0 | 60 | 80 | 110 | 150 | 400 |

| O | E | O−E | (O−E)² | $\frac{(O-E)^2}{E}$ |
|---|---|---|---|---|
| 12 | 11 | 1 | 1 | 0.09 |
| 15 | 13 | 2 | 4 | 0.31 |
| 16 | 15 | 1 | 1 | 0.07 |
| 17 | 21 | − 4 | 16 | 0.76 |
| 15 | 14 | 1 | 1 | 0.07 |
| 17 | 18 | − 1 | 1 | 0.06 |
| 21 | 20 | 1 | 1 | 0.05 |
| 27 | 28 | − 1 | 1 | 0.04 |
| 17 | 19 | − 2 | 4 | 0.21 |
| 26 | 25 | 1 | 1 | 0.04 |
| 26 | 27 | − 1 | 1 | 0.04 |
| 41 | 39 | 2 | 4 | 0.10 |
| 26 | 26 | — | — | — |
| 32 | 34 | − 2 | 4 | 0.12 |
| 37 | 38 | − 1 | 1 | 0.03 |
| 55 | 52 | 3 | 9 | 0.17 |
| 400 | 400 | | | = 2.16 |

Apply tables:

$$V = (\text{Rows} - 1)(\text{Columns} - 1)$$
$$= (4 - 1) \qquad (4 - 1)$$
$$= 9 \text{ degrees of freedom}$$

At 5 per cent significance, the cut off point for 9 degrees of freedom is 16.919. Therefore accept null hypothesis – there is no relationship between the size of the debt and the time taken to settle.


(b)   A hypothesis is a proposition or statement which may be subject to statistical 'hypothesis testing', i.e. comparing observed events with those predicted by the hypothesis.

Observed events are obtained by taking a random samples from the 'population'.

Differences between the observed and the predicted or expected events may be due to the hypothesis being inaccurate or to the sample being biased, i.e. not truly random. 'Significance' is the term used to indicate that any difference between the observed and expected events is not due to change.

Thus 'hypothesis testing' involves the testing of the original proposition or statement whilst 'significance testing' establishes the confidence with which the results may be viewed.

At 5 per cent significance we can have 95 per cent confidence that there is no relationship between debt size and settlement time.

**Further reading**

Bryant, J.W., *Financial Modelling in Corporate Management*, Wiley, 1982.
Jackson, M., *Creative Modelling with Lotus 1–2–3*, Wiley, 1985.
Kaye, G.R., *The Impact of IT on Accountants*, CIMA, 1986.
Kaye, G.R., *Introduction to Financial Modelling Systems*, CIMA, 1988.
Sherwood, D., *Financial Modelling: A Practical Guide*, Gee and Co, 1983.

# Appendix   Mathematical tables

## Table 1   Area under the normal curve

This table gives the area under the normal curve between the mean and a point x standard deviations above the mean. The corresponding area for deviations below the mean can be found by symmetry.

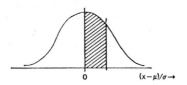

| $\frac{(x - \mu)}{\sigma}$ | 0.00 | 0.01 | 0.02 | 0.03 | 0.04 | 0.05 | 0.06 | 0.07 | 0.08 | 0.09 |
|---|---|---|---|---|---|---|---|---|---|---|
| 0.0 | .0000 | .0040 | .0080 | .0120 | .0159 | .0199 | .0239 | .0279 | .0319 | .0359 |
| 0.1 | .0398 | .0438 | .0478 | .0517 | .0557 | .0596 | .0636 | .0675 | .0714 | .0753 |
| 0.2 | .0793 | .0832 | .0871 | .0910 | .0948 | .0987 | .1026 | .1064 | .1103 | .1141 |
| 0.3 | .1179 | .1217 | .1255 | .1293 | .1331 | .1368 | .1406 | .1443 | .1480 | .1517 |
| 0.4 | .1554 | .1591 | .1628 | .1664 | .1700 | .1736 | .1772 | .1808 | .1844 | .1879 |
| 0.5 | .1915 | .1950 | .1985 | .2019 | .2054 | .2088 | .2123 | .2157 | .2190 | .2224 |
| 0.6 | .2257 | .2291 | .2324 | .2357 | .2389 | .2422 | .2454 | .2486 | .2518 | .2549 |
| 0.7 | .2580 | .2611 | .2642 | .2673 | .2704 | .2734 | .2764 | .2794 | .2823 | .2852 |
| 0.8 | .2881 | .2910 | .2939 | .2967 | .2995 | .3023 | .3051 | .3078 | .3106 | .3133 |
| 0.9 | .3159 | .3186 | .3212 | .3238 | .3264 | .3289 | .3315 | .3340 | .3365 | .3389 |
| 1.0 | .3413 | .3438 | .3461 | .3485 | .3508 | .3531 | .3554 | .3577 | .3599 | .3621 |
| 1.1 | .3643 | .3665 | .3686 | .3708 | .3729 | .3749 | .3770 | .3790 | .3810 | .3830 |
| 1.2 | .3849 | .3869 | .3888 | .3907 | .3925 | .3944 | .3962 | .3980 | .3997 | .4015 |

**Table 1 (Contd)**

| $\dfrac{(x - \mu)}{\sigma}$ | 0.00 | 0.01 | 0.02 | 0.03 | 0.04 | 0.05 | 0.06 | 0.07 | 0.08 | 0.09 |
|---|---|---|---|---|---|---|---|---|---|---|
| 1.3 | .4032 | .4049 | .4066 | .4082 | .4099 | .4115 | .4131 | .4147 | .4162 | .4177 |
| 1.4 | .4192 | .4207 | .4222 | .4236 | .4251 | .4265 | .4279 | .4292 | .4306 | .4319 |
| 1.5 | .4332 | .4345 | .4357 | .4370 | .4382 | .4394 | .4406 | .4418 | .4430 | .4441 |
| 1.6 | .4452 | .4463 | .4474 | .4485 | .4495 | .4505 | .4515 | .4525 | .4535 | .4545 |
| 1.7 | .4554 | .4564 | .4573 | .4582 | .4591 | .4599 | .4608 | .4616 | .4625 | .4633 |
| 1.8 | .4641 | .4649 | .4656 | .4664 | .4671 | .4678 | .4686 | .4693 | .4699 | .4706 |
| 1.9 | .4713 | .4719 | .4726 | .4732 | .4738 | .4744 | .4750 | .4756 | .4762 | .4767 |
| 2.0 | .4772 | .4778 | .4783 | .4788 | .4793 | .4798 | .4803 | .4808 | .4812 | .4817 |
| 2.1 | .4821 | .4826 | .4830 | .4834 | .4838 | .4842 | .4846 | .4850 | .4854 | .4857 |
| 2.2 | .4861 | .4865 | .4868 | .4871 | .4875 | .4878 | .4881 | .4884 | .4887 | .4890 |
| 2.3 | .4893 | .4896 | .4898 | .4901 | .4904 | .4906 | .4909 | .4911 | .4913 | .4916 |
| 2.4 | .4918 | .4920 | .4922 | .4925 | .4927 | .4929 | .4931 | .4932 | .4934 | .4936 |
| 2.5 | .4938 | .4940 | .4941 | .4943 | .4945 | .4946 | .4948 | .4949 | .4951 | .4952 |
| 2.6 | .4953 | .4955 | .4956 | .4957 | .4959 | .4960 | .4961 | .4962 | .4963 | .4964 |
| 2.7 | .4965 | .4966 | .4967 | .4968 | .4969 | .4970 | .4971 | .4972 | .4973 | .4974 |
| 2.8 | .4974 | .4975 | .4976 | .4977 | .4977 | .4978 | .4979 | .4980 | .4980 | .4981 |
| 2.9 | .4981 | .4982 | .4983 | .4983 | .4984 | .4984 | .4985 | .4985 | .4986 | .4986 |
| 3.0 | .49865 | .4987 | .4987 | .4988 | .4988 | .4989 | .4989 | .4989 | .4990 | .4990 |
| 3.1 | .49903 | .4991 | .4991 | .4991 | .4992 | .4992 | .4992 | .4992 | .4993 | .4993 |
| 3.2 | .49931 | .4993 | .4994 | .4994 | .4994 | .4994 | .4994 | .4995 | .4995 | .4995 |
| 3.3 | .49952 | .4995 | .4995 | .4996 | .4996 | .4996 | .4996 | .4996 | .4996 | .4997 |
| 3.4 | .49966 | .4997 | .4997 | .4997 | .4997 | .4997 | .4997 | .4997 | .4997 | .4998 |
| 3.5 | .49977 | | | | | | | | | |

# Table 2   Percentage points of the t-distribution

The values of t given in the body of the table have a probability α of being exceeded for *v* degrees of freedom.

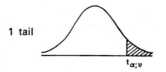

1 tail   $t_{\alpha;v}$

| α | 1 tail 0.10 | 0.05 | 0.025 | 0.01 | 0.005 | 0.001 | 0.0005 |
|---|---|---|---|---|---|---|---|
| *v* | 2 tail 0.20 | 0.10 | 0.050 | 0.02 | 0.010 | 0.002 | 0.0010 |
| 1 | 3.078 | 6.314 | 12.706 | 31.821 | 63.657 | 318.31 | 636.62 |
| 2 | 1.886 | 2.920 | 4.303 | 6.965 | 9.925 | 22.326 | 31.598 |
| 3 | 1.638 | 2.353 | 3.182 | 4.541 | 5.841 | 10.213 | 12.924 |
| 4 | 1.533 | 2.132 | 2.776 | 3.747 | 4.604 | 7.173 | 2.610 |
| 5 | 1.476 | 2.015 | 2.571 | 3.365 | 4.032 | 5.893 | 6.869 |
| 6 | 1.440 | 1.943 | 2.447 | 3.143 | 3.707 | 5.208 | 5.959 |
| 7 | 1.415 | 1.895 | 2.365 | 2.998 | 3.499 | 2.785 | 5.408 |
| 8 | 1.397 | 1.860 | 3.306 | 2.896 | 3.355 | 4.501 | 5.041 |
| 9 | 1.383 | 1.833 | 2.262 | 2.821 | 3.250 | 4.297 | 4.781 |
| 10 | 1.372 | 1.812 | 2.228 | 2.764 | 3.169 | 4.144 | 4.587 |
| 11 | 1.363 | 1.796 | 2.201 | 2.718 | 3.106 | 4.025 | 4.437 |
| 12 | 1.356 | 1.782 | 2.179 | 2.681 | 3.055 | 3.930 | 4.318 |
| 13 | 1.350 | 1.771 | 2.160 | 2.650 | 3.012 | 3.852 | 4.221 |
| 14 | 1.345 | 1.761 | 2.145 | 2.624 | 2.977 | 3.787 | 4.140 |
| 15 | 1.341 | 1.753 | 2.131 | 2.602 | 2.947 | 3.733 | 4.073 |
| 16 | 1.337 | 1.746 | 2.120 | 2.583 | 2.921 | 3.686 | 4.015 |
| 17 | 1.333 | 1.740 | 2.110 | 2.567 | 2.898 | 3.646 | 3.965 |
| 18 | 1.330 | 1.734 | 2.101 | 2.552 | 2.878 | 3.610 | 3.922 |
| 19 | 1.328 | 1.729 | 2.093 | 2.539 | 2.861 | 3.579 | 3.883 |
| 20 | 1.325 | 1.725 | 2.086 | 2.528 | 2.845 | 3.552 | 3.850 |
| 21 | 1.323 | 1.721 | 2.080 | 2.518 | 2.831 | 3.527 | 3.819 |
| 22 | 1.321 | 1.717 | 2.074 | 2.508 | 2.819 | 3.505 | 3.792 |
| 23 | 1.319 | 1.714 | 2.069 | 2.500 | 2.807 | 3.485 | 3.767 |
| 24 | 1.318 | 1.711 | 2.064 | 2.492 | 2.797 | 3.467 | 3.745 |
| 25 | 1.316 | 1.708 | 2.060 | 2.485 | 2.787 | 3.450 | 3.725 |
| 26 | 1.315 | 1.706 | 2.056 | 2.479 | 2.779 | 3.435 | 3.707 |
| 27 | 1.314 | 1.703 | 2.052 | 2.473 | 2.771 | 3.421 | 3.690 |
| 28 | 1.313 | 1.701 | 2.048 | 2.467 | 2.763 | 3.408 | 3.674 |
| 29 | 1.311 | 1.699 | 2.045 | 2.462 | 2.756 | 3.396 | 3.659 |
| 30 | 1.310 | 1.697 | 2.042 | 2.457 | 2.750 | 3.385 | 3.646 |
| 40 | 1.303 | 1.684 | 2.021 | 2.423 | 2.704 | 3.307 | 3.551 |
| 60 | 1.296 | 1.671 | 2.000 | 2.390 | 2.660 | 3.232 | 3.460 |
| 120 | 1.289 | 1.658 | 1.980 | 2.358 | 2.617 | 3.160 | 3.373 |
| ∞ | 1.282 | 1.645 | 1.960 | 2.326 | 2.576 | 3.090 | 3.291 |

# Table 3  The chi-squared distribution ($\chi^2$)

|  |  | Probability level % | | | | | |
|---|---|---|---|---|---|---|---|
|  |  | 99 | 95 | 10 | 5 | 1 | 0.1 |
| | 1 | 0.0³157 | 0.00393 | 2.71 | 3.84 | 6.63 | 10.83 |
| | 2 | 0.0201 | 0.103 | 4.61 | 5.99 | 9.21 | 13.81 |
| | 3 | 0.115 | 0.352 | 6.25 | 7.81 | 11.34 | 16.27 |
| | 4 | 0.297 | 0.711 | 7.78 | 9.49 | 13.28 | 18.47 |
| | 5 | 0.554 | 1.15 | 9.24 | 11.07 | 15.09 | 20.52 |
| | 6 | 0.872 | 1.64 | 10.64 | 12.59 | 16.81 | 22.46 |
| | 7 | 1.24 | 2.17 | 12.02 | 14.07 | 18.48 | 24.32 |
| | 8 | 1.65 | 2.73 | 13.36 | 15.51 | 20.09 | 26.12 |
| | 9 | 2.09 | 3.33 | 14.68 | 16.92 | 21.67 | 27.88 |
| | 10 | 2.56 | 3.94 | 15.99 | 18.31 | 23.21 | 29.59 |
| | 11 | 3.05 | 4.57 | 17.28 | 19.68 | 24.73 | 31.26 |
| | 12 | 3.57 | 5.23 | 18.55 | 21.03 | 26.22 | 32.91 |
| | 13 | 4.11 | 5.89 | 19.81 | 22.36 | 27.69 | 34.53 |
| Degrees of freedom | 14 | 4.66 | 6.57 | 21.06 | 23.68 | 29.14 | 36.12 |
| | 15 | 5.23 | 7.26 | 22.31 | 25.00 | 30.58 | 37.70 |
| | 16 | 5.81 | 7.96 | 23.54 | 26.30 | 32.00 | 39.25 |
| | 17 | 6.41 | 8.67 | 24.77 | 27.59 | 33.41 | 40.79 |
| | 18 | 7.01 | 9.39 | 25.99 | 28.87 | 34.81 | 42.31 |
| | 19 | 7.63 | 10.12 | 27.20 | 30.14 | 36.19 | 43.82 |
| | 20 | 8.26 | 10.85 | 28.41 | 31.41 | 37.57 | 45.31 |
| | 21 | 8.90 | 11.59 | 29.62 | 32.67 | 38.93 | 46.80 |
| | 22 | 9.54 | 12.34 | 30.81 | 33.92 | 40.29 | 48.27 |
| | 23 | 10.20 | 13.09 | 32.01 | 35.17 | 41.64 | 49.73 |
| | 24 | 10.86 | 13.85 | 33.20 | 36.42 | 42.98 | 51.18 |
| | 25 | 11.52 | 14.61 | 34.38 | 37.65 | 44.31 | 52.62 |
| | 26 | 12.20 | 15.38 | 35.56 | 38.89 | 45.64 | 54.05 |
| | 27 | 12.88 | 16.15 | 36.74 | 30.11 | 46.96 | 55.48 |
| | 28 | 13.56 | 16.93 | 37.92 | 41.34 | 48.28 | 56.89 |
| | 29 | 14.26 | 17.71 | 39.09 | 42.56 | 49.59 | 58.30 |
| | 30 | 14.95 | 18.49 | 40.26 | 43.77 | 50.89 | 59.70 |
| | 40 | 22.16 | 26.51 | 51.81 | 55.76 | 63.69 | 73.40 |
| | 50 | 29.71 | 34.76 | 63.17 | 67.50 | 76.15 | 86.66 |
| | 60 | 37.48 | 43.19 | 74.40 | 79.08 | 88.38 | 99.61 |
| | 70 | 45.44 | 51.74 | 85.53 | 90.53 | 100.4 | 112.3 |
| | 80 | 53.54 | 60.39 | 96.58 | 101.9 | 112.3 | 124.8 |
| | 90 | 61.75 | 69.13 | 107.6 | 113.1 | 124.1 | 137.2 |
| | 100 | 70.06 | 77.93 | 118.5 | 124.3 | 135.8 | 149.4 |

The entry in the table is the value of $\chi^2$ which would be exceeded with the given probability by random variations if the null hypothesis were true.

## Table 4  Significant value of the correlation coefficient

If the calculated value of *r* exceeds the table value of '$\alpha$, a significant correlation has been established at the $\alpha$ significance level.

| d.f. | $r_{.1}$ | $r_{.05}$ | $r_{.02}$ | $r_{.01}$ | $r_{.001}$ |
|------|------|------|------|------|------|
| 1 | .98769 | .99692 | .999507 | .999877 | .9999988 |
| 2 | .90000 | .95000 | .98000 | .990000 | .99900 |
| 3 | .8054 | .8783 | .93433 | .95873 | .99116 |
| 4 | .7293 | .8114 | .8822 | .91720 | .97406 |
| 5 | .6694 | .7545 | .8329 | .8745 | .95074 |
| 6 | .6215 | .7067 | .7887 | .8343 | .92493 |
| 7 | .5822 | .6664 | .7498 | .7977 | .8982 |
| 8 | .5494 | .6319 | .7155 | .7646 | .8721 |
| 9 | .5214 | .6021 | .6851 | .7348 | .8471 |
| 10 | .4973 | .5760 | .6581 | .7079 | .8233 |
| 11 | .4762 | .5529 | .6339 | .6835 | .8010 |
| 12 | .4575 | .5324 | .6120 | .6614 | .7800 |
| 13 | .4409 | .5139 | .5923 | .6411 | .7603 |
| 14 | .4259 | .4973 | .5742 | .6226 | .7420 |
| 15 | .4124 | .4821 | .5577 | .6055 | .7246 |
| 16 | .4000 | .4683 | .5425 | .5897 | .7084 |
| 17 | .3887 | .4555 | .5285 | .5751 | .6932 |
| 18 | .3783 | .4438 | .5155 | .5614 | .6787 |
| 19 | .3687 | .4329 | .5034 | .5487 | .6652 |
| 20 | .3598 | .4227 | .4921 | .5368 | .6524 |
| 25 | .3233 | .3809 | .4451 | .4869 | .5974 |
| 30 | .2960 | .3494 | .4093 | .4487 | .5541 |
| 35 | .2746 | .3246 | .3810 | .4182 | .5189 |
| 40 | .2573 | .3044 | .3578 | .3932 | .4896 |
| 45 | .2428 | .2875 | .3384 | .3721 | .4648 |
| 50 | .2306 | .2732 | .3218 | .3541 | .4433 |
| 60 | .2108 | .2500 | .2948 | .3248 | .4078 |
| 70 | .1954 | .2319 | .2737 | .3017 | .3799 |
| 80 | .1829 | .2172 | .2565 | .2830 | .3568 |
| 90 | .1726 | .2050 | .2422 | .2673 | .3375 |
| 100 | .1638 | .1946 | .2301 | .2540 | .3211 |

d.f. = degrees of freedom

## Table 5  The F-distribution

0.01 level

| Degrees of freedom (denominator) | Degrees of freedom (numerator) | | | | | | | | | | | |
|---|---|---|---|---|---|---|---|---|---|---|---|---|
| | 1 | 2 | 3 | 4 | 5 | 6 | 7 | 8 | 10 | 12 | 24 | ∞ |
| 1 | 4052 | 5000 | 5403 | 5625 | 5764 | 5859 | 5928 | 5981 | 6056 | 6106 | 6235 | 6366 |
| 2 | 98.5 | 99.0 | 99.2 | 99.2 | 99.3 | 99.3 | 99.4 | 99.4 | 99.4 | 99.4 | 99.5 | 99.5 |
| 3 | 34.1 | 30.8 | 29.5 | 28.7 | 28.2 | 27.9 | 27.7 | 27.5 | 27.2 | 27.1 | 26.6 | 26.1 |
| 4 | 21.2 | 18.0 | 16.7 | 16.0 | 15.5 | 15.2 | 15.0 | 14.8 | 14.5 | 14.4 | 13.9 | 13.5 |
| 5 | 16.26 | 13.27 | 12.06 | 11.39 | 10.97 | 10.67 | 10.46 | 10.29 | 10.05 | 9.89 | 9.47 | 9.02 |
| 6 | 13.74 | 10.92 | 9.78 | 9.15 | 8.75 | 8.47 | 8.26 | 8.10 | 7.87 | 7.72 | 7.31 | 6.88 |
| 7 | 12.25 | 9.55 | 8.45 | 7.85 | 7.46 | 7.19 | 6.99 | 6.84 | 6.62 | 6.47 | 6.07 | 5.65 |
| 8 | 11.26 | 8.65 | 7.59 | 7.01 | 6.63 | 6.37 | 6.18 | 6.03 | 5.81 | 5.67 | 5.28 | 4.86 |
| 9 | 10.56 | 8.02 | 6.99 | 6.42 | 6.06 | 5.80 | 5.61 | 5.47 | 5.26 | 5.11 | 4.73 | 4.31 |
| 10 | 10.04 | 7.56 | 6.55 | 5.99 | 5.64 | 5.39 | 5.20 | 5.06 | 4.85 | 4.71 | 4.33 | 3.91 |
| 11 | 9.65 | 7.21 | 6.22 | 5.67 | 5.32 | 5.07 | 4.89 | 4.74 | 4.54 | 4.40 | 4.02 | 3.60 |
| 12 | 9.33 | 6.93 | 5.95 | 5.41 | 5.06 | 4.82 | 4.64 | 4.50 | 4.30 | 4.16 | 3.78 | 3.36 |
| 13 | 9.07 | 6.70 | 5.74 | 5.21 | 4.86 | 4.62 | 4.44 | 4.30 | 4.10 | 3.96 | 3.59 | 3.17 |
| 14 | 8.86 | 6.51 | 5.56 | 5.04 | 4.70 | 4.46 | 4.28 | 4.14 | 3.94 | 3.80 | 3.43 | 3.00 |
| 15 | 8.68 | 6.36 | 5.42 | 4.89 | 4.56 | 4.32 | 4.14 | 4.00 | 3.80 | 3.67 | 3.29 | 2.87 |
| 16 | 8.53 | 6.23 | 5.29 | 4.77 | 4.44 | 4.20 | 4.03 | 3.89 | 3.69 | 3.55 | 3.18 | 2.75 |
| 16 | 8.40 | 6.11 | 5.18 | 4.67 | 4.34 | 4.10 | 3.93 | 3.79 | 3.59 | 3.46 | 3.08 | 2.65 |
| 18 | 8.29 | 6.01 | 5.09 | 4.58 | 4.25 | 4.01 | 3.84 | 3.71 | 3.51 | 3.37 | 3.00 | 2.57 |
| 19 | 8.18 | 5.93 | 5.01 | 4.50 | 4.17 | 3.94 | 3.77 | 3.63 | 3.43 | 3.30 | 2.92 | 2.49 |
| 20 | 8.10 | 5.85 | 4.94 | 4.43 | 4.10 | 3.87 | 3.70 | 3.56 | 3.37 | 3.23 | 2.86 | 2.42 |
| 21 | 8.02 | 5.78 | 4.87 | 4.37 | 4.04 | 3.81 | 3.64 | 3.51 | 3.31 | 3.17 | 2.80 | 2.36 |
| 22 | 7.95 | 5.72 | 4.82 | 4.31 | 3.99 | 3.76 | 3.59 | 3.45 | 3.26 | 3.12 | 2.75 | 2.31 |

**Table 5 (contd)**

| Degrees of freedom (denominator) | Degrees of freedom (numerator) | | | | | | | | | | | |
|---|---|---|---|---|---|---|---|---|---|---|---|---|
| | 1 | 2 | 3 | 4 | 5 | 6 | 7 | 8 | 10 | 12 | 24 | ∞ |
| 23 | 7.88 | 5.66 | 4.76 | 4.26 | 3.94 | 3.71 | 3.54 | 3.41 | 3.21 | 3.07 | 2.70 | 2.26 |
| 24 | 7.82 | 5.61 | 4.72 | 4.22 | 3.90 | 3.67 | 3.50 | 3.36 | 3.17 | 3.03 | 2.66 | 2.21 |
| 25 | 7.77 | 5.57 | 4.68 | 4.18 | 3.86 | 3.63 | 3.46 | 3.32 | 3.13 | 2.99 | 2.62 | 2.17 |
| 26 | 7.72 | 5.53 | 4.64 | 4.14 | 3.82 | 3.59 | 3.42 | 3.29 | 3.09 | 2.96 | 2.58 | 2.13 |
| 27 | 7.68 | 5.49 | 4.60 | 4.11 | 3.78 | 3.56 | 3.39 | 3.26 | 3.06 | 2.93 | 2.55 | 2.10 |
| 28 | 7.64 | 5.45 | 4.57 | 4.07 | 3.75 | 3.53 | 3.36 | 3.23 | 3.03 | 2.90 | 2.52 | 2.06 |
| 29 | 7.60 | 5.42 | 4.54 | 4.04 | 3.73 | 3.50 | 3.33 | 3.20 | 3.00 | 2.87 | 2.49 | 2.03 |
| 30 | 7.56 | 5.39 | 4.51 | 4.02 | 3.70 | 3.47 | 3.30 | 3.17 | 2.98 | 2.84 | 2.47 | 2.01 |
| 32 | 7.50 | 5.34 | 4.46 | 3.97 | 3.65 | 3.43 | 3.26 | 3.13 | 2.93 | 2.80 | 2.42 | 1.96 |
| 34 | 7.45 | 5.29 | 4.42 | 3.93 | 3.61 | 3.39 | 3.22 | 3.09 | 2.90 | 2.76 | 2.38 | 1.91 |
| 36 | 7.40 | 5.25 | 4.38 | 3.89 | 3.58 | 3.35 | 3.18 | 3.05 | 2.86 | 2.72 | 2.35 | 1.87 |
| 38 | 7.35 | 5.21 | 4.34 | 3.86 | 3.54 | 3.32 | 3.15 | 3.02 | 2.83 | 2.69 | 2.32 | 1.84 |
| 40 | 7.31 | 5.18 | 4.31 | 3.83 | 3.51 | 3.29 | 3.12 | 2.99 | 2.80 | 2.66 | 2.29 | 1.80 |
| 60 | 7.08 | 4.98 | 4.13 | 3.65 | 3.34 | 3.12 | 2.95 | 2.82 | 2.63 | 2.50 | 2.12 | 1.60 |
| 120 | 6.85 | 4.79 | 3.95 | 3.48 | 3.17 | 2.96 | 2.79 | 2.66 | 2.47 | 2.34 | 1.95 | 1.38 |
| ∞ | 6.63 | 4.61 | 3.78 | 3.32 | 3.02 | 2.80 | 2.64 | 2.51 | 2.32 | 2.18 | 1.79 | 1.00 |

Values of $F$ which would be exceeded with only 1% probability by random variations if the null hypothesis were true. They are valid for two-tailed tests.

**Table 5 (contd)**

0.05 level

| Degrees of freedom (denominator) | Degrees of freedom (numerator) | | | | | | | | | | | |
|---|---|---|---|---|---|---|---|---|---|---|---|---|
| | 1 | 2 | 3 | 4 | 5 | 6 | 7 | 8 | 10 | 12 | 24 | ∞ |
| 1 | 161.4 | 199.5 | 215.7 | 224.6 | 230.2 | 234.0 | 236.8 | 238.9 | 241.9 | 243.9 | 249.0 | 254.3 |
| 2 | 18.5 | 19.0 | 19.2 | 19.2 | 19.3 | 19.3 | 19.4 | 19.4 | 19.4 | 19.4 | 19.5 | 19.5 |
| 3 | 10.13 | 9.55 | 9.28 | 9.12 | 9.01 | 8.94 | 8.89 | 8.85 | 8.79 | 8.74 | 8.64 | 8.53 |
| 4 | 7.71 | 6.94 | 6.59 | 6.39 | 6.26 | 6.16 | 6.09 | 6.04 | 5.96 | 5.91 | 5.77 | 5.63 |
| 5 | 6.61 | 5.79 | 5.41 | 5.19 | 5.05 | 4.95 | 4.88 | 4.82 | 4.74 | 4.68 | 4.53 | 4.36 |
| 6 | 5.99 | 5.14 | 4.76 | 4.53 | 4.39 | 4.28 | 4.21 | 4.15 | 4.06 | 4.00 | 3.84 | 3.67 |
| 7 | 5.59 | 4.74 | 4.35 | 4.12 | 3.97 | 3.87 | 3.79 | 3.73 | 3.64 | 3.57 | 3.41 | 3.23 |
| 8 | 5.32 | 4.46 | 4.07 | 3.84 | 3.69 | 3.58 | 3.50 | 3.44 | 3.35 | 3.28 | 3.12 | 2.93 |
| 9 | 5.12 | 4.26 | 3.86 | 3.63 | 3.48 | 3.37 | 3.29 | 3.23 | 3.14 | 3.07 | 2.90 | 2.71 |
| 10 | 4.96 | 4.10 | 3.71 | 3.48 | 3.33 | 3.22 | 3.14 | 3.07 | 2.98 | 2.91 | 2.74 | 2.54 |
| 11 | 4.84 | 3.98 | 3.59 | 3.36 | 3.20 | 3.09 | 3.01 | 2.95 | 2.85 | 2.79 | 2.61 | 2.40 |
| 12 | 4.75 | 3.89 | 3.49 | 3.26 | 3.11 | 3.00 | 2.91 | 2.85 | 2.75 | 2.69 | 2.51 | 2.30 |
| 13 | 4.67 | 3.81 | 3.41 | 3.18 | 3.03 | 2.92 | 2.83 | 2.77 | 2.67 | 2.60 | 2.42 | 2.21 |
| 14 | 4.60 | 3.74 | 3.34 | 3.11 | 2.96 | 2.85 | 2.76 | 2.70 | 2.60 | 2.53 | 2.35 | 2.13 |
| 15 | 4.54 | 3.68 | 3.29 | 3.06 | 2.90 | 2.79 | 2.71 | 2.64 | 2.54 | 2.48 | 2.29 | 2.07 |
| 16 | 4.49 | 3.63 | 3.24 | 3.01 | 2.85 | 2.74 | 2.66 | 2.59 | 2.49 | 2.42 | 2.24 | 2.01 |
| 17 | 4.45 | 3.59 | 3.20 | 2.96 | 2.81 | 2.70 | 2.61 | 2.55 | 2.45 | 2.38 | 2.19 | 1.96 |
| 18 | 4.41 | 3.55 | 3.16 | 2.93 | 2.77 | 2.66 | 2.58 | 2.51 | 2.41 | 2.34 | 2.15 | 1.92 |
| 19 | 4.38 | 3.52 | 3.13 | 2.90 | 2.74 | 2.63 | 2.54 | 2.48 | 2.38 | 2.31 | 2.11 | 1.88 |
| 20 | 4.35 | 3.49 | 3.10 | 2.87 | 2.71 | 2.60 | 2.51 | 2.45 | 2.35 | 2.28 | 2.08 | 1.84 |
| 21 | 4.32 | 3.47 | 3.07 | 2.84 | 2.68 | 2.57 | 2.49 | 2.42 | 2.32 | 2.25 | 2.05 | 1.81 |
| 22 | 4.30 | 3.44 | 3.05 | 2.82 | 2.66 | 2.55 | 2.46 | 2.40 | 2.30 | 2.23 | 2.03 | 1.78 |

Table 5 (contd)

| Degrees of freedom (denominator) | Degrees of freedom (numerator) | | | | | | | | | | | |
|---|---|---|---|---|---|---|---|---|---|---|---|---|
| | 1 | 2 | 3 | 4 | 5 | 6 | 7 | 8 | 10 | 12 | 24 | ∞ |
| 23 | 4.28 | 3.42 | 3.03 | 2.80 | 2.64 | 2.53 | 2.44 | 2.37 | 2.27 | 2.20 | 2.00 | 1.76 |
| 24 | 4.26 | 3.40 | 3.01 | 2.78 | 2.62 | 2.51 | 2.42 | 2.36 | 2.25 | 2.18 | 1.98 | 1.73 |
| 25 | 4.24 | 3.39 | 2.99 | 2.76 | 2.60 | 2.49 | 2.40 | 2.34 | 2.24 | 2.16 | 1.96 | 1.71 |
| 26 | 4.23 | 3.37 | 2.98 | 2.74 | 2.59 | 2.47 | 2.39 | 2.32 | 2.22 | 2.15 | 1.95 | 1.69 |
| 27 | 4.21 | 3.35 | 2.96 | 2.73 | 2.57 | 2.46 | 2.37 | 2.31 | 2.20 | 2.13 | 1.93 | 1.67 |
| 28 | 4.20 | 3.34 | 2.95 | 2.71 | 2.56 | 2.45 | 2.36 | 2.29 | 2.19 | 2.12 | 1.91 | 1.65 |
| 29 | 4.18 | 3.33 | 2.93 | 2.70 | 2.55 | 2.43 | 2.35 | 2.28 | 2.18 | 2.10 | 1.90 | 1.64 |
| 30 | 4.17 | 3.32 | 2.92 | 2.69 | 2.53 | 2.42 | 2.33 | 2.27 | 2.16 | 2.09 | 1.89 | 1.62 |
| 32 | 4.15 | 3.29 | 2.90 | 2.67 | 2.51 | 2.40 | 2.31 | 2.24 | 2.14 | 2.07 | 1.86 | 1.59 |
| 34 | 4.13 | 3.28 | 2.88 | 2.65 | 2.49 | 2.38 | 2.29 | 2.23 | 2.12 | 2.05 | 1.84 | 1.57 |
| 36 | 4.11 | 3.26 | 2.87 | 2.63 | 2.48 | 2.36 | 2.28 | 2.21 | 2.11 | 2.03 | 1.82 | 1.55 |
| 38 | 4.10 | 3.24 | 2.85 | 2.62 | 2.46 | 2.35 | 2.26 | 2.19 | 2.09 | 2.02 | 1.81 | 1.53 |
| 40 | 4.08 | 3.23 | 2.84 | 2.61 | 2.45 | 2.34 | 2.25 | 2.18 | 2.08 | 2.00 | 1.79 | 1.51 |
| 60 | 4.00 | 3.15 | 2.76 | 2.53 | 2.37 | 2.25 | 2.17 | 2.10 | 1.99 | 1.92 | 1.70 | 1.39 |
| 120 | 3.92 | 3.07 | 2.68 | 2.45 | 2.29 | 2.18 | 2.09 | 2.02 | 1.91 | 1.83 | 1.61 | 1.25 |
| ∞ | 3.84 | 3.00 | 2.60 | 2.37 | 2.21 | 2.10 | 2.01 | 1.94 | 1.83 | 1.75 | 1.52 | 1.00 |

Values of $F$ which would be exceeded with only 5% probability by random variations if the null hypothesis were true. They are valid for two-tailed tests.

# Table 6 The poisson distribution

| | | | | | *m* | | | | | |
|---|---|---|---|---|---|---|---|---|---|---|
| χ | 0.1 | 0.2 | 0.3 | 0.4 | 0.5 | 0.6 | 0.7 | 0.8 | 0.9 | 1.0 |
| 0 | .9048 | .8187 | .7408 | .6703 | .6065 | .5488 | .4966 | .4493 | .4066 | .3679 |
| 1 | .0905 | .1637 | .2222 | .2681 | .3033 | .3293 | .3476 | .3595 | .3659 | .3679 |
| 2 | .0045 | .0164 | .0333 | .0536 | .0758 | .0988 | .1217 | .1438 | .1647 | .1839 |
| 3 | .0002 | .0011 | .0033 | .0072 | .0126 | .0198 | .0284 | .0383 | .0494 | .0613 |
| 4 | .0000 | .0001 | .0002 | .0007 | .0016 | .0030 | .0050 | .0077 | .0111 | .0153 |
| 5 | .0000 | .0000 | .0000 | .0001 | .0002 | .0004 | .0007 | .0012 | .0020 | .0031 |
| 6 | .0000 | .0000 | .0000 | .0000 | .0000 | .0000 | .0001 | .0002 | .0003 | .0005 |
| 7 | .0000 | .0000 | .0000 | .0000 | .0000 | .0000 | .0000 | .0000 | .0000 | .0001 |

| | | | | | *m* | | | | | |
|---|---|---|---|---|---|---|---|---|---|---|
| χ | 1.1 | 1.2 | 1.3 | 1.4 | 1.5 | 1.6 | 1.7 | 1.8 | 1.9 | 2.0 |
| 0 | .3329 | .3012 | .2725 | .2466 | .2231 | .2019 | .1827 | .1653 | .1496 | .1353 |
| 1 | .3662 | .3614 | .3543 | .3452 | .3347 | .3230 | .3106 | .2975 | .2842 | .2707 |
| 2 | .2014 | .2169 | .2303 | .2417 | .2510 | .2584 | .2640 | .2678 | .2700 | .2707 |
| 3 | .0738 | .0867 | .0998 | .1128 | .1255 | .1378 | .1496 | .1607 | .1710 | .1804 |
| 4 | .0203 | .0260 | .0324 | .0395 | .0471 | .0551 | .0636 | .0723 | .0812 | .0902 |
| 5 | .0045 | .0062 | .0084 | .0111 | .0141 | .0176 | .0216 | .0260 | .0309 | .0361 |
| 6 | .0008 | .0012 | .0018 | .0026 | .0035 | .0047 | .0061 | .0078 | .0098 | .0120 |
| 7 | .0001 | .0002 | .0003 | .0005 | .0008 | .0011 | .0015 | .0020 | .0027 | .0034 |
| 8 | .0000 | .0000 | .0001 | .0001 | .0001 | .0002 | .0003 | .0005 | .0006 | .0009 |
| 9 | .0000 | .0000 | .0000 | .0000 | .0000 | .0000 | .0001 | .0001 | .0001 | .0002 |

| | | | | | *m* | | | | | |
|---|---|---|---|---|---|---|---|---|---|---|
| χ | 2.1 | 2.2 | 2.3 | 2.4 | 2.5 | 2.6 | 2.7 | 2.8 | 2.9 | 3.0 |
| 0 | .1225 | .1108 | .1003 | .0907 | .0821 | .0743 | .0672 | .0608 | .0550 | .0498 |
| 1 | .2572 | .2438 | .2306 | .2177 | .2052 | .1931 | .1815 | .1703 | .1596 | .1494 |
| 2 | .2700 | .2681 | .2652 | .2613 | .2565 | .2510 | .2450 | .2384 | .2314 | .2240 |
| 3 | .1890 | .1966 | .2033 | .2090 | .2138 | .2176 | .2205 | .2225 | .2237 | .2240 |
| 4 | .0992 | .1082 | .1169 | .1254 | .1336 | .1414 | .1488 | .1557 | .1622 | .1680 |
| 5 | .0417 | .0476 | .0538 | .0602 | .0668 | .0735 | .0804 | .0872 | .0940 | .1008 |
| 6 | .0146 | .0174 | .0206 | .0241 | .0278 | .0319 | .0362 | .0407 | .0455 | .0504 |
| 7 | .0044 | .0055 | .0068 | .0083 | .0099 | .0118 | .0139 | .0163 | .0188 | .0216 |
| 8 | .0011 | .0015 | .0019 | .0025 | .0031 | .0038 | .0047 | .0057 | .0068 | .0081 |
| 9 | .0003 | .0004 | .0005 | .0007 | .0009 | .0011 | .0014 | .0018 | .0022 | .0027 |
| 10 | .0001 | .0001 | .0001 | .0002 | .0002 | .0003 | .0004 | .0005 | .0006 | .0008 |
| 11 | .0000 | .0000 | .0000 | .0000 | .0000 | .0001 | .0001 | .0001 | .0002 | .0002 |
| 12 | .0000 | .0000 | .0000 | .0000 | .0000 | .0000 | .0000 | .0000 | .0000 | .0001 |

Entries in the table give the probabilities that an event will occur χ times when the average number of occurrences is *m*.

**Table 6 (contd)**

| χ | 3.1 | 3.2 | 3.3 | 3.4 | 3.5 | 3.6 | 3.7 | 3.8 | 3.9 | 4.0 |
|---|-----|-----|-----|-----|-----|-----|-----|-----|-----|-----|
|   |     |     |     |     |  *m* |     |     |     |     |     |
| 0 | .0450 | .0408 | .0369 | .0334 | .0302 | .0273 | .0247 | .0224 | .0202 | .0183 |
| 1 | .1397 | .1304 | .1217 | .1135 | .1057 | .0984 | .0915 | .0850 | .0789 | .0733 |
| 2 | .2165 | .2087 | .2008 | .1929 | .1850 | .1771 | .1692 | .1615 | .1539 | .1465 |
| 3 | .2237 | .2226 | .2209 | .2186 | .2158 | .2125 | .2087 | .2046 | .2001 | .1954 |
| 4 | .1734 | .1781 | .1823 | .1858 | .1888 | .1912 | .1931 | .1944 | .1951 | .1954 |
| 5 | .1075 | .1140 | .1203 | .1264 | .1322 | .1377 | .1429 | .1477 | .1522 | .1563 |
| 6 | .0555 | .0608 | .0662 | .0716 | .0771 | .0826 | .0881 | .0936 | .0989 | .1042 |
| 7 | .0246 | .0278 | .0312 | .0348 | .0385 | .0425 | .0466 | .0508 | .0551 | .0595 |
| 8 | .0095 | .0111 | .0129 | .0148 | .0169 | .0191 | .0215 | .0241 | .0269 | .0298 |
| 9 | .0033 | .0040 | .0047 | .0056 | .0066 | .0076 | .0089 | .0102 | .0116 | .0132 |
| 10 | .0010 | .0013 | .0016 | .0019 | .0023 | .0028 | .0033 | .0039 | .0045 | .0053 |
| 11 | .0003 | .0004 | .0005 | .0006 | .0007 | .0009 | .0011 | .0013 | .0016 | .0019 |
| 12 | .0001 | .0001 | .0001 | .0002 | .0002 | .0003 | .0003 | .0004 | .0005 | .0006 |
| 13 | .0000 | .0000 | .0000 | .0000 | .0001 | .0001 | .0001 | .0001 | .0002 | .0002 |
| 14 | .0000 | .0000 | .0000 | .0000 | .0000 | .0000 | .0000 | .0000 | .0000 | .0001 |

| χ | 4.1 | 4.2 | 4.3 | 4.4 | 4.5 | 4.6 | 4.7 | 4.8 | 4.9 | 5.0 |
|---|-----|-----|-----|-----|-----|-----|-----|-----|-----|-----|
|   |     |     |     |     |  *m* |     |     |     |     |     |
| 0 | .9166 | .0150 | .0136 | .0123 | .0111 | .0101 | .0091 | .0082 | .0074 | .0067 |
| 1 | .0679 | .0630 | .0583 | .0540 | .0500 | .0462 | .0427 | .0395 | .0365 | .0337 |
| 2 | .1393 | .1323 | .1254 | .1188 | .1125 | .1063 | .1005 | .0948 | .0894 | .0842 |
| 3 | .1904 | .1852 | .1798 | .1743 | .1687 | .1631 | .1574 | .1517 | .1460 | .1404 |
| 4 | .1951 | .1944 | .1933 | .1917 | .1898 | .1875 | .1849 | .1820 | .1789 | .1755 |
| 5 | .1600 | .1633 | .1662 | .1687 | .1708 | .1725 | .1738 | .1747 | .1753 | .1755 |
| 6 | .1093 | .1143 | .1191 | .1237 | .1281 | .1323 | .1362 | .1398 | .1432 | .1462 |
| 7 | .0640 | .0686 | .0732 | .0778 | .0824 | .0869 | .0914 | .0959 | .1002 | .1044 |
| 8 | .0328 | .0360 | .0393 | .0428 | .0463 | .0500 | .0537 | .0575 | .0614 | .0653 |
| 9 | .0150 | .0168 | .0188 | .0209 | .0232 | .0255 | .0280 | .0307 | .0334 | .0363 |
| 10 | .0061 | .0071 | .0081 | .0092 | .0104 | .0118 | .0132 | .0147 | .0164 | .0181 |
| 11 | .0023 | .0027 | .0032 | .0037 | .0043 | .0049 | .0056 | .0064 | .0073 | .0082 |
| 12 | .0008 | .0009 | .0011 | .0014 | .0016 | .0019 | .0022 | .0026 | .0030 | .0034 |
| 13 | .0002 | .0003 | .0004 | .0005 | .0006 | .0007 | .0008 | .0009 | .0011 | .0013 |
| 14 | .0001 | .0001 | .0001 | .0001 | .0002 | .0002 | .0003 | .0003 | .0004 | .0005 |
| 15 | .0000 | .0000 | .0000 | .0000 | .0001 | .0001 | .0001 | .0001 | .0001 | .0002 |

Entries in the table give the probabilities that an event will occur χ times when the average number of occurrences is *m*.

**Table 6 (contd)**

| χ | 5.1 | 5.2 | 5.3 | 5.4 | 5.5 | 5.6 | 5.7 | 5.8 | 5.9 | 6.0 |
|---|-----|-----|-----|-----|-----|-----|-----|-----|-----|-----|
| 0 | .0061 | .0055 | .0050 | .0045 | .0041 | .0037 | .0033 | .0030 | .0027 | .0025 |
| 1 | .0311 | .0287 | .0265 | .0244 | .0225 | .0207 | .0191 | .0176 | .0162 | .0149 |
| 2 | .0793 | .0746 | .0701 | .0659 | .0618 | .0580 | .0544 | .0509 | .0477 | .0446 |
| 3 | .1348 | .1293 | .1239 | .1185 | .1133 | .1082 | .1033 | .0985 | .0938 | .0892 |
| 4 | .1719 | .1681 | .1641 | .1600 | .1558 | .1515 | .1472 | .1428 | .1383 | .1339 |
| 5 | .1753 | .1748 | .1740 | .1728 | .1714 | .1697 | .1678 | .1656 | .1632 | .1606 |
| 6 | .1490 | .1515 | .1537 | .1555 | .1571 | .1584 | .1594 | .1601 | .1605 | .1606 |
| 7 | .1086 | .1125 | .1163 | .1200 | .1234 | .1267 | .1298 | .1326 | .1353 | .1377 |
| 8 | .0692 | .0731 | .0771 | .0810 | .0849 | .0887 | .0925 | .0962 | .0998 | .1033 |
| 9 | .0392 | .0423 | .0454 | .0486 | .0519 | .0552 | .0586 | .0620 | .0654 | .0688 |
| 10 | .0200 | .0220 | .0241 | .0262 | .0285 | .0309 | .0334 | .0359 | .0386 | .0413 |
| 11 | .0093 | .0104 | .0116 | .0129 | .0143 | .0157 | .0173 | .0190 | .0207 | .0225 |
| 12 | .0039 | .0045 | .0051 | .0058 | .0065 | .0073 | .0082 | .0092 | .0102 | .0113 |
| 13 | .0015 | .0018 | .0021 | .0024 | .0028 | .0032 | .0036 | .0041 | .0046 | .0052 |
| 14 | .0006 | .0007 | .0008 | .0009 | .0011 | .0013 | .0015 | .0017 | .0019 | .0022 |
| 15 | .0002 | .0002 | .0003 | .0003 | .0004 | .0005 | .0006 | .0007 | .0008 | .0009 |
| 16 | .0001 | .0001 | .0001 | .0001 | .0001 | .0002 | .0002 | .0002 | .0003 | .0003 |
| 17 | .0000 | .0000 | .0000 | .0000 | .0000 | .0001 | .0001 | .0001 | .0001 | .0001 |

$m$

| χ | 6.1 | 6.2 | 6.3 | 6.4 | 6.5 | 6.6 | 6.7 | 6.8 | 6.9 | 7.0 |
|---|-----|-----|-----|-----|-----|-----|-----|-----|-----|-----|
| 0 | .0022 | .0020 | .0018 | .0017 | .0015 | .0014 | .0012 | .0011 | .0010 | .0009 |
| 1 | .0137 | .0126 | .0116 | .0106 | .0098 | .0090 | .0082 | .0076 | .0070 | .0064 |
| 2 | .0417 | .0390 | .0364 | .0340 | .0318 | .0296 | .0276 | .0258 | .0240 | .0224 |
| 3 | .0848 | .0806 | .0765 | .0726 | .0688 | .0652 | .0617 | .0584 | .0552 | .0521 |
| 4 | .1294 | .1249 | .1205 | .1162 | .1118 | .1076 | .1034 | .0992 | .0952 | .0912 |
| 5 | .1579 | .1549 | .1519 | .1487 | .1454 | .1420 | .1385 | .1349 | .1314 | .1277 |
| 6 | .1605 | .1601 | .1595 | .1586 | .1575 | .1562 | .1546 | .1529 | .1511 | .1490 |
| 7 | .1399 | .1418 | .1435 | .1450 | .1462 | .1472 | .1480 | .1486 | .1489 | .1490 |
| 8 | .1066 | .1099 | .1130 | .1160 | .1188 | .1215 | .1240 | .1263 | .1284 | .1304 |
| 9 | .0723 | .0757 | .0791 | .0825 | .0858 | .0891 | .0923 | .0954 | .0985 | .1014 |
| 10 | .0441 | .0469 | .0498 | .0528 | .0558 | .0588 | .0618 | .0649 | .0679 | .0710 |
| 11 | .0245 | .0265 | .0285 | .0307 | .0330 | .0353 | .0377 | .0401 | .0426 | .0452 |
| 12 | .0124 | .0137 | .0150 | .0164 | .0179 | .0194 | .0210 | .0227 | .0245 | .0264 |
| 13 | .0058 | .0065 | .0073 | .0081 | .0089 | .0098 | .0108 | .0119 | .0130 | .0142 |
| 14 | .0025 | .0029 | .0033 | .0037 | .0041 | .0046 | .0052 | .0058 | .0064 | .0071 |
| 15 | .0010 | .0012 | .0014 | .0010 | .0018 | .0020 | .0023 | .0026 | .0029 | .0033 |
| 16 | .0004 | .0005 | .0005 | .0006 | .0007 | .0008 | .0010 | .0011 | .0013 | .0014 |
| 17 | .0001 | .0002 | .0002 | .0002 | .0003 | .0003 | .0004 | .0004 | .0005 | .0006 |
| 18 | .0000 | .0001 | .0001 | .0001 | .0001 | .0001 | .0001 | .0002 | .0002 | .0002 |
| 19 | .0000 | .0000 | .0000 | .0000 | .0000 | .0000 | .0000 | .0001 | .0001 | .0001 |

Entries in the table give the probabilities that an event will occur χ times when the average number of occurrences is $m$.

**Table 6 (contd)**

| χ | | | | | *m* | | | | | |
|---|------|------|------|------|------|------|------|------|------|------|
| | **7.1** | **7.2** | **7.3** | **7.4** | **7.5** | **7.6** | **7.7** | **7.8** | **7.9** | **8.0** |
| 0 | .0008 | .0007 | .0007 | .0006 | .0006 | .0005 | .0005 | .0004 | .0004 | .0003 |
| 1 | .0059 | .0054 | .0049 | .0045 | .0041 | .0038 | .0035 | .0032 | .0029 | .0027 |
| 2 | .0208 | .0194 | .0180 | .0167 | .0156 | .0145 | .0134 | .0125 | .0116 | .0107 |
| 3 | .0492 | .0464 | .0438 | .0413 | .0389 | .0366 | .0345 | .0324 | .0305 | .0286 |
| 4 | .0874 | .0836 | .0799 | .0764 | .0729 | .0696 | .0663 | .0632 | .0602 | .0573 |
| 5 | .1241 | .1204 | .1167 | .1130 | .1094 | .1057 | .1021 | .0986 | .0951 | .0916 |
| 6 | .1468 | .1445 | .1420 | .1394 | .1367 | .1339 | .1311 | .1282 | .1252 | .1221 |
| 7 | .1489 | .1486 | .1481 | .1474 | .1465 | .1454 | .1442 | .1428 | .1413 | .1396 |
| 8 | .1321 | .1337 | .1351 | .1363 | .1373 | .1382 | .1388 | .1392 | .1395 | .1396 |
| 9 | .1042 | .1070 | .1096 | .1121 | .1144 | .1167 | .1187 | .1207 | .1224 | .1241 |
| 10 | .0740 | .0770 | .0800 | .0829 | .0858 | .0887 | .0914 | .0941 | .0967 | .0993 |
| 11 | .0478 | .0504 | .0531 | .0558 | .0585 | .0613 | .0640 | .0667 | .0695 | .0722 |
| 12 | .0283 | .0303 | .0323 | .0344 | .0366 | .0388 | .0411 | .0434 | .0457 | .0481 |
| 13 | .0154 | .0168 | .0181 | .0196 | .0211 | .0227 | .0243 | .0260 | .0278 | .0296 |
| 14 | .0078 | .0086 | .0095 | .0104 | .0113 | .0123 | .0134 | .0145 | .0157 | .0169 |
| 15 | .0037 | .0041 | .0046 | .0051 | .0057 | .0062 | .0069 | .0075 | .0083 | .0090 |
| 16 | .0016 | .0019 | .0021 | .0024 | .0026 | .0030 | .0033 | .0037 | .0041 | .0045 |
| 17 | .0007 | .0008 | .0009 | .0010 | .0012 | .0013 | .0015 | .0017 | .0019 | .0021 |
| 18 | .0003 | .0003 | .0004 | .0004 | .0005 | .0006 | .0006 | .0007 | .0008 | .0009 |
| 19 | .0001 | .0001 | .0001 | .0002 | .0002 | .0002 | .0003 | .0003 | .0003 | .0004 |
| 20 | .0000 | .0000 | .0001 | .0001 | .0001 | .0001 | .0001 | .0001 | .0001 | .0002 |
| 21 | .0000 | .0000 | .0000 | .0000 | .0000 | .0000 | .0000 | .0000 | .0001 | .0001 |

| χ | | | | | *m* | | | | | |
|---|------|------|------|------|------|------|------|------|------|------|
| | **8.1** | **8.2** | **8.3** | **8.4** | **8.5** | **8.6** | **8.7** | **8.8** | **8.9** | **9.0** |
| 0 | .0003 | .0003 | .0002 | .0002 | .0002 | .0002 | .0002 | .0002 | .0001 | .0001 |
| 1 | .0025 | .0023 | .0021 | .0019 | .0017 | .0016 | .0014 | .0013 | .0012 | .0011 |
| 2 | .0100 | .0092 | .0086 | .0079 | .0074 | .0068 | .0063 | .0058 | .0054 | .0050 |
| 3 | .0269 | .0252 | .0237 | .0222 | .0208 | .0195 | .0183 | .0171 | .0160 | .0150 |
| 4 | .0544 | .0517 | .0491 | .0466 | .0443 | .0420 | .0398 | .0377 | .0357 | .0337 |
| 5 | .0882 | .0849 | .0816 | .0784 | .0752 | .0722 | .0692 | .0663 | .0635 | .0607 |
| 6 | .1191 | .1160 | .1128 | .1097 | .1066 | .1034 | .1003 | .0972 | .0941 | .0911 |
| 7 | .1378 | .1358 | .1338 | .1317 | .1294 | .1271 | .1247 | .1222 | .1197 | .1171 |
| 8 | .1395 | .1392 | .1388 | .1382 | .1375 | .1366 | .1356 | .1344 | .1332 | .1318 |
| 9 | .1256 | .1269 | .1280 | .1290 | .1299 | .1306 | .1311 | .1315 | .1317 | .1318 |
| 10 | .1017 | .1040 | .1063 | .1084 | .1104 | .1123 | .1140 | .1157 | .1172 | .1186 |
| 11 | .0749 | .0776 | .0802 | .0828 | .0853 | .0878 | .0902 | .0925 | .0948 | .0970 |

Entries in the table give the probabilities that an event will occur χ times when the average number of occurrences is *m*.

**Table 6 (contd)**

| χ | 8.1 | 8.2 | 8.3 | 8.4 | 8.5 | *m* 8.6 | 8.7 | 8.8 | 8.9 | 9 |
|---|---|---|---|---|---|---|---|---|---|---|
| 12 | .0505 | .0530 | .0555 | .0579 | .0604 | .0629 | .0654 | .0679 | .0703 | .0728 |
| 13 | .0315 | .0334 | .0354 | .0374 | .0395 | .0416 | .0438 | .0459 | .0481 | .0504 |
| 14 | .0182 | .0196 | .0210 | .0225 | .0240 | .0256 | .0272 | .0289 | .0306 | .0324 |
| 15 | .0098 | .0107 | .0116 | .0126 | .0136 | .0147 | .0158 | .0169 | .0182 | .0194 |
| 16 | .0050 | .0055 | .0060 | .0066 | .0072 | .0079 | .0086 | .0093 | .0101 | .0109 |
| 17 | .0024 | .0026 | .0029 | .0033 | .0036 | .0040 | .0044 | .0048 | .0053 | .0058 |
| 18 | .0011 | .0012 | .0014 | .0015 | .0017 | .0019 | .0021 | .0024 | .0026 | .0029 |
| 19 | .0005 | .0005 | .0006 | .0007 | .0008 | .0009 | .0010 | .0011 | .0012 | .0014 |
| 20 | .0002 | .0002 | .0002 | .0003 | .0003 | .0004 | .0004 | .0005 | .0005 | .0006 |
| 21 | .0001 | .0001 | .0001 | .0001 | .0001 | .0002 | .0002 | .0002 | .0002 | .0003 |
| 22 | .0000 | .0000 | .0000 | .0000 | .0001 | .0001 | .0001 | .0001 | .0001 | .0001 |

| χ | 9.1 | 9.2 | 9.3 | 9.4 | 9.5 | *m* 9.6 | 9.7 | 9.8 | 9.9 | 10 |
|---|---|---|---|---|---|---|---|---|---|---|
| 0 | .0001 | .0001 | .0001 | .0001 | .0001 | .0001 | .0001 | .0001 | .0001 | .0000 |
| 1 | .0010 | .0009 | .0009 | .0008 | .0007 | .0007 | .0006 | .0005 | .0005 | .0005 |
| 2 | .0046 | .0043 | .0040 | .0037 | .0034 | .0031 | .0029 | .0027 | .0025 | .0023 |
| 3 | .0140 | .0131 | .0123 | .0115 | .0107 | .0100 | .0093 | .0087 | .0081 | .0076 |
| 4 | .0319 | .0302 | .0285 | .0269 | .0254 | .0240 | .0226 | .0213 | .0201 | .0189 |
| 5 | .0581 | .0555 | .0530 | .0506 | .0483 | .0460 | .0439 | .0418 | .0398 | .0378 |
| 6 | .0881 | .0851 | .0822 | .0793 | .0764 | .0736 | .0709 | .0682 | .0656 | .0631 |
| 7 | .1145 | .1118 | .1091 | .1064 | .1037 | .1010 | .0982 | .0955 | .0928 | .0901 |
| 8 | .1302 | .1286 | .1269 | .1251 | .1232 | .1212 | .1191 | .1170 | .1148 | .1126 |
| 9 | .1317 | .1315 | .1311 | .1306 | .1300 | .1293 | .1284 | .1274 | .1263 | .1251 |
| 10 | .1198 | .1210 | .1219 | .1228 | .1235 | .1241 | .1245 | .1249 | .1250 | .1251 |
| 11 | .0991 | .1012 | .1031 | .1049 | .1067 | .1083 | .1098 | .1112 | .1125 | .1137 |
| 12 | .0752 | .0776 | .0799 | .0822 | .0844 | .0866 | .0888 | .0908 | .0928 | .0948 |
| 13 | .0526 | .0549 | .0572 | .0594 | .0617 | .0640 | .0662 | .0685 | .0707 | .0729 |
| 14 | .0342 | .0361 | .0380 | .0399 | .0419 | .0439 | .0459 | .0479 | .0500 | .0521 |
| 15 | .0208 | .0221 | .0235 | .0250 | .0265 | .0281 | .0297 | .0313 | .0330 | .0347 |
| 16 | .0118 | .0127 | .0137 | .0147 | .0157 | .0168 | .0180 | .0192 | .0204 | .0217 |
| 17 | .0063 | .0069 | .0075 | .0081 | .0088 | .0095 | .0103 | .0111 | .0119 | .0128 |
| 18 | .0032 | .0035 | .0039 | .0042 | .0046 | .0051 | .0055 | .0060 | .0065 | .0071 |
| 19 | .0015 | .0017 | .0019 | .0021 | .0023 | .0026 | .0028 | .0031 | .0034 | .0037 |
| 20 | .0007 | .0008 | .0009 | .0010 | .0011 | .0012 | .0014 | .0015 | .0017 | .0019 |
| 21 | .0003 | .0003 | .0004 | .0004 | .0005 | .0006 | .0006 | .0007 | .0008 | .0009 |
| 22 | .0001 | .0001 | .0002 | .0002 | .0002 | .0002 | .0003 | .0003 | .0004 | .0004 |
| 23 | .0000 | .0001 | .0001 | .0001 | .0001 | .0001 | .0001 | .0001 | .0002 | .0002 |
| 24 | .0000 | .0000 | .0000 | .0000 | .0000 | .0000 | .0000 | .0001 | .0001 | .0001 |

Entries in the table give the probabilities that an event will occur χ times when the average number of occurrences is *m*.

**Table 6 (contd)**

| χ | 11 | 12 | 13 | 14 | m 15 | 16 | 17 | 18 | 19 | 20 |
|---|----|----|----|----|----|----|----|----|----|----|
| 0 | .0000 | .0000 | .0000 | .0000 | .0000 | .0000 | .0000 | .0000 | .0000 | .0000 |
| 1 | .0002 | .0001 | .0000 | .0000 | .0000 | .0000 | .0000 | .0000 | .0000 | .0000 |
| 2 | .0010 | .0004 | .0002 | .0001 | .0000 | .0000 | .0000 | .0000 | .0000 | .0000 |
| 3 | .0037 | .0018 | .0008 | .0004 | .0002 | .0001 | .0000 | .0000 | .0000 | .0000 |
| 4 | .0102 | .0053 | .0027 | .0013 | .0006 | .0003 | .0001 | .0001 | .0000 | .0000 |
| 5 | .0224 | .0127 | .0070 | .0037 | .0019 | .0010 | .0005 | .0002 | .0001 | .0001 |
| 6 | .0411 | .0255 | .0152 | .0087 | .0048 | .0026 | .0014 | .0007 | .0004 | .0002 |
| 7 | .0646 | .0437 | .0281 | .0174 | .0104 | .0060 | .0034 | .0018 | .0010 | .0005 |
| 8 | .0888 | .0655 | .0457 | .0304 | .0194 | .0120 | .0072 | .0042 | .0024 | .0013 |
| 9 | .1085 | .0874 | .0661 | .0473 | .0324 | .0213 | .0135 | .0083 | .0050 | .0029 |
| 10 | .1194 | .1048 | .0859 | .0663 | .0486 | .0341 | .0230 | .0150 | .0095 | .0058 |
| 11 | .1194 | .1144 | .1015 | .0844 | .0663 | .0496 | .0355 | .0245 | .0164 | .0106 |
| 12 | .1094 | .1144 | .1099 | .0984 | .0829 | .0661 | .0504 | .0368 | .0259 | .0176 |
| 13 | .0926 | .1056 | .1099 | .1060 | .0956 | .0814 | .0658 | .0509 | .0378 | .0271 |
| 14 | .0728 | .0905 | .1021 | .1060 | .1024 | .0930 | .0800 | .0655 | .0514 | .0387 |
| 15 | .0534 | .0724 | .0885 | .0989 | .1024 | .0992 | .0906 | .0786 | .0650 | .0516 |
| 16 | .0367 | .0543 | .0719 | .0866 | .0960 | .0992 | .0963 | .0884 | .0772 | .0646 |
| 17 | .0237 | .0383 | .0550 | .0713 | .0847 | .0934 | .0963 | .0936 | .0863 | .0760 |
| 18 | .0145 | .0256 | .0397 | .0554 | .0706 | .0830 | .0909 | .0936 | .0911 | .0844 |
| 19 | .0084 | .0161 | .0272 | .0409 | .0557 | .0699 | .0814 | .0887 | .0911 | .0888 |
| 20 | .0046 | .0097 | .0177 | .0286 | .0418 | .0559 | .0692 | .0798 | .0866 | .0888 |
| 21 | .0024 | .0055 | .0109 | .0191 | .0299 | .0426 | .0560 | .0684 | .0783 | .0846 |
| 22 | .0012 | .0030 | .0065 | .0121 | .0204 | .0310 | .0433 | .0560 | .0676 | .0769 |
| 23 | .0006 | .0016 | .0037 | .0074 | .0133 | .0216 | .0320 | .0438 | .0559 | .0669 |
| 24 | .0003 | .0008 | .0020 | .0043 | .0083 | .0144 | .0226 | .0328 | .0442 | .0557 |
| 25 | .0001 | .0004 | .0010 | .0024 | .0050 | .0092 | .0154 | .0237 | .0336 | .0446 |
| 26 | .0000 | .0002 | .0005 | .0013 | .0029 | .0057 | .0101 | .0164 | .0246 | .0343 |
| 27 | .0000 | .0001 | .0002 | .0007 | .0016 | .0034 | .0063 | .0109 | .0173 | .0254 |
| 28 | .0000 | .0000 | .0001 | .0003 | .0009 | .0019 | .0038 | .0070 | .0117 | .0181 |
| 29 | .0000 | .0000 | .0001 | .0002 | .0004 | .0011 | .0023 | .0044 | .0077 | .0125 |
| 30 | .0000 | .0000 | .0000 | .0001 | .0002 | .0006 | .0013 | .0026 | .0049 | .0083 |
| 31 | .0000 | .0000 | .0000 | .0000 | .0001 | .0003 | .0007 | .0015 | .0030 | .0054 |
| 32 | .0000 | .0000 | .0000 | .0000 | .0001 | .0001 | .0004 | .0009 | .0018 | .0034 |
| 33 | .0000 | .0000 | .0000 | .0000 | .0000 | .0001 | .0002 | .0005 | .0010 | .0020 |
| 34 | .0000 | .0000 | .0000 | .0000 | .0000 | .0000 | .0001 | .0002 | .0006 | .0012 |
| 35 | .0000 | .0000 | .0000 | .0000 | .0000 | .0000 | .0000 | .0001 | .0003 | .0007 |
| 36 | .0000 | .0000 | .0000 | .0000 | .0000 | .0000 | .0000 | .0001 | .0002 | .0004 |
| 37 | .0000 | .0000 | .0000 | .0000 | .0000 | .0000 | .0000 | .0000 | .0001 | .0002 |
| 38 | .0000 | .0000 | .0000 | .0000 | .0000 | .0000 | .0000 | .0000 | .0000 | .0001 |
| 39 | .0000 | .0000 | .0000 | .0000 | .0000 | .0000 | .0000 | .0000 | .0000 | .0001 |

Entries in the table give the probabilities that an event will occur $\chi$ times when the average number of occurrences is $m$.

# Table 7   Present value of £1

The table shows the value today of £1 to be received or paid after a given number of years $V_n r = (1 + r)^{-n}$

| At rate r / After n years | 1% | 2% | 3% | 4% | 5% | 6% | 7% | 8% | 9% | 10% | 11% | 12% |
|---|---|---|---|---|---|---|---|---|---|---|---|---|
| 1 | .99 | .98 | .97 | .96 | .95 | .94 | .93 | .93 | .92 | .91 | .90 | .89 |
| 2 | .98 | .96 | .94 | .92 | .91 | .89 | .87 | .86 | .84 | .83 | .81 | .80 |
| 3 | .97 | .94 | .92 | .89 | .86 | .84 | .82 | .79 | .77 | .75 | .73 | .71 |
| 4 | .96 | .92 | .89 | .85 | .82 | .79 | .76 | .74 | .71 | .68 | .66 | .64 |
| 5 | .95 | .91 | .86 | .82 | .78 | .75 | .71 | .68 | .65 | .62 | .59 | .57 |
| 6 | .94 | .89 | .84 | .79 | .75 | .70 | .67 | .63 | .60 | .56 | .53 | .51 |
| 7 | .93 | .87 | .81 | .76 | .71 | .67 | .62 | .58 | .55 | .51 | .48 | .45 |
| 8 | .92 | .85 | .79 | .73 | .68 | .63 | .58 | .54 | .50 | .47 | .43 | .40 |
| 9 | .91 | .84 | .77 | .70 | .64 | .59 | .54 | .50 | .46 | .42 | .39 | .36 |
| 10 | .91 | .82 | .74 | .68 | .61 | .56 | .51 | .46 | .42 | .39 | .35 | .32 |
| 11 | .90 | .80 | .72 | .65 | .58 | .53 | .48 | .43 | .39 | .35 | .32 | .29 |
| 12 | .89 | .79 | .70 | .62 | .56 | .50 | .44 | .40 | .36 | .32 | .29 | .26 |
| 13 | .88 | .77 | .68 | .60 | .53 | .47 | .41 | .37 | .33 | .29 | .26 | .23 |
| 14 | .87 | .76 | .66 | .58 | .51 | .44 | .39 | .34 | .30 | .26 | .23 | .20 |
| 15 | .86 | .74 | .64 | .56 | .48 | .42 | .36 | .32 | .27 | .24 | .21 | .18 |

| At rate r / After n years | 13% | 14% | 15% | 16% | 17% | 18% | 19% | 20% | 30% | 40% | 50% |
|---|---|---|---|---|---|---|---|---|---|---|---|
| 1 | .88 | .88 | .87 | .86 | .85 | .85 | .84 | .83 | .77 | .71 | .67 |
| 2 | .78 | .77 | .76 | .74 | .73 | .72 | .71 | .69 | .59 | .51 | .44 |
| 3 | .69 | .67 | .66 | .64 | .62 | .61 | .59 | .58 | .46 | .36 | .30 |
| 4 | .61 | .59 | .57 | .55 | .53 | .52 | .50 | .48 | .35 | .26 | .20 |
| 5 | .54 | .52 | .50 | .48 | .46 | .44 | .42 | .40 | .27 | .19 | .13 |
| 6 | .48 | .46 | .43 | .41 | .39 | .37 | .35 | .33 | .21 | .13 | .09 |
| 7 | .43 | .40 | .38 | .35 | .33 | .31 | .30 | .28 | .16 | .09 | .06 |
| 8 | .38 | .35 | .33 | .31 | .28 | .27 | .25 | .23 | .12 | .07 | .04 |
| 9 | .33 | .31 | .28 | .26 | .24 | .23 | .21 | .19 | .09 | .05 | .03 |
| 10 | .29 | .27 | .25 | .23 | .21 | .19 | .18 | .16 | .07 | .03 | .02 |
| 11 | .26 | .24 | .21 | .20 | .18 | .16 | .15 | .13 | .06 | .02 | .01 |
| 12 | .23 | .21 | .19 | .17 | .15 | .14 | .12 | .11 | .04 | .02 | .008 |
| 13 | .20 | .18 | .16 | .15 | .13 | .12 | .10 | .09 | .03 | .013 | .005 |
| 14 | .18 | .16 | .14 | .13 | .11 | .10 | .09 | .08 | .03 | .009 | .003 |
| 15 | .16 | .14 | .12 | .11 | .09 | .08 | .07 | .06 | .02 | .006 | .002 |

## Table 8 Cumulative present value of £1

The table shows the present value of £1 per annum, receivable or payable at the end of each year for *N* Years

| Years | Net rate of interest assumed | | | | | | | | | | | |
|---|---|---|---|---|---|---|---|---|---|---|---|---|
| | 1% | 2% | 3% | 4% | 5% | 6% | 7% | 8% | 9% | 10% | 11% | 12% |
| 1 | .99 | .98 | .97 | .96 | .95 | .94 | .94 | .93 | .92 | .91 | .90 | .89 |
| 2 | 1.97 | 1.94 | 1.91 | 1.89 | 1.86 | 1.83 | 1.81 | 1.78 | 1.76 | 1.74 | 1.71 | 1.69 |
| 3 | 2.94 | 2.88 | 2.83 | 2.78 | 2.72 | 2.67 | 2.62 | 2.58 | 2.53 | 2.49 | 2.44 | 2.40 |
| 4 | 3.90 | 3.81 | 3.72 | 3.63 | 3.55 | 3.47 | 3.39 | 3.31 | 3.24 | 3.17 | 3.10 | 3.04 |
| 5 | 4.85 | 4.71 | 4.58 | 4.45 | 4.33 | 4.21 | 4.10 | 3.99 | 3.89 | 3.79 | 3.70 | 3.61 |
| 6 | 5.80 | 5.60 | 5.42 | 5.24 | 5.08 | 4.92 | 4.77 | 4.62 | 4.49 | 4.36 | 4.23 | 4.11 |
| 7 | 6.73 | 6.47 | 6.23 | 6.00 | 5.79 | 5.58 | 5.39 | 5.21 | 5.03 | 4.87 | 4.71 | 4.56 |
| 8 | 7.65 | 7.33 | 7.02 | 6.73 | 6.46 | 6.21 | 5.97 | 5.75 | 5.54 | 5.34 | 5.15 | 4.97 |
| 9 | 8.57 | 8.16 | 7.79 | 7.44 | 7.11 | 6.80 | 6.52 | 6.25 | 6.00 | 5.76 | 5.54 | 5.33 |
| 10 | 9.47 | 8.98 | 8.53 | 8.11 | 7.72 | 7.36 | 7.02 | 6.71 | 6.42 | 6.15 | 5.89 | 5.65 |
| 11 | 10.37 | 9.79 | 9.95 | 8.76 | 8.31 | 7.89 | 7.50 | 7.14 | 6.81 | 6.50 | 6.21 | 5.94 |
| 12 | 11.26 | 10.58 | 9.95 | 9.39 | 8.86 | 8.38 | 7.94 | 7.54 | 7.16 | 6.81 | 6.49 | 6.19 |
| 13 | 12.13 | 11.35 | 10.64 | 9.99 | 9.39 | 8.85 | 8.36 | 7.90 | 7.49 | 7.10 | 6.80 | 6.42 |
| 14 | 13.00 | 12.11 | 11.30 | 10.56 | 9.90 | 9.30 | 8.75 | 8.24 | 7.79 | 7.37 | 6.98 | 6.63 |
| 15 | 13.87 | 12.85 | 11.94 | 11.12 | 10.38 | 9.71 | 9.11 | 8.56 | 8.06 | 7.61 | 7.19 | 6.81 |

| Years | Net rate of interest assumed | | | | | | | | | | |
|---|---|---|---|---|---|---|---|---|---|---|---|
| | 13% | 14% | 15% | 16% | 17% | 18% | 19% | 20% | 30% | 40% | 50% |
| 1 | .89 | .88 | .87 | .86 | .85 | .85 | .84 | .83 | .77 | .71 | .67 |
| 2 | 1.67 | 1.65 | 1.63 | 1.61 | 1.59 | 1.57 | 1.55 | 1.53 | 1.36 | 1.22 | 1.11 |
| 3 | 2.36 | 2.32 | 2.28 | 2.25 | 2.21 | 2.17 | 2.14 | 2.11 | 1.81 | 1.59 | 1.41 |
| 4 | 2.97 | 2.91 | 2.86 | 2.80 | 2.74 | 2.69 | 2.64 | 2.59 | 2.17 | 1.85 | 1.61 |
| 5 | 3.52 | 3.43 | 3.35 | 3.27 | 3.20 | 3.13 | 3.06 | 2.99 | 2.44 | 2.04 | 1.74 |
| 6 | 4.00 | 3.89 | 3.78 | 3.69 | 3.59 | 3.50 | 3.41 | 3.33 | 2.64 | 2.17 | 1.82 |
| 7 | 4.42 | 4.29 | 4.16 | 4.04 | 3.92 | 3.81 | 3.71 | 3.61 | 2.80 | 2.26 | 1.88 |
| 8 | 4.80 | 4.64 | 4.49 | 4.34 | 4.21 | 4.08 | 3.95 | 3.84 | 2.93 | 2.33 | 1.92 |
| 9 | 5.13 | 4.95 | 4.77 | 4.61 | 4.45 | 4.30 | 4.16 | 4.03 | 3.02 | 2.38 | 1.95 |
| 10 | 5.43 | 5.22 | 5.02 | 4.83 | 4.66 | 4.49 | 4.34 | 4.19 | 3.09 | 2.41 | 1.97 |
| 11 | 5.69 | 5.45 | 5.23 | 5.03 | 4.83 | 4.66 | 4.49 | 4.33 | 3.15 | 2.44 | 1.98 |
| 12 | 5.92 | 5.66 | 5.42 | 5.20 | 4.99 | 4.79 | 4.61 | 4.44 | 3.19 | 2.46 | 1.99 |
| 13 | 6.12 | 5.84 | 5.58 | 5.34 | 5.12 | 4.91 | 4.71 | 4.53 | 3.22 | 2.47 | 1.99 |
| 14 | 6.30 | 6.00 | 5.72 | 5.47 | 5.23 | 5.01 | 4.80 | 4.61 | 3.25 | 2.48 | 1.99 |
| 15 | 6.46 | 6.14 | 5.85 | 5.58 | 5.32 | 5.09 | 4.88 | 4.68 | 3.27 | 2.48 | 2.00 |

# Table 9 Random numbers

```
03 47 43 73 86   36 96 47 36 61   46 98 63 71 62   33 26 16 80 45   60 11 14 10 95
97 74 24 67 62   42 81 14 57 20   42 53 32 37 32   27 07 36 07 51   24 51 79 89 73
16 76 62 27 66   56 50 26 71 07   32 90 79 78 53   13 55 38 58 59   88 97 54 14 10
12 56 85 99 26   96 96 68 27 31   05 03 72 93 15   57 12 10 14 21   88 26 49 81 76
55 59 56 35 64   38 54 82 46 22   31 62 43 09 90   06 18 44 32 53   23 83 01 30 30

16 22 77 94 39   49 54 43 54 82   17 37 93 23 78   87 35 20 96 43   84 26 34 91 64
84 42 17 53 31   57 24 55 08 88   77 04 74 47 67   21 76 33 50 25   83 92 12 06 76
63 01 63 78 59   16 95 55 67 19   98 10 50 71 75   12 86 73 58 07   44 39 52 38 79
33 21 12 34 29   78 64 56 07 82   52 42 07 44 38   15 51 00 13 42   99 66 02 79 54
57 60 86 32 44   09 47 27 96 54   49 17 46 09 62   90 52 84 77 27   08 02 73 43 28

18 18 07 92 46   44 17 16 58 09   79 83 86 19 62   06 76 50 03 10   55 23 64 05 05
26 62 38 97 75   84 16 07 44 99   83 11 46 32 24   20 14 85 88 45   10 93 72 88 71
23 42 40 64 74   82 97 77 77 81   07 45 32 14 08   32 98 94 07 72   93 85 79 10 75
52 36 28 19 95   50 92 26 11 97   00 56 76 31 38   80 22 02 53 53   86 60 42 04 53
37 85 94 35 12   83 39 50 08 30   42 34 07 96 88   54 42 06 87 98   35 85 29 48 39

70 29 17 12 13   40 33 20 38 26   13 89 51 03 74   17 76 37 13 04   07 74 21 19 30
56 62 18 37 35   96 83 50 87 75   97 12 25 93 47   70 33 24 03 54   97 77 46 44 80
99 49 57 22 77   88 42 95 45 72   16 64 36 16 00   04 43 18 66 79   94 77 24 21 90
16 08 15 04 72   33 27 14 34 09   45 59 34 68 49   12 72 07 34 45   99 27 72 95 14
31 16 93 32 43   50 27 89 87 19   20 15 37 00 49   52 85 66 60 44   38 68 88 11 80

68 34 30 13 70   55 74 30 77 40   44 22 78 84 26   04 33 46 09 52   68 07 97 06 57
74 57 25 65 76   59 29 97 68 60   71 91 38 67 54   13 58 18 24 76   15 54 55 95 52
27 42 37 86 53   48 55 90 65 72   96 57 69 36 10   96 46 92 42 45   96 60 49 04 91
00 39 68 29 61   66 37 32 20 30   77 84 57 03 29   10 45 65 04 26   11 04 96 67 24
29 94 98 94 24   68 49 69 10 82   53 75 91 93 30   34 25 20 57 27   40 48 73 51 92

16 90 82 66 59   83 62 64 11 12   67 19 00 71 74   60 47 21 29 68   02 02 37 03 31
11 27 94 75 06   06 09 19 74 66   02 94 37 34 02   76 70 90 30 86   38 45 94 30 38
```

**Table 9 (contd)**

| | | | | | | | | | | | | | | | | | | | | | | | |
|--|--|--|--|--|--|--|--|--|--|--|--|--|--|--|--|--|--|--|--|--|--|--|--|
| 35 | 24 | 10 | 16 | 20 | 33 | 32 | 51 | 26 | 79 | 78 | 45 | 04 | 91 | 16 | 56 | 53 | 92 | 16 | 02 | 75 | 50 | 95 | 98 |
| 38 | 23 | 16 | 86 | 38 | 42 | 38 | 97 | 01 | 87 | 75 | 66 | 81 | 41 | 62 | 91 | 74 | 01 | 40 | 48 | 51 | 84 | 08 | 32 |
| 31 | 96 | 25 | 91 | 47 | 96 | 44 | 33 | 49 | 34 | 86 | 82 | 53 | 91 | 85 | 48 | 43 | 52 | 00 | 27 | 55 | 26 | 89 | 62 |
| 66 | 67 | 40 | 67 | 14 | 64 | 05 | 71 | 95 | 11 | 05 | 65 | 09 | 68 | 90 | 37 | 20 | 83 | 76 | 57 | 16 | 00 | 11 | 66 |
| 14 | 90 | 84 | 45 | 11 | 75 | 73 | 88 | 05 | 52 | 27 | 41 | 14 | 86 | 08 | 22 | 12 | 98 | 22 | 07 | 52 | 74 | 95 | 80 |
| 68 | 05 | 51 | 18 | 00 | 33 | 96 | 02 | 75 | 07 | 60 | 62 | 93 | 55 | 90 | 43 | 82 | 33 | 59 | 49 | 37 | 38 | 44 | 59 |
| 20 | 46 | 78 | 73 | 90 | 97 | 51 | 40 | 14 | 04 | 02 | 33 | 31 | 08 | 36 | 49 | 16 | 54 | 39 | 47 | 95 | 93 | 13 | 30 |
| 64 | 19 | 58 | 97 | 79 | 15 | 06 | 15 | 93 | 01 | 90 | 10 | 75 | 06 | 62 | 89 | 78 | 78 | 40 | 02 | 67 | 74 | 17 | 33 |
| 05 | 26 | 93 | 70 | 60 | 22 | 35 | 85 | 15 | 92 | 03 | 51 | 59 | 77 | 83 | 06 | 78 | 56 | 59 | 52 | 91 | 05 | 70 | 74 |
| 47 | 97 | 10 | 88 | 23 | 09 | 98 | 42 | 99 | 61 | 71 | 62 | 99 | 15 | 93 | 16 | 29 | 51 | 06 | 58 | 05 | 77 | 09 | 51 |
| 68 | 71 | 86 | 85 | 85 | 54 | 87 | 66 | 80 | 73 | 32 | 08 | 11 | 12 | 16 | 63 | 92 | 95 | 44 | 29 | 56 | 24 | 29 | 48 |
| 26 | 99 | 61 | 65 | 53 | 58 | 37 | 78 | 70 | 42 | 10 | 50 | 67 | 42 | 74 | 85 | 55 | 17 | 32 | 94 | 44 | 67 | 16 | 94 |
| 14 | 65 | 52 | 68 | 75 | 87 | 59 | 36 | 41 | 26 | 78 | 63 | 06 | 55 | 50 | 01 | 27 | 08 | 13 | 16 | 29 | 39 | 39 | 43 |
| 17 | 53 | 77 | 58 | 71 | 71 | 41 | 61 | 72 | 12 | 41 | 94 | 96 | 26 | 99 | 36 | 27 | 95 | 44 | 02 | 96 | 74 | 30 | 83 |
| 90 | 26 | 59 | 21 | 19 | 23 | 52 | 23 | 12 | 96 | 93 | 02 | 18 | 39 | 07 | 36 | 18 | 02 | 07 | 25 | 99 | 32 | 70 | 23 |
| 41 | 23 | 52 | 55 | 99 | 31 | 04 | 49 | 96 | 10 | 47 | 48 | 45 | 88 | 20 | 89 | 43 | 41 | 13 | 97 | 17 | 14 | 49 | 17 |
| 60 | 20 | 50 | 81 | 69 | 31 | 99 | 73 | 68 | 35 | 81 | 33 | 03 | 76 | 60 | 48 | 12 | 30 | 24 | 18 | 99 | 10 | 72 | 34 |
| 91 | 25 | 38 | 05 | 90 | 94 | 58 | 28 | 38 | 45 | 47 | 59 | 03 | 09 | 12 | 29 | 57 | 35 | 90 | 82 | 62 | 54 | 65 | 60 |
| 34 | 50 | 57 | 74 | 37 | 98 | 80 | 33 | 91 | 09 | 77 | 93 | 19 | 82 | 04 | 04 | 80 | 94 | 74 | 45 | 07 | 31 | 66 | 49 |
| 85 | 22 | 04 | 39 | 43 | 73 | 81 | 53 | 79 | 33 | 62 | 46 | 86 | 28 | 31 | 46 | 54 | 31 | 08 | 53 | 94 | 13 | 38 | 47 |
| 09 | 79 | 13 | 77 | 48 | 73 | 82 | 97 | 21 | 05 | 03 | 27 | 24 | 83 | 60 | 05 | 44 | 89 | 72 | 35 | 80 | 39 | 94 | 88 |
| 88 | 75 | 80 | 18 | 14 | 22 | 95 | 75 | 49 | 39 | 32 | 82 | 22 | 49 | 37 | 70 | 07 | 48 | 02 | 16 | 04 | 61 | 67 | 87 |
| 90 | 96 | 23 | 70 | 00 | 39 | 00 | 03 | 90 | 55 | 85 | 78 | 38 | 36 | 32 | 69 | 30 | 37 | 94 | 90 | 89 | 00 | 76 | 33 |

# Table 10  Formulae

*Arithmetic mean*

$$\bar{x} = \frac{\Sigma x}{n} \ or \ \bar{x} = \frac{\Sigma fx}{\Sigma f}$$

*Standard deviation*

$$SD = \sqrt{\frac{\Sigma(x-\bar{x})^2}{n-1}}$$

$SD^2$ = variance

*Binomial distribution*

$$Pr(x) = {}^nC_x.p^x.q^{n-x}$$

$${}^nC_x = \frac{n!}{(n-x)!x!}$$

Mean = n.p

Standard deviation = $\sqrt{n.p.q}$

*Normal distribution*

$$.Z = \frac{x-\mu}{\sigma}$$

*Poisson distribution*

$$Pr(x) = \frac{e^{-m}.m^x}{x!}$$

where e = exponential constant

m = mean rate of occurrence

= variance

# Index

Absorption costing, 73–4, 119
  over absorption, 75
  under absorption, 75
Account classification, 26–9
Accounting rate of return, 194–5
Alternative hypothesis, 34–7, 375
Amey, L.R., 138, 173
Analysis of variance, 35, 38–9, 41
Annuities, 201, 204, 233
  table, 406
Argyris, C., 181–2, 189
Arnold, M., 276, 361

Baker, K.R., 113
Barnes, K., 320
Bayes theorem, 249
Becker and Green, 182–3
Behavioural aspects of budgeting, 174–89
Benston, G., 53
Bhaskar, K., 256, 362
Binomial distribution formula, 409
Bowerman, B.L., 173
Breakeven analysis, 19, 78–80, 84
Bromwich, M., 276, 361
Bryant, J.W., 389
Budget, 10
Budget estimate, 31
Budgetary control, 139–89
  budget centres, 141
  budget committee, 141
  budget manual, 141
  budget officer, 141

Budget:
  cash budget, 142, 149
  labour budget, 142, 145
  master budget, 142–3
  materials usage budget, 145
  production budget, 142, 145
  raw material and purchasing budget, 142, 145
  sales budget, 142, 145
  working capital, 166–7

Calculus, 118–22, 343–4
Capital budgeting, 190–256
Capital rationing, 238–41
Carr, J., 362
Carsberg, B., 189, 361
Cash flows, 199–200
Chi-squared, 374–6, 386–9
  table, 393
Coates, J.B., 276
Coch, C., 178
Coefficient of determination, 32–4, 46, 50
Coefficient of variation, 228
Collier, M., 362
Computerized accounting information system (CAIS), 362–88
Confidence interval, 44, 117–18, 301, 388
Contingency theory, 178–9, 183
Contribution, 77–138
Contribution/sales ratio, 80–1, 257
Cooper and Lybrand, 363

Cooper, D., 276, 361
Correlation, 29–52, 61–2, 163–4
 table, 394
Cost behaviour, 3–9
Cost benefit analysis, 192, 338
Cost centres, 9, 257–76, 308–13
Cost classification, 1–20
Cost experience curve, 63
Cost plus pricing, 76, 119
Cost/volume/profit analysis, 90–117
Costs-budgeted cost, 9, 10, 11
 controllable cost, 10
 direct cost, 2
 fixed cost, 3, 10, 11, 15
 incremental cost, 119
 indirect cost, 2
 opportunity cost, 8–9, 109–10, 200
 period cost, 1
 product cost, 1
 relevant cost, 8, 100
 semi-fixed cost, 5–7, 12
 semi-variable cost, 5, 15–16
 standard cost, 9
 sunk cost, 119, 200
 uncontrollable cost, 10
 variable cost, 3, 11–15, 17
Critical path method (CPM), 290–302
 bar chart, 317–19
 dummy activity, 293
 expediting (crashing), 299–300
 free float, 293
 gantt chart, 317–19
 independent float, 293
 project cost control, 293–300
 slack, 292
 total float, 293

Data base, 363, 367, 380–4
Dbase4, 367
Decision support system (DSS), 366
Decision tree, 136–8, 234–7, 246–9
Degrees of freedom, 36–8, 376
Delphi method, 157–8
Demski, J.L., 109
Dev, S., 113
Discoll, D.A., 138
Discounted cash flow, 195–256
DOS, 363
Dury, J.C., 113

Economic order quantity (EOQ or
 EBQ), 13, 130–1
Emmanual, C., 189

Engineering method, 21–2
Expected value, 87–9, 115, 136–8, 227,
 246–9
Expediting, 299–300
Expert systems, 370–1
Exponential smoothing, 159–60

F distribution, 37–9
 table, 395–8
FIFO, 376
Financial modelling, 363, 378–80
Flexible budget, 11, 24, 44–5, 149–52,
 184
Forecasting, 43–8, 156–73
Formulas, 409
French, D., 178

Gee, K.P., 113
Ghosh, B.C., 89
Graphics, 363

Harvey, D.W., 320
Harvey, M., 361
Herbst, A.F., 256
High-low method, 26–9, 49, 51–2
Hirschmann, W.B., 54, 72
Hofstede, G., 178, 182
Hope, A., 189
Hopwood, A.G., 178, 181, 189
Humphreys, R.G., 138

Independent technological
 comparisons, 158–9
Inflation, 222–6, 336
Internal rate of return (IRR), 202–8,
 233
Investment centre, 10, 257–76

Jackson, M., 389
Joint product costing, 124–7
 by-products, 124
 split-off point, 124

Kaplan, R.S., 89
Kaye, G.R., 389
Kennedy, A., 361

Learning curve, 54–72, 314–16
 equation, 58
 tables, 58–9
Levin, R.I., 53
Levy, H., 256
Liao, W.M., 72
Lin, W.T., 138

Linear programming, 91–113
  constraints, 91–3
  feasible region, 93, 107
  iso-profit line, 107
  objective function, 92, 100, 108
  slack variables, 95–9, 111
Lister, R., 189
Lorsch, J.W., 178
Lotus 1–2–3, 367
Lowe, E.A., 189
Lucey, T., 256
Lumby, S., 221

Macros, 363
Madridakis, S., 173
Margin of safety, 19
Marginal costing, 17, 56, 73–138
Martindale, A., 361
Maximin, 136–8
McGee, V.E., 173
McGregor, D., 183
Mean formula, 409
Mepham, M.J., 20
Method study, 155
Middleton, K.A., 89
Minitab, 34–5, 163–4
Modelling process, 371–4
Modelling software, 370
  @Risk, 370
  Forecast, pro, 370–1
  Timestat, 370
  Wizard, 370
Motivation, 175–89
Moving average, 160–2
  residual, 161–2
  seasonal factor, 161–2
  trend, 161–2
Multiple regression, 40–2, 52

Negative exponential distribution, 377
Net present value (NPV), 71–2,
  198–256
  table, 405–6
Network analysis, 290–302, 316–19
Normal distribution, 36, 116, 228–9,
  301
  formula, 409
  tables, 390–1
Null hypothesis, 34–9, 375, 388

O'Connell, R.T., 173
Opportunity costs, 99–100
Otley, D.T., 178, 183, 189

Outlier, 23
Overhead recovery rate, 122

Parametric analysis, 234
Parker, L.D., 173
Payback, 192–4
  bailout payback, 194
Perfect information, 127
Perpetuities, 202
Pert, 290, 300–2
Pike, R.H., 207, 221
Poisson distribution, 374–6
  formula, 409
  table, 399–404
Pricing, 114–37, 243–6
Probability distribution, 37, 116–18,
  129–30, 231–2
Probability tree, 253–6
Process costing, 333–5, 343–6, 352–60
Product mix, 84, 101–2
Profit centre, 9, 257–76
Profit/volume graph, 81–3
Profitability index, 237–8

Queuing, 374–8

Random numbers, 229–31
  tables, 407–8
Regression, 29–52, 61–2, 163–4
Relevant costs, 100
Residual income (RI), 259–76
Return on capital employed (ROCE),
  258–76
Return on investment (ROI), 258–76
Richardson, A.W., 89
Risk, 127, 132, 226–56, 241
Rolling budget, 154, 172–3

Sampling distribution, 34, 43–4
Scapens, R.W., 138, 189, 276, 361
Sensitivity analysis, 99–102, 232–4,
  250–2
Shadow price, 99–102
Sherwood, D., 389
Simmonds, K., 53
Simplex method, 94–8, 111
  pivoting, 96–9
Simulation, 229–32, 250–3, 384–6
Smith, J.E., 276
Soliman, S.Y., 320
Solomon, D., 20
Spreadsheet, 167–8, 363, 367–70
SPSS, 34

SSAP2, 76
SSAP9, 76
Stacey, R.J., 276
Staffurth, C., 320
Standard costs, 62, 277–320
  setting standards, 277–9
Standard deviation, 116–17, 227–9,
  231–2, 301, 337
  formula, 409
Standard error, 34–7
Statistical control charts, 336–8
Statistical packages, 363
Statpack, 34
Stedry, A.C., 178
Subjective curve fitting, 157
Symphony, 363

Targett, P., 320
Taylor, R.E., 113
Test of significance, 34
Theory X and theory Y, 183
Thompson, T., 361
Three point estimates, 87–9, 242–3,
  300
t-distribution, 34–7
  table, 392

Uncertainty, 115–17, 153–4, 242

Value analysis, 155
Van Horne, J.C., 221
Variance, 10, 11, 87
Variance analysis, 277–361
  fixed overhead capacity variance,
    282, 284–90, 302–16
  fixed overhead efficiency variance,
    282, 284–90, 302–16
  fixed overhead expenditure
    variance, 282, 284–90, 302–16
  fixed overhead idle time variance,
    282, 284–90, 302–16
  fixed overhead volume variance in

  hours, 282, 284–90, 302–16
  fixed overhead volume variance in
    units, 282, 284–90, 302–16
  idle time variance, 281, 284–90,
    302–16
  labour efficiency variance, 281,
    284–90, 302–16
  labour rate variance 281, 284–90,
    302–16
  material mix variance, 321, 340–61
  material price variance, 280,
    284–90, 302–16
  material usage variance, 280,
    284–90, 302–16, 323
  material yield variance, 321, 340–61
  operational variance, 328–32,
    340–61
  planning variance, 329–32, 340–61
  sales mix variance, 324–8, 340–61
  sales price variance, 280, 284–90,
    302–16
  sales quantity variance, 324–8, 340–
    61
  sales volume variance, 280, 284–90,
    302–16
  variable overhead efficiency
    variance, 281, 284–90, 302–16
  variable overhead expenditure
    variance, 281, 284–90, 302–16

Watkins, P.R., 138
Wells, M.C., 20
Williams, D., 362
Word processing, 363
Work measurement, 155
Work study, 154

Yelle, L.E., 72

Zero based budgeting, 140, 152–3,
  170–2